As well as being considered the greatest English political philosopher, Hobbes has traditionally been thought of as a purely secular thinker, highly critical of all religion. In this provocative new study, Professor Martinich argues that conventional wisdom has been misled. He shows that religious concerns pervade *Leviathan* and that Hobbes was really intent upon providing a rational defense of the Calvinistic Church of England that flourished under the reign of James I.

Professor Martinich presents a close reading of *Leviathan* in which he shows that, for Hobbes, Christian doctrine is not politically destabilizing and is consistent with modern science. The laws of nature are those commands of God that are deducible by reason, and government requires the laws of nature for its foundation. Moreover, according to Hobbes, a straightforward interpretation of the Bible does not conflict with the science of Galileo: miracles may conform to physical laws; angels need not be immaterial; heaven will be on earth; the damned will suffer for a limited time; and the Kingdom of God will be on earth, sometime in the unspecified future.

This book is sure to become the standard discussion of Hobbes's religion and will be regarded as a model of how to read early modern texts which have hitherto been interpreted in the light of modern interests and preoccupations.

The Two Gods of *Leviathan*

Illustrated title page to the Head edition of Hobbes's *Leviathan* (London, 1651). Photograph courtesy of the Harry Ransom Humanities Research Center, University of Texas at Austin.

The Two Gods
of *Leviathan*

Thomas Hobbes on Religion and Politics

A. P. MARTINICH

DEPARTMENT OF PHILOSOPHY
UNIVERSITY OF TEXAS AT AUSTIN

 CAMBRIDGE
UNIVERSITY PRESS

PUBLISHED BY THE PRESS SYNDICATE OF THE UNIVERSITY OF CAMBRIDGE
The Pitt Building, Trumpington Street, Cambridge, United Kingdom

CAMBRIDGE UNIVERSITY PRESS
The Edinburgh Building, Cambridge CB2 2RU, UK
40 West 20th Street, New York NY 10011–4211, USA
477 Williamstown Road, Port Melbourne, VIC 3207, Australia
Ruiz de Alarcón 13, 28014 Madrid, Spain
Dock House, The Waterfront, Cape Town 8001, South Africa

http://www.cambridge.org

First published 1992
First paperback edition 2002

A catalogue record for this book is available from the British Library

Library of Congress Cataloguing-in-Publication Data
Martinich, Aloysius.
The two gods of Leviathan / A. P. Martinich.
p. cm.
Includes bibliographical references.
ISBN 0 521 41849 6 hardback
1. Hobbes, Thomas, 1588–1679. Leviathan. 2. Hobbes, Thomas,
1588–1679 – Contributions in political science. 3. Hobbes, Thomas,
1588–1679 – Contributions in natural law. 4. Hobbes, Thomas,
1588–1679 – Religion. I. Title.
JC153.H659M37 1992
320.1 – dc20   91–35639

ISBN 0 521 41849 6 hardback
ISBN 0 521 53123 3 paperback

For John and Pinky Scanlan
and
The Peninsula Neighborhood Group

Contents

vii

Contents

Contents

Contents

Acknowledgments

My research was supported by fellowships from the National Endowment for the Humanities and the University Research Institute of the University of Texas at Austin. A grant from the University Research Institute was also helpful in preparing the manuscript for publication. I want to thank the staffs of the British Library (London), the Humanities Research Center of the University of Texas at Austin, the Huntington Library (San Marino, Calif.), and the Newberry Library (Chicago). My thanks are also extended to the following people who commented helpfully on some or all of this book: Donald Becker, Mark Bernstein, Jo Ann Carson, Emmy Edwards, Paul Johnson, Robert Kane, Brian Levack, Leslie Martinich, David Newman, Deborah Nichols, Thomas Seung, Tara Smith, Mark Stoll, David Walker, and Jan Wojcik.

A note on references

References to Hobbes's works are usually to the Molesworth editions (published in 1839) and take the form "EW" for the *English Works* and "OL" for the *Opera Latina*, followed by volume and page numbers. Other works by Hobbes or other editions of his works are cited in the familiar author/year-of-publication style, e.g., (Hobbes, 1643, p. 321) refers to Hobbes's book *Thomas White's De Mundo Examined*.

It may be helpful to have the following correlations for the volumes in the English works:

1	*De Corpore*
2	*De Cive*
3	*Leviathan*
4:1–228	*The Elements of Law*
4:229–278	*Of Liberty and Necessity*
4:279–384	*An Answer to . . . Dr. Bramhall*
6:3–160	*A Dialogue between a Philosopher and a Student of the Commons Laws of England*
6:161–418	*Behemoth*

References to other authors follow the author/year-of-publication style. For pre–nineteenth-century works, I have used the year of original publication whenever reasonable, even when I am quoting from a recent edition. The purpose of this method is to give the reader a sense for how that work fits into Hobbes's own chronology of writings. There are some exceptions. For example, Thomas Aquinas's *Summa Theologiae* is referred to by its name, followed by part, question, article, and the part of the article in which it appears. Thomas Hooker's *Laws of Ecclesiastical Polity* is referred to by book, chapter, and section. When it is difficult to date a work, or if an edition is used that contains several works (such as the collected works of an author), I have sometimes used the date of that edition, even when the date does not accurately reflect the date of composition, especially for non–seventeenth-century authors. For example, William of Ockham's *Quodlibetal Questions* is cited as "Ockham, 1964." I have sacrificed consistency in the interests of making the system of references more helpful.

LEVIATHAN . . . that *mortal god*, to which we owe under the *immortal God*, our peace and defence.

Introduction

HOBBES'S CHRISTIANITY AND RELIGIOUS PROJECTS

Hobbes's theism

In his own day, Thomas Hobbes was accused of atheism and general wickedness. The twentieth century has been much kinder to him in some ways, and the consensus of scholarly opinion now counts him as a tepid theist. My view, in contrast, is that Hobbes was a sincere, and relatively orthodox, Christian. Not only did he believe that God exists and that religion is an important part of human life; he believed that God in some mysterious way has made revelations to various people, believed that Jesus was both God and the Messiah, and believed that there would be a heaven and hell at the end of this world.[1] It is possible that he did not have a strong emotional commitment to religion. He may not have had a strong attachment to the rituals of any denomination, although he went out of his way to worship according to the liturgy of the Church of England (Stephen and Leslie, 1917, 9:936). But he certainly had a strong intellectual commitment to religion. More specifically, he had a strong commitment to the Calvinist Christianity of Jacobean England. I shall be arguing that theological concepts, especially those of English Calvinism, are an inextricable part of his philosophy, especially his moral and political views.[2] Thus, the correct understanding of Hobbes's philosophy must include an expla-

1

nation of the role of characteristically Christian concepts. (On this point, see also Glover, 1965, pp. 142–3.)

When I say that Hobbes was a relatively orthodox Christian, I am using the term "orthodox," as Hobbes did, to mean adherence to the propositions expressed by the authoritative Christian creeds of the first four church councils. This criterion is not chosen arbitrarily. Hobbes adopts it because it is the criterion that Queen Elizabeth had established for orthodoxy when she instituted the High Commission, the court that regulated ecclesiastical matters (EW, 4:405–6). William Chillingworth, the great Protestant apologist and Hobbes's friend, subscribes to the same criterion of orthodoxy (Chillingworth, 1638, p. 16). Furthermore, in his *Historical Narration Concerning Heresy*, Hobbes approvingly explicates the Apostles' Creed (EW, 4:392–401) and in other places commits himself to the creeds of the first four ecumenical councils, those of Nicea, Constantinople, Ephesus, and Chalcedon (EW, 6:14).

Standard and nonstandard religious views

I have said that Hobbes's religious views are relatively orthodox. This is not to say that his views were always the standard religious views of his time, although more of them were standard than is usually thought. To say that a view is orthodox is to make a value judgment, since orthodoxy is normative for a religion. But to say that a view is standard is to make a sociological statement. The standard views are the received, or mainstream, religious opinions of a particular time and place.

Standard views may or may not be orthodox. The view that God exists has always been both orthodox and standard for Christians. But many standard views are transient. Sometimes they come into style and are believed to be orthodox, and sometimes they go out of style and are believed to be heterodox. Transubstantiation was not a standard eighth-century view; it was a standard thirteenth-century view; and again it was not a standard seventeenth-century view in England. It was unknown in the eighth century, considered orthodox in the thirteenth, and thought of as heterodox in the seventeenth. The view that the papacy is the Antichrist was nonstandard in the Middle Ages, standard in sixteenth-century England, and nonstandard in eighteenth-century England (Hill, 1971, pp. 32, 62). Many standard views are neither orthodox nor heterodox, because Christian doctrine does not specify every last belief a Christian must have. The belief in guardian angels was a standard belief, is not now, but has never been declared either orthodox or heterodox.

The failure to recognize the distinction between orthodox and standard undermines many judgments of Hobbes's orthodoxy. About Hobbes's beliefs that "the universe is body, . . . that the Pentateuch and many other books of Scripture are redactions or compilations from earlier sources, . . . [and] that few if any miracles can be credited after the Testamental period," Samuel Mintz says, "their sweeping unorthodoxy is self-evident" (Mintz, 1962, p. 45). Far from being self-evidently unorthodox, none of these is unorthodox, since none is either asserted in or follows from anything in the Bible or in any of the creeds that define orthodoxy, even though they were nonstandard in the seventeenth century. Furthermore, many of these views are held by the most orthodox of Christians today.

While some of Hobbes's views were nonstandard in the sense just explained, especially his view that God is material, most of his views were standard sixteenth- and seventeenth-century Reformation views. In addition to praising Luther and Melanchthon, Hobbes is especially committed to the thought of Calvin and of Puritan theologians such as William Perkins (EW, 5:64–5, 266).[3] Hobbes's determinism, which is often thought to indicate, or even to entail, atheism, is not merely a part of his mechanistic materialism; it is logically tied to Calvin's doctrines of predestination and belief in the omnipotence of God. Hobbes's attempt to minimize the number of miracles in the postapostolic age was a Reformation view, and his attempt to give scientific explanations to many of them was shared by other theologians of his time. Hobbes's supposedly "dark" view of human nature is characteristic of the Bible, as understood by the Calvinist theology he had been taught at Magdalen Hall (EW, 2:xv–xvi). Is there anything in Hobbes's work darker than Calvin's own view of human nature? In *Institutes of the Christian Religion*, Calvin says, "[I]t is futile to seek anything good in our nature. Indeed, I grant that not all these wicked traits appear in every man; yet one cannot deny that this hydra lurks in the breast of each. For as the body, so long as it nourishes in itself the cause and matter of disease . . . will not be called healthy, so also will the soul not be considered healthy while it abounds with so many fevers of vice; . . . the soul, plunged into this deadly abyss, is not only burdened with vices, but is utterly devoid of all good" (Calvin, 1559, II.3.2).[4] Although Hobbes's remarks about human beings in the state of nature are intended to be purely descriptive, whereas Calvin's remarks about human nature are intended to be normative, the basic view is the same.

Accusations of heterodoxy need to be evaluated with the great Christian theologians in mind. In other words, Hobbes has been the victim of a double standard. Scholars often build much of their case for Hobbes's alleged irreligiousness upon his adherence to doctrines that Reformation leaders also held, but their adherence to the doctrine is not used to attack their faith in Christianity. For example, both Luther and Calvin denied free will, but this is never used as evidence that they were atheists. Similarly, Hobbes's attacks on Aristotelian philosophy should not be construed as anti-Christian. Reformation theologians from Tyndale to Calvin (and beyond) frequently attacked Aristotle. The express objective of both these theologians and Hobbes was to eliminate what they considered pagan accretions to Christian doctrine (e.g., Tyndale, 1526, p. 328).

Many of Hobbes's views which may have been nonstandard in the seventeenth century were at least not unprecedented. Like Hobbes, Milton held that angels have bodies

(Elledge, 1975, p. 394); Luther held that humans are not conscious after death (Burns, 1972, pp. 27–32); and Tertullian held that God is material. In any case, Hobbes always presented a two-pronged defense of the acceptability of his nonstandard views: that his own view is philosophically or scientifically necessary and that the standard view is not biblical (e.g., EW, 3:381–8, 4:61–2).

Hobbes's religious projects

However extensive his divergences from standard seventeenth-century views may or may not be, it is more important to understand what motivates them. I shall argue that, in addition to his obvious political intentions, Hobbes was trying to answer the challenge that the new science of Copernicus and Galileo posed for religion[5] and to prevent the abuse of religion for political purposes. Hobbes's goal with respect to these two issues was (1) to show that the distinctively religious content of the Bible could be reconciled with the new science and (2) to prove that religion could not legitimately be used to destabilize a government. Each of these issues required a new way of looking at some of the old truths. According to the Old Testament,[6] the earth is the center of the universe; according to the Copernican view it is not. According to Presbyterians and Roman Catholics, people can revolt for religious reasons; according to the royalist, Church of England view in the Elizabethan and Jacobean periods, they cannot. It is not surprising that Hobbes's religious theories were challenged. Most of his critics either did not appreciate the challenge of modern science or themselves wanted to use religion for their own partisan purposes. Thus, Hobbes was bent on initiating a cultural transformation (cf. Johnston, 1986, pp. xix–xx); his philosophy was Janus-faced. It looked back to the past for its religious content and forward to the future for its theoretical foundations.

Introduction

Fact and theory

More needs to be said about the theories that Hobbes devised to support the orthodox religious doctrines that he tried to preserve. The Christian creeds – for example, the Nicene creed – specify what may be called "first-order propositions." By "first-order propositions," I mean nontheoretical ones. Propositions such as that God exists, that he is almighty, that there is one God, and that three persons are God, are nontheoretical. They articulate the content of a religious faith, but they do not explain it. Rather, they need some theory to make them intelligible or to explain how they could possibly be true.[7] The doctrine of the Trinity is the most prominent example of a doctrine that needs to be explained. One theory supporting it might be that every intelligent being must have a mind, a will, and a memory, and that God the Father is the mind, the Holy Spirit is the will, and the Son is the memory. Augustine of Hippo argued for something very much like this. Another theory might be that identity is relative: that the Father, the Son, and the Holy Spirit are identical, relative to being God, but not identical relative to being persons. These are two competing theories supporting the same dogma. Or consider another doctrine, one that does not appear in the creeds already mentioned. According to the doctrine of papal infallibility, the pope is infallible when he makes pronouncements to the entire church about matters of faith or morals. How this could be so needs an explanation. One theory might be that whenever the pope makes such a pronouncement, after praying to the Holy Spirit for guidance, the Holy Spirit itself guarantees that the pope will speak truly. Quite a different theory is that the pope's pronouncements are infallible because they are not empirical statements but a kind of declarative speech act. What is peculiar about declarations is that they are true in virtue of being uttered by the right person in the right circumstances about the right topic. That is, the declarative speech act creates the fact that makes it true. For example, when the president of the Olympic

6

Games says, "I declare the Olympic Games open," his utterance creates the fact that makes the utterance true. When a jury says, "We find the defendant guilty," then the defendant is guilty in the relevant sense of legal guilt (Martinich, 1980, 1982).

Neither the distinction between first- and second-order propositions nor the one between fact and theory is peculiar to theology. It is a fact that the sun illuminates various parts of the earth each day in a predictable sequence. But there have been various theories to explain this fact: that Apollo drives the sun across the sky each day; that the sun moves in a circular path around the earth; and that the earth rotates on its axis with respect to the sun. The choice between theories is not always between mythic and scientific, or between good scientific or bad scientific theory. The wave and particle theories of light are both good theories; but they cannot both be true.[8] First-order propositions do not specify any particular theory that can explain them, and in the history of Christianity, various theories have been proposed to support Christian doctrine. The two most basic theories are the Platonic theory of Augustinianism and the Aristotelian theory of Thomism. Hobbes thought that the Platonic influence on Christianity was innocuous, but he detested the influence of Aristotelianism. One of Hobbes's chief projects was to create a new theory for Christianity, a theory that would make it compatible with the modern science of Copernicus, Galileo, and Harvey.

To exploit a biblical metaphor, I am maintaining that Hobbes thought that the Roman Catholic Church had poured the new wine of Christianity into the old skins of Aristotelianism, which were now cracked and leaking doctrine.[9] His project was to pour the old wine of biblical Christianity into the new skins of scientific theory.[10] As it came to be worked out historically, the new skins turned the old wine into the vinegar of atheism. But I do not see that Hobbes should be faulted for his ingenious efforts, since it is doubtful whether any theory has succeeded where his has failed.

THE FAILURE OF HOBBES'S RELIGIOUS PROJECTS

Hobbes would have come to be a religious hero if his projects had succeeded. But they did not. (For an explanation of some of the logical deficiencies of Hobbes's views, see Hepburn, 1972.) Thus, his critics were correct, to a large extent, in sensing that his attempt to salvage religion would not work. Rather than supplying an adequate conceptual foundation for religion, on the whole his views fit into a long tradition that tended to undermine it, often contrary to the intentions of the authors. In short, while his views did contribute to the secularization of philosophy, I maintain that this was an unintended and (for Hobbes) unforeseen consequence of his work. Don Cameron Allen has written a history of the same kind of failed attempt to give theoretical support to a religious doctrine, namely, the story of Noah and the Flood. Allen says that "the efforts of the theologians to prove that this legend was completely credible in every detail ended with almost a complete disavowal of the story itself." Speaking more generally, he then says that the "progress of mankind often depends more on glorious failures than on brilliant successes" (Allen, 1949, p. 66).[11]

I am claiming that Hobbes's philosophy is one of those glorious failures, and that it and the attempt to establish the truth of the story of Noah are part of the early modern project of trying to reconcile Christianity with modern science. Hobbes is often misinterpreted because only those parts of his theories that are congenial to contemporary philosophers have been emphasized, while the rest has been downgraded or explained away. If his jaundiced view of human nature is abstracted from its Calvinistic underpinnings of the total depravity of mankind; if his determinism is abstracted from his predestinationism; if his social contractarianism is abstracted from his absolutism; then he looks very contemporary. Such interpretations are the philosophical equivalent of writing Whig history. Taken as a whole and in their historical context, Hobbes's doctrines look quite different.

I have suggested that in addition to his departure from

many standard first-level religious views, part of the animus against him by his contemporaries can be attributed to the apparent failure of his theories to justify orthodox Christian views. Of course, this is not the whole story. For many other intellectuals who concocted theories that were at least as inadequate as Hobbes's were dealt with much more kindly than Hobbes. The whole story is quite complicated. Part of it has to do with his acerbic personality; part of it has to do with the peculiar politics of the time. Much of this story will be detailed in the following chapters. What I want to mention here is an irony in the history of claims that Hobbes was either an atheist or a tepid theist. His contemporaries said that he was an atheist as a way of maligning him; our contemporaries say it as a way of praising him.

Whether successful or not, some of Hobbes's ideas were developed and accepted by later religious thinkers. His view that faith belongs to the will, not the intellect, which is characteristic of the Reformation tradition, was fully developed by Søren Kierkegaard. His method of dating passages and determining authorship of various parts of the Bible is now widely accepted by biblical scholars. His explanations for the stories of miracles and healings in the Bible have been adopted by some theologians.

HOBBES'S MODERNISM

In emphasizing Hobbes's orthodoxy over his nonstandard views, I am not saying that his theories are conservative or lack novelty. To the contrary, a large part of the contemporary opposition to him was directly attributable to his novelty. The seventeenth century was still emerging from deeply rooted medieval views. For example, writing fifty years before Hobbes, Richard Hooker had used scholastic philosophy to defend state control of the Church of England (Wootton, 1986, pp. 217–21). Also, at least two of Hobbes's most famous critics, John Whitehall and Alexander Ross, rejected Copernicanism. Whitehall tended to conflate Hobbes's scientific and political views. He wrote that Hobbes is "positive for *Copernicus*, and would have the Earth it self turn'd upside down in Nature, (just as he hath been indeavoring to deal with the Policy of it," (Whitehall, 1679, p. 162; Ross, 1646, p. 57; Ross, 1653, pp. 93–4, 101).

Perhaps the most important element of Hobbes's greatness is his distinctively modern theories of both the natural and social worlds.[12] To a great extent, this involved inverting or reversing medieval priorities. For example, for medieval thinkers the primary object of knowledge is God. Even if people want to know what human nature is like, they should study the nature of God, according to medieval thinkers, because God made man in his own image and the original has more reality than an image. Hobbes rejects this line of thought. He is part of the humanistic tradition that was to come to full bloom in the eighteenth century: the proper study of mankind is man. What people know about God must come for the most part from revelation. Hobbes does not abandon belief in God, but he does transform the character of those discussions. Thus, while Hobbes is not medieval, he has the same concerns as medieval philosophers, as I shall show in later chapters (cf. Laird, 1934).

In addition to reversing or inverting medieval priorities, Hobbes also transformed religious concepts into secular concepts. For example, the biblical and medieval model of God's method of creating the world becomes the model for creating the commonwealth. The biblical and medieval idea that salvation comes after death is changed into the view that the commonwealth provides salvation in this life.

None of these reversals or transformations is evidence that Hobbes was nonreligious or antireligious. To the contrary, they indicate how important he thought these religious concepts were, not merely for some remote or invisible spiritual life but here and now. So, in addition to emphasizing Hobbes's adherence to orthodoxy and his novel theoretical foundation for religion, I shall be pointing out how he adapts traditional religious concepts to a modern view of reality.

Introduction

A HISTORICAL APPROACH TO HOBBES

Hobbes scholarship, over the last twenty-five years, has been as impressive as any in modern philosophy. However, the best of it has typically been ahistorical (e.g., Gauthier, 1969; Kavka, 1986). These philosophers have been concerned with the logical skeleton of Hobbes's argument. They have abstracted from both the larger conceptual issues of his philosophy, especially his views of religion and history, and their historical context, for example, the English Civil War. They do so out of a strange kind of respect for him. Since they aspire to ascertain the best argument for a certain position and read Hobbes because they think that he can often help them attain their aspiration, they are happy to abandon his own argument when they think he fails them. Kavka, for example, says, "This book is less concerned with what Hobbes said for its own sake than with what may be learned from what he said. In particular, it is concerned with his moral and political ideas insofar as they are relevant today. So the text corrects, modifies and departs from Hobbes where necessary" (Kavka, 1986, p. xiv). By focusing exclusively on the narrowly logical structure of his thought, they present a bloodless model of Hobbes's philosophy.

One of my goals in this book is to flesh out Hobbes's thought and to restore its historical and religious muscle. So this work belongs to the history of philosophy. That does not make my book history as opposed to philosophy. On the contrary, I believe that the work of W. V. Quine, and other recent philosophers of language, has shown that to understand a person's language is not to assign independently existing "meanings" to the speaker's words, without regard to the context. Interpreting or understanding what a person meant equally involves attributing certain beliefs and intentions to the speaker (Davidson, 1984, p. 141), and the basis for attributing these beliefs and intentions depends to a great extent on contextual features: who the person is, where and when he or she said it, to whom he or she said it, and so on.

In the case of historical figures, understanding these beliefs and intentions requires a historical understanding of the subject's life, times, and circumstances. Hobbes himself made the point a bit more simply: "Though words be the *signs* we have of one another's *opinions* and intentions, because the *equivocation* of them is so *frequent according to* the *diversity of contexture*, and of the company wherewith they go, . . . it must therefore be *extremely hard* to find the *opinions* and meaning of those *men* that are *gone from us long ago*, and have left us no other signification thereof than their books, which cannot possibly be understood without *history*, to discover those aforementioned circumstances" (EW, 4:75).[13]

My intentions, then, are philosophical, and they can be achieved only by taking extra-logical elements into account; in particular, I must take historical elements into account.[14] The history of philosophy is the way philosophy teaches by examples.[15] Because I combine analytic techniques with the history of philosophy, I would describe my work as an essay in analytic history of philosophy.

In urging the importance of a historically informed interpretation of philosophers, I am not suggesting that a nonhistorical interpretation has no value. Rather, I am suggesting that a purely nonhistorical approach is virtually impossible. Every scholar has some historical knowledge of a philosopher's context and uses it in his or her interpretation. Every Hobbes scholar either presupposes that seventeenth-century English means the same as twentieth-century English or assumes that it means something different (and must discover the divergences). In either case, a historical judgment has been made. Thus, rather than arguing that a historical interpretation of Hobbes is superior to a non-historical interpretation, I am arguing that a more historical interpretation is needed in order to understand Hobbes's thought correctly. Sometimes just a little more historical information can radically change one's interpretation of a text. But I am not suggesting that extensive historical awareness will determine a specific interpretation. Quentin Skinner is as knowledgeable as anyone about both the philosophical and nonphilosophical context surrounding Hobbes, yet his interpretation is the opposite of mine, and I shall have to explain in what way I think he misuses the historical evidence.

SECULAR AND RELIGIOUS INTERPRETATIONS

Hobbes scholars can be divided into two groups: those that give a secular interpretation to his philosophy and those that give a religious interpretation. A religious interpretation is one that holds that the idea of God and other religious concepts play an important part in Hobbes's philosophy. A secular interpretation is not a religious one. I shall sometimes refer to proponents of these two views as "secularists" and "religionists," respectively. These terms are meant to be nontendentious. They do not indicate a pre-judgment as to the value of the views in question, nor do they indicate the personal religious convictions of the scholar involved.

For my purposes, the most important secularists are Quentin Skinner, David Gauthier, and Edwin Curley. (Skinner has already been mentioned; his views are discussed at length in Appendix B.) Gauthier, in *The Logic of Leviathan*, has presented an impressive and rigorous treatment of Hobbes's political philosophy that explicitly excludes what Hobbes says about God. I discuss Gauthier's views primarily in Chapters 2 and 5. Curley has presented the strongest case that Hobbes, like Spinoza, intended to undermine the idea of revealed religion and was probably an atheist. I discuss Curley's views in Appendix A. The most significant religious interpreters are A. E. Taylor, Howard Warrender, and F. C. Hood.[16] While I am in general sympathy with Taylor and Warrender, I differ from them in many important respects. For now, it is most essential for me to dissociate myself from the work of Hood.

Contrary to Hood, I maintain that Hobbes is not assuming the truth of Scripture and drawing conclusions from it

(Hood, 1964, p. 1); rather, he is trying to supply a theoretical justification for believing in Scripture, which he thinks is under subtle attack from both incipient modern science and self-appointed interpreters with disruptive political motives. Further, I think that Hood is mistaken in holding that the laws of nature are a "philosophic fiction," that they are "not yet laws properly so-called" and "as such . . . do not oblige" (Hood, 1964, pp. viii, 4). I shall argue that, according to Hobbes, the laws of nature are properly laws and are such because God commands them. Another difference between Hood's treatment and mine is that I treat the full range of religious and theological concepts that Hobbes discusses, including angels, heaven, hell, miracles, and redemption, not merely the obviously political ones.

Most Hobbes scholars are secularists. One consequence of this is that they present a bowdlerized version of his philosophy from which all the religious elements have been expurgated. After mentioning that the last two of *Leviathan*'s four parts explicitly deal with religion, contemporary scholars typically claim that these parts are not important for understanding his philosophy and thus ignore them. When religious topics or theological terms are introduced in the first two parts, these are typically passed over without mention or with a perfunctory and dismissive discussion, most notably in Hobbes's discussion of the laws of nature. One of the most popular editions of *Leviathan* excises parts III and IV completely. When his religious views are discussed, only a select few are quoted. At least 95 percent of Hobbes's remarks about religion are either obviously consonant with orthodox Christianity, typical of seventeenth-century Christianity, or directed specifically against Presbyterianism and Catholicism. It is not surprising that scholars can make some of Hobbes's remarks seem to say just the opposite of what he intended them to mean, when they are removed from their literary contexts and when the historical context is either unmentioned or unknown. An example of Hobbes's orthodox expression of a central Christian doctrine is the following:

To the office of a Redeemer, that is, of one that payeth the ransom of sin, which ransom is death, it appertaineth, that he was sacrificed, and thereby bare upon his own head and carried away from us our iniquities, in such sort as God had required. Not that the death of one man, though without sin, can satisfy for the offenses of all men, in the rigour of justice, but in the mercy of God, that ordained such sacrifices for sin, as he was pleased in his mercy to accept. . . . [T]he death of the Messiah, is a sufficient price for the sins of all mankind, because there was no more required. Our Saviour Christ's sufferings seem to be here figured, as clearly as in the oblation of Isaac, or in any other type of him in the Old Testament. He was both the sacrificed goat, and the scapegoat. . . . Thus is the lamb of God equivalent to both those goats; sacrificed, in that he died; and escaping, in his resurrection; being raised opportunely by his Father, and removed from the habitation of men in his ascension. (EW, 3:476–7)

There is nothing maudlin or saccharine in this passage. But it is reverent and orthodox, although clearly committed to a specific theology – authentic Calvinism – insofar as it emphasizes that the Atonement is achieved through the mercy, in contrast with the justice, of God.

Like most interpreters, I will focus on Hobbes's greatest work, *Leviathan*. Because I do not want to be sidetracked by the need to explain minor differences between Hobbes's various works, I will discuss these other works only insofar as they complement the project of interpreting *Leviathan*.

CONCLUSION

In the chapters that follow I will be arguing that Hobbes effects a number of important reversals in the traditional understanding of the way Christianity should be conceived. His motivation for these reversals was twofold: he wanted to preserve orthodox Christian beliefs by reconciling them with the modern science of Copernicus, Galileo, and others; and he wanted to neutralize religion politically so that it would serve the cause of peace rather than war.

Some of the reasons why his project received such opposition in his own time include: (1) his rejection of some standard religious beliefs of the seventeenth century, beliefs that are not part of orthodoxy; (2) the presence of partisan religious and political organizations among his opponents; (3) the novel ability of his theoretical apparatus to account for various religious propositions; (4) the philosophical ineptitude of his critics; and (5) the ultimate inadequacy of that theoretical apparatus. Other reasons could be added. Hobbes was contentious. His remarks were often barbed and harsh, and sometimes vulgar (e.g., EW, 4:440; see also 5:212). Although he was not unusually abusive for the time, when he struck personally at an enemy he was brutal. Fed up with Bishop John Bramhall's self-righteous airs, Hobbes says that Bramhall's case would have been stronger if he had devoted more time to thinking rather than trying to gain preferment and to increase his personal wealth (EW, 5:63). He had a rapier wit, and his style is often inflammatory and hyperbolic. I shall provide illustrations of these qualities in the chapters that follow.

From a different perspective, my thesis is that for the most part Hobbes meant what he said. According to the dominant interpretations, Hobbes did not mean that the laws of nature are literally laws; did not mean that they literally impose an obligation on humans; did not mean that God literally commands them; did not mean that the Kingdom of God is literally a kingdom; and did not literally mean that God rules. According to me, the correct understanding of his moral and political philosophy depends upon interpreting what he said literally, when he writes *ex professo* on a topic. Some scholars have found it odd that Hobbes's radically new political theory should result in such conventional moral laws. But it is no more surprising than to find that Copernicus's cosmological system did not change the fact that night and day follow each other, that there are twenty-four hours in a day, and that there are 365 days in a year. Both Hobbes and Copernicus presented new theories to account for old facts.

Part I

The religious background to Hobbes's philosophy

Chapter 1

Considerations upon the reputation and religion of Mr. Hobbes

Natus erat noster servator Homo-Deus annos
Mille et quingentos, octo quoque undecies.
(O.L., 1:lxxxv)

THE USE OF THE TERM "ATHEISM"

Since few philosophers today think that Hobbes was an atheist, proving that he was a theist is not a pressing matter. Nonetheless, investigating the grounds for the charge against him will motivate the introduction of certain methodological principles that are commonly used in interpreting Hobbes's works. Unlike Nietzsche and Sartre, for example, Hobbes never says that he is an atheist. To the contrary, he affirms his belief in God on many occasions. The case against him, then, is at best indirect. It is based upon inferences that his contemporaries and scholars have made about his work.

One piece of prima facie evidence that Hobbes was an atheist is the fact that some of his contemporaries called him an atheist.[1] But this is not strong evidence. The term "atheist" was used indiscriminately in Hobbes's day as a term of abuse, as some observers of the contemporary scene recognized. In his essay "Of Atheism," Francis Bacon wrote, "[A]ll that impugn a received religion, or superstition, are, by the adverse part, branded with the name of atheists." An article in a newspaper edited by Marchamont Nedham says that the priests "call every thing that squares not with their corrupt *Clergy-Interest*" atheism (*Mercurius Politicus*, no. 84,

19

January 8–15, 1652). A theologian who was trying to improve the theoretical underpinnings of Christianity was especially likely to be tagged an atheist. James I called the distinguished Dutch theologian Konrad Vorst "a wretched Heretique, or rather Atheist" (Milward, 1978, p. 34) and "an enemie of God" (Tyacke, 1987a, p. 88).[2] Protestants and Catholics called each other "atheists."[3] Protestants called each other "papists" and "heretics" in the same breath: John Caius, Master of Gonville and Caius College, was called both "a Romanist and an atheist." The basis for the charge was that Catholicism logically leads to atheism (Chillingworth, 1638, p. 5; see also pp. 12–13, 409). Even Ralph Cudworth, the Cambridge Platonist, author of *The True Intellectual System of the Universe* and critic of Hobbes's materialism, was accused of atheism (Passmore, 1951, p. 27). Charles I called his enemies "Brownists, Anabaptists and Atheists," and it is clear from the context that "Atheists" is being used appositively (quoted from Kenyon, 1985, p. 153). In *Paradise Lost*, Milton called the rebellious angels "atheists" (Milton, 1674, book 6, line 370). Not in the same class, but also accused of atheism, were certain members of the Royal Society, some of whom, notably Robert Boyle, were motivated to pursue their scientific investigations by their desire to prove the truth of Christianity (Lyons, 1944, p. 60; Evelyn, 1669, entry for July 9, 1669).

Not even Christian monarchs escaped the epithet. Queen Elizabeth was called an atheist by John Bakeless, and James I the same by Martin Becanus, a Jesuit. It is not surprising, then, that a lay subject of a monarch could be called an atheist. Sir Walter Raleigh was accused of atheism, even though the theme of his *History of the World*, which begins with the Genesis account of creation, is that divine providence directs human history.[4]

Since religion and politics were closely tied in the seventeenth century, "atheist" was also a quasi-political term. In 1647, *Mercurius Pragmaticus* attributed atheism to Scots, Jesuits, Independents, and everyone else opposed to the king:

A Scot and Jesuite joyn't in hand,
First taught the World to say,
That Subjects ought to have Command,
And Princes to Obey.

These both agree to have NO KING,
The Scotch-man he cries further,
NO BISHOP; 'Tis A godly thing
States to Reform by Murther

Then th' Independents meeke and slie,
Most lowly lies at Lurch,
And so to put poore Jockie by
Resolves to have NO CHURCH.

The King Dethron'd! The Subjects bleed!
The Church hath no aboad;
Let us conclude They're all agreed,
That sure there is NO GOD.
(Quoted from Nedham, 1650, p. xxii; see also EW, 4:294;
Dillenberger, 1960, p. 55 n. 7)

"Atheist" was only one of a cluster of words used in a
similar way. "Heretic," "Antichrist," and "papist" are three
others. Concerning heresy, Bishop John Stillingfleet made
the accusation against John Locke. Whereas "heretic" was a
generic epithet, Socinianism was a preferred brand of heresy
to attribute to one's opponent. Edward Knott, a Catholic
apologist, accused all Protestants of Socinianism (Chillingworth, 1638, p. 6). Among themselves, Protestants were
more discriminating. The Calvinist Theophilus Gale accused
Hugo Grotius of "rank *Socinianisme* and *Arianisme.*"[5] The
term "Antichrist" was liberally applied: the institution of the
papacy, individual popes, Protestant bishops and monarchs,
ministers, Presbyterians, and all laymen were so called, by
someone at some time (see Hill, 1971, pp. 1–40). "Papists"
included Charles I, Archbishop William Laud, and Arminians[6] in general (Trevor-Roper, 1989, pp. 63, 68). Even
Hobbes was called a papist (Whitehall, 1679, p. 147). If the
words of his contemporaries are taken in an uncritical way,
then Hobbes was an atheistical papist.[7] So much for the

21

precision and reliability of the term "atheist," coming from the pen of an opponent.

Although these terms were meant to be abusive and were applied rather freely, they did not lack cognitive content. It is important to try to realize that there is often a gap between the meaning or definition of a word and the way it is applied. I shall explain this distinction in the next section.

ATHEISM BY CONSEQUENCE

There is a difference between the meaning of a word and the criteria for its application. The meaning of the word "strong" is having the power to do much work and not easily broken, worn, or injured. But there are various criteria for its application. Some humans, elephants, and machines are strong in the same senses. But the criteria for applying that property to those three kinds of things differ. An elephant that could do only as much work as a human being would not be a strong elephant. This is not to suggest that there is only one criterion of strength for elephants and only one criterion of strength for humans. There are many criteria for each, and many of them are ad hoc and sometimes inappropriate. According to one criterion, a human is strong if he or she can do fifty pushups; according to another, a strong human can benchpress at least 200 pounds. Fruitless arguments can arise among people who agree about the meaning of a word if they do not realize that they disagree about the proper criterion for its application.

This problem arises with the word "atheist." The meaning of "atheist" is a person who believes that God does not exist. But various criteria compete with each other in the application of the term. In Elizabethan England, the criterion for atheism was variously skepticism, agnosticism, Machiavellianism, unitarianism, or immorality (Strathmann, 1951, pp. 96–7). For the sake of simplicity, let's consider the following three criteria for atheism: saying that one does not believe in God; acting as if one does not believe in God; and espousing beliefs that entail that one does not believe in God. Both

Hobbes's seventeenth-century critics and his twentieth-century defenders favor the last of these criteria. They claim that Hobbes is what he himself would call "an atheist by consequence." This criterion is defensible to the extent that a person sees all the logical consequences of his or her own view. Unfortunately, most people, even philosophers, do not.[8]

Also, sometimes it is unclear what consequences a principle does have. Hobbes argued at some length with Bishop Bramhall over just this issue. Bramhall, like certain others, thought that atheism was a logical consequence of some of Hobbes's philosophical principles. In the seventeenth century, charges of atheism were often raised on these general grounds. A man might be accused of atheism, not because he had ever professed such a view, but because he had espoused a view that his critics thought led by logical consequence to atheism. One of the original objections to the doctrines of Luther was that they were thought to lead to atheism (Montaigne, 1588, p. 320). Chillingworth believed that Roman Catholicism, because of its "weak and silly Ceremonies & ridiculous observances . . . , [logically leads to] Atheisme and impiety" (Chillingworth, 1638, p. 5; see also p. 409). In the eighteenth century Thomas Paine lumped Catholics and Protestants together and claimed that Christianity is "a species of Atheism" because of its mean-spirited portrayal of God (Paine, 1795, p. 36). In most cases it is unfair for critics to insist that their own deductions about their opponents' principles take precedence over the latter's own explicit assertions of their beliefs and their own claims about what does and does not follow from their principles (EW, 4:284). Sometimes a person's conscious beliefs and explicit assertions about God are inconsistent with the unrecognized consequences of his or her principles; that is, that the person is a sincere, though inconsistent, theist.

Not long after the publication of *Leviathan*, Henry Hammond, who had perhaps known Hobbes at Great Tew in the 1630s and who was destined to be a Restoration bishop, wrote in a letter that *Leviathan* was "a farrago of Christian atheism" (N. Pocock, 1850, p. 294). The phrase "Christian atheism" is oxymoronic and not completely clear. By using the word "farrago," Hammond indicated that Hobbes's doctrine was confused; this suggests he meant that although Hobbes intended to be a Christian, his principles in fact led to atheism. This interpretation of the phrase is more plausible than construing it to mean that Hobbes intended to present an atheistic doctrine, because if Hammond had thought that that was Hobbes's intent, he would not have said the work was a "farrago," and it would have been pointless to call it "Christian" (cf. Tuck, 1991a). In a subsequent letter, Hammond said of *Leviathan* that it was "a farrago of all the maddest divinity that ever was read, and . . . destroyed Trinity, Heaven, Hell" (N. Pocock, 1850, p. 295). Since Hobbes purported, in *Leviathan*, to defend the Trinity, heaven, and hell and since Hammond thought that these attempts were a farrago, he must have thought that Hobbes was an atheist as a consequence of his principles rather than wittingly. Finally, Hammond's epithets should not be taken too seriously, because they are offhand remarks that appear in letters devoted to other subjects, and he displays no substantive knowledge of *Leviathan*.

Not being in contact with Hobbes, Hammond was not in a good position to judge whether Hobbes was secretly an atheist. Other people, including those of religiously unimpeachable reputations, knew Hobbes better and never suggested that Hobbes was irreligious. For example, Robert Payne, a friend of Hammond and most other royalist Anglicans, explained that Hobbes resented the fact that Anglican clergy were undercutting his friendship with Charles II. Writing to Gilbert Sheldon, future archbishop of Canterbury, Payne said, "I am sorry to hear any of our coat have had the ill fortune to provoke so great a wit [Hobbes] against the church" and thought that Sheldon himself would not have opposed Hobbes (N. Pocock, 1848, p. 170). Although he regretted that Hobbes's religiopolitical views offended the royalist Anglicans, Payne never suggested that Hobbes was irreligious.

The weakness of the thesis that a philosopher's intended

views can be read off simply from the logical consequences of his or her propositions can be explained (ironically) by appealing to a hermeneutic or interpretive principle that Hobbes formulated independently of the controversy with Bramhall: "[W]hen it happeneth that a man signifieth unto two *contradictory* opinions, whereof the *one* is *clearly* and directly *signified*, and the *other* either drawn from that by *consequences*, or not known to be contradictory to it; then, when he is not present to explicate himself better, we are to take the *former* for his opinion; for that is clearly signified to be his, and directly; whereas the other might proceed from error in the deduction, or ignorance of the repugnancy" (EW, 4:75–6; see also Gauthier, 1969, pp. 179–80). In other words, Hobbes is pointing out that an author's own explicit assertions should be favored over a proposition derived from the author's principles by an interpreter. For one thing, the interpreter may have misunderstood what the author said or mistaken its consequences (making an "error in deduction"). Also, the author may have not realized that his or her principles had the consequences that the interpreter deduced ("ignorance of the repugnancy").[9] The second possibility is especially important, because it sets a limiting condition on atheism.

An atheist must be a person who is to some degree conscious of his disbelief in God; a person who subscribes to principles that entail atheism must intend those principles to entail atheism. Hobbes calls people who are not aware that their principles lead to atheism "atheists by consequence."[10] Hobbes thinks it is relatively easy to be an atheist by consequence. He thought he had proven that the principles of his Roman Catholic friend Thomas White led to the conclusion that there is no God and hence that White was an atheist by consequence (Hobbes, 1642, p. 326). He also tries to show, near the end of his *Answer to Bishop Bramhall*, that his accuser Bramhall is himself one (EW, 4:383–4; see also pp. 294 and 427). According to Hobbes, anyone who believes that God is an incorporeal spirit is a consequent atheist, because he is committed to the following syllogism: Nothing that is incorporeal exists; God is incorporeal; therefore, God does not exist.[11] The major premise is philosophically necessary, according to Hobbes, since the phrase "incorporeal existence," like "incorporeal substance," is contradictory. The minor premise is explicitly held by Bramhall and all scholastic philosophers.[12] However Hobbes, unlike Bramhall, thinks it is unfair to call atheists by consequence "atheists" *simpliciter* and thus forebears from condemning Bramhall on this ground. Concerning people in general who unwittingly subscribe to principles that he thinks in fact entail atheism, Hobbes says, "Were they atheists? No. For though by ignorance of the consequence they said that which was equivalent to atheism, yet in their hearts they thought God a substance. . . . So that his *atheism by consequence* is a very easy thing to be fallen into, even by the most godly men of the church" (EW, 4:383–4).

Robert Boyle also was slower than Bramhall to call someone an atheist. In *The Christian Virtuoso*, he says, "I do not think there are so many speculative atheists, as men are wont to imagine. . . . I am very apt to think, that mens want of due information, or their uncharitable zeal, has made them mistake or misrepresent many for deniers of God, that are thought such, chiefly because they take uncommon methods in studying his works, and have other sentiments of them than those of vulgar philosophers" (Boyle, 1690, p. 515). Whether Boyle had Hobbes in mind or not, his words certainly apply to Hobbes.[13]

If Hobbes was an atheist, then he was also an anarchist. His seventeenth-century critics used the same form of argument to establish that his principles led to both atheism and the destruction of all government. At that time, politics and religion could be distinguished but not very easily separated. The earl of Clarendon said that he had "never read any Book that contains in it so much Sedition, Treason, and Impiety as this *Leviathan*. . . . [Its principles] dissolving all the ligaments of Government, and undermining all principles of Religion" (Clarendon, 1676, p. 319; see also Ross, 1653, "To the Reader"). Another early critic said, "Mr *Hobbes* is generally for Positions that tend to unhinge all the foundations of Government" (Whitehall, 1679, p. 69). Atheism and anarchism stand or fall together, for several reasons. Clarendon and others think that Hobbes's principles have these things *as their consequences*, independently of what Hobbes thinks the consequences are. The same principles seem both atheistic and anarchic to Clarendon: humans are by nature self-interested, and humans have a right to their own life which can never be alienated.[14] Even if Hobbes's principles do lead to anarchism, it is misleading and inflammatory to refer to him as an "anarchist" when his obvious intentions are quite different. Further, no one who thinks that Hobbes's principles logically lead to anarchism thereby argues that this is evidence that he was conveying a secret message that anarchy is preferable to any government. Neither should people conclude that Hobbes was a secret atheist if his defense of theism does not succeed.

Implicit in the foregoing discussion are two reasons why Hobbes ought to be counted a theist. First, before ever being accused of atheism, Hobbes presented several versions of the traditional cosmological proofs for the existence of God, with no hint of sarcasm, parody, or satire. So, to judge him on the basis of the consequences of his principles, he is a theist. Second, after being accused of atheism by Bramhall, Hobbes explicitly denied the charge and tried to show that the pernicious consequences that Bramhall derived from Hobbes's principles were not genuine consequences but non sequiturs.

There is still a third reason for holding that Hobbes was a theist, and this reason is important for understanding why I interpret Hobbes as a sincere Christian and not a fifth columnist. Much of what he wrote presupposes, not merely the existence of God, but the existence of the Christian God. The most prominent examples of this are Parts III and IV of *Leviathan*, which deal with the full range of theological concepts. If in these sections Hobbes merely expressed conventional views about the matters or if there were undertones of sarcasm or irony, then a good case against his theism could

be built. But just the opposite is true. Far from being perfunctory or hackneyed, sarcastic or ironic, his treatments of
such issues as the Trinity and the Redemption of humankind
by Christ are ingenious and novel. It would have been absurd for Hobbes to concoct original theories for Christian
doctrines if he were not intellectually committed to them
(J. G. A. Pocock, 1971, pp. 167–8).

I shall be arguing, especially in Part III, "Religion within
the Limits of Science and Politics," that a close analysis of
Hobbes's views about the theological topics reveals that he is
trying to reconcile orthodox Christian doctrine with modern
science and a tenable political theory. The challenge was
great – perhaps impossible to achieve – and there were no
other models that Hobbes could draw on. If his theories are
logically absurd, it is not because he wanted them to be
absurd but because he was struggling with an enormous
problem and could not see anything better.[15] Pocock has put
a related point strongly: "Although esoteric reasons have
been suggested why Hobbes should have written what he
did not believe, the difficulty remains of imagining why a
notoriously arrogant thinker, vehement in his dislike of 'insignificant speech,' should have written and afterwards defended sixteen chapters of what he held to be nonsense, and
exposed them to the scrutiny of a public which did not consider this kind of thing nonsense at all" (Pocock, 1971, p.
162).

Some may object that, far from presupposing religious beliefs, Parts III and IV of *Leviathan* are designed to undermine
religion in a clever way. According to David Wootton, there
are systematic ambiguities in Hobbes's text. On one reading
of them, Hobbes is a theist; but on another reading, Hobbes
is an atheist. Given this contradiction and the fact that
Hobbes was a perceptive philosopher, it is clear that Hobbes
is using the contradiction to communicate something by implication. It cannot be that Hobbes is a theist, for he could
have produced a text that communicated that unambiguously. Therefore, given that as a practical matter professions of atheism were impossible in seventeenth-century En-

gland, Hobbes must have been communicating that he was an atheist, or at least antireligious. Here is a summary of that view:

> Charron, Hobbes, and Boyle seem systematically ambiguous. One can read them as either defending or criticizing religion. But why would they write ambiguously if their real intent was to defend religion? Their ambiguity can best be explained by the thesis that they intended to convey both an exoteric and an esoteric message. The only alternative would seem to be to provide a complex account in each case of how a pious author could be misread as impious by both contemporaries and later generations, an account that would have to include an explanation of why such an author would be unable or unwilling to correct the misapprehensions of his contemporaries when they became known to him. (Wootton, 1988, p. 711; see also Skinner, 1988, p. 53)

There are several ways to reply to this argument. First, I do not think that Hobbes's views are "systematically ambiguous." There are certainly some ambiguous passages and some that are difficult to reconcile with theism, for example, his definitions of religion and revelation. But it is non-controversial that every distinguished philosopher has written ambiguous passages. I think that the kind of difficulties that Wootton alludes to are relatively few compared to his work as a whole and can be explained in ways that are not ad hoc. That is, they can be explained in ways that are simple and not "complex." There is no mystery about "how a pious author could be misread as impious." The history of Christianity is full of examples. Aquinas and Meister Eckhart were condemned as impious in their own times. As for philosophers of later generations, they have to a large extent relied upon the judgment of Hobbes's contemporaries.[16] Finally, it is simply not true that Hobbes was "unable or unwilling to correct the misapprehensions of his contemporaries when they became known to him." Hobbes's replies to Bramhall (*An Answer to a Book Published by Dr. Bramhall* . . . *"Catching of Leviathan,"* *Of Liberty and Necessity*, and *The Questions Concerning Liberty and Chance*), his reply to John Wallis (*Consider-*

ations upon the Reputation, Loyalty, Manners, and Religion of Thomas Hobbes), his *Historical Narration Concerning Heresy*, which is an indirect response to charges that he was a heretic, and his *Historia Ecclesiastica Carmine Elegiaco Concinnata*, another indirect defense, are extended, largely cogent replies to misinterpretations. In general, Hobbes thought that his opponents often did not try to refute him but merely quoted him out of context. He also thought that they were philosophically inept (e.g., EW, 4:280–93). Finally, he also seemed to be largely unaware of published objections to his work (ibid., pp. 237, 281).

INTELLECTUAL COURAGE AND PHYSICAL COWARDICE

To hold that Hobbes professed Christianity but believed in atheism requires some explanation for the discrepancy between profession and belief. The obvious explanation is that Hobbes felt compelled to misrepresent his views because he feared that his life would be endangered by telling the whole truth.[17] Evidence of this is that Hobbes himself said that he was born a twin with fear and was the first of those who fled the Civil War. I am willing to concede that he was a physical coward. Hobbes attributed his premature birth to the impending invasion of the Spanish Armada. Some scholars think that he was exaggerating, since he was born on April 5, 1588, and the Spanish fleet did not sail until May. They do not take into account that the invasion was expected and that there was widespread fear in that year because it had been prophesied that 1588 would be a year of great disasters by many biblical and millenarian scholars (Firth, 1979, p. 150; see also Rogow, 1986, pp. 17–18). Hobbes may be alluding to these prophecies in his autobiography when he writes: "Fama ferebat enim diffusa per oppida nostra, / Extremum genti classe venire diem. / Atque metum tantum concepit tunc mea mater, / Ut pareret geminos, meque metumque simul" (For a rumor was spreading through our villages / that the last day of our nation would come from the fleet./

30

And my mother was then filled with so much fear / that she simultaneously gave birth to twins, both me and fear; OL, 1:lxxxvi).

There is little evidence that he was an intellectual coward. That is, although he would certainly flee from immediate physical danger, there is little evidence that he misrepresented his most important doctrines in writing, in order to escape danger. If Hobbes had been an atheist, he could have preserved his integrity in other ways; for example, by not publishing works about religion at all or by publishing anonymously, as many people of the time did. Even though anonymous authors were often identified, a person intent on anonymity could preserve it without too much difficulty. I agree with Willis Glover when he says, "The most plausible explanation for his discussion of these [controversial] matters is that he took his opinions on them seriously enough to risk the criticisms they were bound to draw. If Hobbes's purpose had been to avoid persecution, this purpose would have been better served by a clear and unqualified Erastianism without elaboration" (Glover, 1965, p. 148).

Hobbes certainly knew that his novel views would cause him trouble: "That which perhaps may most offend, are certain texts of Holy Scripture, alleged by me to other purpose than ordinarily they use to be by others" (EW, 3, "Epistle Dedicatory"). But he presents these novel interpretations "with due submission." Further, if he is the coward these scholars imply that he is, then he shows literally unbelievable fortitude in the face of the attacks of Bramhall, Wallis, and others. If Hobbes had been an intellectual coward, then he either would have not written about religion at all or would have made his religious views sound as conventional as possible. All of these counterfactual conditional sentences should make clear that I do not believe for a moment that Hobbes was an atheist, an intellectual coward, or a liar. Later I shall explain why an orthodox Christian, as I claim Hobbes was, should present novel biblical interpretations and why he felt compelled to write about religion at all.

My defense of Hobbes's theism has an important conse-

31

quence. The same kind of reasons that have been used to defend him in this context can be used to defend the claim that he tried to be a completely orthodox Christian. His discussions of such topics as the Trinity, redemption, grace, miracles, heaven, and hell presuppose belief in them. When he was presented with doubts of his orthodoxy, his affirmed his belief in the propositions of the Christian creeds. And, presented with Bramhall's objections, he explained why Bramhall's interpretations were incorrect and elaborated on his views. In short, without strong reasons to the contrary, Hobbes must be taken at his word on religious matters (cf. J. G. A. Pocock, 1971, pp. 167–18).

ATHEISTS AND ARMINIANS

Ceteris paribus, if a person's contemporaries call him an atheist, it is plausible that he is an atheist. I have already given some reasons why the *ceteris paribus* condition fails. In the seventeenth century "atheist" was more readily used as a term of abuse than it is these days, and more often attributed to a person whose philosophical or religious principles entailed atheism in the opinion of the critic. There is still another reason why the *ceteris paribus* condition fails. In seventeenth-century England, religious disagreements were more acrimonious than they are in the twentieth century. Religious views were more parochial, partisan, and politically charged. In order to talk informatively about the seventeenth century, it is simply not good enough to rely solely on the distinction between theist and atheist. While there is nothing wrong with this distinction, more fine-grained distinctions are needed in order to understand the disputes between intellectuals in that period. Most attacks of one person against another were highly parochial. Indeed, these attacks, far from indicating that the target of criticism lacked religion, are strong evidence for it. A Calvinist attack on an Arminian is no evidence that the Arminian was any less Christian than the Calvinist, and vice versa.

This point bears directly on Hobbes's religious views. He

subscribed to a Calvinist theology, whereas his most famous critics – for example, Bramhall and Clarendon – were Arminians. For his own part as a critic, Hobbes had highly specific denominational and sectarian targets in *Leviathan*. He attacked Roman Catholic and Presbyterian doctrines by name, because they were his most powerful opponents. But he had other groups in mind too. In *Behemoth* he criticized Baptists and Quakers, which at the time were disreputable sects, not to mention the millenarian Fifth Monarchy men[18] (EW, 6:167, 333, 357, 391).

Many of his contemporaries called Hobbes a heretic or atheist, not because he aspired to heresy or atheism, but because he was advancing a theoretical case for a politically charged religious view with which they disagreed. In particular, he was supporting a case for a state-controlled Church of England that would be episcopal in polity and Calvinist in theology. If this sounds strange, it is nonetheless not. He was supporting in effect the Elizabethan and Jacobean Church of England, which had become unpopular in the 1640s. To a great extent, he was trying to do for the Stuart Church of England what Hooker had done for the Elizabethan church a half century earlier. Hooker argued both from reason and the Bible that the secular and religious authorities need to be the same, just as it was institutionalized in the Church of England. The major differences between Hooker and Hobbes are that while Hooker was using a scholastic philosophy and theology to attack Puritans, Hobbes used what he understood to be modern scientific methods and a Calvinist theology to attack, primarily, Roman Catholics and Presbyterians. Those who object that Hobbes wanted a state-run religion need to understand that at least since the Act of Supremacy of Henry VIII in 1534, such a view was the official English view and the law of the land. This supremacy was reaffirmed during the reign of Edward VI and then again in the Act of Supremacy of 1559, during the reign of Elizabeth. Uniformity in church liturgy was dictated by the Uniformity Act of the same year. In 1572, the Oath of Supremacy for all new bishops began, "I, A. B., now elect bishop of C., do utterly testify and declare that the Queen's Highness is the only supreme governor of this realm . . . as well in all *spiritual and ecclesiastical things or causes as temporal*" (Dickinson and Donaldson, 1954, 3:13). Thus, the content of Hobbes's religious views was quite conservative and traditional and was sometimes recognized as such by his contemporaries (e.g., Clarendon, 1676, pp. 232–3). While many people were seemingly scandalized by Hobbes's theoretical arguments that the church and state ought to be governed by the same person, Clarendon agreed completely and even claimed that no bishop or priest holds anything different (ibid., p. 249). After the Restoration, the union of civil and ecclesiastical authority in the monarch was the official theory of Charles II's court when he was trying to promote his claim to absolute sovereignty (Ashcraft, 1986, pp. 39–74).

As I said, I shall be arguing that in theology, Hobbes was a Calvinist; and in liturgy and ecclesiastical polity episcopal. This is not to say that his defenses of his views are conservative or traditional. Hobbes introduced new theories and new ways of reasoning about both politics and religion, in order to save the old doctrines of Christianity and absolute sovereignty. Hobbes has been called a "radical in the service of reaction" (Tulloch, 1874, 2:26). Robert Filmer, one of Hobbes's earliest critics, essentially agreed. He said that although he liked Hobbes's political conclusions, he did not like the arguments Hobbes used to prove them (Filmer, 1655, p. 239). Implicit in Filmer's remark is a distinction between doctrine (conclusions) and theory (arguments). That is, Filmer approved of Hobbes's conservative doctrine but rejected his liberal theory. By "conservative" and "liberal" here, I mean "traditional" and "innovative." I shall be arguing that the same distinction between conservative doctrine and liberal theory applies to Hobbes's religious views. Hobbes's conclusions in religion are conservative, but he used liberal arguments.

Many of the defenders of the Church of England were also conservative philosophically and thus found any innovation objectionable. In this way, Hobbes, in the seventeenth century, was in the same position as Aquinas in the thirteenth century. For it must be remembered that many of Aquinas' views were condemned in 1270 and 1277. One difference between Hobbes and Aquinas is that Hobbes's theory, unlike Aquinas' Aristotelian theory, never gained acceptance by those who wrote the theological history of the period. Baptists, Quakers, and Brownists (the latter of whom evolved into Congregationalists) were excoriated in the seventeenth century but achieved respectability over time. It was Hobbes's misfortune never to have been adopted by a sect that was promoted to church status or to have espoused the theology of the Restoration Church of England. His theory lost out to antipredestination Arminian theologians, in part because they made themselves appear to be uncompromising royalists, while Hobbes had been compromised during the Interregnum. Hobbes recognized the political disability he suffered in defending authentic Calvinism against the Arminians, whose position he described as "the readiest way to ecclesiastical promotion" (EW, 5:2). The ecclesiastical dominance and political advantage of the Arminians during the 1630s and then again after 1660, was well known. George Morley was a close friend of Clarendon and member of the circle that met at Great Tew. When he was asked by someone trying to understand the niceties of Reformed theology, "What do the Arminians hold?," he replied, "All the best bishoprics and deaneries in England" (quoted from Ollard, 1988, p. 37).[19] If Hobbes had been a member of the Dutch Reformed Church, his reputation might have fared better.

Most of the so-called contemporary critics of Hobbes were either Arminian Anglicans who opposed Hobbes's Calvinism, or uncompromising royalists who would not forgive Hobbes for his acceptance of Cromwell's rule and preferred a divine right of kings theory of government (Clarendon, 1676). Scholars rely too heavily and too uncritically upon these political and theological partisans. To accept their interpretation of Hobbes would be like relying on the anti-Christian Roman Historians Livy and Suetonius for our understanding of early Christian views if the empire had not fallen. Hobbes is a victim of having his place in the history of religion first written by the victors of the theological battles he lost.

I have never seen it mentioned, in connection with their debates with Hobbes, that his critics had their faults: that Archbishop Laud's protégé Bishop Bramhall, who called Hobbes "an atheist," was an Arminian; or that Alexander Ross, who called him "a Sabellian, Mahumetan, Manichies (Manichaean), Tertullian, and a Jew"[20] was an anti-Semite (Ross, 1653, "To the Reader"); or that Clarendon, who thought him an ingrate to the class that financially supported him, was an impeached and exiled former minister to Charles II; or that Wallis was arguably a traitor, rebel, and double agent (EW, 4:415–17). My point is not to smear these men but to indicate that in the volatile political world of the seventeenth century almost every thinker of any note was called a criminal or heretic at some time and to urge that charges made by each of Hobbes's critics be used discriminately. When a person makes a charge against Hobbes, it must be weighed against what Hobbes said, and most likely meant, in the relevant texts. This is all that he himself requested in these matters (EW, 4:281).

The same caution must be used with institutions. Although Parliament appointed a committee in 1666 to investigate Hobbes for possible atheism, the committee never reported, and no action was taken against him. If this investigation of Hobbes is an indictment of his work for the crime of atheism, then the failure of that committee to report is tantamount to an acquittal. However, it would be a mistake to make too much of the committee, no matter how one judges its action or inaction. Considering the frequency of beheadings, hangings, mutilations, and imprisonment suffered by dozens of religious figures in the seventeenth century, the absence of any trial or penalty against Hobbes suggests that he was not, by and large, considered a genuinely irreligious figure. In contrast, Laud was accused of heresy by the House of Commons, convicted of treason, and executed.

It is also important to consider the historical context within which the committee was formed. Bubonic plague had raged in London in 1665, and a large part of London burned the next year. Many thought the disasters were signs of the judgment of God, and many blamed papists and atheists. The committee that was formed to investigate Hobbes was also instructed to investigate Thomas White, a priest, although the latter was no apologist for the pope (*Journals of the House of Commons*, 8:636). In short, the appointment of the committee to investigate Hobbes's work had less to do with Hobbes than with a general mood that "national repentance and moral reformation" was needed (Seaward, 1989, p. 256).

One can only speculate as to why Hobbes (along with White) was a target. One factor may have been that the committee was formed at the instigation of moralizing ministers who would not have approved of Hobbes's tough language. Here are two other suggestions. First, many members of the Cavalier Parliament were Arminians and opposed to Hobbes's Calvinistic views. Second, many members may have been upset that Hobbes had returned to England during the Interregnum and apparently had provided in *Leviathan* a justification for obeying the Interregnum government. Hobbes and White had long been opposed to the claims of Parliament. Even though this Parliament did not make the same claims for itself as earlier ones, it still thought of itself as more significant than Hobbes did. In *Behemoth*, written about the time the committee was appointed, he argued that Parliament had no legal authority for its actions and that it should offer only advice to the king (EW, 6:258–62). He also criticized Parliament's role in the Civil War. About one hundred members of the Cavalier Parliament had served in the Long Parliament (Coward, 1980, p. 246).

Hobbes was even harder on the universities than on Parliament, calling them hotbeds of sedition (EW, 3:330, 4:219, 6:233, 236; 7:344). The universities themselves were highly political institutions, both wide-ranging and indiscriminate in their dislikes. The condemnation of Hobbes by Oxford University in 1683 should be assessed in the context of knowing who else was condemned with him at the same time. In addition to those by Hobbes, the books or opinions of Knox, Milton, Richard Baxter (who wanted dissenters to be allowed to remain in the church), John Owen (a puritan theologian who had supported Cromwell), Henry Parker (who had criticized the king's advisers), Godfrey Goodman, (bishop of Gloucester, accused of being a papist), and Philip Hunton (a clergyman, who argued for corporate sovereignty, that is, a sovereignty shared by king and parliament) were ordered burned in 1683.[21] Quakers, Fifth Monarchy men, and subscribers to the Presbyterian Solemn League and Covenant were also condemned. Among the propositions condemned were that "all civil authority is derived originally from the people." On the other hand, the condemnation implies the Hobbesian view that a sovereign may impose requirements "in the worship of God" beyond what is strictly necessary for salvation. This condemnation was an ideological book burning against thinkers to the right and left of Restoration, Anglican views. On another occasion, the university orator of Oxford University even condemned the Royal Society for fostering atheism through its scientific researches (Evelyn, 1669, diary entry for 9 July, 1669). John Locke was condemned by Oxford University and by the Middlesex grand jury (Hunter, 1981, pp. 186–7). Hobbes was merely one of several religiously committed intellectuals who accused Oxford and Cambridge of corrupting Christians with pagan thought. John Webster thought that humanistic learning was un-Christian. As a consequence, Webster was attacked by Seth Ward in his book *Vindiciae Academiarum*, which contained an appendix in which two additional people were criticized: the Puritan chaplain William Dell, who had made similar charges against humanistic learning, and Hobbes (Ward, 1654; Green, 1964, p. 139; Mallet, 1924, 2:398). If reformers are people who criticize institutions for failing to live up to their high-minded mission, then Hobbes was a reformer.

Hobbes was also the victim of his philosophical astuteness, as he himself recognized (EW, 4:288–9, 291, 330). Many of his critics saw him as a theological fifth columnist, because he recognized, as they could not, that certain propositions did not have the consequences traditionally attributed to them (Clarendon, 1676, p. 195). For example, virtually everyone thought that if there are angels, then they are immaterial substances; if there is a heaven, then there is a dimension other than the spatiotemporal one; if the flames of hell are eternal, then the damned suffer eternally; and if the Kingdom of God exists, then it exists now. Hobbes showed that none of these consequences holds and thus was taken by some of his contemporaries and even by later scholars to be in effect denying the existence of angels, heaven, hell, and the Kingdom of God, even though he not only asserted them but showed how these biblical ideas could be fitted into a modern world-view. Not to see the force of Hobbes's logical point is sad enough, but then to infer that he was secretly denying religion is to compound the outrageously fallacious interpretation.

There was also a political dimension to each of the seemingly theological and logical issues. The establishment clergy in general were committed to defending the traditional interpretations of these ideas, because to concede any of Hobbes's interpretations would be to admit that they themselves were fallible, and even though they were not Roman Catholics they were loath to admit their own fallibility. More particularly, they wanted to be the superintendents over an eternal bliss of heaven and an eternal wretchedness of hell immediately after death, in order to maintain their coercive influence over the laity, as Hobbes himself says.[22] Of course, Hobbes was fully aware of the political dimension of these views and wanted to exploit them. But from that it does not follow that he insincerely espoused them only for their political value.

Chapter 2

Religion

In this chapter I want to discuss religion rather generally. I shall first discuss the importance of the idea of God in seventeenth-century philosophy. Next I shall consider, in a preliminary way, the role that theological concepts play in the introduction to *Leviathan* and in the book's title. The last section of the chapter is about Hobbes's treatment of the concept of religion.

GOD IN SEVENTEENTH-CENTURY PHILOSOPHY

It was more difficult for a person to be an atheist in the seventeenth century than it is for someone today, simply because there are so many atheists now.[1] It was even more difficult to be a theoretical atheist – that is, a thinker who could given an explanation for reality that did not include God as an essential part. For there were virtually no atheistic models of reality from which a philosopher might draw inspiration to construct his own. I am not denying the possibility of a seventeenth-century atheistic philosopher. I am saying that it is unlikely and that the burden of proof is on those who say that Hobbes was an atheist.[2]

Many historians have shown how pervasive religion was in all areas of intellectual and practical life during the seventeenth century (e.g., Popkin, 1987b; Hill, 1986, vol. 2). It is not within the scope of this book to rehearse the evidence for that view in any detail. Rather, I shall mention some of the most superficial and obvious facts about seventeenth-century philosophy, in order to jog the reader's memory, singling out the philosophies of Descartes, Spinoza, Locke, and Leibniz.

The full title of Descartes's greatest work is *Meditations on First Philosophy, in which are Demonstrated the Existence of God and the Immortality of the Soul.* The word "meditations" is distinctively religious, and the method of the *Meditations* resembles the meditations of Descartes's patron Cardinal Berulle and the *Spiritual Exercises* of Saint Ignatius, a Counter-Reformation work that Descartes had read at the Jesuit school La Fleche (Popkin, 1987b, pp. 41–2). In addition to its method, the content of the *Meditations* is essentially theistic. After doubting everything that he had previously believed and then proving that he himself exists, Descartes argues that it is necessary to prove that God exists, in order to defeat the claim that possibly there is a being that pervasively deceives human beings. He offers two proofs, one in the third and one in the fifth meditation. (The fifth also includes a proof that the soul is immortal.) So important is belief in the existence of God that Descartes claims that no atheist mathematician can properly be said to know that his mathematical proofs are correct, since no atheist can be certain that he is not the subject of deception. Descartes tried to reconcile his philosophy with the doctrine of transubstantiation,[3] and Hobbes thought him a hypocrite for doing so; but of course Descartes was a Catholic and Hobbes anti-Catholic.

Spinoza is quite different. He rejects the possibility of revealed religion. He denies the basic tenets of Judaism, although he is more sympathetic to the doctrine of Christianity. He was, by most accounts, an atheist. Nonetheless, it is possible to consider his philosophy a radically nonstandard theism. He is a pantheist, and it is not obvious that pantheism is not a limiting case of theism. Spinoza's ontological proof for the existence of God should be taken seriously. What Spinoza did was to show that the concepts of God and substance have consequences far different from the ones the scholastic philosophers attributed to them. He argues that substance is what exists from itself; only God exists from himself; therefore, God is the only substance.

Although his philosophy does not depend upon religious concepts, John Locke was intellectually committed to religion. We know from his friend James Tyrell that Locke's original motivation for writing his *Essay Concerning Human Understanding* was a discussion about the foundation of "revealed religion," an issue that gets discussed in book IV (Cranston, 1957, pp. 140–1). The *Essay* also contains a proof for the existence of God. Locke defended the rationality of Christianity in his book *The Reasonableness of Christianity* and also authored *A Discourse of Miracles*, as well as a two-volume paraphrase of and commentary on the Epistles of Saint Paul which remained unfinished at his death.

The only book that Leibniz published in his lifetime was *Theodicy*, an attempt to show that the existence of God is not inconsistent with the existence of evil. His *Discourse on Metaphysics* begins by defining God as "an absolutely perfect being" and continues by exploring the consequences of this idea for various philosophical issues.

It would be easy to present more evidence of the pervasively theistic character of seventeenth-century philosophy by discussing the work of Malebranche, Grotius, More, Cudworth, and Newton. But the point has been made. Many of the major philosophical works of the most famous philosophers of the seventeenth century had distinctively religious content.

I have rehearsed these familiar facts to indicate the intellectual milieu within which Hobbes worked, because these roughly set the boundaries for what Hobbes would likely mean if he said that he believed in God. Quentin Skinner has rightly emphasized how important it is to understand the historical context within which an author wrote in order to understand what he or she could have meant (Skinner, 1988a, pp. 29–67). Since virtually every major seventeenth-century philosopher was a theist, any philosopher who wanted to communicate that atheism was true would most likely have to do so in some fairly direct way. This is a consequence of what it is to communicate something. For communication requires that the speaker intend to get the audience to recognize that the speaker openly intends the audience to believe something. In Hobbes's day, anyone saying or implying that God exists would have been understood as trying to communicate that he truly believed that God exists, since that would have been the simplest, most plausible construal of what he meant. The intention to get someone to believe that the speaker was an atheist simply could not have been achieved by asserting his belief in God and by articulating theories that presupposed that he believed in God, such as a divine command theory of morality, a theory of the Trinity, and a theory of redemption. In particular, if Hobbes says that he holds certain religious views, he should be taken at his word unless there is compelling evidence to the contrary. The existence of private letters or journals that would indicate atheism or hypocrisy would be such compelling evidence. Gauthier, who does not think that the concept of God plays a significant role in Hobbes's philosophy, endorses this position (Gauthier, 1969, p. 180).

My theory of meaning may seem too restrictive because it seems to exclude irony and sarcasm. That is not correct. Interpreting an utterance or text as having some nonliteral meaning is possible, but this course is justifiable only when a literal interpretation is not plausible. In other words, a literal interpretation of a text is the default mode, and a nonliteral interpretation is acceptable only when a literal interpretation does not make sense. One of my goals is to show that much more of Hobbes's text can be interpreted literally than most scholars recognize.

THEOLOGICAL CONCEPTS IN THE INTRODUCTION TO LEVIATHAN

Gauthier's interpretation

If Hobbes had never said anything in *Leviathan* about God or never used distinctively Christian concepts, or if he had mentioned them only in passing or in inessential contexts, or if he had disparaged belief in them, then the secular interpretation of Hobbes would be greatly strengthened. But that is not the case. *Leviathan* is divided into four parts: "Of Man," "Of Commonwealth," "Of a Christian Commonwealth," and "Of the Kingdom of Darkness." Almost half of *Leviathan* is devoted to exclusively religious topics. Many scholars explain away this fact by claiming that the third and fourth parts are not essential to the logic of the first two – that they are a kind of extended afterthought or sop to non-philosophers who were genuinely religious. Gauthier and others attempt to substantiate this view by developing from the first two books of *Leviathan* a Hobbesian political theory that does not make use of the concept of God (Gauthier, 1969, p. 178).

I intend to show, in a later chapter, that the secular interpretation of Hobbes's political philosophy is mistaken. Indeed, God plays a central role in the entire scheme of the first two books. What Gauthier and others have done is to expurgate Hobbes's views in the following way. Whereas Hobbes argues for a certain set of conclusions C, from premises $P_1, P_2, \ldots, P_n$, they purport to show that these conclusions are derivable from a subset of premises, $P_1, \ldots, P_i$, which do not contain the concept of God. They then conclude that this proves that Hobbes himself did not rely upon the concept of God in proving C.

This line of reasoning is explicit in Gauthier, who says that "theistic suppositions are logically superfluous" in Hobbes's system. Perhaps they are, but it is fallacious to conclude that Hobbes does not rely upon them. The secular interpretation of Hobbes may make for a neater philosophical theory, but it does not follow that it is the one that Hobbes presented or intended. For example, suppose that the first logician to prove functional completeness for the propositional calculus proved that the sentential connectives for conjunction, negation, and disjunction, taken jointly, are functionally complete. It would be a mistake for a scholar to argue that the logician proved that conjunction and negation are functionally complete, even though they are. The logician's own proof is logically less neat than the one attributed to him, but it is the one he intended. Similarly, without trying to settle the issue of whether the secular interpretation of Hobbes by Gauthier and others is philosophically superior to my interpretation of him, I will be arguing that mine is truer to what Hobbes said and meant.

Gauthier suggests that God is discussed only in Parts III and IV of *Leviathan* and hence is secondary to the system (1969, p. 178). While a large part of my argument will amount to a refutation of Gauthier's position on Parts III and IV, my preliminary treatment of the early passages of *Leviathan* will show that far from being absent, theological concepts pervade them.

Leviathan: A Bible for modern man

Not only do a variety of theological concepts play a central role in *Leviathan;* I would even claim that because of its comprehensiveness and its broadly accurate description of modern attitudes and behavior *Leviathan* deserves to be called "A Bible for modern man." For it includes a metaphysics; an epistemology; a philosophy of man; ethics and theories of politics; a philosophy of religion; and a philosophy of history.[4]

Genesis opens with the words, "In the beginning of creation, when God made heaven and earth," and goes on to express an ancient cosmology. The Gospel of Saint John consciously echoes Genesis by beginning with the very same words, "In the beginning," and describing Jesus as present at the creation of the world. *Leviathan* similarly begins by linking the two themes of God and nature: "Nature, the art whereby God hath made and governs the world" (EW, 3:ix). Notice that Hobbes's first affirmation is couched in religious language. There are, however, some radical differences between the Old Testament creation stories and Hobbes's opening line. Hobbes promotes nature above God, at least rhetorically, insofar as "nature" is mentioned before "God."

45

This is analogous to Saint John's promotion of Jesus ("the Word") over "God" in the opening of his gospel: "In the beginning was the Word, and the Word was with God" (John 1:1–2). Also, the contrast that was traditionally drawn between nature and art is explicitly rejected by Hobbes. In postmodern terms, Hobbes wants to "deconstruct" the art – nature dichotomy.[5] His point is that, far from their being opposed to each other, nature is artificial. The interplay between art and nature segues into an interplay between art, man, and the state. "Nature . . . is by the *art* of man, as in many other things, so in this also imitated, that it can make an artificial animal" (EW, 3:ix).

This artificial animal is the commonwealth, which Hobbes later calls "that *mortal god*, to which we owe under the *immortal God*, our peace and defence" (EW, 3:158). The idea that the sovereign is akin to a divinity was common. It is obvious in the theory of the divine right of kings. Hobbes's description of the sovereign as a "mortal god" is even stronger, and its precedent for him, I believe, is more immediate and more specifically English than any abstract political theory. James I, in a speech to Parliament, compared himself to a god in vivid terms:

> The state of monarchy is the supremest thing upon earth. For kings are not only God's lieutenants upon earth, and sit upon God's throne, but even by God himself they are called gods. . . . Kings are justly called gods for that they exercise a manner or resemblance of divine power upon earth. For if you will consider the attributes to God, you shall see how they agree in the person of a king. God has power to create, or destroy, make, or unmake at his pleasure, to give life, or send death, to judge all, and to be judged nor accountable to none; to raise low things, and to make high things low at his pleasure, and to God are both soul and body due. And the like power have kings: they make and unmake their subjects; they have power of raising and casting down, of life and of death; judges over all their subjects, and in all cases, and yet accountable to none but God only. They have power to exalt low things and abase high things, and make of their subjects

like men at the chess: a pawn to take a bishop or a knight, and to cry up or down any of their subjects, as they do their money. And to the king is due both the affection of the soul and the service of the body of his subjects.[6] (James I, 1610, p. 107, or James I, 1616, pp. 529–30)

This speech continues themes that James had expressed earlier. In his popular *Basilikon Doron*, a handbook that he wrote for his son on the subject of how to be a king, James summarizes the book's themes in a sonnet, which ends with a statement of the similarity between God and the sovereign. Referring to his son, James says, "And so ye shall in Princelie vertues shine / Resembling right your mightie King Divine" (James I, 1603, 1:5). The entire sonnet is an extended metaphor in the same vein; it begins "God gives not Kings the stile of Gods worship in vaine, / For on his throne his Scepter doe they swey," and James again, like Hobbes, refers to the sovereign as God's lieutenant (ibid.). I think that in his political works Hobbes was trying to give a theoretical foundation to the claims that James made about his monarchy in his books and speeches (cf. Grover, 1990, 101–3). (The same holds for James's religious views, as I shall explain later.) One difference between Hobbes and James is that the latter subscribed both to the theory of the divine right of kings and to a patriarchal justification of monarchy, whereas Hobbes realized that these theories were untenable. Thus he saw the need to invent a new theory to justify the monarchy that existed from the time when he was becoming a young adult until he was almost middle-aged. In short, I shall argue that Hobbes takes the analogy between God and the sovereign most seriously in several ways. Only two will be mentioned here. First, Hobbes grounds the obligation imposed by the state and enforced through its irresistible power in the obligation humans have to God in virtue of his irresistible power. Second, Hobbes sees the civil government as saving humans from bodily death in the state of nature; just as God saves humans from spiritual death.

It is prima facie implausible that theological concepts are

47

not important to Hobbes, when he begins his book as he does. But there is much more. Unlike Genesis, which begins with a cosmology, Hobbes's focus is on the nature of human beings and the principal work of human beings, the commonwealth. This is in keeping with his humanistic strain, according to which the proper study of mankind is man. But he is not a garden-variety humanist; he explains the world mechanistically: "For seeing life is but a motion of limbs, the beginning whereof is in some principal part within; why may we not say, that all *automata* (engines that move themselves by springs and wheels as doth a watch) have an artificial life? For what is the *heart*, but a spring; and the *nerves*, but so many *strings*; and the *joints*, but so many *wheels*, giving motion to the whole body, such as was intended by the artificer?" (EW, 3:ix). There are elements in the commonwealth analogous to bodily parts and functions. But Hobbes completes the analogy by returning to the account of creation in Genesis. He says that just as God created the world by saying, "*fiat, . . . let us make man*" (EW, 3:x), so the commonwealth is created by the speech act performed in making the civil covenant.

What is Leviathan?

We have noticed several inversions or reversals of biblical themes in the opening lines of *Leviathan*. One of the most important is Hobbes's selection of the name "Leviathan" for the commonwealth. For in the Bible, Leviathan is a monster, a principle of chaos and disorder, whom God either will destroy or has already destroyed (see Job 3:8, 40:25; Isa. 27:1, 51:9; Amos 3; Psalms 74:14, 104:26). In contrast, Hobbes presents Leviathan as the principle of rule and order. Hobbes explains his selection of the term in this way:

> Hitherto I have set forth the nature of man, whose pride and other passions have compelled him to submit himself to government: together with the great power of his governor, whom I compared to *Leviathan*, taking that comparison out of the last two verses of the one-and-fortieth of *Job;* where God having set forth the great power of *Leviathan*, calleth him king

of the proud. *There is nothing,* saith he, *on earth, to be compared with him. He is made so as not to be afraid. He seeth every high thing below him; and is king of all the children of pride.* (EW, 3:307)

Not only is Leviathan not an enemy of God; he is a *"mortal god"* (EW, 3:158).[7]

Although Hobbes is reversing the standard interpretation of Leviathan from a principle of disorder to a principle of order and from an enemy of God to an agent of God, his use of Leviathan is thoroughly biblical, not merely in that he derives the name from the Bible but because he understands the root of human trouble to be pride. Many of the great stories of sin in the Bible and in Christian mythology, from Adam and Eve to the revolt of the angels, are stories of disobedience that have their root in pride: the refusal of human beings to be subordinate. Hobbes's account of the original condition of human beings confirms this.[8]

Pride and human misery

According to Hobbes, if one takes both strength and intelligence into account, almost all human beings are equal in the state of nature.[9] This equality, Hobbes says, leads each person to think that he has an equal chance against another to fulfill his desire (EW, 3:111). That is, no one, or virtually no one, is willing to subordinate himself to another person. Further, some people enjoy dominating others; thus each person needs to watch out for these, possibly few, people. However, because no one can be certain who might turn out to enjoy dominating other people, because the consequences of being dominated are so dire, and because no one can look for protection from the government – for in the state of nature there is no government – each person must be wary of every other person. One reasonable course of action to take in such a situation is to attack others preemptively (EW, 3:111–12, 2:16) or at least to be on the defensive. Worse, each person knows that he himself is being viewed suspiciously as a possible attacker by everyone else and hence is subject to preemptive attack. He also realizes that, because of everyone's defensive attitude, his own behavior, even if innocent, may be misinterpreted and hence provoke an attack. Thus, each person must fear everyone else (EW, 3:112). In short, in the state of nature there is a war of all against all, not because each person is actively fighting with every other person but because each person has a standing suspicion of attack by some other person. To quote Hobbes, "For WAR, consisteth not in battle only, or the act of fighting; but in a tract of time, wherein the will to contend by battle is sufficiently known; . . . so the nature of war, consisteth not in actual fighting; but in the known disposition thereto, during all the time there is no assurance to the contrary. All other time is PEACE" (EW, 3:113). That is why man's "pride and other passions have compelled him to submit himself to government" (EW, 3:307).

I have not tried to present Hobbes's complete explanation of the causes of war in the state of nature. Rather, I have shown that on Hobbes's view the biblical notion of pride, combined with modest assumptions about the human condition – equality, ignorance, occasional aggressiveness, and absence of government – are sufficient to explain human misery and to suggest that relief is available only from a creature of biblical proportions, such as Leviathan.

The title of *Leviathan* and the central theme of its introduction are all directly intertwined with theological concepts. This is good prima facie evidence that the rest of the book will contain important theological components. The proof of this must be a detailed consideration of these topics, which I begin in the next chapter. For the remainder of this chapter, I shall discuss Hobbes's views about religion in general.

RELIGION

The definition of "Religion"

Immediately preceding the four chapters devoted to justifying a commonwealth is a chapter titled "Of Religion" (chapter 12). It would be odd, then, if religion had nothing to do with justifying the commonwealth. Of course, one might argue that Hobbes's views about religion are negative and that he views religion as a problem against which all rational people must strive. There is no doubt that much of what he says about religion appears to be negative and, as a matter of fact, can be used by opponents of religion to make their case against it. However, on several occasions Hobbes says that religion is one of the two things that are distinctive to human beings, reason being the other (EW, 3:44, 94). If Hobbes thought that religion was inherently pernicious, one would expect him to say something to this effect, perhaps by denigrating it in comparison with reason. But he never does.

Hobbes's explicit introduction of the concept of religion occurs earlier than chapter 12. A basic tenet of his philosophy is that everything that exists is matter in motion, and in the early chapters of *Leviathan* Hobbes tries to show how such concepts as sensation, imagination, reasoning, and science are analyzable and reducible to complex forms of matter in motion (chapters 1–5). This general project of materialistic reductionism continues in chapter 6, "Of the Interior Beginnings of Voluntary Motions; Commonly Called the Passions; and the Speeches by which they are Expressed." The definition of "religion" is preceded by the definition of "curiosity" as "*Desire* to know why, and how" (EW, 3:44). The reason for this juxtaposition is revealed only later, in the chapter "On Religion" when Hobbes says that curiosity is the cause of religion (EW, 3:94).[10]

Hobbes then defines religion as "*Fear* of power invisible, feigned by the mind, or imagined from tales publicly allowed" (EW, 3:45). This definition of religion is neutral on the issue of whether any religion is true or not. Although "feigned" often suggests something counterfeit, it is not part of the meaning of the word. "Feigned" means only that something is constructed, as every idea must be constructed, according to Hobbes. Also, "imagination," which is cognition of an object that has been sensed in the past (EW, 3:5), can be true or false, depending upon whether it corresponds with reality. The phrase "tales publicly allowed" is prob-lematic, because the word "allowed" is ambiguous. It can mean either tales that are approved by the government or merely tales that are generally accepted by people. In *An Answer to Bishop Bramhall*, Hobbes indicates that he intends the former interpretation (EW, 4:328).

The syntactic structure of his definition gives the impres-sion that Hobbes is defining religion as a genus. Religion is any kind of fear of invisible power. The definition further suggests that there are two species of religion, one of which is defined by the specific difference "feigned by the mind" and the other of which is defined by the specific difference "imagined from tales publicly allowed." If this is correct, then it would be necessary to define "superstition" as re-ligion "feigned by the mind," where "feigned" is taken in the strong sense of "inventing something with no basis in fact." This is a plausible definition of "superstition." And Hobbes had given a similar definition in *De Cive:* "Now the fear of invisible things, when it is severed from right reason, is superstition" (EW, 2:227). Defending himself against Bramhall's attacks, Hobbes expatiates on his definition of superstition: "Fear of invisible powers, what is it else in savage people, but the fear of somewhat they think a God? What invisible power does the reason of a savage man sug-gest unto him, but those phantasms of his sleep, or his dis-temper, which we frequently call ghosts, and the savages thought gods. . . . I said superstition was fear without rea-son" (EW, 4:292).

If he had said nothing else about superstition, Hobbes would have saved himself much grief. Unfortunately, imme-diately after defining "religion," Hobbes's explicitly defines "superstition" in a way quite at variance with the one just described. He says "superstition" is religion "not allowed" (EW, 3:45; cf. 4:292). From the context this must mean that superstition is religion that is imagined from tales not al-lowed. This is a relativistic definition of "superstition" that has the consequence that whether a religion is a superstition or not depends upon time and place. For example, Roman

Catholicism in Elizabethan England would be a superstition, but not under Elizabeth's half-sister Mary or in sixteenth-century Spain. On the other hand, the Church of England would not be a superstition in Elizabethan England but would be one in Spain at the same time. And every denomination of Christianity would be a superstition in pre-Constantinian Rome, but not afterward.

There is thus an incompatibility between the two definitions of superstition. The same kind of incompatibility infects his definitions of "true religion." Hobbes's explicit definition of "true religion" is innocuous: true religion is "fear of power invisible" in which "the power imagined, is truly such as we imagine" (EW, 3:45). This is an appropriately descriptive definition. But the definition that is implied by his definition of religion and the specific difference mentioned earlier is objectionable, namely, true religion is "fear of power invisible, . . . imagined from tales publicly allowed" (EW, 3:45).

It is a logical principle that from a contradiction anything follows. But it cannot be an interpretive principle that any doctrine can be imputed to a philosopher who falls into a contradiction. For virtually every philosopher, like everyone else, involves him or herself in some contradiction or other. It is hard to know what can be imputed.

According to Leo Strauss, whenever a great philosopher expresses an inconsistent or incoherent doctrine about an issue for which one could be persecuted, the interpreter should judge that the philosopher subscribes to the dangerous doctrine. David Berman gives a Straussian interpretation to the passage under discussion. He says that the sentence that defines religion "can be and was read as a superbly condensed statement of unbelief." Further, he says that the sentence that defines "true religion" as invisible power corresponding to the way people imagine it "covers up and effectively denies the first provocative statement" (Berman, 1988, p. 65).[11] Although the passage can be read in this way, in the sense that it is not impossible to do so, the issue is whether this is a compelling or a plausible way to

53

read it. To me it seems no more plausible than holding that the definition of true religion is a superbly condensed statement of belief and that the definition of religion reveals a confusion in Hobbes's thought. Also, if Hobbes's definition of true religion as religion corresponding to the way invisible powers are "*effectively denies* the first provocative statement [my italics]," – and Berman says it does – then the provocative statement is not to be taken as indicative of Hobbes's considered views at all.

Berman thinks that there is evidence for his interpretation five chapters and forty-five pages farther into *Leviathan*. In chapter 11, Hobbes explains how it is possible for people to know that there is a God even though they cannot imagine him. He says,

> For as a man that is born blind, hearing men talk of warming themselves by the fire, and being brought to warm himself by the flame, may easily conceive, and assure himself, there is somewhat there, which men call *fire*, and is the cause of the heat he feels; but cannot imagine what it is like; nor have an idea of it in his mind, such as they have that have see it: so also by the visible things in this world, and their admirable order, a man may conceive there is a cause of them, which men call God; and yet not have an idea, or image of him in his mind. (EW, 3:92–3)

The clear thrust of this passage is that people can conceive of God even though they have no sense experience of him. Hobbes gives essentially the same explanation of how humans conceive of God in his objections to Descartes's *Meditations*. In this latter work, Hobbes explicitly contrasts conceiving of God with having an "idea or image *corresponding to the sacred name of God*" (Descartes, 1984, p. 127). The intent is not to deny that humans can conceive of God, nor even that humans have some sort of image when they conceive of him. The intent is to deny that the image that humans have corresponds to or is a faithful representation of God. I think this is strong evidence of a sincere attempt to justify religion philosophically and firmly within the Christian theological tradition, as I shall explain at greater length in Chapter 7. But Berman ignores the main thrust of the passage from *Leviathan*. He focuses on Hobbes's remark that people cannot have an idea or image of God (Berman, 1988, p. 66). He holds that Hobbes expects the reader to recall that five chapters earlier "true religion" had been defined as one in which God is truly "imagined" and that since it is now being affirmed that God cannot be imagined, Hobbes must be secretly communicating that no religion is true.[12]

To the objection that his interpretation "seems just too clever," Berman replies that "Hobbes *was* clever enough" (ibid., p. 67). But Hobbes's cleverness is not the issue here. The issue is whether Hobbes would expect his audience to associate texts almost fifty pages apart in order to interpret both passages in a way that directly contradicts what appears to be their main thrust.[13] Apparently Berman thinks this is plausible. I do not. I think that only a person who has already made up his or her mind about what Hobbes means, regardless of what Hobbes says, would come up with such an interpretation.[14] The general point I want to make here is one that Hobbes articulated: "[S]ubtle conjectures at the secret aims and inward cogitations of [authors] . . . cannot often be certain, unless withal so evident, that the narration itself [the text] may be sufficient to suggest the same also to the reader" (EW, 8:viii).

Another problem with Berman's argument is that it is too strong. For if it can be used to show that Hobbes was an atheist, it can also be used to show that Bishop Berkeley was one. For he also held that we have ideas only of what we can sense and that God cannot be sensed. A general problem with Straussian interpretations is that they overestimate the ability of philosophers and underestimate their problems. Philosophers are not infallible, nor are they logic machines. They make mistakes. This is vividly demonstrable in Hobbes's case with regard to his geometrical theories. Speaking of the benefits of using the correct philosophical method, he says, "For all men by nature reason alike, and well, when they have good principles. For who is so stupid, as both to mistake in geometry, and also to persist in it, when another detects his error to him" (EW, 3:35). It is sadly ironic that Hobbes was unable to recognize his errors in squaring the circle, even after John Wallis had explained them to him several times.[15]

Mathematical reasoning is relatively straightforward. Philosophy is much more difficult. As Hobbes said, the people "most subject" to subscribing to absurdities are those who "profess philosophy" (EW, 3:33; see also pp. 31–2). Although Hobbes would not put it this way, the reason that absurdity stalks philosophers is that they deal with concepts about which there is little theoretical clarity, so every mistake is liable to be one that involves transgressing the limits of some concept. What may be an obvious truth about some concept to later generations of philosophers may have been quite obscure to the earlier ones who helped make that clarity possible. The Straussian interpretation also assumes that a person as proud and dogmatic as Hobbes would deliberately risk submitting himself to public ridicule for expressing contradictory opinions and trust that certain astute readers would see through the contradiction and attribute only the controversial and correct position to him. (See also John Pocock, 1971, p. 162.)

There is a much simpler way of handling the admitted difficulties of Hobbes's definitions of superstition and true religion. Earlier I explained the difference between the definition of a word and the criteria for applying the definition. That distinction can help us here. Recall that in the seventeenth century "atheist" meant a person who believes that God does not exist but that the term was applied, roughly, as a term of opprobrium, to one's religious or political enemy. Catholics were atheists to Protestants, just as Protestants were atheists to Catholics, and Arminians were atheists to Calvinists, just as Calvinists were atheists to Arminians.

I suggest that Hobbes succumbed to the same confusion of definition and criteria of application with regard to the terms "true religion" and "superstition." The correct Hobbesian definitions are these: *True religion is religion in which the power imagined is such as people imagine it. Superstition is not true religion; that is, it is fear of power invisible, feigned by the mind.* There is nothing objectionable in either of these definitions. But he also realized that both of the defined terms were often applied loosely or in ways that were not logically tied to the definitions. He had these criteria in mind when he implied: *True religion is fear of power invisible, imagined from tales publicly allowed. Superstition is religion that is not allowed.* There is textual evidence for my interpretation. Later in *Leviathan* Hobbes says that "every one in himself calleth [true] religion" whatever he worships but that "in them that worship, or fear that power otherwise than they do, superstition" (EW, 3:93). Henry Hammond used the term "superstition" in the latter way when he wrote, "*Superstition* [is] the worship and prayers to Saints departed," attributing this kind of activity to the outlawed Roman Catholics (Hammond, 1650a, p. 53).

It is worth mentioning that what I have suggested are Hobbes's definitions of true religion and superstition are consistent with his criteria of application. A true religion may be the one that is approved by the government. And superstition may be prohibited by the government. Indeed, Hobbes would consider such a situation to be ideal, even though he recognized that reality often falls short of that.

In addition to the textual evidence from Hobbes, my suggested interpretation makes sense within the context of seventeenth-century England. There was a strong tradition of religious intolerance during and prior to the time that Hobbes was writing. Anglicans had suppressed Presbyterians.[16] Presbyterians had suppressed the Anglicans. Both groups had suppressed Roman Catholics. All three groups would have agreed about the definition of "true religion." But each was free to apply it publicly to its own religion only when it was in power, and each was free to think that superstition was the religion that was "not allowed." Since each of these religious groups at one time was in power, each would in fact have applied these terms in just this way. Further, whether in power or not, each of these groups would have applied these terms in their thoughts to the others.

The tension between the objectiveness of the definition of "true religion" and the subjectiveness of its application is reflected in a certain way of talking about one's own religion. Attached to professions of one's own faith, which was presumably the "true religion," were sometimes expressions of the contingency of that faith. For example, Queen Elizabeth, professing her faith in the English Church, told Parliament in 1586 that the Church of England was the one "I was born in, bred in, and, I trust, shall die in" (quoted from Neill, 1976, p. 100).[17] James I talked about "the Religion wherein I was brought up" and then, as something of an afterthought, described it as "the onely true forme of Gods worship" (James I, 1603, 1:14). In the century in which Hobbes was born, English Christians were required to change their religion no fewer than three times. Seemingly unaffected by the dizzying changes in the prescribed religion, many people egocentrically viewed their own religion as the sole truth and every other religion as heresy or superstition. Parliament itself had recognized this situation before Hobbes wrote the passage under discussion. Resisting the attempt of the Assembly of Divines to dictate religious uniformity in the 1640s, Parliament made the following declaration:

> We know how apt men are to make that blasphemy and heresy which is contrary to what they hold, and to esteem their actions heinous whose persons they hate. We see how ready men are in our days to brand one another with the names of incendiaries, covenant-breakers, children of Belial, and fighters against the Kingdom of God, because they do not agree with them in every particular, or consent presently to what they desire in things which in their own nature are indifferent or at least very disputable. (Quoted from Jordan, 1938, p. 73)

That is, Parliament is saying that people consider heresy to be anything they hate. People call others who disagree with them, even over the most trivial matter, "covenant-breakers," "children of Belial," and "fighters against the Kingdom of God." Surely "atheist" and "superstitious" fit into this cluster of abusive terms. In short, Hobbes was echoing in 1651 what Parliament had said a decade earlier.

An alternative to thinking of every view other than one's own as heresy was toleration. The general drift of religious opinion after 1650 was in that direction. The earl of Clarendon was an ardent member of the Church of England. But his daughter married James II and converted to Catholicism, and Clarendon acknowledged, in his "laste will and Testament," that other religions might be legitimate and offer its members salvation, even as he professed his faith in the Church of England (Ollard, 1988, p. 347). Although Hobbes was not enthusiastic about toleration, his attitude, I have suggested, is a jaundiced version of Clarendon's. And it led him confusedly to combine an explicit definition of "true religion" with a description of the criterion for the use of the term "superstition." There is no doubt that my interpretation attributes some cynicism to Hobbes, but the cynicism is justified, I think, and consonant with what we know of Hobbes's personality. It also does not suggest any irreligion on his part. Whether I am right about this or not, Hobbes's logical confusion makes conjectural any inference about his intent based upon these definitions. A final judgment about Hobbes's religious beliefs cannot be based on them.

Heresy

Among those who would concede that Hobbes was a theist, many would hold that he was a heretic. Hobbes was as sensitive about this charge as he was about the charge of atheism, and he responded to it by treating the issue explicitly both in *Leviathan* and in *An Historical Narration Concerning Heresy and the Punishment Thereof*. Consequently, I shall discuss his treatment of heresy before proceeding to his treatment of the nature of religion. He says, "For *heresy is nothing else but a private opinion obstinately maintained, contrary to the opinion which the public person, that is to say, the representant of the commonwealth, hath commanded to be taught"* (EW, 3:579; see also p. 90; cf. Kraynak, 1990, pp. 40–1). Hobbes is not being sarcastic. He is exploiting the Greek etymological roots of the term "heresy." He points out that in ancient Greece various philosophical schools, such as the Pythagoreans and the Peripatetics, were called "heretical" (EW, 4:387, 6:98, 174). And in part, Hobbes is describing the current understanding of heresy in seventeenth-century England. In 1640, Parliament voted against religious canons that had been proposed by the clergy, on the grounds that the clergy had no authority to decide religious issues such as heresy. As Nathaniel Fiennes described it in a speech in the House of Commons, the clergy had presumed to take for themselves "a parliamentary power, in determining an heresie not determined by law, which is expressly reserved to the determination of a parliament" (Fiennes, 1641, p. 9). In short, Parliament, which is the public person that represents the commonwealth, is the only institution with the authority to decide what heresy is.

In works written after *Leviathan*, Hobbes omits the reference to what the sovereign commands. In *An Historical Narration Concerning Heresy*, Hobbes begins by pointing out that a heretic was originally anyone who held his own opinion, such as Pythagoras, Plato, Aristotle, or Zeno. Hobbes is no doubt pleased to be able to say that Aristotle was a heretic in the original sense of the term (EW, 4:388). "Heretic" came to be a term of abuse only when people began to follow these philosophers merely in order to make money or to appear clever (ibid., pp. 387–8). In the early church, to be a heretic was to disagree with the majority: "So that *catholic* and *heretic* were terms relative; and here it was that *heretic* came to be a name, and a name of disgrace, both together" (p. 390). However, no sanctions for heresy were imposed at this time by any sovereign, and the church did not have the authority to do so itself. The first heresies concerned the Trinity. The chief theological purpose of the early creeds was to insist that there is only one God, who is three persons. And the chief political purpose of them was peace (p. 393; see also pp. 399, 402). After delivering a learned disquisition on the meaning of the Apostles' Creed relative to the various heresies it was meant to counteract, Hobbes discusses the history of heresy in England. He says that there was no punishment of heretics prior to the condemnation of Wyckliffe in the reign of Richard II (p. 403). Subsequently, different laws were passed by different kings in order to control heresy; and under Edward VI there was again no punishment for heretics at all. The situation changed under Queen Mary, a Roman Catholic, who executed some Protestants for their faith. Hobbes's telling of the checkered story of heresy has many morals: that what counts as heresy changes; that someone accused of heresy in the past can come to be seen as an orthodox reformer later (Wyckliffe); that some accusers of heresy can later come to be seen as heretics themselves (Mary I); and that, often, though not always, heresy was not considered an especially heinous offense. In short, his history provides him with one defense of his views.

A second defense is that under Queen Elizabeth "the commissioners were forbidden to adjudge anything to be heresy, which was not declared to be heresy by some of the first four general Councils" (p. 405). Judgment had to be made by the High Commission, and no punishment was prescribed except ecclesiastical censure. This puts Hobbes in the clear, in several ways. First, he professes belief in the creeds produced by all of these councils. Second, even if he were a heretic, he would not have to fear any physical harm.

A third way in which the consequences of heresy are minimized or eliminated is ironic. Hobbes says that when the Scottish Presbyterians forced Charles I to abolish the High Commission, they thereby eliminated the only body competent to judge heresy. Thus, there were no "human laws left in force to restrain any man from preaching or writing any doctrine concerning religion that he pleased. And in this heat of the war, it was impossible to disturb the peace of the state, which then was none" (p. 407). This was precisely the time when Hobbes was writing *Leviathan*. So, the rebels themselves had immunized Hobbes and everyone else from the charge of heresy. Hobbes has given the rebels their comeuppance.

The nature of religion

As mentioned earlier, Hobbes states that the source of religion, which is peculiar to humans,[18] is the desire to learn
the causes of things (EW, 3:94). Often the cause is visible,
and when it is a person will either fear it or not, depending
upon the nature of the cause. But when the cause is invisible, a person will invariably fear it. Following some of "the
old poets," Hobbes suggests that the pagan gods were "created by human fear" (ibid., p. 95). But belief in the true God,
who is "eternal, infinite, and omnipotent," is more easily
derived from a straightforward inference from observable
effects to an invisible cause. Hobbes goes on to give a brief
and completely conventional cosmological proof for the existence of the God who is the proper object of religion:

> For he that from any effect he seeth come to pass, should
> reason to the next and immediate cause thereof, and from
> thence to the cause of that cause, and plunge himself pro-
> foundly in the pursuit of causes; shall at last come to this, that
> there must be, as even the heathen philosophers confessed,
> one first mover; that is, a first, and an eternal cause of all
> things; which is that which men mean by the name of God.
> (EW, 3:95–6; see also 4:59–60)

A constant theme of *Leviathan* is the difference between the
proper elements of religion – that is, the elements of true
religion – and pagan variations, as is the case here, where
fear of the unknown as a source for belief in gods is contrasted with a human curiosity about the origins of things.
Hobbes continues this point by explaining that this proof for
the existence of God proceeds without any mention of the
fortunes of human beings, in contrast with the pagans' concern about their own fate. He thinks that this sort of self-
interested search for causes accounts for polytheism (EW,
3:96). Later it becomes clear that polytheists think that each
thing they fear is a different god: thus chaos, heaven, the

ocean, fire, earth, wind, crocodiles, dogs, and all sorts of places were called "gods" (ibid., p. 99).

Although Hobbes is willing to affirm that God is literally "infinite, omnipotent, and eternal" (p. 97; see also p. 95), there is no more that humans can know about God's nature. Any other properties attributed to God's nature must be construed not as cognitively meaningful but as pious expressions (p. 97).[19] Pagan religions, however, are not content with these modest results of human reasoning. They manufacture anthropomorphic models of their gods (EW, 3:96, 4:292) and devise an incoherent phrase to describe them: "incorporeal spirit." Human beings are in such a deprived state that it "was almost impossible for men, without the special assistance of God, to avoid both rocks of *atheism* and *superstition*" (EW, 2:227). This emphasis on the tendency of humans to pervert true religion and develop multifarious superstitions places Hobbes in the center of the Calvinist tradition, which attacks Roman Catholicism in particular and all non-Reformed Christian religions in general.

In the *Institutes* Calvin says that "scarcely one man in a hundred is met with who fosters" true religion (Calvin, 1559, I.4.1). The source of the problem is twofold, according to Calvin: human depravity and religion itself. This leads Calvin to say, in his *Commentary on Psalms*, "Religion is thus the beginning of all superstitions, not in its own nature, but through the darkness which has settled down upon the minds of men, and which prevents them from distinguishing between idols and the true God" (quoted from Eire, 1986, p. 205). This theme is repeated in many places in Calvin's work: "[E]very man's conscience is capable of distinguishing good from evil. But then, what happens except that religion degenerates into a thousand chimeras of superstition; and consciences pervert every act of judgment, so that one cannot tell vice from virtue" (Calvin, 1958, p. 132, and Eire, 1986, pp. 195–275). Robert Bellarmine, the champion of the Counter-Reformation, said that Protestants list as abuses "the sacrifice of the Mass, the celibacy of the priesthood, fasting at Lent, the invocation of the saints, prayers for the dead, the veneration of images, and other practices" (quoted from Wootton, 1983b, p. 49). This list is virtually identical with the items Hobbes attacks at various places in *Leviathan*. In short, there is no need to see Hobbes as doing anything more than participating in the Protestant tradition of resisting superstition. This interpretation is also supported by Hobbes's upbringing in the Calvinistic Church of England of his youth, the Calvinistic orientation of Magdalen Hall, which he attended in his adolescence, and his own expressed admiration for Calvin.

Hobbes is especially hard on pagan religions – religions that divinize objects of nature, attribute polytheistic causes to natural events (e.g., saying that Venus causes fertility or that Aeolus causes tempests), worship images or engage in degenerate activities in the name of religion, and rely on oracles, astrology, augury, and necromancy. Scholars who suspect Hobbes of subversive motives claim that he intended his readers to see the same kind of behavior in Christianity. But the textual evidence is just to the contrary. For when he discusses religion he contrasts proper Judeo-Christian practice with improper pagan practice. From the seed of religion, common to all humans, some have created a religion "according to their own invention." But others "have done it, by God's commandment, and direction." The founders of this kind of religion were "Abraham, Moses and our blessed Saviour" (EW, 3:98–9). There is no hint of irony or sarcasm in this passage.

At times Hobbes's tone is strident, and he sounds like the prophet Jeremiah. Jeremiah condemned pagan practices such as divination and the casting of lots, even though Judaism had similar ones. Since no one suggests that Jeremiah was cynically condemning Judaism, no one should suggest that Hobbes was cynically condemning Christianity, without hard evidence to the contrary. Consider a passage such as this, on the nature of the pagan gods:

They have attributed to them, not only the shapes, some of men, some of beasts, some of monsters; but also the faculties, and passions of men and beasts: as sense, speech, sex, lust, generation, and this not only by mixing one with another, to propogate the kind of gods; but also by mixing with men, and women, to beget mongrel gods, and but inmates of heaven, as Bacchus, Hercules, and others; besides anger, revenge, and other passions of living creatures, and the actions proceeding from them, as fraud, theft, adultery, sodomy, and any vice that may be taken for an effect of power, or a cause of pleasure; and all such vices, as amongst men are taken to be against law, rather than against honor. (EW, 3:101)

Taken at face value, these are the words of a prophet inveighing against false religion, not a libertine intent on undermining all religion. Given the Judeo-Christian tradition of anathematizing the pagan religions, exemplified by men such as Jeremiah and Calvin, and Hobbes's staunch upbringing in that tradition, taking his words at face value is the simplest, most plausible interpretation of them. One might object that Hobbes, as a philosopher, must have seen that Christianity has its own "mongrel god" as a redeemer. But this interpretation is conjectural, based upon a dubious premise and a dubious inference of a priori reasoning.[20] As a matter of fact, there are numerous contemporary philosophers who know pagan mythology, know of Hobbesian arguments against pagan religions, and do not infer that Jesus is a mongrel god. The view that this passage from Hobbes has a secret message does not jibe with the text itself. The clear thrust of the passage is to attack promiscuity, carnality, and wholesale licentiousness in pagan religion. To suggest that the unique and passionless conception of Jesus is an instance of such promiscuity is to transmogrify the text.

After his condemnation of pagan religion, Hobbes then endorses Judeo-Christian religions, in which God "gave laws, not only of behaviour towards himself, but also towards one another" (EW, 3:105). A little later he ends the chapter by attacking, not all priests, but "unpleasing priests," who shape religion for their own self-interest. He mentions Catholic priests explicitly, but implies that Presbyterian presbyters are as bad (ibid., p. 109). This leaves the priesthood of the

Church of England uncriticized, even if individual priests of that denomination might be criticizable for subscribing to papist or presbyterian corruptions.[21]

Hobbes often labored to pluck out the pagan elements of Greek philosophy that had been intertwined with biblical doctrines. For example, at the beginning of *De Corpore*, a work that has nothing ostensibly to do with religion, Hobbes condemns what passed as philosophy in Greece. He denies that it was properly philosophy; it was "a certain phantasm, for superficial gravity, though full of fraud and filth." Hobbes says that the church fathers are responsible, for they began "with the decrees of Holy Scripture to mingle the sentences of heathen philosophers; . . . and bringing in the enemies, betrayed unto them the citadel of Christianity" (EW, 1:x). He regards Plato's views as harmless, but he thinks Aristotle's were "foolish and false." He sets himself the task of performing an "exorcism" and restoring "the rules of honouring God, . . . and to yield what is due to religion to the Holy Scriptures" (ibid., p. xi). Hobbes's attitude is typical of the Protestant Reformers, who wanted to strip away the Aristotelian scholasticism of the Middle Ages in order to reveal the true religion of the Bible. To think that Hobbes wants the reader to transfer his criticisms of Greek philosophy to the Christian religion is an extravagant hypothesis, given what he says and the historical context.

Like Calvin, Hobbes devotes more attention to the dangers of superstition than to the requirements of true worship. One reason for this is that true worship is a simple affair. The chief idea is that the proper worship of God must be shaped by the sort of reverent behavior a person would exhibit toward a revered human being; "gifts, petitions, thanks, submission of body, considerate addresses, sober behavior, premeditated words" should be offered to God (EW, 3:98). Reason cannot be more specific than this. Again like Calvin, Hobbes does not think that there is one liturgy, which is required for all Christians at all times. The determination of a proper liturgy is best left to those a person believes to be "wiser." Hobbes must be using this term euphemistically and proleptically; for later it will be clear that the wisest person in matters of religion is the sovereign.

There are many other religious elements in the early pages of *Leviathan* of a more incidental nature, but even these are telling. When Hobbes gives an example of a thought "unguided, without design," he says that during a discussion of the Civil War, a person asked him what the value of a Roman penny had been. Even though these two things may seem wholly unconnected, Hobbes traced the thinking from the Civil War, through the execution of an innocent king, through "the thought of the delivering up of Christ," through the price paid to Judas, to the value of the Roman penny – "and all this in a moment of time; for thought is quick" (EW, 3:12–13).[22] It is more likely than not that Hobbes was preoccupied with religious concepts and attentive to the interrelation between politics and Christianity, when even his example of a random thought concerns the Civil War and connects the execution of Charles I with the crucifixion of Jesus.[23] But these examples are, as I said, incidental (see also ibid., 3:18–19, 24). More important is his religious theory of the underpinnings of moral and political philosophy, which I shall be discussing in the next four chapters.

Part II

Law, morality, and God

Chapter 3

Power, obligation, and justice

TWO INTERPRETATIONS

There are two opposing interpretations of Hobbes's moral theory, one supported by the secularists and one supported by the religionists. According to the secularists, Hobbes's moral theory is based upon self-interest. Moral laws are egoistic or prudential prescriptions. According to this view, Hobbes holds the following:

> An action *a* is moral if and only if *a* is derivable by reason alone as conducive to self-preservation.[1]

This is the received view of Hobbes's moral theory. The problem for this interpretation is to explain why Hobbes's theory should count as a moral theory if Hobbes's laws of nature merely codify maxims of self-interest. Some secularists simply deny that Hobbes has a moral theory. Others have ingenious explanations for why his theory should count as a moral theory. According to the religionists, Hobbes holds a divine command theory of morality. The principal proponents of this view are A. E. Taylor, Howard Warrender,[2] and F. C. Hood. According to their rendition of it, a divine command theory holds the following:

> An action *a* is moral in virtue of a law of nature if and only if God commands that *a* be done.

The phrase "in virtue of a law of nature" is necessary, in order to separate the issue of what makes something moral

71

for any human being from the issue of whether God may have imposed some moral obligations on certain human beings. The problem for the religionists' theory is to explain the role that self-interest plays. Taylor and Warrender separate it completely from morality, on the grounds that self-interest provides the motivation to be moral without contributing anything to morality itself.

I think that there is something right, and something wrong, about each of these views. The religionist interpretation is correct insofar as the commands of God play an essential role in Hobbes's theory. But the religionists are mistaken in thinking that God's command is both a necessary and a sufficient condition for morality. I shall argue that a weaker thesis is correct, namely:

> An action *a* is *moral* in virtue of a law of nature only if God commands that *a* be done.

That is, God's command is a necessary, not a sufficient, condition for natural morality. This proposition is compatible with something not being part of the natural moral law even though God commands it. For example, God commanded the Jews to practice circumcision. This practice is now part of the positive moral law of the Jews but is not part of the natural moral law. According to Hobbes, if God commands something, then it is either part of the law of nature or part of the positive law of some people.

A second problem with the interpretation of the standard religionists is that they separate the moral character of the laws of nature from Hobbes's psychology of human motivation. Taylor is content to point out that there is "no logically necessary connection" (1938, pp. 36–7) between a psychological theory and a moral theory. Warrender tries to take some of the sting out of this claim by holding that the two systems are consistent with each other and that the psychology "validates" the morality (Warrender, 1957, pp. 87–97).

The secularist interpretation can account for the motivational element in morality; it is also correct in holding that

Hobbes intends to elevate self-interest to morality and that the laws of nature are derivable by reason alone. But these are necessary, not sufficient, conditions for morality, according to Hobbes. Thus, the secularist thesis should be weakened to the following:

> An action *a* is moral only if *a* is derivable by reason alone as conducive to self-preservation.

What the secularist interpretation leaves out is the contribution that God's command makes to morality, according to Hobbes. Although secularists admit that there is textual evidence for the opposing view, they do not see either the need or any coherent way to incorporate God's command into the theory (Hampton, 1986, p. 29).

My interpretation will give due place to the textual evidence for both the secularist and the standard religionist interpretation of Hobbes's moral theory but will avoid the flaws in each. In short, I shall be arguing that according to Hobbes

> An action *a* is moral in virtue of a law of nature if and only if God commands that *a* be done and *a* is derivable by reason alone as conducive to self-preservation.

Critics of divine command theories of morality have claimed that such theories are not genuine theories of morality. They hold that nothing can be made good merely by command. If God commands something, it must be because it is good; it is not good simply because he commands it. Thus, if Hobbes holds a divine command theory of morality (and no other moral theory), then he does not have a theory of morality at all.

In order to reply to this criticism, we need to distinguish between a theory of morality and a correct theory of morality, just as we need to distinguish between a theory of science and a correct theory of science. Ptolemy's theory is incorrect, but it is a theory nonetheless. It is tendentious, or at least misleading, to argue that Hobbes does not have a moral

73

theory because he holds a theory of kind *K* and nothing of kind *K* is a moral theory, even though he thinks that morality exists and that his theory of kind *K* is the correct account of morality. There is a difference between arguing that morality should be analyzed in terms of either self-interest or God's commands, on the one hand, and arguing that there is no such thing as morality, only self-interest or God's commands. Hobbes argues for the former, not the latter. It is, at the least, misleading to use a definition of morality to rule out traditional theories of morality.

One last preliminary point: it is possible that there is no (psychologically) simple and descriptively adequate definition of morality, and I shall not try to define the term. Morality may be a cluster concept made up of various, sometimes overlapping, concepts. For me, morality deals with (1) what it is for a person to be good or bad, and just or unjust; and (2) the nature of, and the means to, human happiness. Hobbes certainly has a theory of morality in this sense.

THE STATE OF NATURE AND JUSTICE

I introduced the background to Hobbes's discussion of the laws of nature in the last chapter, when I explained that the source of human misery is pride, in the biblical sense of the refusal to be subordinate to authority. I pointed out that Hobbes's proof that in the state of nature humans are engaged in a war of each against all can be stated using very modest assumptions. If even a few people are aggressive, then, because the consequences of an undefended attack are so dire and because no one can be sure who might attack, each person must be suspicious of everyone (EW, 2:16).[3] However, Hobbes tends to overstate his case and to attribute aggressiveness to everyone.

> Let him [the reader] therefore consider with himself, when taking a journey, he arms himself, and seeks to go well accompanied; when going to sleep, he locks his doors; when even in his house he locks his chests; and this when he knows

there be laws, and public officers, armed, to revenge all injuries shall be done him; what opinion he has of his fellow-subjects, when he rides armed; of his fellow citizens, when he locks his doors; and of his children, and servants, when he locks his chests. Does he not there as much accuse mankind by his actions, as I do by my words? (EW, 3:114)

A traveler locks his doors because he believes some people are robbers, not because he believes all are.[4] Hobbes invalidly generalizes to all people when he suggests that the traveler accuses "mankind" by such behavior. Hobbes may have been motivated by his Calvinistic view of humans. But that is not the important point in this context. What is important is Hobbes's observation that neither the desires that lead to aggression nor the actions that proceed from those passions are in themselves sinful (ibid.).

Sin can be taken in a broad or a narrow sense. In the narrow sense, to sin is to disobey a command of God. This is the traditional Judeo-Christian understanding of sin. Furthermore, since the laws of nature are commands of God, according to Hobbes (as I shall argue in Chapter 4), to disobey a law of nature is a sin. In the broad sense, sin is not restricted to disobedience to God. To sin is to act, or even intend to act, against a law (EW, 3:277). God can punish people for sins in this sense. But civil sovereigns should punish only those sins that are also crimes, where a crime is understood to be the actual commission of an act that violates a law.

So far nothing has been said about justice. Nowhere in this passage does Hobbes say that to sin is to act unjustly. The concepts of justice and injustice do not appear until the next page. I believe that no interpretation of Hobbes's remarks about the origin of justice can be made plausible or consistent unless these concepts are understood within the relatively narrow context in which they occur. There are three different passages in *Leviathan* in which Hobbes talks explicitly about the origin of justice and injustice.

The first is in chapter 13 in the context of explaining what things are like in the state of nature, before there has been any mention or consideration of the laws of nature. Speaking about the "Natural Condition of Mankind" as a war of all against all, Hobbes says that "nothing can be unjust" (EW, 3:115). This utterance alone leaves it open that everyone is just in the state of nature, because no one can break a law in a condition in which there are no laws; at least, Hobbes has not yet mentioned the existence of any laws at all. However, this suggested interpretation is undermined by his next remark. He says, "The notions of right and wrong, justice and injustice have there no place. Where there is no common power, there is no law: where no law, no injustice" (ibid.). Later we shall discover that the laws of nature operate in the state of nature. But, according to the compositive method that Hobbes is following here, the state of nature is being considered in isolation (or abstracted) from all laws, including the laws of nature. Since there is no law, there can be no injustice. Let's call the state of nature, considered in isolation from the laws of nature, the "primary state of nature."

In the primary state of nature, it seems that not even the existence of God is considered. For whether one accepts the religionist or the secularist interpretation of Hobbes, God is a power over all people, and Hobbes says that "there is no common power" in this primary state of nature (EW, 3:343–6). I would suggest, although this cannot be demonstrated in the present context, that it is precisely because the common power of God is absent from the primary state of nature that there is "no law" at all and "where no law, no injustice." For we shall see shortly that justice and injustice do exist in what I shall call the "secondary state of nature," in which the only common power is God and the only laws are the laws of nature.

Before proceeding to what Hobbes says about the secondary state of nature, one further point that he makes about justice and injustice should be mentioned. Hobbes holds that justice and injustice are not fundamentally qualities or properties. For if they were, then a person might be just or unjust "alone in the world." Rather, to be just is a relation that holds between people "in society, not in solitude" (EW, 3:115). One traditional definition of justice can be expressed in the following way: x is just if and only if for all y, x pays y what x owes y. The relational and social element in justice is evident from the analysans. Hobbes's treatment of justice fits into this traditional idea.

Hobbes ends this chapter about the primary state of nature with a proleptic remark. He says that the way out of the (primary) state of nature is through the "Laws of Nature" (p. 116). Hobbes begins the next chapter by introducing the idea of the right of nature, which is enjoyed by everyone in the state of nature, independent of any lawful constraints on them. He then introduces the idea of the law of nature. His purpose is to add another element to his rational reconstruction of civil government, in keeping with his compositive method. The law of nature is not derived from the state of nature. Rather, having explained what the (primary) state of nature is in isolation from the idea of the law of nature, he can now introduce the former idea and analyze the consequences of doing so. As I indicated earlier, I shall call the state of nature considered in conjunction with the law of nature the "secondary state of nature."

One of the principal consequences of adding the law of nature to the state of nature is that it permits Hobbes to discuss the origin of justice and injustice. Hobbes introduces the idea of injustice in two contexts in the secondary state of nature. Both are problematic, though in different ways. Let's begin with the first. Hobbes says that a person may "lay aside his right" to something, and that when he does so he cannot interfere with others who wish to exercise their right to that thing without being guilty of "injustice" (EW, 3:119). He does not explain why laying down a right could put one in jeopardy of being unjust. At this stage of explaining the law of nature, every laying down of right could be unilateral, and, if it is unilateral, it is not clear why there would be any exposure to the possible committing of injustice. A person could lay down his right either to everyone or to one other particular person without receiving any consideration from anyone else. Such a free laying down of right would not be conditional upon any reciprocation on the part of the beneficiary of the act, even though the person laying down his right may hope for some benefit in return (p. 120). That is, a person P_1 could transfer a right to a person P_2 with the hope of receiving a future benefit from P_2. But, because P_2 is not himself obliged to act kindly toward P_1, the action of P_1 is unilateral. Thus it is not clear how the action of P_1 could expose him to the possibility of being unjust, unless perhaps he thinks that God would judge the action in this way. Even if P_1 withdrew his laying down of right, what injustice could there be in that, unless again God would judge the action to be unjust? What may lie behind Hobbes's odd introduction of the idea of injustice is his anticipation of a specific kind of laying down of right, namely, the making of a covenant.

The origin of justice and injustice in the secondary state of nature is introduced for a second time in *Leviathan* chapter 15 when he states the third law of nature: "that men perform their covenants made" (EW, 3:130). This law would seem to presuppose that covenants can be made in the state of nature; otherwise the law would be vacuous and have no application. It is not the actual existence of covenants but the possibility of their existence, that gives rise to justice and injustice. Laws should be construed as conditional expressions, not categorical ones. Although the law "All trespassers will be prosecuted" has the grammatical form of a categorical proposition, it is not logically categorical, because it does not entail that there are trespassers. Like physical laws, as Hobbes understands them, the law in question should be understood to mean: "If someone is a trespasser, then he will be prosecuted." Similarly, the law "Men perform their covenants" should be construed conditionally: "If a man makes a covenant, then he performs it."

Hobbes says the following: "[I]n this law of nature, consisteth the fountain and original of JUSTICE. For where no covenant hath preceded, there hath no right been transferred . . . ; and consequently, no action can be unjust" (EW, 3:130).[5] Injustice presupposes the existence of a covenant. Injustice is "the not performance of a covenant"; justice is what is "not unjust" (p. 131). It is clear from this manner of definition that "just" and "unjust" are contradictory terms for Hobbes. However, the terms apply only in the secondary state of nature, because only in this state of nature are there laws which may be broken. The terms "just" and "unjust" do not apply at all in the primary state of nature, because absolutely no law, not even the law of nature, is posited to exist there.

There is no reason to hold that Hobbes equivocates on the definition of the term "just." Being just always means that one is not breaking a covenant; it never means that there is no covenant which might be broken (cf. Barry, 1968, p. 41). If one were to ask whether a person who in fact never made a covenant in the secondary state of nature were just, unjust, or neither, the answer would be "just" (by default). For, in avoiding covenants one avoids not keeping any covenants, and from this it follows that one is just. Since the state of nature is not primarily (if at all) a historical reality, it is not apposite to ask when the first covenant was made (EW, 3:114). The issue of whether a person is just or unjust in the secondary state of nature is a conceptual issue, and there is nothing logically odd about attributing justice to a person who has never done anything that would count as "good" or "just" in conventional terms. For what it is worth, it was standardly held that Adam was created just, even though he had not done anything to deserve being born with that attribute.[6]

The next question to be asked is this: if justice and injustice require a law, and law requires a common power, as Hobbes claimed in his discussion of the primary state of nature, what law and what common power make justice and injustice possible in the secondary state of nature? The only law in the state of nature is the law of nature. And the only common power in the state of nature is God. Consequently, justice and injustice exist in the (secondary) state of nature, because there is a law, established by a common power, namely, God (EW, 3:114).

Roughly, for Hobbes, a covenant is words that a person utters with the intention of being bound or obliged to do what one says one will do. What can bind or oblige a person who makes a covenant in the state of nature? It cannot be the strength of the words themselves, for words do not have any force in that sense. Although the words of a covenant are literally its bonds, these bonds "have their strength, not from their own nature, for nothing is more easily broken than a man's word, but from fear of some evil consequence upon the rupture" (EW, 3:119).

Later Hobbes says that what "helps to strengthen" the words of a covenant is fear (ibid., p. 128). In the state of nature, people have only two things to fear: "one, the power of spirits invisible; the other, the power of those men they shall therein offend" (p. 129). Since everyone in the state of nature is roughly equal and already at war, there is little more to fear from an offended individual than from an unoffended one. Although humans are often irrational, and thus often do fear other humans more than the greater power of God, it is the fear of God that objectively obliges or ties people in the state of nature to their covenants. Hobbes says, "So that before the time of civil society, or in the interruption thereof by war, there is nothing can strengthen a covenant of peace agreed on, against the temptations of avarice, ambition, lust, or other strong desire, but *the fear of that invisible power, which they every one worship as God; and fear as a revenger of their perfidy*" (ibid., my italics).[7]

Without a civil government, every agreement between humans is warranted by God: "All therefore that can be done between two men not subject to civil power, is to put one another to swear by the God he feareth: which *swearing*, or OATH, is a form of speech, added to a promise; by which he that promiseth, signifieth, that unless he perform, he renounceth the mercy of his God, or calleth to him for vengeance on himself" (EW, 3:129).[8] Some scholars have mistakenly interpreted Hobbes to hold that God plays no part in an oath, but the force of his remarks is just the opposite, namely, that because nothing other than God has the unfailing strength to enforce a covenant made in the state of nature, God's support is always implied by the words of the covenant. This is why it is not necessary to turn a covenant into an explicit oath by calling on God by name: "For a covenant if lawful, binds in the sight of God, without the oath, as much as with it: if unlawful, bindeth not at all; though it be confirmed with an oath" (ibid., p. 130). Anthony Ascham is sometimes presented as an authentic Hobbesian. If that is correct, then his view confirms my interpretation of Hobbes, for Ascham defines an oath as "a religious attestation of God with an imprecation of his wrath when we assert or promise." He goes on to say that God is the only being "who by right of government hath also a right of punishing alwayes, and every where" (Ascham, 1649a, p. 46).

The necessity of believing in divine punishment in order to control humans was a common seventeenth-century doctrine. The mathematician Thomas Hariot wrote, "The belief in heaven and the fiery pit makes the simple folk give obedience to their governors, and behave with great care, so that they may avoid torment after death and enjoy bliss" (Hariot, 1588, p. 268). The marquis of Newcastle, one of Charles II's tutors, told the prince, "Were there no heaven or hell you shall see the disadvantage for your government" (quoted from Hill, 1986, 2:12). And Bishop Samuel Parker said, "Nothing can so effectively enslave them [the common people] as the fear of invisible power and the dismal apprehensions of the world to come" (quoted from ibid., p. 16). There is no need to think that any of these people thought that his views implied that there was no hell or that his sentiments betrayed religious insincerity. They probably thought that God made hell because it was a necessary part of the entire universe, given that sinful humans were part of it. Many intellectuals of the time, notably Thomas Sprat, thought that even science served the political function of maintaining "order and stability." It did this by teaching humility, discouraging enthusiasm, and showing citizens how difficult it is to govern anything (Jacob, 1976, pp. 37–9).

There is a serious objection to the interpretation I have
been developing about the existence of covenants in the state
of nature. Immediately after saying that the third law of
nature is that men [ought to] perform their covenants, and
saying that justice and injustice arise out of the performance
or nonperformance of covenants, Hobbes seems to say that
there are in fact no valid covenants in the state of nature and
consequently no injustice (and, presumably, no justice), because before a commonwealth is established there is no coercive power to take away the kind of fear that invalidates all
covenants. Here is the passage:

> But because covenants of mutual trust, where there is a fear of
> not performance on either part, as hath been said in the for-
> mer chapter, are invalid; though the original of justice be the
> making of covenants; yet injustice actually there can be none,
> till the cause of such fear be taken away; which while men are
> in the natural condition of war, cannot be done. (EW, 3:131)

This passage is difficult for several reasons. First, one clause,
"though the original of justice be the making of covenants,"
seems to presuppose that valid covenants are made in the
state of nature. But the clauses immediately following it
seem to deny the possibility. This apparent denial also
makes the third law of nature, which is stated immediately
before this passage, very difficult to understand. If no covenants can be made in the state of nature, then the third law
("that men perform their covenants made") is vacuous, as I
have said earlier. The law would never have any application.
This is one good reason for arguing that Hobbes, upon reflection, would not want to mean what his words literally
say.

There is even a sharper way of putting the problem of
interpreting Hobbes to mean that it is impossible for people
to make covenants in the state of nature. If he is interpreted
in this way, then his account of the origin of government is
hopelessly incoherent. According to Hobbes, the origin of
civil government requires a covenant. If every covenant requires a coercive power, and if there is no coercive power in

the state of nature, then no covenant can be made in the state of nature. In particular, no covenant creating a government could be made in the state of nature. The upshot of this argument is that if Hobbes's philosophy is to have any chance for success, he must allow that some covenants can be made in the state of nature. (We shall see later on that he says exactly this.)

I do not want to minimize the apparent textual support for the objection that there are no covenants in the state of nature. In chapter 14, Hobbes says, "If a covenant be made, wherein neither of the parties perform presently, but trust one another; in the condition of mere nature, which is a condition of war of every man against every man, upon any reasonable suspicion, it is void" (EW, 3:124). One might argue that since there is always "reasonable suspicion" in the state of nature, apparent covenants in the state of nature are in fact always void.

One can reply to this interpretation of the passage in various ways. First, it is subject to the same problems that were described when the first passage to the same effect was discussed: it does not allow for any exit from the state of nature. Second, even though there is a state of war of everyone against all, it is not at all clear that everyone always has reasonable suspicion of everyone else in the state of nature in any way that would preclude at least temporary covenants. In other words, the phrase "upon reasonable suspicion" need not mean that one always has a reasonable suspicion. For example, suppose there is a small group of people who are actively being harassed by one person, Gloria. The people are far enough apart from each other so that they know that each can flee from all of the other members of the group if the necessity arises. This group can covenant to form a circle around Gloria and to stone her whenever she comes near any one of them. (The circle can contract and expand as needed to achieve this aim.) In this time and place, none of the members of the group has any reasonable suspicion of any other member of that group. Each can fulfill his or her covenant, and they can then disband. Hobbes himself recognized that covenants are possible in the state of nature because he knew that nations have covenants with each other and that nations are in the state of nature.

In contrast to the two passages that seem to say that covenants are impossible in the state of nature, there are other passages that clearly say the opposite: "Covenants entered into by fear, in the condition of mere nature, are obligatory" (EW, 3:126). On many occasions Hobbes says that making a covenant under fear or duress in the state of nature is not an invalidating condition. The most famous of these passages concerns the ransom case. According to Hobbes, if a person returns to the state of nature by being captured by pirates and promises to pay ransom upon release, that person incurs an obligation to make the payment even after he is out of the power of the pirates. Hobbes makes clear that this applies in the state of nature. The entire passage is worth quoting:

> Covenants entered into by fear, in the condition of mere nature, are obligatory. For example, if I covenant to pay a ransom, or service for my life, to an enemy; I am bound by it: for it is a contract, wherein one receiveth the benefit of life; the other is to receive money, or service for it; and consequently, where no other law, as in the condition of mere nature, forbiddeth the performance, the covenant is valid. Therefore prisoners of war, if trusted with the payment of their ransom, are obliged to pay it: and if a weaker prince, make a disadvantageous peace with a stronger, for fear; he is bound to keep it; unless, as hath been said before, there ariseth some new, and just cause of fear, to renew the war. (EW, 3:127)

Two examples of covenants made in the state of nature are presented in this passage. One is expressed in the clause "if a weaker prince, make a disadvantageous peace with a stronger, for fear; he is bound to keep it." The other concerns the ransom. Each example is quite easy to explain on the view I attribute to Hobbes. Anyone in the state of nature is subject to the laws of nature, which are the same as the laws of God; and when breaking them also involves a breach

84

of contract, then the action is unjust. Ascham, the alleged Hobbesian, said, "In an oath made to a Pirate or a Tyrant wee contract with God himselfe. . . . [W]e are bound to make the oath good, by reason of our obligations to God" (Ascham, 1649a, p. 55).

Notice that Hobbes gives no indication that prisoners of war are obliged to pay only so long as they fear the person who had kept them captive. The prisoners of war are already released and "trusted with the payment of their ransom." Since trust, not fear, operates in the payment, the former prisoners are out of the clutches of the former captor. Nothing rules out the possibility that the former prisoner returns to a civil state that is stronger than the former captor, since Hobbes is speaking of the ransom case quite generally. However, to say that fear of the former captor is not operative is not to say that the fear of no one is operative. In the state of nature, God is the most powerful object to be feared, even though he is not always feared most.

Moreover, fear is invariably what motivates covenants in the state of nature. At the end of chapter 13, when Hobbes is preparing to explain how it is possible for humans to get out of the state of nature, he says that "fear of death" is one of the things that inclines a person to peace. That is, fear motivates one to enter into the covenant that is made to create a civil government. Also, the object of fear is often the very people with whom one makes the covenant.

Fear can invalidate a covenant in only one circumstance, namely, if the fear is one that arises from "some new fact, or other sign of the will not to perform" after the covenant has been made (EW, 3:125). But it is not so much the fear itself as the realization that the other party will not perform as he promised that voids the covenant. No fear that existed prior to and during the making of the covenant is an invalidating condition. Thus, a person cannot legitimately try to invalidate a covenant by saying, "I only covenanted to pay for fire insurance because I feared that my in-laws would burn down the house; since I no longer have that fear, my covenant to pay for the coverage is void."

The upshot of this discussion is that it is mysterious why Hobbes seems to have said in the passages just quoted that fear is an invalidating condition. The best I can do is (1) to acknowledge their existence; (2) to try to give a psychological explanation for their occurrence; and (3) to deny that Hobbes would have wanted to stand by the words if he had understood their consequences. I have already done the first. Concerning (2), I suggest that he was so intent upon establishing the importance of civil authority that he exaggerated the difficulty of covenanting in the state of nature. Concerning (3), Hobbes himself recommended this course. Trying to explain why someone might seem to give up his right to life (contrary to what Hobbes will allow), he says the person is not to be taken at his word: "And therefore if a man by words, or other signs, seem to despoil himself of the end, for which those signs were intended; he is not to be understood as if he meant it, or that it was his will; but that he was ignorant of how such words and actions were to be interpreted" (EW, 3:120).

I have argued that justice exists in the (secondary) state of nature. Furthermore, since justice presupposes the existence of law, the laws of nature are in effect there. Often a covenant that was attempted to be enacted in the state of nature becomes void because one party reasonably suspects that the other party will not fulfill his side of the bargain. This kind of case often arises when something that seems to be required by some higher-numbered law of nature, say the third (Keep your covenants), fourth, or fifth, contradicts the second ("by all means we can, to defend ourselves"). But this apparent contradiction cannot be a real one, because the higher-numbered laws are entailed by the lower-numbered laws (EW, 3:117–18, 130). (It is assumed that the first two laws are consistent.) Thus, all the laws of nature are always in effect, in the sense that they are always on the books and must be followed when all of their preparatory conditions are met. But the preparatory conditions are rarely met in the state of nature. That is, many actions that would seem to be required by the third, or some later, law of nature are voided by the widespread danger of particular circumstances in the state of nature.[9]

OBLIGATION

Law and obligation

Although it has been mentioned in passing, I have not treated the concept of obligation explicitly. In this section I shall argue that the laws of nature and obligation are conceptually tied. The laws of nature "oblige," or obligate, human beings.

The term "laws of nature" is equivocal. It could refer to the physical laws of nature or to laws pertaining specifically to human behavior when it is judged to be just or unjust, good or bad. Let's tentatively call these latter laws "behavioral laws of nature." In Hobbes's time the physical laws of nature were typically understood to be purely descriptive of how bodies operate. Since Hobbes was a determinist, one might have expected him to assimilate the behavioral laws of nature to the physical laws of nature. If he had, then all laws of nature would be purely descriptive, and the issue of whether the behavioral laws of nature are moral laws or prudential rules would have been moot. But he does not. Hobbes never says that the behavioral laws of nature are a special case of the physical laws of nature. If the physical laws are descriptive, what should the behavioral laws be said to be? Normally, the laws of nature are said to be "prescriptive," but that term would be tendentious. Whether they are moral laws or prudential rules, the behavioral laws of nature may be said to be "directive," in contrast with the physical laws of nature. Hereafter, when I use the term "laws of nature" it will mean the behavioral laws of nature.

When it is applied to the laws of nature, the word "law" is typically defined partially in terms of the word "obligation," or a cognate term. Thus *Webster's Third New International Dictionary* begins its definition of "law": "a binding custom or practice of a community: a rule . . . that is . . . made obligatory by a sanction . . . or enforced by the controlling authority." Not only does this definition incorporate the idea of obligation; it also specifies that the obligation holds in virtue of some "controlling authority." I maintain that it is Hobbes's view that God is the controlling authority for the laws of nature and that his irresistible power enforces the required sanction.

Brian Barry denies that Hobbes's laws of nature have either of these features. One reason he thinks that the laws of nature need not have the ordinary features of laws is that he believes that Hobbes is not using the term "law" in its ordinary sense. Barry's view is at variance with Hobbes's own claim that he is talking about "law" and associated words in their ordinary sense (EW, 3:359). It also trivializes Hobbes's project. If he were using "law" in a stipulative sense, unconnected with its ordinary use, then his conclusions would have no consequences for the issues that concern moral and political philosophers, for they are trying to understand the foundations of precisely the notion that functions in the interpersonal relations of people, and that notion is expressed by the ordinary use of "law," which requires that laws be obligatory.

Barry claims that most of Hobbes's use of the word "obligation" are intelligible simply by taking it to mean "renunciation of right." Even if this is true, it is not sufficient to establish his thesis. If Hobbes defined "obligation" in terms of "renunciation of right," then all of his uses of "obligation" and cognate terms should be intelligible in this sense. But they are not. In numerous places and in various contexts, Hobbes says that the laws of nature oblige, and his utterances cannot be taken to mean simply that someone has renounced his right (EW, 3:130, 145, 257, 322, 324, 342, 377, 461, 470, 514, 522). The reason is that the laws of nature oblige in the (secondary) state of nature, whether or not anyone has laid down his right. As the page references just given indicate, Hobbes's uses of "obligation" and its cognates are not mostly clustered around one page, contrary to Barry's claim (1968, p. 59). If Hobbes does not often say that the laws of nature oblige, it is because it is unnecessary to do so. People do not often say that all humans are mortal or that all bachelors are unmarried, even though they clearly believe such.

Barry claims that when "obliges" does not mean "renounces a right," then Hobbes uses it to mean "conduces to self-preservation." This seems quite unlikely. For if "obliges" ever had this meaning, then that meaning would be virtually the opposite of the meaning it usually has. This can be shown by considering what happens if Barry's explication of "obligation" in the figurative sense (and Hobbes's explication of "liberty") are substituted into Hobbes's claim that "law and right differ as much as obligation and liberty." If we make the suggested substitutions, then Hobbes's claim is this: "Law and right differ as much as what conduces to self-preservation and the absence of external impediments to preserve one's own nature." This is a distinction without a difference.

It is not even plausible that "obliges" could mean "conduces to self-preservation" in the very passage that leads Barry to this view: "The laws of nature oblige *in foro interno;* that is to say, they bind to a desire they should take place: but *in foro externo;* that is, to the putting them in act, not always" (EW, 3:145). On Barry's interpretation, this passage says: "The laws of nature conduce to self-preservation *in foro interno;* . . . but *in foro externo;* that is, to the putting them in act, not always." It is implausible that in this passage Hobbes was trying to convey that what leads to self-preservation is what we desire should happen, but that what leads to self-preservation does not always do so. What Hobbes did mean, as I have suggested, is that the laws of nature are always in effect in the (secondary) state of nature but the preparatory conditions required for having them constrain one's actions are not always satisfied. I am not denying that the laws of nature conduce to self-preservation, but that is not what "obliges" means here.

There is an even stronger objection to Barry's interpretation of the passage. If "obliges" did mean "conduces to self-preservation" in this passage, then one would expect

Hobbes to have phrased the "that is" clause like this: "The laws of nature oblige *in foro externo;* that is to say, they conduce to self-preservation." But he did not say this. Barry cannot reply that Hobbes was not thinking explicitly about self-preservation in this context, for clearly Hobbes was. Shortly after the passage under consideration, he says that modest and tractable behavior in the state of nature would lead to one's own ruin, "contrary to the ground of all laws of nature, which tend to nature's preservation" (EW, 3:145).

One of the sources of Barry's mistake is that he thinks that Hobbes defines the concept of obligation in the following passage: "Right is laid aside, either by simply renouncing it; or by transferring it to another. . . . And when a man hath in either manner abandoned, or granted away his right; then he is said to be OBLIGED, or BOUND, not to hinder those, to whom such right is granted, or abandoned, from the benefit of it. . . . " (EW, 3:118–19). But there is no reason to take it in that way. The passage may be indicating no more than that laying down of right is one way of picking up an obligation. Taken strictly, the passage is a remark about how people talk. The clausal form "When a person does *x*, he is said to be *y*" is used too loosely to be interpreted as introducing a definition. Consider these examples: a person who gives a large amount of money to charities is said to be good; a person who protests against his country's war is said to be a traitor; a person who drives while intoxicated is said to be reckless. There is no plausibility in holding that any of these examples is meant to define the term following "is said to"; similarly, there is no need to take Hobbes to be defining "obliged" as meaning "laying aside right."

There would be some plausibility in taking Hobbes to be defining the idea of obligation in this context if he had not already introduced that concept in connection with law in general. Hobbes had said that law and right differ as much as obligation and liberty. In other words, every law involves obligation, just as every right involves liberty (EW, 3:119).

Furthermore, Hobbes's own statements about when a person is obliged do not support the idea that obligation is the consequence of laying down one's right. He says that a sovereign is "obliged by the law of nature" to procure the safety of his people, even though the sovereign lays down no right (EW, 3:322). Again, the laws of nature "oblige all mankind, in respect of God," even though no human lays down any right to God (p. 343).

It is at least as plausible to read the passage as stating a sufficient condition for obligation. That is, if a man has in any way abandoned his right, then he is said to be obliged. This leaves it open that a person may be obliged in some other way.

Justice and obligation

Not only does Barry claim that obligation is divorced from law in Hobbes's theory; he also claims that obligation is divorced from justice. He maintains this position even though the passage just quoted continues as follows: A person who has an obligation "*ought*, and it is his DUTY, not to make void that voluntary act of his own: and . . . such hindrance is INJUSTICE, and INJURY, as being *sine jure*; the right being before renounced, or transferred" (EW, 3:119). The clear import of this passage is that necessarily, if a person ought or is obliged to do something, then not to do it is unjust. That is, obligation and injustice – and hence obligation and justice – are connected to each other. Barry tries to escape from this consequence in the same way that he did earlier: he claims that Hobbes equivocates on his definition of "just." According to one definition, something is just if and only if it is not unjust, but according to a second definition, something is just if and only if it does not break a covenant. While Barry may be willing to concede that being just is logically tied to obligation in the latter sense, he denies that it is so tied in the former (Barry, 1968, pp. 41–2). There is no textual justification for attributing an equivocation to Hobbes. Barry resorts to this argument primarily to save his interpretation.

In order to give a smooth interpretation to Hobbes's views, there is no need to detach being just from obligation. If

Hobbes means what he says, namely, that God commands
the laws of nature, and the laws of nature specify acting to
preserve one's own life, then anyone who does not act unjustly is fulfilling the obligations inherent in the laws of nature
and is thereby just. In short, a secularist interpretation of the
laws of nature, such as Barry's, requires elaborate revisionary
readings of Hobbes's texts, while the kind of religious interpretation that I have been presenting gives a straightforward, literal reading.[10]

Power and obligation

Traditionally, Hobbes has been interpreted as holding that
might makes right. If this is taken to mean that Hobbes
thinks that the use of overwhelming power is justified in any
circumstance, then the interpretation is not correct. But a
different interpretation of this traditional view is correct:
namely, irresistible power creates obligation where no prior
obligation exists. I want to defend this interpretation against
the objections of Barry, who denies that there is any connection between obligation and power, just as he had denied
any connection between obligation and justice and between
obligation and law.

One text often used to prove that Hobbes did think that
irresistible power engenders obligation is the following from
De Cive:

> Now if God has the right of sovereignty from his power, it is
> manifest that the *obligation* of yielding him obedience lies on
> men by reason of their weakness. For that *obligation* which
> rises from contract . . . can have no place here . . . when it
> [liberty] is taken away by hope or fear, according to which the
> weaker, despairing of his own power to resist, cannot but
> yield to the stronger. From this last kind of obligation, that is
> to say, from fear or conscience of our own weakness in respect
> of the divine power, it comes to pass that we are obliged to
> obey God in his natural kingdom. (EW, 2:209)

Barry is not persuaded. He thinks that because Hobbes
calls this "natural obligation," it cannot be moral obligation.

I think that Barry misinterprets the force of "natural." "Natural" indicates the origin of the obligation, not its logical character. That is, Hobbes thinks that moral obligation can arise in one of two ways. When the people involved are equal, obligations with respect to each other are created by making a covenant: these are the ordinary obligations that humans incur in social intercourse. In contrast, when one of the parties is overwhelmingly more powerful than the other, the latter person has a natural obligation to the former.

Barry thinks that God's natural right means the same thing as each person's right in the state of nature (Barry, 1968, p. 44). But that is not what Hobbes says; God's right by nature is the "same right" as "the sovereign right [that] ariseth from pact" (EW, 3:346). God's right is not the same as the right of nature, because God's natural power is irresistible and no individual's power is (ibid.). Hobbes says, "Power irresistible justifies all actions, really and properly, in whomsoever it be found; less power does not, and because such power is in God only, he must needs be just in all actions" (EW, 4:250). The phrase "really and properly" indicates that irresistible power is the fundamental ground for obligation. All other obligation derives from it. Thus, God by his omnipotence generates the primary kind of obligation. I am not trying to determine whether Hobbes's view is cogent, but only what it is.

Many philosophers seem to think that the connection between power and basic moral obligation that I have been discussing is either too abhorrent or too obviously false for Hobbes to have espoused it. In addition to judging what Hobbes holds on the basis of what his texts say, it is important to consider the historical possibility that someone could have held such a view. Historically, it is quite probable. Christians have traditionally held that God is radically unlike his creatures and thus that many things that would be impossible for humans are possible for God. Similarly, many things that would be unjust for humans to do would not be unjust for God to do. It would be unjust for a human to order a man to kill his innocent son in order to prove his faithfulness, but it was not unjust for God to order Abraham to kill Isaac. The same rules that apply to humans do not apply to God, because he is sovereign. This idea of sovereignty was sometimes analyzed in terms of his supreme power and sometimes in terms of his ability to create. At bottom I think they are the same, since the ability to create – to make something from nothing – is the greatest power. Sometimes this sovereignty was expressed by identifying God's will with justice. Calvin, for example, says, in *Articles Concerning Predestination*, that "the pure will of God alone . . . is the supreme rule of justice" and in another place that "whatever he [God] wills and decrees is right and just" (Calvin, 1954, pp. 179, 334). Faced with the question presented in Plato's *Euthyphro*, whether something is just because it is willed by the gods or willed by the gods because it is just, Calvin answers, "Just because it is willed by God." I think that Hobbes is following Calvin in this regard, and I shall be showing in later chapters that Hobbes is trying to give a philosophical justification for many of Calvin's other views. In Chapter 4, I will explain how Hobbes's views about obligation, power, and law fit into the wider tradition of voluntarism and rationalism.

Hobbes is trying to give an account of the traditional claim that all of God's actions are just even though they do not always satisfy the demands of ordinary morality. Irresistible power justifies, that is, makes an action just or good, according to Hobbes, so long as there is no previous obligation prohibiting that action. When he discusses the problem of evil, he always mentions the same element of the Book of Job, namely that God can justly do whatever he wants to do, because of his power (EW, 2:207–8; 3:346–7; 4:249; 5:115–16). In short, Hobbes did hold that irresistible might makes right and that anyone overwhelmed by someone has a natural obligation to that person. It is not the absolute quantity of power but the relative inequality of power that generates an obligation: Hobbes says that if two beings were omnipotent, then neither one would have an obligation to the other. But where one being is omnipotent and the other is not, then the latter is obliged to the former (EW, 2:209).

Bishop Bramhall understood Hobbes in the same way.[11] This comes out in his dialogue with Hobbes when Bramhall expresses his horror at Hobbes's claim that atheists deserve to die not because they are sinners but because they are God's enemies. Since atheists do not believe that God exists, Hobbes argues, they cannot recognize the laws of nature as laws, and thus they cannot strictly be culpable for being ignorant of the laws of nature. If they fail to follow them, they are merely acting imprudently, not immorally. This does not satisfy the good bishop, who thinks that Hobbes is being too soft on atheists. He wants culpability attributed to atheists. Describing Hobbes's view, Bramhall says, "His reason [for not attributing culpability] is, because *the atheist never submitted his will to the will of God, whom he never thought to be* [exist]. And he concludeth that man's obligation to obey God proceedeth from his weakness . . . : *Manifestum est obligationem ad prestandam ipsi (Deo) obedientiam, incumbere hominibus propter imbecilitatem*" (EW, 4:290).

Barry thinks that the interchange between Bramhall and Hobbes on this point bolsters his interpretation, but we shall see that he is mistaken. He asks us to notice that Bramhall is quoting *De Cive*, even though Bramhall's book is entitled *The Catching of Leviathan*. He then claims that Hobbes's reply to Bramhall involves some rhetorical legerdemain. He claims that Hobbes ignores the quotation from *De Cive* and cleverly turns the discussion back to *Leviathan* and away from the idea that power is related to obligation. Here is Barry's discussion of the point.

> In his reply, Hobbes coolly replaces the sentence quoted by Bramhall with a quite different one, writing, "to the same sense I have said in my *Leviathan*, that the right of nature whereby God reigneth over man, is to be derived not from his creating them, as if he desired obedience, as of gratitude; but from his irresistible power" [EW, 4:295]. And then he argues that this is not discreditable to God. But notice that by his

maneuver of citing *Leviathan*, Hobbes has neatly avoided having to defend the words quoted by Bramhall, which spoke of
obligation. (Indeed it is hard to see any other point in making
the substitution.) (Barry, 1968, p. 40)

The two major claims that Barry makes about Hobbes's reply, namely, that Hobbes avoids talking about obligation
and that he does not comment on the passage from *De Cive*,
are both false. The falsity of the first claim can be gleaned
even from the small portion of Hobbes's text that Barry
quotes: "to the same sense I have said in my *Leviathan*." That
is, Hobbes claims that the doctrine in both books is the same.
Thus, if the passage in *De Cive* is about obligation and the
passage from *Leviathan* is its correlative, then to comment on
the passage in *Leviathan* is tantamount to commenting on
obligation in the passage from *De Cive*. This may seem suspiciously indirect, so it is important to add that Hobbes also
directly comments on the passage from *De Cive* and does not
ignore it, *pace* Barry. This becomes clear if a bit more of the
relevant passage is quoted: "In the seventh paragraph of
chapter xv, of my book *De Cive*, he [Bramhall] found the
words in Latin, which he here citeth. And to the same sense
I have said in my *Leviathan*, that the right of nature whereby
God reigneth over men, is to be derived not from his creating
them, as if he required gratitude; but from his irresistible
power" (EW, 4:293–4). That is, Hobbes is asserting that he
holds the same view of obligation in *Leviathan* as he held in
De Cive, and he repeats essentially the same phrase, "irresistible power." In order to appreciate the falsity of Barry's
second claim, also notice that Hobbes thinks "the words in
Latin" that Bramhall quoted are important. Hobbes says that
Bramhall misinterprets or mistranslates the Latin. Hobbes
had used the word *incumbere*, in the phrase "obedientiam,
incumbere hominibus propter imbecilitatem," in order to express the necessity of human submission to God, whereas
Bramhall had understood Hobbes to have obedience to God
"*depend* upon our weakness" (EW, 4:291). In other words,
Hobbes accuses Bramhall of quoting the Latin of *De Cive*,

instead of the English of *Leviathan*, in order to fool people into thinking that there was something objectionable hidden in the Latin version of Hobbes's theory. That explains why Hobbes complains about Bramhall's fishing for a doctrine in the Latin text that is obviously not there in the English. And Hobbes argues that there is no objectionable doctrine in the Latin either. That is the correct explanation for why Hobbes says this:

> He saw he could not catch *Leviathan* in this place, he looks for him in my book *De Cive*, which is Latin, to try what he could fish out of that: and says I make our obedience to God, depend upon our weakness; as if these words signified the *dependence*, and not the *necessity* of our submission, or that *incumbere* and *dependere* were all one. (EW, 4:295)

Barry's tactic was to make Hobbes's reply to Bramhall look as if it were evasive and deceptive, when Hobbes was in fact clearly focused on Bramhall's text. And Barry did this supposedly in the interests of trying to make Hobbes look better than the religious interpreters do. Hobbes really does not need friendly interpreters like this.

Barry also claims that Hobbes had abandoned in *Leviathan* the earlier connection he had made between irresistible power and obligation in *De Cive*. The falsity of this is suggested by the fact that Hobbes maintains the connection in two of his other post-*Leviathan* tracts, both of which were written in reply to Bramhall's criticisms, *Of Liberty and Necessity* and *The Questions Concerning Liberty, Necessity, and Chance* (EW, 4:250, 5:116, 146).

I have discussed Barry's interpretation at some length because it is widely accepted. But the details of my refutation should not obscure the main point. Hobbes takes the omnipotence of God as the basis of all obligation. God's power creates a natural obligation, not because it is omnipotent, but because it is irresistible; that is the property that ties one to a course of action.[12] As Hobbes said, if there were two omnipotent beings, then neither one would have an obligation to the other. It is the radical inequality of power between

God and humans that gives rise to the obligaticn. No human has any natural obligation to any other human, not because no human is omnipotent but because all humans are roughly equal in power. Thus, Hobbes says, "[I]f there had been any man of power irresistible, there had been no reason, why he should not by that power have rule and defended both himself and them [all other people], according to his own discretion. To those therefore whose power is irresistible, the dominion of all men adhereth naturally by their excellence of power" (EW, 3:346). By the last sentence, Hobbes probably is referring to the domination of a parent over a child. That power is like God's, and it is his power that makes him sovereign: "[C]onsequently it is from that power, that the kingdom over men, and the right of afflicting men at his pleasure, belongeth naturally to God Almighty; not as Creator, and gracious; but as omnipotent" (ibid.).

Since humans are roughly equal and hence not naturally sovereign, no human is naturally obliged to anyone else. However, people can create obligations, by manufacturing a creature that imitates God and does have irresistible power. This artificial being is Leviathan, the civil government, which acquires irresistible power through each prospective citizen's transfer of power to the designated sovereign: "Power unlimited is absolute sovereignty. And the sovereign in every commonwealth, is the absolute representative of all the subjects" (EW, 3:211). Scholars have not taken as seriously as he intended it Hobbes's remark that Leviathan is the *"mortal god,* to which we owe under the *immortal God,* our peace and defence" (ibid., p. 158). The ground of all obligation is the irresistible power of God. Humans are able to enter into covenants that create a mortal god, which has its own irresistible power and which can maintain human obligations in virtue of the laws of nature, which are God's commands and underwritten by his power. God primes the pump of obligation. Once a human authority with overwhelming power is in place, God can be relegated to the background.

The reason that it is necessary to create a civil government

98

is that, notwithstanding God's omnipotence, humans are more afraid of what they do see than of what they do not see, and more afraid of what is close to them than of what is remote. Thus, it is a practical necessity for humans to create a civil government, which can enact laws and impose obligations, but only because God stands behind and commands the laws of nature. His power and the fear that humans have of his power is sufficient to get people to enact covenants of peace, which establish an earthly sovereign of such overwhelming strength that the teeth of obligation are bared and razor sharp at the necks of the citizens.

Chapter 4

Law

In the last chapter, I argued that Hobbes believes that the root of all obligation is God's omnipotence, because irresistible power directed to an object literally binds, ties or constrains that object to a certain course of action. Because humans are roughly equal to each other, they are not naturally obliged to anyone other than God. They can create obligations, however, by using the laws of nature, which are God's commands, to create a human sovereign who acquires irresistible power. In this chapter, I shall discuss those laws of nature. The distinction between right and law is crucial to this discussion. Once that distinction is explained, I shall discuss the nature of law and say why it is important to distinguish between the form and the content of law. I conclude by discussing the consequences of my view for the secularist interpretation of Hobbes and for the Taylor–Warrender theses. I shall begin by presenting part of the textual basis for my view.

THE TEXTUAL EVIDENCE

To a large extent the purpose of this chapter is to prove that Hobbes almost always means what he says about the laws of nature, namely, that the laws of nature are literally laws; more precisely, they are moral laws in the same way in which they are divine laws. Hobbes says or implies as much in each of the following quotations:

1. "[W]e are to consider next, what are the Divine Laws, or

dictates of natural reasons; . . . the same laws of nature, of which I have spoken already in the fourteenth and fifteenth chapters of this treatise; namely, equity, justice, mercy, humility, and the rest of the moral virtues" (EW, 3:348).

2. "[O]bedience to his [God's] laws, that is, in this case to the laws of nature, is the greatest worship of all" (EW, 3:355).

3. "The *word of God*, is then also to be taken for the dictates of reason and equity, when the same is said in the Scriptures to be written in man's heart" (EW, 3:412).

4. "The same law which is *natural* and *moral*, is also wont to be called *divine*, nor undeservedly; as well because reason, which is the law of nature, is given by God to every man for the rule of his actions. . . ." (EW, 2:50-1).

5. "Because the *word of God*, ruling by nature only, is supposed to be nothing else but right reason, . . . it is manifest that the laws of God, ruling by nature alone, are only the *natural laws*; namely those which we have set down in chaps. II. and III. and deduced from the dictates of *reason, humility, equity, justice, mercy*; and other *moral virtues*. . . ." (EW, 2:209-10).

6. "[The sovereign] never wanteth right to anything, otherwise, than as he himself is the subject of God, and bound thereby to observe the laws of nature" (EW, 3:200).

7. "[T]he laws of nature, there is no doubt, . . . are the laws of God, and carry their authority with them, legible to all men that have the use of natural reason: but this is no other authority, than that of all other moral doctrine consonant to reason; the dictates whereof are laws, not *made*, but *eternal*" (EW, 3:378).

8. "God . . . governeth as many of mankind as acknowledge his providence, by the natural dictates of right reason" (EW, 3:345).

These are not the only passages in which he makes such affirmations. (I shall quote and discuss others later.) I am not pretending that the interpretive issue is settled by quoting these statements. I would simply like the reader to understand that the textual basis for the view that Hobbes believes that the laws of nature are divine laws is substantial, and that, given his repetition of the point, it is prima facie plausible that he means what he says unless strong countervailing reasons are presented. Contrary to the dominant scholarly view, I do not believe that such reasons exist. In the next section, I shall begin my interpretation of Hobbes's view of the laws of nature by discussing the distinction between right and law.

RIGHT AND LAW

Suarez on ius

Hobbes says that "they that speak of this subject [the laws of nature], use to confound *jus*, and *lex*" (EW, 3:117), but he does not say about whom he is thinking. Even though other philosophers disagreed with Hobbes about the meanings of these terms, and even though they sometimes decided to use them synonymously for their own purposes, some philosophers did try to distinguish them in ways that bear upon Hobbes's own use of the terms. Francisco Suarez,[1] for example, devotes the second chapter of *De Legibus* to the alleged distinction. He thinks there are good grounds for distinguishing these concepts. Most importantly, he says that *ius* "is properly wont to be bestowed upon a certain moral power which every man has, either over his own property or with respect to that which is due to him. For it is thus that the owner of a thing is said to have a right (*ius*) in that thing" (Suarez, 1612, p. 30). This is a weaker version of Hobbes's own claim that each person has the right (*ius*) to anything that he can possess. Although the word *ius* probably is etymologically connected with *iurare* ("to swear" or "to take an oath"), Suarez, like many medieval and early modern philosophers, derived it from *iustitia* ("justice"), *iustum* ("just"), or "*iussum*" ("ordered" or "commanded") (ibid., p. 29). In any case, it has a deontic force, as it is ordinarily used. We shall see that Hobbes contradicts this deontic use.

Deontic and nondeontic terms

In order to be clear about what the law of nature is, Hobbes contrasts it to the thing with which it is often confused, namely, the right of nature. The sole difference between the two is that the law of nature is deontic and the right of nature is not. By "deontic" I mean having the force of an obligation. This force can be expressed by the term "oblige" and its cognates, as well as by the terms "owe," "ought," and "bind." Some philosophers have distinguished between moral and nonmoral obligations. Hobbes does not make such a distinction; he distinguishes between natural and artificial obligations and says that they are equally binding. He also holds, I shall argue, that artificial obligation logically depends upon natural obligation. Some philosophers have also distinguished between having an obligation and being obliged. For example, if a bandit with a gun says, "Give me your money, or I'll kill you," the victim is obliged to hand over the money, even though he has no obligation to do so. I think that Hobbes would be irritated with this rather scholastic distinction, built upon an inexact idiom. In his view, if the victim is obliged, then he has an obligation. A person may feel obliged without having an obligation and even say (incorrectly) that he is obliged when he has no obligation, just as a person may feel guilty or say he is guilty (perhaps from a scrupulous conscience) when he is not guilty.

In Hobbes's usage, although "right" is a nondeontic term, it is normative – that is, it is a value-laden term.[2] Whatever is desired is good, according to Hobbes, and people desire precisely that to which they have a right, namely, their self-preservation. The normativity of right is also inherent in the word "liberty," which helps define "right": the right of nature (*jus naturale*) is "the liberty each man hath, to use his own power, as he will himself, for the preservation of his own nature; that is to say, of his own life; and consequently, of doing any thing, which in his own judgment, and reason, he shall conceive to be the aptest means thereunto" (EW,

3:116). And liberty is the unimpeded exercise of one's own power. Liberty can be total or partial. If there are no impediments whatsoever, one has total liberty, but if there is an impediment which prevents the exercise of some powers but not others, then one maintains partial liberty. In the dedication to *Leviathan*, Hobbes explained his project as a search for a middle ground between "too great liberty" and "too much authority" (EW, 3:[v]). The total right of nature is a variant of "too great liberty," while the laws of nature protect against "too much authority." The right of nature is unlimited and nondeontic, because by definition it is the opposite of the laws of nature. In the primary state of nature, there are no laws that restrict what a person can legitimately possess or appropriate. In the secondary state of nature, the laws do not impose any restrictions until people enter into covenants. The laws of nature are in effect in the state of nature, but their primary job is not to restrict what people possess. They serve a different function.[3]

A law of nature (*lex naturalis*), in contrast with the right of nature, "is a precept or general rule, found out by reason, by which a man is forbidden to do that, which is destructive of his life, or taketh away the means of preserving the same; and to omit that, by which he thinketh it may be best preserved" (EW, 3:117).[4] Implicit in this definition is the content of the right of nature. Hobbes says that the law of nature is the sum of the right of nature (ibid.). The difference between the two is that the law of nature adds obligation to the content of the right of nature. The right of nature says what is the case; the law of nature says what ought to be the case. How can one make this transition from "is" to "ought"? Hobbes's goal in chapter 14 of *Leviathan* is to answer that question.

Initially, three aspects of Hobbes's definition of a law of nature suggest that a law of nature is a genuine law. First, there is its name: "law of nature." If Hobbes thought that a law of nature was not a genuine law, then one would expect him to say that he is using the term figuratively. But he does not. Second, every law, according to Hobbes, must have someone to command it, and this is suggested in the phrase "by which a man is forbidden to do that." Nothing is forbidden unless someone forbids it. Third, the immediate context of the definition indicates that Hobbes believes that the laws of nature are genuinely deontic, as laws are, not merely descriptive or prudential. For, immediately after defining a law of nature, he says that right "consisteth in liberty to do, or to forbear." In contrast, "LAW determineth, and bindeth to one of them: so that law, and right, differ as much, as obligation, and liberty; which in one and the same matter are inconsistent" (EW, 3:117). The only thing that could bind or constrain humans to a course of action in the state of nature is God.

As we saw in Chapter 3, these commands are obligatory; that is, they bind a person to a course of action because God has the power to enforce them. This straightforward interpretation of Hobbes's text is opposed by most Hobbes scholars, who adopt a secularist interpretation, according to which a law of nature is not a genuine law.[5] They hold that Hobbes's use of the term "law," in the phrase "law of nature," is metaphorical and often argue that the laws of nature are not genuinely moral but only prudential.

In order to sustain the thesis that the laws of nature are merely prudential, that is, that they provide merely the knowledge a person needs in order to further his own well-being, narrowly understood, one must claim that Hobbes intends his phrase "the laws of nature" metaphorically. There are several problems with this claim. One is that Hobbes never purports to explain the metaphor and never suggests that he is using the term in any way figuratively. Further, it is implausible that Hobbes would use "laws of nature" metaphorically when his purpose is to define the key term in his moral and political philosophy explicitly. It would be a serious defect if that key term were being used metaphorically.[6] His theory would then be based upon a kind of fraud, for he would be using the fundamental term of his moral theory in a metaphorical way, when only a strictly literal understanding of it is philosophically acceptable. Phi-

losophy is getting rid of the metaphors. Granted that Hobbes
sometimes spoke metaphorically, as everyone does, he was
insistent that the use of metaphor in philosophy was pernicious. He says, "[T]he light of human minds is per-
spicuous words, . . . [and] metaphors, and senseless and
ambiguous words, are like *ignes fatui;* and reasoning upon
them is wandering amongst innumerable absurdities; and
their end, contention and sedition, or contempt" (EW, 3:36–
7). In light of this attitude and the fact that in the context of
defining "law" he emphasizes that the terms "right" and
"law" have been misused by philosophers, it is highly unlikely that he would have used "law" metaphorically.

There are still other problems with interpreting the term
"laws of nature" metaphorically. One problem is that it
would make certain arguments in Hobbes's work patently
unsound. For example, consider this passage: "For seeing
punishments are consequent to the breach of laws; natural
punishments must be naturally consequent to the breach of
the laws of nature; and therefore follow them as their natural, not arbitrary effects" (EW, 3:357). The argument here is
sound only if natural laws are genuine instances of laws;
otherwise Hobbes is equivocating on the term "law," and
the fallacy would be a howler. Another problem is that there
is a passage in which Hobbes explicitly considers metaphorical and nonmetaphorical uses of words, points out one
metaphorical sense of the term "God's kingdom," and in
effect asserts that God's rule through the laws of nature does
not involve a metaphor. Hobbes says that the word "kingdom" has a metaphorical sense when it is applied to God's
power as it extends "not only to man, but also to beasts, and
plants, and bodies inanimate." The reason is that the subjects of a king must understand his precepts. Consequently,
all who recognize that God "governeth the world, and hath
given precepts, and propounded rewards, and punishments
to mankind, are God's subjects" (EW, 3:344). He then says
that the way of "promulgation" of God's laws is "by the
dictates of *natural reason*," which he had earlier identified
with the laws of nature. Given that he is contrasting this

sense in which God governs and has a kingdom with the previous metaphorical sense of "kingdom," there should be no doubt that Hobbes holds that the laws of nature are literally laws.

On another issue related to the literalness of the "laws of nature," the secularist interpretation also does not have any good way of explaining who or what forbids what is forbidden in a law of nature.[7] It is not persuasive to claim that since laws of nature are "rules of reason," reason is the authority or the thing that commands them. For reason is not literally able to do anything,[8] other than calculate: that is its sole nature and function (EW, 3:30). On this matter, as on several other telling issues, Hobbes's view is the same as that of John Selden, the great jurist whom Hobbes admired. Selden says, "For pure, unaided reason merely persuades or demonstrates; it does not order, nor bind anyone to their duty" (quoted from Tuck, 1979, p. 93; see also Sommerville, 1984, pp. 442–3).

Suppose that the secularist responds that Hobbes and Selden's explicit views about reason notwithstanding, in this context Hobbes means that it is reason that forbids metaphorically. Then the secularist has dug a deeper hole for himself. For then he is committed to holding that a second key term of Hobbes's definition is metaphorical. An interpretation that attributes the literal meaning to Hobbes's definition is surely preferable to one that attributes a figurative meaning to it. The necessity of attributing metaphorical interpretations to Hobbes's key terms becomes patently absurd in Hood's defense of the claim that according to Hobbes the laws of nature do not oblige:

> In Hobbes's thought obligation always implies an obliger. He had to exclude from his philosophy the only moral obliger, God, and yet had to ground all civil obligations upon the natural obligation to perform covenants. He did this, by defining a law of nature as a precept by which man is forbidden. Obligation without an obliger is a consequence of command without a commander. A command without a commander seems an absurdity. (Hood, 1964, p. 87)

To say that "a command without a commander seems an absurdity" is too weak. It is an absurdity, and Hobbes does not hold it. Typically, Hood uses language that gives the impression that Hobbes was speaking literally: "In saying that law binds or obliges Hobbes means that every law binds or obliges" (ibid., 86); for that is the only kind of language that makes sense.

There is additional evidence against the claim that Hobbes is arguing that the laws of nature cannot be genuine laws because the laws of nature are rules of reason. There are many kinds of genitive in English, and it is as plausible to take "rules of reason" to mean rules that reason discovers as it is to take it to mean rules that reason commands. Further, it is unlikely that Hobbes would have used a metaphor that makes reason command or have authority over a person, since he thinks that people are driven by passions (EW, 3:82, 116). It is the job of reason to suggest the means to satisfy one's desires. To say that reason commands is analogous to saying that the will is free. It is not reason that commands but the person who has the reason, just as it is not the will that is free but the person who has the will.

The secularist interpretation of the definition of "the laws of nature" also does not make sense in the context. When Hobbes defines the term, his intention is to contrast right and law. The basis for the contrast is obligation: "For though they that speak of this subject, use to confound *ius*, and *lex*, *right* and *law:* yet they ought to be distinguished; because RIGHT consisteth in liberty to do, or to forbear; whereas LAW, determineth, and bindeth to one of them: so that law, and right, differ as much, as obligation, and liberty; which in one and the same matter are inconsistent" (EW, 3:117; see also pp. 323–4). The right of nature is not deontic; it is a principle of freedom; it does not bind anyone to anything. In contrast, the laws of nature are deontic; they are principles of restraint; they bind everyone to certain actions.

There is another problem with the secularist view that the laws of nature are not properly laws. Whenever Hobbes divides laws into types, he always includes the laws of nature as laws in the same sense as positive civil laws, as in the following passage:

> Another division of laws, is into *natural* and *positive*. *Natural* are those which have been laws from all eternity; and they are called not only *natural*, but also *moral* laws; consisting in the moral virtues, as justice, equity, and all habits of the mind that conduce to peace, and charity; of which I have already spoken in the fourteenth and fifteenth chapters. (EW, 3:271)

If Hobbes ever wanted to convey that he did not intend his use of "law" to be taken literally, this would have been the place to do it. There would be a more urgent reason for making this clear. If natural laws were not literally laws, then to divide laws into natural and positive would be analogous to dividing horses into saw horses and living horses. Since saw horses are not literally horses, it would be absurd to classify them with living animals.

The same difficulty prohibits interpreting "law" metaphorically in this passage: "But God declareth his laws three ways; by the dictates of *natural reason*, by *revelation*, and by the *voice* of some *man*, to whom by the operation of miracles, he procureth credit with the rest" (EW, 3:345). If the laws of nature were not genuine laws, then it would be absurd to include them in the same category with the laws declared by revelation and by prophets.

Earlier, in *Elements of Law*, Hobbes had divided laws into three types: divine, natural, and civil. And, immediately after making the division, Hobbes remarks that divine law and the laws of nature are actually "one and the same law" (Hobbes, 1640, p. 187). Such a division and such a remark would be semantically absurd if Hobbes were equivocating on the word "law." To draw upon the example of horses again, it would be as if one said that saw horses and living horses are equally horses. It is not sensible to suggest that divine laws are also only metaphorically laws, because

Hobbes is explicit in holding that the divine laws are God's commands. The only way to make sense of his language is to take him to mean what he says, namely, that the laws of nature are laws and hence need a lawgiver.

A similar semantic argument can be made when the laws of nature are discussed in the same context as other kinds of laws: "The law of nature excepted, it belongest to the essence of all other laws, to be made known, to every man that shall be obliged to obey them, either by word, or writing, or some other act, known to proceed from the sovereign authority" (EW, 3:259). This passage would not make any sense if Hobbes were equivocating on "law." If the laws of nature were not laws but counsels or something else, then it would be absurd to exempt them from the requirement that laws be promulgated orally or by writing. Of course, the reason that they are exempted from the normal modes of promulgation is that they are promulgated by God through human reason. Hobbes says this: "[T]o the nature of laws belongest a sufficient, and clear promulgation, such as may take away the excuse of ignorance; which in the laws of men is . . . promulgation by the voice of man. But God declareth his law . . . by the dictates of *natural reason* [as regards the laws of nature]" (EW, 3:345).

To say that the law of nature differs from the right of nature with respect to obligation is not to say that they have nothing in common. To the contrary, they are identical in a certain respect. The content of the laws of nature is precisely the right of nature. The content of both the right of nature and the laws of nature is to defend oneself by any means one can. Consequently, Hobbes says, the second branch of the first law of nature is "the sum of the right of nature" (EW, 3:117). The difference between the right of nature and the law of nature consists in the fact that the laws of nature have something that the right of nature does not have; it is something that transforms the nondeontic right of nature into the deontic law of nature: it has the command of a person in authority prefixed to it. The only one with such authority over humans in the state of nature is God.

Precepts

Some secularists say that the laws of nature are not laws but precepts (e.g., Zagorin, 1954, p. 175). Without further explication of what a precept is, this is not helpful. In the seventeenth century, the term "precept" was more or less synonymous with "law" in its basic use. The *Oxford English Dictionary* defines "precept" variously as "an authoritative command to do some particular act; an order, mandate . . . . A general command or injunction; an instruction, direction or rule for action or conduct, *esp.* an injunction to moral conduct; a maxim. *Most commonly applied to divine commands* [my italics]. . . . A written or printed order issued by a constituted authority." The idea of command, moral command, and even divine command is prominent in this definition. There was also a long tradition that contrasted a precept with a counsel: a precept is a command that imposes an obligation; a counsel is an admonition about what is best to do (Swinburne, 1989, 132–3; Kirk, 1931, 240–57; and the section entitled "Counsels and Commands" later in this chapter). In this sense of the word, to say that the laws of nature are not laws but precepts is self-contradictory.

There is another sense in which a law and a precept can be distinguished. But even in this second sense, "law" and "precept" are not mutually exclusive terms. Although he sometimes seems to use them synonymously (e.g., EW, 6:231), Hobbes also does distinguish between them. "Precept" is the more general term. A precept is something "by which a man is guided and directed in any action whatsoever" (ibid., 3:512). A law and a counsel are two different kinds of precepts. A law is an obligatory precept, and a counsel is, roughly, a nonobligatory precept (3:512, 489, 490, 563). Hobbes uses "precept" in its generic sense in the definition of "law of nature" that we have been considering: a law of nature is "a precept or general rule."[9] If a law of nature were nothing but a precept, then his definition should have terminated at that point. But it continues, in order to identify the specific difference between this kind of precept and others: "found out by reason, by which a man is forbidden. . . ." The general point I want to make is that the terms "law" and "precept" are not contrary terms and that merely to say that the laws of nature are precepts does not rule out the possibility that they are literally laws.

Other secularists claim that laws of nature are not laws because they are dictates of reason. The problems with this interpretation are best examined after we discuss the definition of "law" and the difference between a command and a counsel.

THE NATURE OF LAW

Law in general

Hobbes's definition of "law of nature" has already been quoted and briefly discussed. I now turn to the topic of law in general. Hobbes says that "the law is a command" (EW, 3:257) and, more explicitly, "Every law is a command to do, or to forbear" (EW, 6:64). He does not say or imply in either context that the laws of nature are excepted. Since a command is a speech act, and every speech act requires a speaker, there must be some speaker for every law; that is, there must be a lawgiver for every law. This is implicit in his remark that laws are "rules authorized" (EW, 3:335).

I have already suggested that the only possible lawgiver for the laws of nature is God.[10] For if something is authorized, it has an author. A second element of a law follows from its being a speech act. Since a law is a speech act, it must be communicated. Traditionally, this element of a law has been captured in the requirement that a law must be promulgated. And Hobbes concurs when he says, "[T]o the nature of laws belongeth a sufficient, and clear promulgation, such as may take away the excuse of ignorance" (EW, 3:344–5; see also pp. 257–8). That is, unless a law is promulgated, and hence communicated, no one can be blamed for not observing it.

In addition to promulgation, theorists traditionally have

required that laws be in accord with reason. Many scholars think that Hobbes does not accept this condition, because he seems to say that anyone with sovereign power can command anything he wants to command, even things contrary to reason. But that is not Hobbes's view. Human sovereigns can legitimately command only things that do not contravene the laws of nature, which are themselves derived from reason (EW, 3:256). Anything against reason is something that tends toward one's death, and no one is obliged to do what causes his own death. Thus, although a sovereign may utter the words "I command that you kill yourself" and intend those words to express a command, the sovereign would fail in this attempt, because the content of the seeming command contravenes the laws of nature. Hobbes did not sufficiently consider the fact that the content of other seeming commands may not be legitimate for the same reason. The content of "I command that you give up all your private property, or your vote, or your right to public education" is arguably contrary to the laws of nature, even though not as obviously or directly as "I command that you kill yourself." Hobbes did not want to give any potential malcontent grounds for sedition.

A law in general, then, according to Hobbes, includes at least these elements: (1) it has an author; (2) it is promulgated; and (3) it is not against reason. This is virtually identical with what Aquinas says about law, which he defines as "an ordinance of reason for the common good, promulgated by him who has the care of the community" (*Summa Theologiae* I-II, 90, 4, c; cf. Fuller, 1990).

The definition of law

Let's now consider Hobbes's definition of a law of nature and see how it specifies these same three elements. Recall Hobbes's definition: a law of nature (*lex naturalis*), in contrast with the right of nature, "is a precept or general rule, found out by reason, by which a man is forbidden to do that, which is destructive of his life, or taketh away the means of preserving the same; and to omit that, by which he thinketh it may be best preserved" (EW, 3:117). The first element is only implied by the word "forbidden." It is an invariant part of the natural law tradition that if that laws of nature have an author, it is God. So, if something is forbidden by the laws of nature, it must be God who is doing the forbidding. Admittedly, this is not explicit in the definition, and Bramhall complained that Hobbes had not explicitly said that the laws of nature are the commands of God when he deduced the laws of nature. Alluding to his statement that the laws of nature "as delivered in the word of God . . . are properly called laws," Hobbes defended himself by saying, "I thought it fittest in the last place, once for all, to say they [the laws of nature] were the laws of God" (EW, 4:284; cf. p. 147).

This brings us to the second element of law: promulgation. The method of promulgation is implicit in the phrase "found out by reason." Later he makes this explicit: "To rule by words, requires that such words be manifestly known; for else they are no laws. . . . God declareth his laws . . . by the dictates of *natural reason*. . . . . [God governs] by the dictates of right reason" (EW, 3:345; see also pp. 258, 359). The third element is not problematic, since all scholars agree that the content of the laws of nature are dictates of reason and thus deducible by reason.

It might be urged that yet a fourth element is required for law: punishment for violations of the law. Although this issue will be discussed further in Chapter 5, it is at least worth mentioning here that Hobbes considers punishments "consequent" to laws, not elements of them. And he thinks that there are natural punishments for breaking the laws of nature:

> There is no action of man in this life, that is not the beginning of so long a chain of consequences. . . . And in this chain, there are linked together both pleasing and unpleasing events; . . . and these pains, are the natural punishments of those actions, which are the beginning of more harm than good. And hereby it comes to pass, that intemperance is naturally punished with diseases; rashness, with mischances; in-

justice, with the violence of enemies; pride, with ruin; cowardice, with oppression; negligent government of princes, with rebellion; and rebellion, with slaughter. For seeing punishments are consequent to the breach of laws; natural punishments must be naturally consequent to the breach of the laws of nature; and therefore follow them as their natural, not arbitrary effects. (EW, 3:356–7; see also p. 344)

One might object to Hobbes that if certain injuries naturally follow certain behavior, then that behavior ought to be avoided, whether or not it is forbidden by an authority. Thus, it is irrelevant whether God forbids naturally injurious behavior.[11] In reply, it should be conceded that one has a reason to avoid certain behavior if it is injurious, whether or not it is forbidden. However, this is only one reason why certain behavior ought to be avoided. Other considerations can override such a reason. If naturally injurious behavior were commanded by a legitimate authority, then one would have an obligation to engage in it. Thus, whether God commands or forbids certain behavior is relevant to determining whether one should engage in it or not. Also, the relevant issue in this context is the status of an injury as a punishment. An injury is a punishment only if it is "inflicted by . . . authority" (EW, 3:297). Thus, determining whether God forbids an action that naturally results in injury is relevant to determining whether performing that action breaks a law and consequently whether the resulting injury is a punishment or not. Finally, it is interesting that Hobbes has a moral view of the universe. God, who creates and governs the world, has built punishments into its very structure.

Let's now return to Hobbes's definition of law. In addition to specifying the same elements as Aquinas's definition, Hobbes's definition is also similar in syntax and content to that of his older contemporary, Hugo Grotius. Compare Hobbes's definition to this one by Grotius: "The law of nature is a dictate of right reason, which points out that an act, according as it is or is not in conformity with rational nature, has in it a quality of moral baseness or necessity; and that, in consequence, such an act is either forbidden or enjoined by the author of nature, God" (Grotius, 1646, pp. 38–9).[12]

Grotius, like Hobbes, holds explicitly that the laws of nature are dictates of reason and implies that they are promulgated by reason. And he, like Hobbes, makes God the author of the laws. Nonetheless, there is an important difference. While God plays an essential role in Hobbes's notion of law, just as in his notion of obligation, Grotius thinks that God is dispensable. He says that the laws of nature would hold even if "there is no God, or that the affairs of men are of no concern to Him" (ibid., p. 13). However, Grotius continues, since God did as a matter of fact command them, since humans owe him everything that they have, and since those who obey him will be rewarded eternally, the law of nature can rightly be attributed to him (p. 14).

Thus far I have been concentrating on the similarities between Hobbes's definition of law in general and the law of nature and the definitions of Aquinas and Grotius, but there is one big difference. The content of the law, according to Aquinas, is the common good; according to Grotius, it concerns moral baseness or necessity (that is, goodness). Such value-laden content seems to be worthy of the law. In contrast, the content of Hobbes's law appears at first sight to be petty and mean-spirited, because it concerns one's own self-preservation. It is this feature that caused Hobbes so much grief. In the next section, we shall consider the extent to which Hobbes deserved to be abused for this change.

LAW AND SELF-INTEREST

I doubt that Hobbes thought he was changing the idea of law by eliminating the concept of the common good from the definition of law. Rather, he believed that he had discovered precisely what the common good was: each person's self-preservation. That is, what is good for everybody is what is each person's own good. If everyone were to work for what is in his or her own best interest, then everyone would benefit. That is enlightened self-interest, and Hobbes wanted to make it the content of law. He is explicit in revealing the unacknowledged self-interested character of morality:

> [A]ll men agree on this, that peace is good, and therefore also the way, or means of peace, which, as I have shewed before, are *justice, gratitude, modesty, equity, mercy,* and the rest of the laws of nature, are good: that is to say *moral virtues;* and their contrary *vices,* evil. Now the science of virtue and vice, is moral philosophy; and therefore the true doctrine of the laws of nature, is the true moral philosophy. But the writers of moral philosophy, though they acknowledge the same virtues and vices; yet not seeing wherein consisted their goodness; nor that they come to be praised, as the means of peaceable, sociable, and comfortable living, place them in a mediocrity of passions. . . . (EW, 3:146–7)

Notice how Hobbes contrasts his own "science of virtue and vice" and "true moral philosophy," both of which are based upon the principle of self-preservation, with that of the "writers of moral philosophy," who did not see "wherein consisted their [virtues'] goodness." Rousseau is the person who is remembered for saying that his project was to establish a civil order taking men as they are and laws as they might be, but the idea was first Hobbes's (EW, 4:256). What Hobbes thinks he sees is that long-term self-interest is the common good, the content of morality.

There is nothing inherently non-Christian in this view, even if it is offensive to pious ears. All Christians have the responsibility to safeguard their own souls in this world in order to be with God in the next. This was Hobbes's view. When Bramhall denied that Saint Paul or Moses acted in his own self-interest, Hobbes replied that both of those holy men "did for a good to themselves, which was eternal life" (EW, 4:378). It is doubtful whether Moses had any such intention, but Hobbes had no better response available. Much later, Nietzsche used the doctrine that Christians act for their own eternal happiness as evidence that Christians are egoists. He was outraged by what he took to be the hypocrisy of using the ideology of altruism to camouflage the egoism. Nietzsche disdained Christians, but disdain is largely a matter of attitude. It is a Christian principle that the laborer is worth his pay, and if eternal bliss is the pay, what is wrong with accepting it? And consider the alternative. Of course, acting in one's own self-interest, to the detriment of others, is not laudable, but neither Christianity nor Hobbes's laws of nature direct that. To the contrary, both are intended to help people achieve their own good. Christianity is a religion of individual salvation, in contrast, say, with Judaism, for which the salvation of the entire nation is primary, so it is important for Christians to understand that their own long-term self-interest lies in helping other people. Hobbes tried to show that this doctrine need not be known solely through divine revelation. It could be proven along the lines he proposed.

If Hobbes had approved of unmitigated self-interested behavior, then he would have approved of anyone who pursued his or her own self-interest no matter what the laws of nature say. But he argues against this position, which, following the Psalms, he attributes to the fool, who does not believe in God. Hobbes says that there are three reasons why a person should observe the laws of nature even if it is not seemingly in his self-interest. First, in the long run people who break their promises are found out and suffer for it. Even though some liars get away with their deceptions, this is a matter of luck, and luck is not a solid foundation upon which to build a life. Second, in the state of nature people at least occasionally need confederates to survive, and no one will be inclined to help a known liar. The third reason is of most interest to us, because it is explicitly theological. Hobbes says that people should keep their promises in the state of nature because that is the only sure way "of gaining the secure and perpetual felicity of heaven" (EW, 3:134). In *Behemoth*, Hobbes ties together obedience to the laws of the commonwealth, prudence, and eternal happiness. He says that people "without discipline" mistakenly consider only the short-term consequences of their actions and do not appreciate the long-term consequences. They calculate the good or bad things "of this present life only, which are in their sight, never putting into the scales the good and evil of the life to come, which they see not" (EW, 6:231; see also p. 219). In short, Hobbes does not approve of all self-interest, only long-range, rule-governed self-interest.[13]

A stronger defense of Hobbes can be made against his critics who want to oppose God's commands and self-interest. To say that God's commands must be different from human self-interest is to slander him. Traditionally, God is said to have created the world because he wanted to share his happiness with creatures. If God, having made humans, imposed harsh laws on them, he would not be a gracious and merciful God. His laws are intended to make humans flourish, not suffer. God's yoke is gentle; his burden is light. His laws are designed to help humans achieve happiness, and happiness is in every person's self-interest. If God's laws conflicted with human self-interest, then they would conflict with human good.

Hobbes is not trying to overthrow morality nor trying to replace an old morality with a new morality. His laws of nature are statements of conventional morality: make peace; do unto others as you would have them do unto you; keep your covenants; be gracious; be accommodating; pardon trespasses (EW, 3:117–18, 130–9). Hobbes is trying to provide a new foundation or theory for the content of the old morality, a theory that is consistent with orthodox Christianity.

Although Hobbes's revised definition of the law of nature may seem shocking, it is consonant with his revised understanding of what is goodness and what is happiness. Before Hobbes, goodness was defined objectively as something that exists independently of the desires of people. Coordinately, happiness was thought to be a state in which desires are extinguished. But Hobbes defines goodness in terms of actual desires: goodness is "the object of any man's appetite or desire" (EW, 3:41). And happiness is not the same as being sated; it is the process of satisfying an unending sequence of desires.

THE LAWS OF NATURE AS DICTATES OF REASON

Dictates of reason

I have already argued that the laws of nature are the laws of God, not merely dictates of reason. Rather, the role of reason is to discover the natural laws that God commands. However, the view that the laws of nature are nothing but dictates of reason is so widespread that I shall not assume what I have already proven. In my discussion of the laws of nature as dictates of reason, I show in another way that Hobbes intends them to be essentially God's commands.

After emphasizing the difference between the nondeontic character of right versus the deontic character of law, Hobbes proceeds to derive the first two laws of nature by reason. About the first he says that since everyone in the state of nature has a right to everything, even the lives of every other person, it follows that "as long as this natural right of every man to everything endureth, there can be no security to any man, how strong or wise soever he be, of living out the time, which nature ordinarily alloweth men to live." From this, Hobbes infers that "it is a precept or general rule of reason, *that every man, ought to endeavor peace, as far as he has hope of obtaining it; and when he cannot obtain it, that he may seek, and use, all helps, and advantages of war*" (EW, 3:117). This first law of nature entails a second law: "*that a man be willing, when others are so too, as far-forth, as for peace, and defence of himself he shall think it necessary, to lay down this right to all things; and be contented with so much liberty against other men, as he would allow other men against himself*" (ibid., p. 118). The formal structure and soundness of the arguments for these or any of the other laws of nature that Hobbes purports to derive are not relevant to my purposes and will not be discussed. What is relevant is their relation to my general claim that they are part of a divine command theory of morality. There is prima facie evidence that the laws of nature are connected with God's command, for Hobbes says that the second law is the same as the law of the Gospel, "[W]hatsoever you require that others should do to you, that do ye to them" (ibid.). Before Hobbes, the twelfth-century jurist Gratian had made the same observation (Edwards, 1981, p. 38).

Every law consists of two parts: a *form* that expresses the command of some authority, and a *content* that expresses what is to be done. I maintain that for Hobbes the authority for the law of nature is God. Since all of his Christian predecessors who thought that law was a command agreed that God was the one who commanded the law of nature (e.g., Aquinas, *Summa Theologiae* I-II, 97, 3, c), there was no reason for Hobbes to say it at the beginning of his discussion of the laws of nature, especially since he says it often in other places. His focus on chapters 14 and 15 is not the form but the content of the law of nature. Since it is the law of nature that is at issue, not God's positive law, God cannot speak directly to humans. Rather, he must promulgate the content of the law in a natural way, that is through reason (EW, 3:359). This was a standard view of natural law in the seventeenth century.

In chapter 15, Hobbes proceeds to derive seventeen additional laws.[14] Only three of the twenty laws of nature in the English version of *Leviathan* contain the word "ought," namely the first, sixth, and eighteenth. In the Latin version, only the first and eighteenth have the equivalent force; each contains a gerundive construction (OL, 3:103, 120). This does not mean that the laws of nature are not literally laws or that they are not deontic. Rather, since only the content of the laws of nature is being derived, they appear in purely propositional form. The "oughtness" or obligatory character of a law attaches to the proposition in virtue of the authority of the one who commands it, not in virtue of its derivability from reason. For geometrical propositions are equally derivable from reason but do not have any obligatory character.

So it is a mistake to think that because Hobbes derives the content of his laws of nature from features of self-interest he has no genuine morality, if morality is understood as a set of rules applying to each person equally in his relations with others and conducive to his happiness. The content of most of the twenty laws of nature should make this obvious. The third law is to keep one's covenants; the fourth is to show gratitude; the fifth is to be cooperative; the sixth is to pardon injuries; the seventh is not to be cruel; the eighth is not to be abusive; the ninth is not to be proud; the tenth is not to be arrogant; and so on. Hobbes constructed a very conventional morality on the basis of self-interest. Hobbes is conservative in the content of morality; he wants to preserve the traditional morality but to establish it on a rigorous foundation.

So there is no special problem in explaining why Hobbes's theory ought to be considered a moral theory. The content of the laws of nature is the traditional morality and concerns the right sort of human interaction. But this is not the whole of a moral theory, according to Hobbes. A moral theory must impose obligations. And for him there is only one possible ultimate source: an irresistible force. That is, the content of morality only becomes a complete moral system if it acquires the character of being obligatory, and the only way for something to become obligatory is for it to be commanded by an irresistible force. Only God is such a force.

Some philosophers think that a divine command morality is not a genuine morality, because not even divine might can make right. Although I cannot settle the general question about such theories here, three remarks are appropriate. One is that when critics claim that Hobbes does not have a genuine moral theory, it is because they believe he has only a theory of prudential behavior. The second is that if it should turn out that divine command theories are not genuine moral theories, Hobbes is no worse off than the many obviously decent philosophers who are committed to them, and it is tendentious to declare a person immoral or nonmoral because his moral theory is incorrect. The third remark is that Hobbes's theory is not subject to some of the standard criticisms made against divine command theories. For example, although God in the abstract could command anything, only commands that are promulgated can be laws. Furthermore, according to Hobbes, the only way all humans can receive such promulgations is through deducing them by reason, and the only content of morality that is deducible are the precepts that instruct a person about self-preservation. Thus, the content of morality cannot be arbitrary in the ordinary understanding of "arbitrariness" but must have the "natural" desirable content of traditional morality.

For all of these reasons, I believe that the ingenious and elaborate explanations of those secularists who deny that the laws of nature are literal laws for Hobbes but who proceed to try to prove that, this notwithstanding, he has a genuine moral theory are misguided. In addition to the other problems mentioned, these secularists do not have any simple explanation for the absence of deontic language in most of the laws of nature. In contrast, my own interpretation has a ready explanation, namely, that the laws of nature, as formulated, specify only the content of the laws, not their form. As stated and as derived by reason, the laws of nature are theorems only, not laws. They have the force of law only because God commands them and promulgates them through reason. Hobbes explicitly says this at the conclusion of his derivation of the laws of nature at the end of chapter 15, although the passage in which he does so is often misinterpreted. He says,

> These dictates of reason, men used to call by the name of laws, but improperly: for they are but conclusions, or theorems concerning what conduceth to the conservation and defence of themselves; whereas law, properly, is the word of him, that by right hath command over others. But yet if we consider the same theorems, as delivered in the word of God, that by right commandeth all things; then they are properly called laws. (EW, 3:147)

This passage is usually taken to mean that the laws of nature are nothing but dictates of reason, not properly laws. A care-

ful reading, however, indicates just the opposite. Just as he
had criticized earlier philosophers for confusing "right" with
"law" and for thinking that right was deontic, Hobbes in this
passage is criticizing earlier philosophers for confusing the
content of a law of nature with the law itself. Every law must
have the proper form ("I command") either explicitly or implicitly (EW, 3:561; see also p. 257). When Hobbes says that
"men used to call [dictates of reason] by the name of laws,
but improperly," he is dissociating himself from that improper usage. If he were going to adopt the improper use of
the word "laws," then he would have said something such
as "I, like men before me, shall use the term 'laws of nature'
improperly." The past tense of the phrase "men used to
call . . ." makes sense only if Hobbes is going to use the
phrase "the laws of nature" in a different and proper sense,
which he goes on to explain ("law, properly"). In short, by
choosing the phrase "men used to call by the name of laws,
but improperly" he intends to dissociate himself from this
past usage.

Further, Hobbes does not say in this passage that what he
has derived are "laws of nature." Rather, he uses the term
"dictates of reason," in order to draw a distinction between
the content of a law of nature (which is derivable from reason) and the entire law. The theorems of geometry are just as
much dictates of reason as the theorems that form the content of the laws of nature. A dictate is simply something that
is said, not necessarily something that is commanded. Aquinas makes clear that a dictate of reason can form the content
of various kinds of speech acts when he says, "Just as an
assertion is a dictate of reason asserting something, so is a
law a dictate of reason commanding something" (*Summa
Theologiae* I-II, 92, 2, c: "[S]icut enuntiatio est rationis dic-
tamen per modum enuntiandi, ita etiam lex per modum
praecipiendi"). Often only the propositional content of what
a speaker intends to communicate is expressed. If this content (a dictate) is issued by an authority, then a command is
indirectly issued, because the force of the command is conveyed by the fact that it was an authority who issued it, not

because what was uttered was a dictate (Searle, 1979, pp. 30–57).

It is a mistake, then, to equate "dictates of reason" with "laws of nature," as many scholars do. Kavka, for example, claims that Hobbes says that "the laws of nature are not 'laws'" (1986, p. 361). But Hobbes does not say this. He says that the "dictates of reason" are not properly laws. A law has to have the force of authority, but a dictate need not. Granted that the term is often used in connection with laws, that is because typically one focuses on the content of a law, not its authority, which is presupposed in the context. Grotius uses the same language when he is explaining that the laws of nature are demonstrable: "The law of nature is a dictate of right reason" (Grotius, 1646, p. 38). Also, although "dictate" is substitutable for "law" in many contexts, it is not always so, and thus they are not synonymous. The term, "the crown" is substitutable for "the king" in many contexts, for example, "The crown imposed a new tax." Analogously, "dictate" is sometimes used for "law." Such a use is an instance of synecdoche.

Let's now consider the remainder of the passage under consideration: "law, properly, is the word of him, that by right hath command over others. But yet if we consider the same theorems, as delivered in the word of God, that by right commandeth all things; then they are properly called laws." Since Hobbes is using the term "laws of nature" properly, he must hold that they are commanded by the person with the authority to command them, namely, God. How are these dictates expressed? When he says that these theorems are "delivered in the word of God," he does not mean that they are a matter of special revelation. The phrase "the word of God" here refers to God's natural revelation to humans through right reason, as he says elsewhere (EW, 3:345; see also p. 271).

I will end this section with one final argument. If Hobbes thought that the laws of nature were not literally laws but strictly speaking only dictates of reason, then, although it would make sense for him to say that the laws of nature are dictates, it would not make sense for him to say the converse, namely, that the dictates are laws. But he does: "[T]he dictates [of reason] . . . are laws, not *made*, but *eternal*" (EW, 3:378; see also p. 271).[15]

God's command and dictates of reason in De Cive

In *De Cive* there is a passage relevant to the dictates of reason which deserves a separate discussion, because it is even more susceptible to misinterpretation than the central passage from *Leviathan* that I have just discussed. Hobbes says,

> But those which we call the laws of nature, (since they are nothing else but certain conclusions, understood by reason, of things to be done and omitted; but a law, to speak properly and accurately, is the speech of him who by right commands somewhat to others to be done or omitted), are not in propriety of speech laws, as they proceed from nature. Yet, as they are delivered by God in holy Scriptures, as we shall see in the chapter following, they are most properly called by the name of laws. For the sacred Scripture is the speech of God commanding over all things by greatest right. (EW, 2:49–50)

It is easy to think that Hobbes is saying that the laws of nature are not genuinely laws unless they are communicated to humans by a special revelation. But that is not the force of this passage at all. When Hobbes says that the laws of nature are not "laws, as they proceed from nature," he does not mean that they simply are not laws. To draw this inference – namely, that "Laws of nature are not laws, as they proceed from nature" entails "Laws of nature are not laws" – is to commit the fallacy of accident. One simply cannot detach the phrase "as they proceed from nature," any more than one can detach the phrase "considered as a child" from the proposition "No human, considered as a child, is a mathematician" and infer "No human is a mathematician." The former proposition is true (even if some children are mathematicians), but the latter is false. In short, Hobbes's claim that the laws of nature are not laws is qualified, not categorical. He means that, as demonstrated by reason, they have no force of law. What, then, gives them force?

His next sentence is misleading: "Yet, as they are delivered by God in holy Scriptures, as we shall see in the chapter following, they are most properly called by the name of laws." This gives the impression that the laws of nature depend upon God's command as a special revelation to Jews and Christians. But the text of the following chapter belies that interpretation. What Hobbes does there is to quote the Scriptures as saying that anyone can prove to himself by reason alone what God commands. He quotes from Psalms, Proverbs, Jeremiah, Deuteronomy, and the Gospel of John passages like the following: "The mouth of the righteous will be exercised in wisdom, and his tongue will be talking of judgment: the law of God is in his heart" (EW, 2:51, quoting Psalm 37:30–1; see also EW, 3:412). This passage says that the law of God is in a person's heart. Since, according to the Bible, the seat of reason is the heart, the law of God is in a person's reason. That is to say, Hobbes quotes the Bible for its testimony that God's law is demonstrable by reason. Since the law of nature is the only law that is demonstrable by reason, it follows that God's law is the law of nature. This interpretation is confirmed by the title of chapter 4, "That the Law of Nature Is a Divine Law."

All of the biblical passages quoted by him are, Hobbes says, "descriptions of right reason, whose dictates, we have showed before, are the laws of nature" (EW, 2:51). As derived by right reason, they do not depend upon revelation to be credible. Their occurrence *in* the Bible does not mean that they are legitimized *by* the Bible, considered as a book revealing the special word of God. For each of the twenty laws of nature that he had demonstrated in *De Cive*, Hobbes purports to show that there is a demonstration of it in the Bible also. Not all of these proof texts may be persuasive, but Hobbes's intent is unmistakable in this chapter: to show that the laws of nature are properly laws because they are derivable by reason as the laws of God, just as the Bible itself argues: "[T]he law of nature is all of it divine" (EW, 2:62).

COUNSELS AND COMMANDS

Hobbes distinguishes between commands and counsels. A command is supposed to benefit the one who issues it; a counsel is supposed to benefit the one to whom the counsel is given, according to Hobbes. Although his discussion of this distinction in *Leviathan* is split between chapter 24, "Of the Nutrition, and Procreation of a Commonwealth," and chapter 26, "Of Civil Laws," it is relevant to the laws of nature, because, since all law is command (EW, 3:257; see also p. 226), it would seem to follow that the laws of nature ought to benefit God. But this consequence is absurd, for at least two reasons. First, since God is self-sufficient, nothing that humans do can benefit him. Second, since the laws of nature benefit humans, these laws would seem to be counsels, not commands. And if they are not commands, then they are not literally laws. In this section, I shall argue that the source of the problem is Hobbes's mistaken analysis of commands.

Since commands and counsels are speech acts and Hobbes had an inchoate speech act theory, it will be helpful to begin our discussion with some background about speech act theory. According to the standard theory, paradigmatic sentences consist of two parts: an *illocutionary force* that is expressed by an *illocutionary act verb* in performative form,[16] and a propositional content expressed in a "that" clause or something similar. Consider these sentences:

> I state that Mary will be at the party.
> I ask whether Mary will be at the party.
> I promise that Mary will be at the party.
> I guess that Mary will be at the party.

The verbs "state," "ask," "promise," and "guess" express the force that the speech act is supposed to have. They indicate the kind of intention, attitude, and purpose the speaker is taking toward his audience and toward the proposition that is forthcoming. The proposition in each of the examples just given is expressed by the clause "Mary will be at the party." Thus, the same content can be expressed with different illocutionary forces ("forces," for short). These particular examples are paradigmatic cases. Usually propositions are expressed with no explicit illocutionary force indicated,[17] and the specific force must be gathered from the context or is indeterminate within a certain range of forces. For example, if a bull is about to charge Adam and Sally says, "That bull is about to charge," Adam can gather from the context that Sally's utterance has the force of a warning. If Sally says the same thing to Adam when both are securely behind a wall, the force may be indeterminate between a statement, assertion, guess, or conjecture. In most cases, no confusion results from utterances that lack an explicit force, and the frequent absence of a force-indicating device is a mark of the efficiency of ordinary language. However, it can cause problems, and Hobbes is particularly exercised over the absence of a force-indicating device for sentences of the form "Do x," which may signal either a counsel or a command:

> How fallacious it is to judge of the nature of things by the ordinary and inconstant use of words, appeareth in nothing more, than in the confusion of counsels, and commands, arising from the imperative manner of speaking in them both, and in many other occasions besides. For the words *do this*, are the words not only of him that commandeth; but also of him that giveth counsel; and of him that exhorteth. (EW, 3:240; see also 4:343)

It is easy enough to make the force of a bare proposition determinate by adding an expression that indicates that illocutionary force. Thus, the indeterminate utterance "Do this" can be given a force by adding either "I command that you . . ." or "I counsel that you . . ." Hobbes says essentially the same thing: "The style of a law is *We command:* but, *we think good* is the ordinary style of them, that but give advice" (EW, 3:561; see also p. 257).

So much for preliminaries. We can now turn to the serious

philosophical issue of figuring out the difference between a command and counsel. Hobbes says,

> COMMAND is, where a man saith, *do this*, without expecting other reason than the will of him that says it. From this it followeth manifestly, that he that commandeth, pretendeth thereby his own benefit: for the reason of his command is his own will only, and the proper object of every man's will, is some good to himself.
>
> COUNSEL, is where a man saith, *do*, or *do not this*, and deduceth his reasons from the benefit that arriveth by it to him to whom he saith it. And from this it is evidence, that he that giveth counsel, pretendeth only, whatsoever he intendeth, the good of him, to whom he giveth it.[18] (EW, 3:241; see also 4:74–5)

According to this passage, the difference between a command and a counsel is the person who is supposed to benefit from the action performed. In a command, the speaker benefits; in a counsel, the addressee benefits. Although Hobbes is correct about counsels, he is obviously mistaken about commands. The speaker may benefit and may intend his own benefit, but this is not necessarily the case. Suppose a mother commands his child to brush his teeth. She intends the action to benefit the child. If she also intends to benefit from reduced dental bills, this is an indirect and inessential component of the command itself.[19] What is characteristic of commands is that the speaker has authority over the addressee and that the addressee acts because he recognizes that the speaker has that authority. Who the beneficiary of the act commanded may be is not relevant to the issue.

Bramhall saw that Hobbes's view about commands was mistaken and criticized him for it. Bramhall says that if commands need to benefit the commander, then the Ten Commandments could not be commands but only counsels, since they benefit the humans who observe them (EW, 3:341). Unfortunately, Hobbes failed to appreciate the criticism. He did not see that his view about commands was mistaken in itself and inconsistent with his views about the laws of nature.

One way to explain the source of his mistake is to point out that Hobbes introduced the distinction between commands and counsels long after he had discussed the laws of nature and with quite different purposes. And he never explicitly relates his theory of commands and counsels to the laws of nature, which he had discussed ten chapters earlier. But this is only an explanation of the mistake, not an excuse or justification for it.

The broad purpose of the distinction is twofold. The first is political. He is in essence giving advice to the sovereign.[20] He says that a sovereign should not criticize or punish the people he asks for advice which it turns out he does not like. For "he that demandeth counsel, is author of it" (EW, 3:242). Hobbes may have been thinking of the case of Thomas Wentworth, earl of Strafford, who was executed on the grounds that he had given bad counsel to Charles I (EW, 6:245–53; esp. p. 248). Sovereigns should choose counselors with various kinds of expertise and listen to them in private (EW, 3:248). Hobbes criticizes exhortations and dehortations as spurious forms of commands that masquerade as counsels. For "counsels vehemently pressed" are draped in emotive language and designed to get what the speaker wants, not what is good for the person counseled. He also gives advice to counselor. A counselor "ought to propound his advice, in such form of speech, as may make the truth most evidently appear; that is to say, with a firm ratiocination, as significant and proper language, and as briefly as the evidence will permit. . . . [The counselor should avoid] *obscure, confused, and ambiguous expressions, also all metaphorical speeches, tending to the stirring up of passions*" (EW, 3:246).

The second purpose for the distinction between counsels and commands is religious. Hobbes draws many of his examples of commands and counsels from the Bible. He says that God's commandments are commands, not counsels, because they "are drawn from the will of God our king, whom we are obliged to obey" (EW, 3:244). Although this is a sensible reason, it is not the reason that he should have expressed, given his theory of commands and the laws of nature. As I have already explained, he is committed by his views about the nature of a command to the idea that God benefits from his commandments. But this consequence is so obviously absurd for an orthodox Christian that Hobbes shrinks from it and gives the sensible but theoretically unwarranted answer just mentioned.

There is another reason that Hobbes wants the Ten Commandments to be genuine commands or laws. He wants to draw a sharp distinction between God's relation to the Jews under the Old Covenant and his relation to Christians under the New Covenant. Because God had a special sovereignty over the Jews, God's utterances to them were commands. But because God later ended that special sovereignty, the utterances of Jesus in the New Testament are not commands but counsels. This explains why Hobbes holds that the precept "Repent and be baptized in the name of Jesus" is a counsel, not a command; the reason is that repenting does not provide any benefit to God (EW, 3:244). Hobbes wants to emphasize that Jesus was not a king and that the promised Kingdom of God is not yet established. This is part of his view of Jesus and Christianity. Later, when the office of Jesus is discussed, Hobbes argues at great length that Jesus is a counselor. More generally, he argues that the apostles and all genuine preachers of Christianity, other than the sovereign, counsel Christians; they do not command them. Command belongs to the sovereign only. Even later, in a slightly different context, he refers back to the distinction when he is criticizing Bellarmine's defense of the legislative powers of the pope (EW, 3:561).

RATIONALISM AND VOLUNTARISM

In the medieval and early modern tradition of natural law theorists, there were two camps: those who thought that natural law is purely demonstrative, and those who thought that it is voluntaristic (see Edwards, 1981, pp. 46–65).

According to the first view, the law of nature is a law simply because reason can prove that it specifies things that are good for all humans. Suarez explains this view in the following way: "[This view holds that] even if God did not exist or if He did not judge of things correctly, nevertheless, if the same dictates of right reason dwelt within man, constantly assuring him, for example, that lying is evil, those dictates would still have the same legal character which they actually possess, because they would constitute a law pointing out the evil that exists intrinsically in the object condemned" (Suarez, 1612, p. 196). This group consisted of rationalistic scholastics and included Aquinas, although Suarez denies it. Hobbes may have been inclined to this view in *De Cive*. For Hobbes, in line with Aquinas, indicates there that right reason is a kind of law:

> But since all do grant, that is done by *right*, which is not done against reason, we ought to judge those actions only *wrong*, which are repugnant to right reason, that is, which contradict some certain truth collected by right reasoning from true principles. But that which is done *wrong*, we say it is done against some law. Therefore *true reason* is a certain *law*; which, since it is no less a part of human nature, than any other faculty or affection of the mind, is also termed natural. Therefore the *law of nature*, that I may define it, is the dictate of right reason, conversant about those things which are either to be done or omitted for the constant preservation of life and members, as much as in us lies. (EW, 2:15–16, see also p. 31; Hobbes, 1640, p. 82)

I have been arguing that the doctrine of *Leviathan* is significantly different in that it espouses a divine command theory.[21]

The passage in which Hobbes explains that men used to confuse the dictates of reason with the laws of nature may be an unconscious reference to his own earlier view. The theory of *Leviathan* puts him in the second, or voluntarist, camp, which consisted primarily of nominalists such as William of Ockham. (Descartes, however, is a voluntarist.) According to this view, something is good only if God commands it (Idziak, 1979, pp. 51–73).

The conflict between the rationalist and voluntarist theorists of the late medieval and early modern period is strictly
analogous to the conflict between secularist and religionist
interpreters of Hobbes. But Hobbes holds a middle view: he
has both a rationalist and a voluntarist component in his
theory. That is, he holds that a law of nature must both be a
command of God and be deducible as conducive to self-
preservation. Suarez had devised a "middle way," according to which the laws of nature oblige insofar as God wills
them, and their content is demonstrably good. It is possible
that Hobbes was partially inspired by Suarez: Hobbes refers
to him in other contexts and must have known that James I
had been attacked by him (Suarez, 1612, pp. 188–9).

The importance of God for morality in the state of nature
can also be shown in another way. At the end of chapter 14,
Hobbes says that in the state of nature "a covenant, if lawful,
binds in the sight of God" (EW, 3:130) and that a person
cannot swear an oath in the state of nature unless he does
believe in God. That is why Hobbes ends Part II of *Leviathan*
with an explanation of what the "Kingdom of God by
Nature" is. His point, in short, is that atheists should not be
allowed in any country, because, not seeing the laws of
nature as God's laws, they do not acknowledge any obligations (EW, 3:344).[22] In his reply to Bramhall's *Catching of the
Leviathan*, he makes the same point when he says that atheists cannot be punished too severely, because "there is no
living in a commonwealth with men, to whose oaths we
cannot reasonably give credit" (EW, 4:294). The clear implication is that oaths depend upon the laws of nature and
the laws of nature depend upon the command of God.

WHAT SURVIVES OF THE SECULARIST AND THE
TAYLOR–WARRENDER THESES

At the beginning of the preceding chapter, I sketched the
two standard interpretations of Hobbes's moral theories: the
secularist interpretation and the Taylor–Warrender version
of the religious interpretation. The upshot of my view is that

an important part of each interpretation survives and a less important part must be discarded. What survives from the Taylor–Warrender thesis is that God's command is a necessary condition for the laws of nature. What must be discarded is the claim that God's command is sufficient. Also, the claim that Hobbes's psychology or motivation is independent of his moral theory must also be discarded, for God commands that people act in their genuine self-interest.

Concerning the secularist interpretation, what must be discarded is the denial that God's command is a necessary condition for a law of nature. I believe that my explication of the passages that distinguish between the right of nature and the law of nature and the passages that define the relation between the dictates of reason and the laws of nature shows decisively that Hobbes thinks the laws of nature are, properly speaking, laws. Gauthier and Kavka are mistaken not only in their interpretation of this passage but also in their general view that "God plays *no substantive role* in Hobbes's moral and political philosophy" (Kavka, 1986, p. 362) and that "God plays only a secondary part in the system" (Gauthier, 1969, p. 178). However, most of what they say about the content of the laws of nature, in contrast with their form ("I command"), insofar as that content is demonstrable by reason, remains valuable. For the laws of nature, *qua* dictates of reason, form the content of morality.

In Chapter 5, I shall show that Hobbes does not try to derive the laws of nature from the right of nature, as if he were trying to derive an "ought" from an "is." The right of nature is the content of the laws of nature, and the laws of nature exist and are obligatory in the state of nature. Their obligatoriness depends upon God's irresistible power, which literally binds or "obliges" action. Because of possible equivocation, it is misleading to say that Hobbes holds that might makes right. And he does not hold that all uses of overwhelming human force are justified. However, he does believe that irresistible power is the source of all obligation.

Chapter 5

The history and idea of covenants

In Chapter 2, I argued that from the very beginning of *Leviathan* Hobbes's thought is steeped in a biblical understanding of humans and nature. In Chapters 3 and 4, I argued that Hobbes subscribes to a divine command theory of morality, according to which the laws of nature consist of two elements: the command of God and propositions about self-preservation. Because these are laws of *nature*, not special revelation, the only way they could be promulgated by God is through human reason. That is, humans are informed of God's law by reasoning about what it would contain. God is an essential component of the moral laws, according to Hobbes, because laws involve obligation and the only person with the irresistible power necessary to create obligation is God. To put this the other way round, if God did not exist, then no being would have the power necessary to serve as the source for the obligation required for moral laws. The laws of nature could still be deduced by reason, but then they would be only prudential maxims, just as many scholars think they are for Hobbes. But I have argued that Hobbes considers the laws of nature to be genuine moral laws and that he believes they have this character because the almighty God commands them. So, according to Hobbes, the existence of God is essential to morality.

Although the laws of nature operate in the state of nature, they are not sufficient to guarantee human preservation. For although God's power is irresistible, as a matter of fact people fear other people more than they fear God. What the laws of nature do provide is the wherewithal that humans need in order to establish a civil government, and the latter has the means to preserve humans rather well. Since civil government depends upon the laws of nature and the laws of nature are God's commands, civil government depends upon God. This is a relatively thin dependence. In this chapter I want to show that much more is involved. Hobbes relies on a cluster of thick theological concepts which revolve around the biblical idea of a covenant. In the first section, I explain how Hobbes relates the idea of covenant to those of faith, grace, and merit. This leads to a discussion, in the second section, of the theologico-political use of the concept of covenant by seventeenth-century Scots and an explanation, in the third section, of the idea of covenant in Reformation covenant theology. This completes the historical part of the chapter. In the fourth section, I explain the distinction between renouncing a right and transferring one, because all covenants require a transfer of right. In the fifth section, I explain how God's irresistible power underwrites the force of covenants. In the sixth section, I explain that, according to Hobbes, violations of natural laws are punished by God through the bad consequences that naturally follow them according to the physical laws that God has established.

COVENANT, FAITH, AND MERIT

Contract and covenant

For our purposes, we can take "social contract" to refer to "the act by which men are assumed to establish a communally agreed form of social organization. . . . [And it] is often thought of as a pact that all men make with each other as equals" (Levin, 1973, p. 251b). It is generally accepted that Hobbes belongs to the social contract tradition of political theory. But scholars never comment on the peculiarity of Hobbes's use of the term "covenant" where others use "contract."[1] Both Locke and Rousseau speak of the social contract, but Hobbes does not, even though he defines "covenant" in terms of "contract." A contract is "the mutual transferring of right" (EW, 3:120).

A "covenant" is a contract in which one party receives the other party's right to something when the contract is made but receives the thing itself only at some future time. If someone says, "I hereby give you *x*, which will be delivered tomorrow" (EW, 3:122), the other person acquires the right to the thing but not the thing itself. So there is a difference between acquiring a right to something and actually acquiring the thing. Covenants look to the future for performance of the conditions specified in the present. As we shall see later in greater detail, this is also one essential element of biblical covenants, which always involved the promise of some future good, as when God in his covenant with Noah promised never to destroy the world by flood again and in his covenant with Abraham promised to make him the father of a great nation.

Faith and grace

The word "covenant" is a distinctively biblical term. Perhaps not much could be made of this if Hobbes himself did not reinforce its theological associations in many ways. One of the most obvious is the fact that he follows up his discussion of the notion of contract, which forms part of the notion of a covenant, with three other distinctively theological concepts: faith, grace, and merit. This is all the more striking when one considers that Hobbes had, shortly before this, deduced the first two laws of nature, the second of which he identifies with "the law of the Gospel," and is in the process of developing the machinery that will create the civil government, which he calls "the mortal god." It is at this point that he defines faith. Faith, Hobbes explains, is keeping the promise made in a covenant (EW, 3:121). This remark should be compared with that of the biblical translator and theologian William Tyndale (c. 1494–1536): "Faith . . . according to the covenants . . . is our salvation. . . . [W]here thou findest a promise . . . there must thou understand a covenant" (Tyndale, 1536, p. 471).[2]

Hobbes then mentions that when a transfer of right is not mutual, one person has given a gift to the other. But a gift, as he indicates, is the same concept as grace in theology. Thus, it is possible for one party unilaterally to give up his right to an object, either in order to initiate a friendship or to gain future consideration, such as "hope of reward in heaven" (EW, 3:121). Any such unilateral transfer of right, done for the immediate benefit of someone else – that is, any act of grace – is also done for the agent's own long-term benefit. Although I take Hobbes's intention here to be religious – he wants to found government on theological concepts – his effort is odd. For his definition attributes grace to humans, not to God. When a human unilaterally transfers his right to something, then he is the origin of grace, according to Hobbes's definition, even though traditionally God should be the source. Hobbes's problem is that he knows that God does not profit from his own actions. Everything that God does that is good for humans benefits humans only, not God, who is self-sufficient. So Hobbes cannot get his definition of grace to fit his conception of God. Although his treatment of grace has gone awry, I do not see any feature of his account that should lead one to think that Hobbes is consciously trying to subvert the idea of grace. Later we shall find many places in which Hobbes defends the idea of God's mercy, which is tantamount to God's grace.

Meritum congrui *and* meritum condigni

Hobbes then proceeds, still in the context of preparing the ground for his explanation of what a covenant is, to explain what "merit" is. In the scholastic theology of the Middle Ages and early modern period, a distinction was drawn between satisfaction and merit. Satisfaction is repaying a just debt.[3] Thus, Jesus had to make satisfaction to God in order to redeem humans from their sins. But Jesus' redemptive act additionally had merit; that is, it was an action that was good in itself, since he did not require redemption himself but acted only for the sake of sinful humanity. Since every good action deserves a reward, Jesus deserved a reward. On some accounts, human beings themselves deserved to be rewarded, because Jesus was the representative of humankind. That is, since Jesus' good action was directed toward God, humans came to merit the reward from God. God then seemed to become a debtor to humans. But this presented a problem. How can God, who is self-sufficient and beholden to no one, become a debtor?

In order to solve this problem, theologians manufactured a distinction between two kinds of merit: *meritum condigni* and *meritum congrui*. The first, *meritum condigni*, is a kind of merit that requires a reward out of justice. That is, if x merits a reward *ex condigno* from y, then y ought, as a matter of obligation and justice, to give x a reward. *Meritum congrui* is a kind of merit that requires a reward only out of propriety. That is, if x merits a reward *ex congrui* from y, then it is appropriate for y to give x a reward, even though there is no obligation based upon justice for y to do so. This distinction allowed theologians to say that Jesus' redemptive act secured for humans *meritum congrui*, not *meritum condigni*. That is, God freely rewards humans for the redemptive act of Jesus but at no point owes a legal debt to anyone.

My explanation of the distinction is simpler and clearer than the medieval or modern scholastic discussions, as is Hobbes's.[4] He relates his distinction between two kinds of merit directly to the idea of contract. He says that there are two kinds of merit. A person who performs his part of a contract merits the transfer of right that was promised by the other party. This is a matter of justice and corresponds to *meritum condigni*. This kind of merit needs to be distinguished from the kind that is involved if someone offers a gift (grace) to anyone who is able to get it. In such a case, a person merits the prize "only by the benignity of the giver" (EW, 3:123). Hobbes takes the orthodox and Calvinist position that "no man can demand a right to it [Paradise], by his own righteousness, or any other power in himself, but by the free gift of God only" (EW, 3:124; 4:380–1). People merit heaven only in the sense of *meritum congrui:* "For God Almighty, having promised Paradise to those men, hoodwinked with carnal desires, that can walk through this world according to the precepts, and limits prescribed by him; they say, he that shall so walk, shall merit Paradise *ex congruo*" (EW, 3:124).[5] Bishop Bramhall accused Hobbes of not understanding the distinction between the two kinds of merit but prudently did not try to give any alternative explanation. Hobbes defended himself by saying that no one knew what the Schoolmen meant by the terms and that he had done his best to make sense of them (EW, 4:380–1).

Although the issues may appear to be bizarre from the perspective of the twentieth century, they had a special relevance to the seventeenth century, a relevance rooted in the debates at the beginning of the Reformation between Luther and John Eck. Eck defended the view of Aquinas, according to which humans do have *meritum ex condigno* (*Summa Theologiae* I-II, 114, 3, c). According to Luther, this is a form of Pelagianism, the view that humans can do something to deserve their own salvation. To hold that humans enjoy *meritum congrui* is non-Pelagian. For, according to this view, God saves those who do good works because it is the appropriate thing to do, not because he is required out of justice to do so. God cannot be required to do anything out of justice, because God cannot be subject to anything whatsoever. The distinction was also discussed by Suarez and Bellarmine, whose views were important to Hobbes. However, I believe that Hobbes's immediate concern with the distinction may stem from the views of the sixteenth- and seventeenth-century covenant theologians, who were trying to soften the sting of Calvin's predestinationism. They held that God voluntarily submitted himself to claims of justice through a covenant of grace that he entered into with humans. By the terms of that covenant, God would reward those people who had faith in Jesus Christ. Referring to God's covenant with Abraham, John Preston, master of Emmanuel College, Cambridge, says, "[T]hese words containe the *Covenant* on both sides, sayeth the *Lord*, this is the *Covenant* that I will make on my part, *I will be thy God* . . . you shall have all things in me that your hearts can desire: The *Covenant* againe, that I require on your part, is, that you be *perfect with me*, that you be *upright*, that you be without *hypocrisie*" (Preston, 1629a, p. 38). As in a Hobbesian covenant, there is mutual obligation. In 1632, Richard Sibbes, a famous Calvinist divine, wrote, "God, for his part, undertakes to convey all that concerns our happiness, upon our receiving of them, by believing on him" (Sibbes, 1862, 1:civ). According to Thomas Goodwin's version, Christ "was truly and indeed God's hired servant in his work [of satisfaction], and God covenanted to give him the salvation of those he died for as his wages and reward. . . . So that, if God be just, he must give forth salvation, otherwise Christ's obedience would cry as the work of an hireling doth for wages" (quoted from Hill, 1986, 3:306; see Hill for other examples of this attitude). The covenant theologians in effect made human salvation a matter of God's justice, rather than mercy, and imposed obligations on the ultimate sovereign, God, through a covenant. Hobbes opposes both views in favor of Calvin's own brand of Calvinism. Hobbes always maintains that salvation was an act of God's mercy (e.g., EW, 3:476) and that no sovereign incurs obligations to his subjects, because the sovereign is never a party to their covenants.

I believe that Hobbes raises this issue of *meritum congrui* versus *meritum condigni* in the context of laying the theoretical foundations of civil government because he is resting his case upon theological concepts and because he cares about the correct theological doctrine of salvation. There is no explanation for his attempt to understand these terms other than a deep intellectual commitment to theology. I would be willing to rest my entire thesis about Hobbes's religious thought on the fact that he weaves these theological concepts into his initial discussion of a covenant, if there were not so much other evidence for his commitment to the Christian religion.[6]

COVENANT THEOLOGY

The Scottish Covenanters

I have already discussed two reasons why Hobbes used distinctively theological terms in his discussion of the establishment of the civil state. One is an intrinsic interest in them. Another is that some of his most influential Continental opponents, namely Suarez and Bellarmine, had discussed them. I have also introduced a third reason, namely, that Hobbes thinks that covenant theologians were perverting Calvinism. This theme will be taken up again in the following section. In this section, I will discuss still a fourth reason for Hobbes's use of the idea of a covenant: his negative reaction to the Scottish Covenanters.

In 1581 and 1596, Scottish nobles and clergy had "covenanted" with God to defend the Reformed Church.[7] These covenants were a transformation by the Presbyterian Church of the traditional "bonds," or mutual-defense leagues, that Scots had entered into in order to defend themselves prior to the existence of a stable police force in Scotland. These covenants were equally religious and political, as indicated by the Leith Covenant of 1572, in which the nobles supported James VI against his mother, Mary Queen of Scots. The nobles committed themselves

> in the fear of God the Father, of His Son our Lord Jesus Christ, and of the Holy Spirit . . . that we in all times hereafter, with our lives, lands, and goods, and all that we may make, shall set forward and promote the blessed Evangel of our Lord Jesus Christ, professed by us within this realm . . . and maintain with the King's Majesty, our sovereign Lord authority, his Regent and nobility, assisters to his grace. . . . (Quoted from Burrell, 1958, pp. 340–1)

In 1596, the covenant idea came back to haunt James. The general assembly of the Scottish kirk established a covenant to sustain the presbyterian system of church government against what it took to be James's intention of reestablishing the Catholic Church. The idea of a covenant, first between God and the elect and then later between God and the people of Scotland, grew rapidly.

In 1637, the Scottish nobility, as Hobbes himself described it, entered "into a covenant amongst themselves, which impudently they called a covenant with God, to put down episcopacy" (EW, 6:37). This covenant was widely thought of as "the justification for a special divine bond between God and the people of Scotland" (Burrell, 1958, p. 342). Many Scots thought that "the kingdom of Scotland supplanted ancient Israel as God's covenanted nation" (ibid., p. 343). In 1634, Samuel Rutherford even claimed to have discovered that Scotland is mentioned in the Bible:[8]

> Now, O Scotland, God be thanked, thy name is in the Bible. Christ spoke to us long since, ere ever we were born. Christ said, "Father, give me the ends of the earth, put in Scotland and England, with the isles-men in the great charter also: for I have them among the rest." . . . Believe in the name and authority of the Son of God, I pray you believe, and read Scotland's Charter. Psalm ii. 8, xlv, and lxxii. Will ye then believe? (Quoted from Burrell, 1958, p. 348; see also Burrell, 1964, p. 16)

These covenants were used by the Scots to justify their opposition to Charles I. In 1638, the Scots, who were presbyterian in church polity and puritan in liturgy, built upon this prior covenant to oppose an order of Charles I to adopt the liturgical book that he had authorized for them. The Scots resisted on the grounds that the prescribed rituals were "popish" and had been thrust upon them illegally by the Scottish bishops. In response, the Scots formulated the National Covenant, which begins,

> We, Noblemen, Barons, Gentlemen, Burgesses, Ministers, and Commons . . . by the providence of God living under one King, and being of one reformed Religion, Having before our eyes the glory of God, and the advancement of the Kingdom of our Lord and Saviour Jesus Christ, the Honour and Happinesse of the Kings Majesty and his Posterity, and the

true publick Liberty, Safety, and Peace of the Kingdoms wherein every ones private condition is included; And calling to minde the treacherous and bloody plots, conspiracies, attempts and practices of the Enemies of God against the true Religion: . . . We have now . . . according to the commendable practice of . . . Gods people in other Nations, . . . resolved and determined to enter into a mutuall and solemn League and Covenant: Wherein we all subscribe, and each one of us for himself, with our hands lifted up to the most high God, do Swear

1. That we shall sincerely, really and constantly, through the grace of God, endeavor in our several places and callings, the preservation of the Reformed Religion in the Church of Scotland, in Doctrine, Worship, Discipline and Government, against our common Enemies. (Dickinson and Donaldson, 1954, 3:122–3; variant text in Gardiner, 1884, 8:330)

There is no concept of covenant in Scottish secular law. For the Scots, the National Covenant was exactly like the Old Testament covenant. In 1638, Archibald Johnston of Wariston, one of the leaders of the Covenanters, wrote that there was "a veries near paralel betwixt Izrael and this Church [of Scotland], the only tuo suorne nationes of the Lord" (Wariston, 1632–9, p. 344). Slightly more than a century later, Hume described the Scots' feelings about this covenant as follows: "And none but rebels to God and traitors to their country, it was thought, would withdraw themselves from so salutary and so pious a combination" (Hume, 1754, p. 315; see also Gardiner, 1884, 8:336). After many futile attempts to bring the Scots back into line, Charles decided to draw up his own covenant for them to sign. The Scottish people refused, on the grounds that they had already committed themselves to a covenant and it would be blasphemous to reject it (Hume, 1754, pp. 316–17; Gardiner, 1884, 8:362–3). A lunatic, Margaret Michelson, considered an inspired prophetess by the people, claimed that the National Covenant came from heaven and that the King's covenant was the work of Satan (Gardiner, 8:365). In the end, Charles made an uneasy peace with the Scottish Covenanters.

There is no doubt that Hobbes had these Scottish covenants in mind when he was writing both *De Cive* and *Leviathan*. Those documents were issued shortly before the composition of these works; their formulations were significant events bearing upon the foundations of Charles's sovereignty; they were inspired by the kind of politically destabilizing use of religion that Hobbes so consistently opposed; and finally, Hobbes expresses his disgust for the Covenanters (EW, 3:160–1, 4:418).[9] Hobbes regularly mentions Presbyterians as one of the two religious groups most menacing to political stability. He alludes to them in the following passage:

> And whereas some men have pretended for their disobedience to their sovereign, a new covenant, made, not with men, but with God; this also is unjust: for there is no covenant with God, but by mediation of somebody that representeth God's person; which none doth but God's lieutenant, who hath the sovereignty under God. But this pretence of covenant with God, is so evident a lie, even in the pretenders' own consciences, that it is not only an act of an unjust, but also of a vile, and unmanly disposition. (EW, 3:160–1)

Earlier, in chapter 14, when he was explaining the nature of a covenant, he had condemned the same concept without the historical allusion. Immediately after explaining why there cannot be a covenant with brute beasts, he says,

> To make covenant with God, is impossible, but by mediation of such as God speaketh to, either by revelation supernatural, or by his lieutenants that govern under him, and in his name: for otherwise we know not whether our covenants be accepted, or not. (EW, 3:125–6)

Notice that rather than denying that covenants with God are possible, he is specifying the conditions under which they occur. While supernatural revelation is always theoretically possible, the more usual way is to go through the proper channels, namely through God's lieutenant, the sovereign.

Reformation covenant theology

The Scottish Presbyterians' use of the term "covenant" was deeply rooted in the theology of the Reformed Church. Covenant was a central concept in the theology of Tyndale. In the preface to his 1534 edition of the Pentateuch, Tyndale writes, "[A]ll the promises throughout the whole scripture do include a covenant" (Tyndale, 1526, p. 41), and in his preface to the New Testament he writes, "The general covenant wherein all other are comprehended and included, is this. If we meek ourselves to God, to keep all his laws, after the example of Christ: then God hath bound himself unto us to keep and make good all the mercies promised in Christ, throughout all the scripture" (Tyndale, 1534, p. 4).

The development of covenant theology was different in Scotland and England. The Scottish version is closely tied to the native Scottish idea of bonds, and the Scottish theologians were influenced primarily by Continental Reformers (Burrell, 1958). Although Hobbes was surely influenced by the Scottish Covenanters, he was not influenced by their theologians, and thus they need not be discussed. The English version did influence Hobbes. In England the idea of covenant was developed between 1570 and 1573 by Thomas Cartwright (c. 1535–1603), who wanted to eliminate the episcopal system completely from England, and then by William Perkins, whom Hobbes admired.[10] According to Perkins, God made two kinds of covenant with human beings: a covenant of grace and a covenant of works. By the terms of the covenant of works, which was made with Adam, humans would enjoy eternal happiness if they obeyed God. All humans violated the covenant of works through the agency of Adam's sin. Thus a new covenant had to be established in order to restore a relation between God and humans; this is the covenant of grace. By the terms of this covenant, which was originally made with Abraham and renewed with Isaac, Jacob, David, and others, humans were required to put their faith in God, and God would save them through his grace. On this view, the covenant that God made with Jesus is the same as the one he made with the great Old Testament figures; God simply administered or "dispensed" his grace in different ways to the ancient Jews and the Christians (Perkins, 1596, p. 94).

Central to the idea of covenant theology is the idea that humans sinned in virtue of Adam's sin and that they are saved through Jesus. In other words, humans are federated with these two figures, and hence covenant theology is also called "federal theology."[11] I have used the indefinite form "humans" in the last two sentences, rather than the universal term "all humans," because, although all covenant theologians agreed that all humans had sinned through the sin of Adam, they were divided over whether Jesus had died for all humans or only for the elect. In either case, people were federated in Adam and Jesus, both of whom were representative or public persons (Hill, 1986, 3:300–1, 304). Thomas Goodwin says that "the notion of a public representative to do acts that in law are counted as theirs whom he represents, is common among all nations" (quoted from ibid., p. 305). Their acts are the acts of everyone whom they represent, just as Hobbes would say that the acts of the sovereign are the acts of his subjects.

Calling a representative person "a public person," the Larger Catechism issued by the Westminster Assembly of Divines in 1648 declares that "the covenant being made with Adam as a public person not only for himself but for his posterity" gave way to the covenant of grace with Christ "as a public person." This doctrine is Pauline. Just as all humans sinned in Adam, so also are all humans (the elect?) redeemed in Christ.[12] The terms of covenant theology had been institutionalized two years earlier in the Westminster Confession of 1646:

> The first covenant made with man was a covenant of works, wherein life was promised to Adam, and in him to his posterity upon condition of perfect and personal obedience. . . . Man by his fall having made himself incapable of life by that covenant, the Lord was pleased to make a second, commonly called the covenant of grace; wherein he freely offered unto

sinners life and salvation by Jesus Christ, requiring of them faith in him that they may be saved, and promising to give unto all those that are ordained unto life his Holy Spirit, to make them willing and able to believe. (Leith, 1982, p. 202)

Although Hobbes condemns the political use that the Scots made of the Reformation idea of covenant, he uses essential elements of covenant theology in his own political theory.[13] Just as Adam and Jesus are representative persons in virtue of whom humans are either punished or saved, so the sovereign is a representative person in virtue of whom citizens are saved from the dangers of the state of nature. The political connection had also been made by the covenant theologian Peter Bulkeley, who said that "the covenant which passeth between God and us is like that which passeth between a king and his people" (Bulkeley, 1651, p. 435). Hobbes explains how a sovereign can be a representative person in his theory of authorization, according to which each citizen appoints the sovereign to be his agent and to work for him to preserve his life. Because the sovereign is an agent of the citizen, according to this aspect of Hobbes's theory, the citizen is the author of all that the sovereign does. That is, the actions of the sovereign are owned by the citizens. Thus, the saving behavior of the sovereign is the saving action of the citizen.

This is not to say that Hobbes accepted the doctrine of covenant theology. In its English version, as presented by John Preston, God and humans are equal parties to the covenant (Preston, 1629a, p. 38); the covenant created "a kind of equality" between God and man (cf. Hooker, 1638a, p. 460; Hill, 1986, 3:307; Miller, 1935, pp. 60–1). Similarly, Bulkeley held that in a covenant between a king and his people, "[T]he king promiseth to rule and govern in mercy and righteousness, and they again promise to obey in loyalty and faithfulness" (Bulkeley, 1651, p. 436).[14] Hobbes avoided this consequence by insisting that the sovereign is not a party to the political covenant.

Not only does Hobbes adapt the idea of a representative

person to his political theory; he also espouses aspects of the doctrine of covenant theology in his theology, although he does not use exactly those terms. Hobbes says that Christianity stands on two great doctrines: obedience, and faith in Christ. These correspond respectively to the covenant of works and the covenant of grace. He holds that if humans had not disobeyed, faith in Christ would not have been necessary.[15]

HOBBES ON LAYING DOWN OF RIGHT

Renouncing and transferring right

In Chapter 4, we saw that Hobbes distinguishes between the deontic concept of law and the nondeontic concept of right. Hobbes effects the transition from "is" to "ought" by holding that in the laws of nature God commands that each person preserve his own life and reveals through reason the principles for doing so. The laws of nature are prerequisites for getting out of the wretched state of nature, but they alone are not sufficient. For even though all the laws of nature are always in effect, the circumstances of the state of nature are such that the law that usually guides behavior is the second branch of the first law, namely, "by all means we can, to defend ourselves" (EW, 3:117). In order to break out of the cycle of suspicion and impending violence that Hobbes so eloquently describes, humans need to come to an agreement (that is, to establish a covenant) that will engender peace. This covenant requires that each party lay down either all or part of his right in a particular manner.

For a person to lay down a right, as we have seen, is for him to "*divest* himself of the *liberty*, of hindering another of the benefit of his own right to the same" (EW, 3:118). Since each person already has a right to everything in the state of nature, a person does not gain any additional right to anything when someone else lays down a right. If someone lays down his right to something, then someone else will encounter less opposition in attempting to exercise his own right. How much a person may benefit from someone else's action of laying down of a right depends upon whether the right is *renounced* or *transferred*.

To renounce a right is to divest oneself of a right to some thing and not to aid anyone else in the exercise of his right to it. Thus, if there is one apple available to ten people and one person renounces his right to it, then each person's chance of getting the apple for himself, *ceteris paribus*, improves from one-tenth to one-ninth. The person who renounces his right does not exercise his right to that apple but also does not assist any of the remaining nine people to exercise theirs. The situation is quite different with transfer of right.

To transfer a right to something is for a person to assist someone else to exercise the latter's own right to that thing; it is to transfer "the means of enjoying" the object transferred (EW, 3:125). As Hobbes says, "[W]hosoever has right to the end, has right to the means" (ibid., p. 164). Thus, if one person P_1 transfers his right to the apple to a person P_2, then P_1 must assist P_2 to obtain it, since when a person transfers a right he intends some particular person or persons to benefit (p. 119). In other words, to transfer a right is to transfer the power to exercise that right. Sovereigns acquire irresistible power through transfers of power, not renunciations (p. 169). When each citizen transfers his rights to the sovereign, the sovereign acquires tremendous power to fulfill his office. This would not be possible if each citizen merely renounced his right to things. For renunciations of rights do not increase the sovereign's power to do the things he is appointed to do, such as build roads and bridges and protect all the citizens from marauding invaders. Indeed, if each citizen merely renounced his rights, the sovereign's power would be dissipated among all the citizens, each of whom he is supposed to protect, and he would be more vulnerable than any other person. The secret to the sovereign's irresistible power is that each citizen transfers his right to the sovereign. That is, each person uses his power to enable the sovereign to do his duty. With everyone working together to do the sovereign's bidding, the sovereign has a good chance of getting the roads and bridges built and defending against invaders. This is Hobbes's point when he says that the "only way to erect such a common power, as may be able to defend them [citizens] from the invasion of foreigners, and the injuries of one another, and thereby to secure them in such sort, . . . is to confer all their power and strength upon one man, or upon one assembly of men, that may reduce all their wills, by plurality of voices, unto one will" (p. 157). Taxes are one concrete way that the sovereign gets the power he needs to exercise the rights that get transferred to him, and taxes may be considered "the wages, due to them that hold the public sword to defend private men" (pp. 333–4).

Hobbes is not always consistent in his explanation of transfer of right. Sometimes he explains his view in such a way that it requires only that a person "not . . . oppose the exercise of some right by the other" (Gauthier, 1969, p. 41). This makes transfer of right a special case of renunciation of right. When a person renounces his right, he lays down his right to everyone, but when a person transfers his right, he lays down his right to only one person (ibid., p. 58). Although this interpretation, which is defended by Gauthier, has some textual basis, there are several reasons for not taking it as Hobbes's most considered view. First, Hobbes clearly intends the terms "renunciation of right" and "transfer of right" to be mutually exclusive. But Gauthier's interpretation does not preserve this feature. Second, Gauthier's interpretation attributes a seriously flawed idea to Hobbes when an interpretation that attributes a better idea to him is available. If transferring a right is merely laying down a right to one person, as Gauthier would have it, then the sovereign would have no way to acquire the power he needs to do his job. So Gauthier's interpretation does not provide Hobbes with a way of explaining how the sovereign acquires the power he must have in order to function as a sovereign. On his interpretation, renouncing a right is passive; it is standing out of the way of someone else's exercising his power. But a transfer of right needs to be active; to transfer something means to give something. What is given in a transfer of right is power. To transfer a right is to contribute one's own power to someone else in order for the latter person to be better able to exercise his right. My account explains how a sovereign increases his power to become irresistible by the small increments contributed by each citizen's transferring his right. Gauthier's mistake leads him to speak inappropriately. He often employs the phrase "use of a right," as in the clause "the subject actually assigns to the sovereign the use of his right" (ibid., pp. 111, 157). The problem with Gauthier's remark is that rights are had, not used.[16] What is appropriately said to be used is power. So Gauthier should have said, "The subject actually assigns to the sovereign the use of his power when he transfers his right." Another objectionable feature of the remark that "the subject actually assigns to the sovereign the use of his right" is that, in order to govern, the sovereign does not need any additional right. By the right of nature, he, like everyone else, has the right to everything. What the sovereign needs is not right but power.

As I said, Gauthier's interpretation is encouraged by Hobbes, who sometimes did confuse transfer of right with renunciation of right, as in *De Corpore Politico*. He says that transfer of power and strength is nothing but "to lay by, or relinquish his own right of resisting him to whom he so transfereth" (EW, 4:123). Yet three paragraphs earlier he had explained transfer of power in what I take to be the superior way. He said that a person who covenants gives "his strength and means to him, whom he covenanteth to obey; and hereby, he that is to command may by the use of all their means and strength, be able by the terror thereof, to frame the will of them all to unity and concord amongst themselves" (ibid.). Since the transfer of right creates a power that may induce "terror," it is clear that the power of the person acquiring the right is greatly increased.

Mutual and reciprocal transfer of right

Hobbes develops the idea of a transfer of rights in order to be able to explain what contracts are. He says that a contract is the "mutual transferring of right" (EW, 3:120). Although he intends this remark to be a definition, it is subject to misunderstanding. An exchange of gifts between friends could be understood to be a mutual transferring of rights. But Hobbes would not want to say that an exchange of gifts creates a contract. For the sake of simplicity, let's stipulate that the term "reciprocal transfer of rights" will cover the case of an exchange of gifts and understand Hobbes's term "mutual transfer of rights" in the following stronger sense: a mutual transfer of rights consists of a person P_1 transferring his right to something O_1 in consideration of a person P_2 transferring his right to something O_2 and vice versa, where P_1, O_1, P_1, and O_2 are not identical. This explication of "mutual transfer of right" is merely designed to explain the term in the sense that Hobbes clearly intended to express.

It is important to notice that the phrase "mutual transfer of right" continues after our explication to contain a certain indeterminacy. The meaning of the phrase does not require that any party to the contract transfer his right to any other party to the contract, even though it would be normal to do so. This indeterminacy is necessary in order to allow for contractual situations like the following: Suppose that the United States and El Fatah make a covenant with the following provisions: the United States transfers its right to $1 million to the government of Iran on the condition that El Fatah transfer its right to imprisoned French citizens to the government of France. One reason that Hobbes must allow his parties to a covenant to transfer their rights to people who are not parties to the covenant is that the sovereign-making covenant is just such a mutual transferring of right to a noncovenanting person.

154

THE ORIGIN OF OBLIGATION

Hobbes says that when a person either renounces or transfers his right, he communicates this fact to other people in some visible way (EW, 3:119). Such communication constitutes a covenant with these other people, and thereby human obligation is born. For, not to keep one's promise as expressed in the renunciation or transfer would be to violate the third law of nature, "that men perform their covenants made" (EW, 3:130). This is the most straightforward way to interpret Hobbes's text:

> And when a man hath in either manner abandoned, or granted away his right; then is he said to be OBLIGED, or BOUND, NOT TO HINDER THOSE, to whom such right is granted, or abandoned, from the benefit of it: and that he *ought*, and it is his DUTY, not to make void that voluntary act of his own: and that such hindrance is INJUSTICE, and INJURY, as being *sine jure;* the right being before renounced, or transfered. (EW, 3:119).

Hobbes's rhetoric makes no sense unless laying down of right establishes obligation. Gauthier agrees, but thinks that there is nothing more to this account than that obligations are self-imposed by humans. He says that Hobbes's doctrine is simply

> *A* has an obligation not to do x = *A* has laid down the natural right to do x

and that, by this definition, "at one blow Hobbes can, and does, cut away the arguments of those who say that political obligation – which is what Hobbes wishes primarily to explain – must be derived from some prior obligation to obey the will of God, or to follow the laws of nature, or what have you" (Gauthier, 1969, p. 41). The religious interpreter need not be moved by Gauthier's assertion. For nowhere in his explanation of laying down a right is there any indication of a power that ties or binds a person to his action. On

Hobbes's account, there is obligation in the state of nature but no human power to enforce it, and without force, covenants are but so many words (EW, 3:119, 128). Gauthier's interpretation cannot explain how laying down a right is anything more than words, and so his claim that political obligation is a purely "human creation" (Gauthier, 1969, p. 41) is nothing but words. It is no good for Gauthier to say that obligations are "self-imposed" (ibid., p. 40). Given the fact that whatever burden a person takes on himself he can put down, a self-imposed obligation is no obligation at all.

Further, nothing about Hobbes's passage compels one to take it as asserting an identity between having an obligation and laying down a right. As explained in Chapter 3, the language is consistent with interpreting it as nothing more than the assertion that *if* one lays down a right, *then* one has an obligation. And the possibility of laying down a right may depend upon something else, namely, God's underwriting power. In the absence of a human power to tie one's behavior to the promised course of action, there is only one way to explain the origin of obligation here. The parties to the covenant trust that God, the author of the laws of nature, will guarantee performance (EW, 3:128–9). All of this is part and parcel with interpreting Hobbes as a divine command theorist. Consequently, Hobbes says that obligations "have their strength, not from their own nature, for nothing is more easily broken than a man's word, but from fear of some evil consequence upon the rupture" (EW, 3:119; see also Sommerville, 1984, p. 442).

It should be fairly obvious that the passage under discussion does not tell the whole story about obligation. Intuitively it seems odd that laying down a right, that is, letting go of something, should create an obligation, that is, should impose something on someone. Duties are the result of picking something up, not laying something down. Gauthier's explication of Hobbes's notion of laying down a right slides over this problem. It does not indicate the source of the power that ties or binds the person who lays down his right. It is implausible that Hobbes, who was so adamant that safety requires irresistible power and that philosophers should use words in their literal senses, should have built the foundations of his theory of sovereignty on a metaphorical meaning of "obligation" that is devoid of all reference to power.

LAWS OF NATURE AND NATURAL PUNISHMENTS

There are two ways in which God might punish in his natural kingdom.[17] Either he arranges things so that the violator of the covenant will fare badly in this life, or, failing that, will suffer in the next. Hobbes is rightly loath to rest his moral and political theory on the prospect of an afterlife, since this is a matter of supernatural revelation (EW, 3:135). Thus, he explains the connection that God, who "governs the world" (ibid., p. ix), has established between the "natural punishments" of "the natural kingdom of God, and his natural law" (EW, 3:356). Every human action begins a long chain of consequences which no human can infallibly predict. Often some act will immediately cause pleasure, but later pain; and the pain may be much more severe than the pleasure, which is immediately associated with the action. Thus,

> there are linked together both pleasing and unpleasing events; in such manner, as he that will do anything for his pleasure, must engage himself to suffer all the pains annexed to it; and these pains, are the natural punishments of those actions, which are the beginning of more harm than good. And hereby it comes to pass, that intemperance is naturally punished with diseases; rashness, with mischances; injustice, with the violence of enemies; pride, with ruin; cowardice, with oppression; negligent government of princes, with rebellion; and rebellion, with slaughter. For seeing punishments are consequent to the breach of laws; natural punishments must be naturally consequent to the breath of the laws of nature; and therefore follow them as their natural, nor arbitrary effects. (Ibid., pp. 356-7)

This line of reasoning also underlies Hobbes's response, which was discussed earlier, to the fool who thinks it is in his self-interest to violate his covenants. Yet Hobbes is neither so naïve nor so unbiblical as to think that there is a perfect correlation between goodness or wickedness and, respectively, success or failure in this life. Citing a complaint in Psalm 72, he raises one of the problems of evil by asking "why evil men often prosper, and good men suffer adversity" and appeals to the Book of Job for his answer. God has the right to do whatever he wants to do with humans, because of his power. People often find this answer abhorrent, yet Hobbes is correct in holding that this is God's own answer, given in his theophany (Job 38:4; EW, 3:346). This may be a hard doctrine, but Hobbes is orthodox in asserting it. John Wilkins said that if the good were invariably rewarded with earthly happiness, then "virtue would lose its merit" (quoted from Thomas, 1971, p. 109).

Hobbes also appeals to God's power, which transcends justice and injustice, in the answer that Jesus gave to the question of why a particular person was born blind. His disciples thought that the explanation must be that either the man or his parents had sinned, but Jesus rejects this answer: "Neither hath this man sinned, nor his fathers; but that the works of God might be made manifest in him" (quoted by Hobbes, EW, 3:347).[18]

Hobbes presents a different perspective in his comments on Thomas White's *De Mundo*. He explains that when people prosper they think it is either because they are being rewarded for their goodness or because God is rational. But when they suffer they attribute the evil either to chance or to the irrationality of God. The reason is that "no-one admits his own depravity, and that, out of jealousy, the virtues of those whom one envies for their good one calls wickedness" (Hobbes, 1642, p. 461). The upshot is that there are fewer events in life that legitimately give rise to the problem of evil than most people think. One may consider Hobbes's point of view jaundiced, but his principal purpose in the context was to deny the existence of chance and to affirm the rationality of God. Hobbes affirms that the universe operates according to laws and that typically, though not invariably, goodness in this life is rewarded and evil punished. As for the apparent exceptions, God is free to do as he pleases, and sometimes humans are mistaken about the ultimate outcome of good or evil.

Secular theorists are baffled by Hobbes's derivation of obligation from laying down rights in a prepolitical situation. Gauthier thinks that Hobbes is guilty of "confusion" when "he does speak of the laws of nature as obliging" (Gauthier, 1969, p. 55). If this were a confusion, then it would be one in which Hobbes wallowed. For he says that the laws of nature oblige at the beginning of chapter 15 and twice later in that chapter, and he also says that they bind (e.g., EW, 3:130, 145). I do not believe that Hobbes was confused about what he thought on this matter. On my interpretation, two sets of obligations must be distinguished. First, the laws of nature oblige with respect to God in virtue of being commands of God, prior to any social intercourse. Second, the actions that result from the laying down of a right oblige with respect to humans in virtue of falling under the laws of nature. In the passage quoted earlier from chapter 14 about the origin of obligation and justice, Hobbes is speaking only of the origin of human obligation and justice, for this is the chapter in which he is trying to ground the civil covenant. In chapter 15, he is speaking of the laws of nature in themselves and is thinking about how they oblige as God's laws.

My interpretation of the foundations of Hobbes's political theory does not rest on inferences from general principles that he espouses in various places, but on his own words when he is presenting his theory. He says, "The force of words, being, as I have formerly noted, too weak to hold men to the performance of their covenants; there are in man's nature, but two imaginable helps to strengthen it" (EW, 3:128). One, the glory or pride of not wanting to appear so weak as to need to break a covenant, cannot be relied upon because too few people have this kind of self-respect. The other help is fear: "The passion to be reckoned upon, is fear; whereof there be two very general objects: one, the power of spirits invisible; the other, the power of those men they shall therein offend. Of these two, though the former be the greater power, yet the fear of the latter is commonly the greater fear." Hobbes relies upon both of these fears. In the state of nature, it is the fear of God that operates, and it is his power that makes covenants obligatory. Hobbes says it is this fear "which hath place in the nature of man before civil society." The fear of men is less important in the state of nature, because each person, being roughly equal in power, is not sufficiently afraid of others, except in actual combat (ibid., p. 129). This does not seem consonant with Hobbes's usual view about the state of nature. I think he adopts it because he believes that he needs the fear of God to ground all obligation. Hobbes concludes, "So that before the time of civil society, or in the interruption thereof by war, there is nothing can strengthen a covenant of peace agreed upon, against the temptations of avarice, ambition, lust, or other strong desire but the fear of that invisible power, which they every one worship as God; and fear as a revenger of their perfidy" (ibid.). In short, God puts the obligation into covenants in the state of nature. It is only God who will take revenge on those who break their covenants. For obligations "have their strength, not from their own nature, for nothing is more easily broken than a man's word, but from fear of some evil consequence upon the rupture" (EW, 3:119).

Since there is no one other than God to obligate the parties to a covenant in the state of nature, it is logically superfluous for a person to appeal to God expressly in such circumstances: "For a covenant, if lawful, binds in the sight of God, without the oath, as much as with it: if unlawful, bindeth not at all; though it be confirmed with an oath" (EW, 3:130). Hobbes is not saying that oaths to God have no power. Rather, he is saying that the power of God is already underwriting any covenant made in the state of nature. Thus, the oath of an atheist is worthless, according to Hobbes, and no punishment is too great for such men (EW, 4:294). All of this is part and parcel with interpreting Hobbes as a divine command theorist.

Chapter 6

Sovereign-making covenants

In this chapter I shall explain how humans are able to transfer their right of nature to a separate person and thereby institute a commonwealth. In *Leviathan*, the institution of the commonwealth is supposed to depend upon an interplay between authorization and authority. I shall argue that Hobbes's idea of authorization is confused. Hobbes also claims that there are two ways in which a commonwealth can be instituted. The first way results in what he calls "sovereignty by institution." The second way results in what he calls "sovereignty by acquisition." I shall argue that Hobbes is correct to say that so far as sovereignty is concerned, the differences between them are insignificant. Finally, since the model for these sovereign-making covenants comes from the biblical idea of a covenant, I shall briefly discuss Hobbes's treatment of the covenants in which God figures.

SOVEREIGN-MAKING COVENANTS AND THE KINGDOM OF GOD BY NATURE

I have been arguing that sovereign-making covenants rest upon the power of God, because covenants need to be binding. They are binding only if the laws of nature are literally laws; and the laws of nature are literally laws only if God's power underwrites them.[1] In addition to this chain of power reaching from the earthly sovereign up to the heavenly God, there is an analogy between the earthly sovereign and God. The earthly sovereign is sovereign only because he has overwhelming power to accompany his natural right to all things. God is sovereign because he naturally has the irresistible power to accompany his natural right to all things. Given these interconnections between the artificial sovereignty of earthly sovereigns and the natural sovereignty of God, one might expect Hobbes to say something about them. I claim that he does in chapter 30, "Of the Office of the Sovereign Representative," and chapter 31, "Of the Kingdom of God by Nature."

While most scholars find these two chapters either mysterious or an embarrassment, they confirm my interpretation of Hobbes's theologically based political theory. Since Hobbes says that a sovereign does not incur any obligations or duties as a result of the sovereign-making covenant, most scholars think that Hobbes should hold that the sovereign has no duties at all. But Hobbes contradicts this view. He says at the beginning of chapter 30 that because the sovereign has been trusted with the safety of the people, "he is obliged by the law of nature, and . . . [must] render an account thereof to God, the author of that law, and to none but him" (EW, 3:322). This passage either says or presupposes that God is the author of the law of nature and that the sovereign has obligations to God under that law. The sovereign is further obliged to protect his subjects from injuries and to exercise "general providence" (ibid.), just as God exercises providence over creation. Here, then, is an explicit linking of the earthly sovereign to the authority of God by a duty incurred through the laws of nature. And it occurs prominently, at the beginning of chapter 30.

The following chapter, "Of the Kingdom of God by Nature," is even more significant. It occupies the conspicuous position of being the last chapter of the second part of *Leviathan*, "Of Commonwealth." If God's role in Hobbes's political theory were either minimal or nonexistent, then this chapter would have been misplaced and should have been the first chapter of the third part, "Of a Christian Commonwealth." Of course, on my view, Hobbes's placement of this chapter is exactly right.

Since the civil government rests upon the laws of nature, which are "the laws of God," it is important to know what these laws of God are (EW, 3:343). For if one is ignorant of them, then one cannot know whether the command of a sovereign is legitimate or not, "and so, either by too much civil obedience, offends the Divine Majesty; or through fear of offending God, transgresses the commandments of the commonwealth" (EW, 3:343; 2:204). Hobbes is probably more worried about people disobeying the sovereign than about what they think would amount to disobeying God, because so many Englishmen had been using the alleged laws of God to justify their seditious behavior. Nonetheless, he is concerned to have people obey the laws of God. Since the laws of God are the laws of nature and since the laws of nature enable people to get out of the state of nature, it is important for people to know what the laws are. For example, it would be disastrous if people thought that it were not part of God's law that they seek peace. However, in this context, Hobbes is not thinking of these laws of nature at all. He says, "And seeing the knowledge of all law, dependeth on the knowledge of the sovereign power, I shall say something in that which followeth, of the KINGDOM OF GOD" (EW, 3:344). That is, the ultimate sovereign is God, from whom the earthly sovereign derives his authority. To leave no doubt that this is what he means, Hobbes then says, "*God is king, let the earth rejoice* saith the psalmist (xcvii.1). And again, *God is king, though the nations be angry; and he that sitteth on the cherubims, though the earth be moved.* Whether men will or not, they must be subject always to the divine power" (ibid.).

Some scholars claim that Hobbes does not mean that the Kingdom of God is literally a kingdom or that God literally reigns. They support this interpretation by quoting this statement from *De Cive:* "Now although God governs all men so by his power, that none can do anything which he would not have done; yet this, to speak properly and accurately, is not to reign" (EW, 2:204). But to use this quotation as evidence that God does not literally reign in his kingdom is to quote out of context. Hobbes's point is to deny that God literally reigns over plants, beasts, or atheists, because they lack the intelligence to recognize God's existence. (Notice the company that atheists keep.) This is the way he leads into affirming that God "is properly said to reign," because "he governs his subjects by his word, and by promise of rewards to those that obey it, and by threatening them with punishment that obey it not" (EW, 3:344).[2] In short, Hobbes is explaining that it is proper to say that God's kingdom is literally a kingdom.

Atheists are not governed by God, because they deny that he exists. This makes them enemies of God and subject to being killed. Although this idea bothered his contemporaries, Hobbes was not disturbed. There were no professed atheists to worry about, and, as for the dissimulating ones, the death sentence is sufficient, as Hobbes explained in *De Cive:* "Those only therefore are supposed to belong to God's kingdom, who acknowledge him to be the governor of all things, and that he hath given *his commands* to men, and appointed *punishments* for the transgressors. The rest we must not call subjects, but enemies of God" (EW, 2:205). In the parallel passage in *Leviathan,* Hobbes makes clear that the commands he is speaking of here are the "natural dictates of right reason," or the laws of nature (EW, 3:345).[3] The source of God's sovereignty is the irresistible power he has by nature (ibid.). If any human had had irresistible power, he, like God, would have been naturally sovereign (ibid., pp. 345–6). But because humans are roughly equal in the state of nature, they must artificially create a person who has overwhelming power.

Although Hobbes does not hold a divine right of kings theory, he often says that sovereigns serve by the right of God (e.g., EW, 6:236). I have tried to explain what he means by this by arguing that civil sovereignty depends upon the law of nature, which depends upon the natural power of God. This means that the foundations for the civil sovereign belong to natural right, not to civil right, and Hobbes says precisely this in the Latin version of *Leviathan:* "[*J*]urium fundamenta . . . juris naturalis sunt, non civilis" (OL, 3:241).

PERSON, AUTHOR, ACTOR

The sovereign-making covenant occurs when persons in the state of nature mutually transfer certain rights to some person who is not himself a party to the covenant (EW, 3:158). In *Leviathan*, Hobbes uses the technical ideas of authorization and authority to explain how these rights are transferred and what they amount to. And these ideas are explained in terms of two roles that persons can play: author and actor. In this section, I shall begin explaining some of these terms.

Hobbes defines a person as he "whose words or actions are considered, either as his own, or as representing the words or actions of another person, or of any other thing, to whom they are attributed, whether truly or by fiction" (EW, 3:147). This is convoluted writing, and Hobbes's meaning is clearer in Latin: "Persons est *is qui suo vel alieno nomine res agit*" (a person is someone who does something in his own name or in the name of someone else) (OL, 3:123). If a person acts in his own behalf, then he is a natural person; if he acts in behalf of someone or something else, then he is an artificial person. I say, "something else" because an artificial person can represent buildings and institutions (EW, 3:149–50). However, it should be emphasized that the artificial person is the human being who represents the building and institution, not the building or institution itself.

Hobbes's idea that a person can represent the words and actions of another person is, I believe, derived from the covenant theologians, for whom the idea of a representative or public person was a key concept (Hill, 1986, 3:300–24; Trinterud, 1951).[4] According to that concept, all humans sinned through Adam, because he represented all humanity. That is the downside. The upside is that humans are able to be redeemed through Jesus because he also represented all humans.[5] The view that Jesus is the representative person for mankind could assume a grotesque form. Commenting on Galatians 3:13, Luther says, "And all the prophets saw this, that Christ was to become the greatest thief, murderer, adulterer, robber, desecrator, blasphemer, etc., there has ever been anywhere in the world. He is not acting in His own Person now" (Luther, 1535, p. 277; see also Calvin, 1559, II.16.10). Since there is no sin of one person against another in the state of nature, the sovereign will not take any sin upon himself. Nonetheless, he does represent all his subjects, and it is through him that they will be saved, not from the evils of eternal damnation, which was the work of Christ, but from the immediate evil of death lurking in the state of nature. Thus, Hobbes transmutes a theological idea into a secular one.

Central to the idea of a representative person is that he acts for others. When he does something, he is *acting* for someone else, and that other person is credited with being the *author*, or originator, of the action. For example, if Adam represents Beth in a real estate transaction, then Adam acts for Beth by doing the work of finding a house and negotiating the contract, and Beth is the author (the buyer) of the transaction. Thus, there is a difference between an actor and an author. Of course, a person can be an author by acting for or representing himself. In such a case he owns his actions directly. But Hobbes is more interested in the cases in which a person authorizes someone else to act for him. In such cases, the person authorized to act is called an "actor," and the actions resulting from his behavior are not owned by him but owned indirectly by the person giving the authorization (the author).

It is analytic that if a person P_1 authorizes a person P_2 to act for him, then P_1 is superior to P_2 with regard to that action. Although P_2 acquires the authority to act for P_1 and can be said to have authority, he remains subordinate to P_1, and his authority is derivative. By authorizing someone, a person does not give up any of his rights. In particular, a citizen should not suffer any loss of right by authorizing a sovereign to defend himself. This is important, because in the next section we shall see that Hobbes will illicitly slide from holding that *the sovereign is authorized to act by his subjects* to *the sovereign has authority* to *the sovereign has authority over his subjects.*

AUTHORIZATION AND AUTHORITY

A contradiction in the sovereign-making covenant

The sovereign-making covenant is a mutual transferring of rights to govern oneself to some person who is not himself a party to the covenant (EW, 3:158). There is one novelty and one traditional element to this account. The novelty is Hobbes's insistence that the sovereign is not a party to the covenant. For those who thought of civil government as arising from a contract or covenant, a sovereign-making covenant held between the sovereign and the people. This was the understanding of the relationship in the National Covenant. Such an understanding allows one to talk about the duties of sovereigns toward their subjects. Hobbes consciously eschews this idea. He thinks that if a sovereign were to have duties to his citizens, his authority would be effectively undermined.

I believe that Hobbes was inspired to introduce this novelty by the conception of God he formulated from his Calvinistic reading of the Bible. According to Hobbes, because of his irresistible power, God has the authority to do whatever he wants to do to anyone (Eire, 1986, pp. 197–203). He is unbounded, not just in the rightness of his actions, but in the lawfulness of them. Thus, Hobbes said that God can "justly" afflict his creatures in any way he chooses (EW, 3:347).[6]

Hobbes puts the distinction between authorization and authority to work in chapter 17 when he formulates the sovereign-making covenant in these words: "I authorise and give up my right of governing myself, to this man, or to this assembly of men, on this condition, that thou give up thy right to him, and authorise all his actions in like manner" (EW, 3:158). This formula for the sovereign-making covenant is in explicit performative form. The verb phrase "I authorize and give up" specifies the alleged illocutionary force of the utterance, and the phrase "my right of governing myself" specifies the propositional content, which can be made more explicit if expressed in the form "I have the right to govern myself."

Typically, an explicit illocutionary act has only one performative verb prefixed to the propositional part. But there is no objection in principle to having a speech act that has two forces, so long as they or the conditions for their performance do not contradict each other. When two or more illocutionary-act verbs are joined together, each is usually a variant of the other. Thus, it is possible to have illocutionary-force verbs such as "I swear and avow" or "I declare and define," since the two words in each case have roughly the same meaning in the context and can either disambiguate or emphasize the illocutionary force that is intended to be expressed. The question now is whether the verbs in the performative formula "I authorize and give up" are roughly synonymous or not. I shall argue that they are not. But the issue is complicated, because Hobbes may have equivocated on "authorize." For the sake of simplicity, let's consider two possibilities separately: first, that "authorize" is used to mean something similar to "give up"; second, that it means something dissimilar.

If Hobbes intended to use "authorize" in a meaning close to the meaning of "give up," then, in this context, to authorize a person P to do something is to set up P to make the final decision on the matter. If this is what Hobbes meant, then his authorization formula means simply that the way out of the state of nature is for each person to give up his right to govern himself. If the idea of governing oneself means anything, it must partially mean having the right to defend oneself from force. Unfortunately, this is precisely what it cannot mean without attributing a basic contradiction to Hobbes, for he said earlier that a "covenant not to defend myself from force, by force, is always void" (EW, 3:127). The fact that the phrase "authorise and give up my right of defending myself" seems to communicate that the speaker is giving up precisely this right is not supposed to matter, according to Hobbes. Thus, he says,

And therefore there be some rights, which no man can be understood by any words, or other signs, to have abandoned, or transferred. As first a man cannot lay down the right of resisting them, that assault him by force, to take away his life; because he cannot be understood to aim thereby, at any good to himself. The same may be said of wounds, and chains, and imprisonment; both because there is no benefit consequent to such patience. . . . And therefore if a man by words or other signs, seem to despoil himself of the end, for which those signs were intended; he is not to be understood as if he meant it, or that it was his will; but that he was ignorant of how such words or actions were to be interpreted. (EW, 3:120)

Consequently, Hobbes cannot be understood to intend that "authorize" have virtually the same meaning as "give up" (cf. May, 1980, p. 200). Let's then consider what other meaning it might have.

Coming as it does after his discussion of person and personating, I take Hobbes to mean by "authorize" that if one person authorizes another, then the latter person is to represent the former. On this meaning of authorize, if one person authorizes another person, then the first person has authority over the second and does not give up his right to do what he authorizes the second to do. The first person is superior to the second person with respect to the authorization, and the second person remains subordinate to the first after the authorization is given. This explains why Hobbes can say that in the authorization of the sovereign "there is no restriction at all, of his [the citizen's] former natural liberty" (EW, 3:204). Even though it may be imprudent for the first person to undo or otherwise subvert the efforts of the second person, there is no legal or logical impossibility involved in such action. In contrast with authorization, if one person gives up his right to do something to some second person, then the first person has, *ipso dicto*, given up his right. To give up a right is to lose it. The problem with Hobbes's sovereign-making formula is that the first illocutionary-act verb, "to authorize," expresses that no right has been given up, whereas the second illocutionary-act verb, "to give up [my right]," expresses that it has.

What has led Hobbes to incorporate a contradiction into his sovereign-making formula is his deep-seated ambivalence about the foundations of political theory. On the one hand, he wants the citizens themselves to be the immediate source of their sovereign's power and authority, for various reasons. Notwithstanding his abhorrence of democracy, he had even held, in the *Elements of Law*, that every government begins as a democracy (EW, 4:139). Hobbes probably thinks that if citizens believe that they are the immediate source of authority, then they will feel responsible for their form of government and will be less inclined to revolt or to claim that God is instructing them about how to treat the sovereign. Also, if citizens authorize the actions of their sovereign, then his actions are their actions. That is, each person has to avow the actions of his sovereign and cannot complain about them. It is this attitude that partially explains why Hobbes can seemingly paraphrase the original sovereign-making formula as follows: "I authorize, or take upon me, all his [the sovereign's] actions" (EW, 3:204).[7] This formula, unlike the original one, is perfectly consistent, because "give up my right to govern myself" has been eliminated. It is analogous to the examples "I swear and avow" and "I declare and define."

On the other hand, Hobbes also has a different view about the foundations of political theory. He wants political stability above all. In addition to not wanting citizens to rebel, because of his fear of any disruption of domestic tranquillity, he does not want citizens to be able to withdraw their authority from the sovereign, even though the possibility of withdrawing authorization is inherent in that idea. Thus, he wants citizens to give up whatever is necessary in order to ensure political stability. That is why the phrase "I give up [my right]" is in the original formula. But by adding that phrase, he undoes what he did with the phrase "I authorize." In short, Hobbes has a theory of authorization and a theory of authority; and they are incompatible.[8]

Authority, authorization, and a semantic shift

Hobbes has been able to deceive many of his readers, and very likely himself, about the contradiction in his sovereign-making formula largely because of a subtle semantic shift. After he says that one person can authorize another, he says that when one person authorizes another person to do something, the second person has authority; and he implies that the second person is an authority. If this meant that the second person has authority to act for the first person, there would be no problem. In such a case, the second person would be a *deputy* for the first person, and as such would be subordinate to him. But this is not the meaning that Hobbes intends. When he says that the second person has authority or is an authority, he means that the second person acquires authority *over the first person* (EW, 3:148). But this is absurd. If P_1 gives authority to P_2, then the authority of P_2 is derivative; P_1 retains his authority or superiority over P_2 and cannot become subordinate in that regard, *pace* Hobbes. Beginning with the predicate "*x* authorizes *y*," which entails that *x* is superior to *y*, he argues that since *x* authorizes *y*, *y* is an authority, and hence *y* is an authority over *x*. Depending upon one's other views about language and logic, the fallacious inference occurs either in the move from "*x* authorizes *y*" to "*y* is an authority" and is an instance of *dicto simpliciter*, or it occurs in the move from "*y* is an authority" to "*y* is an authority over [every] *x*" and is an instance of invalid universal generalization.

The contradiction in Hobbes's sovereign-making formula can be illustrated with four propositions to which he is committed:

(1) If P_1 authorizes P_2 to do an action A, then P_1 has authority over P_2 with respect to A.

(2) P_1 authorizes P_2 to govern P_1.

(3) If P_1 has authority over P_2 with respect to A, then P_2 cannot have authority over P_1 with respect to A.

(4) If P_1 authorizes P_2 to govern P_1, then P_2 has authority over P_1 with respect to governing P_1.

From (1) and (2), (5) follows:

(5) P_1 has authority over P_2 with respect to governing P_1.

And from (5) and (3), (6) follows:

(6) P_2 cannot have authority over P_1 with respect to governing P_1.

But from (2) and (4), (6') follows:

(6') P_2 has authority over P_1 with respect to governing P_1.

But (6) and (6') are contradictory. The source of the contradiction is (4), which, as I explained above, is false. Hobbes asserts it because he wants some way to subordinate citizens to the sovereign. In other words, Hobbes tries to effect a kind of Heglian master–slave reversal. He wants the citizen, who is the source of the sovereign's authority and power, to alienate both and to become the slave of the sovereign. But this mover *from authorized by* to *authority over* is illegitimate.[9]

Earlier in this chapter (in "Person, Author, Actor"), I concentrated on the contradiction in the performative formula "I authorize and give up." There are also problems with the propositional content. Hobbes does not specify any for "authorize." Every authorization is an authorization for a particular action or range of actions that must be specified in order to communicate what the actor is supposed to do for the author. If Hobbes had supplied a propositional content for "authorize," it would have to be conveyed by the phrase "my right of governing myself." But it makes no sense to say either "I authorize my right of governing myself" or the more explicit "I authorize that I have the right of governing myself." One might want to change the syntax and claim that Hobbes means "I authorize [the sovereign] to govern me," even though that is not what Hobbes says. However, one who takes this tack is committed to holding that Hobbes's formula means "I authorize [the sovereign] to govern me, and I give up my right of governing myself," and the contradiction between the first illocutionary-act verb and the second reappears. My own guess is that Hobbes confusedly did not intend to specify any propositional content for "I authorize." He intended to give the sovereign carte blanche to do with his subjects what he will, as indicated by Hobbes's variation on the sovereign-making covenant: "I authorize, or take upon me, all his [the sovereign's] actions" (EW, 3:204).

Let's now consider the propositional content of "I give up." What does "governing" mean in the phrase "my right of governing myself"? In its central, ordinary sense, "to govern" means to rule with authority. If this is its meaning here, then the contradiction just discussed is again confirmed. For then the formula means "I authorize and I give up my right to rule with authority."[10]

Gauthier's interpretation

My interpretation of Hobbes's sovereign-making formula is contrary to that of Gauthier. Gauthier's way of avoiding the problems in connection with the phrase "giving up my right to govern myself" is to deny that Hobbes means either "give up my right" or "govern" literally. Gauthier's denial that Hobbes means what he says should be seen in the context of the entire secularist interpretation of Hobbes, according to which "law of nature" does not literally mean law of nature; "obligation" does not literally mean obligation; "forbidden" does not literally mean forbidden; and, when applied to God, "rule" does not literally mean rule, and "kingdom" does not literally mean kingdom.

As an alternative to the literal meaning of the phrase "giving up my right to govern myself," Gauthier gives a Pickwickian interpretation. According to Gauthier, contrary to all appearances, the phrase means "give up the right to make decisions which are to be counted as mine" (Gauthier, 1969, p. 154). It may appear that this substituted phrase means that the person gives up his right to determine what happens to him. But if that were what Gauthier meant, then his interpretation would be of no help to Hobbes, because the limit Hobbes had set on the laying down of right would still be exceeded. In fact, Gauthier seems to mean by the phrase that the person gives up the right to cancel the authorization of the sovereign (p. 157). But this also does not help Hobbes, for the same reason. If an authorization he has given should ever threaten a person's own life, it can be canceled. This example is only a special case of Hobbes's general claim that a person can never be obliged to do anything that threatens his own life.

A suggested revision

Given that Hobbes's account of the sovereign-making covenant is contradictory and confused in the ways described, it is not clear how he would want to revise his account. My own suggestion is inspired by Hobbes's gloss on the sovereign-making formula. Near the end of chapter 17 of *Leviathan*, Hobbes says that the essence of a commonwealth is "one person, of whose acts a great multitude, by mutual covenants one with another, have made themselves every one the author, to the end he may use the strength and means of them all, as he shall think expedient, for their peace and common defence" (EW, 3:158; see also 2:68–9). Hobbes wants all people to agree to act in such a way that all are made safe from the dangers of the state of nature. This agreement must be compatible with the facts that each person has a right to everything; that no one can lay down his right to defend himself; and that a sovereign with overwhelming power must be set up. These conditions can be met if one exploits the idea that, in addition to the right to defend oneself, each person has the right to defend every other person. Hobbes explicitly subscribes to this position when he tries to justify the institution of punishment: "In the making of a commonwealth, every man giveth away the right of defending another; but not of defending himself" (EW, 3:297). Thus, each person ought to covenant to transfer to the sovereign his right to defend every other person. Since to transfer a right to someone is to use one's power to enable that person to exercise his rights, each citizen will commit himself to use his power to enable the sovereign to defend everyone else.[11] In this way, the sovereign acquires immense power, because he is receiving the power of each person to defend every other person. As Hobbes says, "The greatest of human powers, is that which is compounded of the powers of most men, united by consent, in one person, natural, or civil" (EW, 3:74). *Mirabile dictu*, while each person thereby retains his right to defend himself, he also acquires the collective power of every other person to defend him, because they have also transferred their rights to defend him to the sovereign. In effect, one must lose one's right to defend others in order to gain the security of being defended by others.

On the revision I am suggesting, the citizens retain authority over the sovereign whom they authorize, but he acquires the power he needs to do the job for which he is appointed. Most scholars sympathetic with Hobbes's greatness as a philosopher should be willing to sacrifice his explicit theory of authorization for the one he implies in other places.

SOVEREIGNTY BY INSTITUTION AND SOVEREIGNTY BY ACQUISITION

Covenants originate in two ways: either at the initiation of the covenanters or at the initiation of a person who has the power to dictate who the sovereign will be.[12] When the covenanters themselves initiate the covenant, they covenant because they can foresee that their long-term prospects in the state of nature are bad. The resulting government is called "sovereignty by institution." When a person with irresistible power initiates the covenant, the covenanters act because they are threatened with immediate death from the person with power. The resulting government is called "sovereignty by acquisition."

The difference between them is insignificant at bottom, because "the rights, and consequences of sovereignty, are the same in both" (EW, 3:186; see also p. 185). If the difference appears significant, it may be because the cases of sovereignty by acquisition are the historically more conspicuous ones. To take England as an example, the government of William the Conqueror was achieved through sovereignty by acquisition, as was that of Oliver Cromwell, on one interpretation of what happened as the eventual result of the Civil War. Thus, the distinction would seem not to be problematic. Unfortunately it is (e.g., Gauthier, 1969, p. 113). The responsibility lies in large part with Hobbes, because he does not treat the matter as clearly as he might have, and in no small part with the scholars, because they have not attended to the religious context of Hobbes's theory.

Here is Hobbes's summary account of the distinction:

> The attaining to this sovereign power, is by two ways. One, by natural force; as when a man maketh his children, to submit themselves, and their children to his government, as being able to destroy them if they refuse; or by war subdueth his enemies to his will, given them their lives on that condition. The other, is when men agree amongst themselves, to submit to some man, or assembly of men, voluntarily, on confidence to be protected by him against all others. This latter may be called a political commonwealth, or commonwealth by *institution*; and the former, a commonwealth by *acquisition*. (EW, 3:159)

The example of a father threatening his children with death may be misleading, since Hobbes also says that children, like madmen, are incapable of making contracts (EW, 3:257). One way of reconciling the two discussions is to hold that the children being threatened with death are adolescents, old enough to make covenants but not yet strong enough to challenge the father, whereas the children incapable of making contracts have not yet attained the age of reason. In any case, the distinction between the two ways of achieving sovereignty is clear enough.

Hobbes's discussion of sovereignty by institution in chapters 18 and 19 is inconsequential and unexceptionable, for our purposes. The problems arise solely in connection with his discussion of sovereignty by acquisition in chapter 20, "Of Dominion Paternal and Despotical."

Here is what Hobbes might have said: in sovereignty by acquisition, some force, either a person or group of people, successfully attacks another person or a group of people. (For the sake of simplicity, I shall hereafter assume that many people are attacked.) When the defeated people are at the brink of death, they have two options. They can either covenant with the attackers, or they can die.[13] If they choose death, that is the end of the matter. If they choose to covenant, then they covenant *with each other*, just as in sovereignty by institution, to make someone their sovereign. Who that "someone" will be is dictated by the conquerors.

Hobbes's account becomes confusing at this point, because he does not make explicit that the conqueror can dictate either of two possible arrangements. One possibility is for the conquerors to incorporate the defeated people as citizens into the nation of the attackers. Hobbes says that the ancient Romans sometimes did this. And James I tried to do this when he became king of both England and Scotland (EW, 3:184, 6:43–4). But he failed, because the Scots demanded that they keep their own Parliament, separate from the English Parliament (EW, 6:43). Nonetheless, Hobbes thinks that any two nations that are ruled by the same sovereign ought to be treated in the same way by that sovereign (EW, 3:190–1, 6:44). The United States incorporated a conquered people as citizens when it captured Puerto Rico from the Spanish but does not treat them the same as citizens. In any case, when the conquered are incorporated into the conquering nation, there is in effect a new covenant made among all of the people involved, both the conquerors and the conquered, and one expanded nation results.

The other arrangement that the conquerors can dictate is this. They can require that the conquered people covenant among themselves to choose as their sovereign only the entire conquering people. Often the conquerors appoint a "governor" or "president" or "procurator" to administer the government, but this person is only a minister or agent of the genuine sovereign, who, according to Hobbes, is the entire population of the conquerors. Although this may give the impression that the government of the conquered people is a democracy, that cannot be correct, says Hobbes, because a democracy is a kind of self-rule and a conquered people under this arrangement is not ruling itself. Rather, as Hobbes explains, the conquered people are ruled by a monarch: "For though where the people are governed by an assembly, chosen by themselves out of their own number, the government is called a democracy, or aristocracy; yet when they are governed by an assembly, not of their own choosing, it is a monarchy; not of *one* man, over another man; but of one people, over another people" (EW, 3:180; see also pp. 178–9). On this account, although the sovereign dictates the terms of the covenant, neither he nor the citizens that he represents are parties to it. That is, a new government is established among the defeated people. Hobbes sometimes suggests that this is his preferred account (EW, 3:178; see also pp. 179–80). He says that in this situation the new government is always a monarchy, no matter what form of government the attacking nation may have had. According to Hobbes, a new civil state comes into existence with the conquest. That is, suppose England had conquered French Canada and forced the French Canadians to take George I as their sovereign. In this situation, the man George I would have been sovereign over two nations. This situation also seems to have obtained when William I conquered England. The English did not become Normans, and the Normans did not become Englishmen.[14] To move to a sublime case, God seems to have been in this situation three or four thousand years ago, insofar as he was sovereign over all humans by his natural power but sovereign over the Jews only by his covenant with them. (The fact that sovereigns are not supposed to be parties to the covenant does not seem to bother Hobbes in this context.)

Hobbes's view of sovereignty by acquisition is not difficult in itself, even though his presentation of it is unclear. However, the proper interpretation of his view also requires an understanding of the religious content of his thought. I have already shown various ways in which Hobbes either validates his view by appealing to biblical or standard Christian doctrines or adapts these doctrines to his own moral and political theory. He does the latter here.

Scholars sometimes comment on the apparent oddity of Hobbes's use of the term "servant" to refer to a citizen, in his discussion of sovereignty by acquisition, since his preferred term in other contexts is "subject." Hampton attributes this usage to his view that citizens lack all political rights. This leads her to slide from Hobbes's term "servant" to the term "slave," even though Hobbes is careful to distinguish between servants and slaves. While Hampton is correct to think that Hobbes wants to emphasize the absoluteness of the sovereign, she does not appreciate what lies behind Hobbes's use of the word "servant," namely, his intention to validate his view by appealing to certain biblical events. And the biblical account of these events uses this word.

Halfway through the chapter on sovereignty by acquisition, Hobbes says, "Let us now consider what Scripture teacheth in the same point" (EW, 3:191). "The same point" ought to be the point discussed in the immediately preceding paragraph. But it is not. The preceding paragraph talks about the difference between a family and a kingdom, and I conjecture that Hobbes inserted this paragraph after the rest of the chapter had been written. For if one excises that paragraph, then the chapter coheres. The paragraph containing "the same point," and the entire second half of the chapter, concern biblical events and injunctions bearing upon the nature of sovereignty. If we delete the paragraph about the difference between a family and a kingdom, then the preceding paragraph discusses "the rights and consequences of both *paternal* and *despotical* dominion," which Hobbes says "are the very same with those of a sovereign by institution" (EW, 3:190). That is, the second half of chapter 20 is a biblically based proof of his views about sovereignty by acquisition.

Hobbes begins his biblical proof with a quotation from Exodus: "Speak thou to us, and we will hear thee; but let not God speak to us, lest we die" (Ex. 20:19; EW, 3:191). He says that this expresses the Hebrews' "absolute obedience" to Moses, although it could also have been used to require that no covenant be made with God except through the sovereign. His next quotation, the longest in the chapter, comes from 1 Samuel (8:11–17):

> This shall be the right of the king you will have to reign over you. He shall take your sons, and set them to drive his chariots, and to be his horsemen, and to run before his chariots; and gather his harvest; and to make his engines of war, and instruments of his chariots; and shall take your daughters to make perfumes, to be his cooks, and bakers. He shall take your fields, your vine-yards, and your olive-yards, and give them to your servants. He shall take the tithe of your corn and wine, and give it to the men of his chamber, and to his other servants. He shall take your man-servants, and your maid-servants, and the choice of your youth, and employ them in his business. He shall take the tithe of your flocks; and you shall be his servants.

It is ironic that Hobbes should use this quotation in this context. For the speaker, the prophet Samuel, is arguing against instituting Saul as monarch because of the possible sad consequences, which he rehearses. Later Hobbes quotes the same passage as evidence that the Jews rebelled against God as their sovereign and instituted Saul as their monarch in order to be "like the nations." Hobbes does not seem to be aware that there are in the Bible two different but parallel accounts of Samuel's attitude toward the appointment of Saul as king, one favorable and one unfavorable. And, to repeat, it is ironic that Hobbes should draw upon the unfavorable account in his discussion of the nature of sovereignty. It is ironic, but understandable; his purpose here is to emphasize the absoluteness of the sovereign.

Many of the other biblical quotations that he adduces for support of his view are predictable, especially: "Servants, obey your masters in all things" (Col. 3:30) and "give to Caesar that which is Caesar's" (EW, 3:193).

GOD AND COVENANTS

I have already argued that Hobbes's idea of covenants was influenced by the idea in covenant theology and by the politicoreligious covenants of the Scottish Covenanters. In particular, Hobbes's concept of the sovereign as a representative person was so influenced. I have further suggested that the paradigm of Hobbes's idea of sovereignty is biblical. Just as God has sovereignty over humans in virtue of the natural, irresistible power of his omnipotence, a human sovereign has sovereignty over citizens in virtue of the artificial, overwhelming power contributed by the citizens.

God and human sovereigns are also similar in that neither one has duties toward his subjects, and consequently neither can act unjustly toward his subjects. The human sovereign is above justice, because he is not a party to the sovereign-making covenant. Since he does not transfer any right to anyone through a covenant, he does not lose his natural right to all things but only gains the right and power contributed by the covenanting people. God's situation is different. He is above justice simply by virtue of his natural omnipotence.

It would seem that God could not enter into covenants at all, or at least would not, since he has nothing to gain from them. However, God's role in covenants is central to both Judaism and Christianity, and Hobbes has a lot to say about them. Prior to reading his accounts of these covenants, we might expect him to try to make them consistent with what he has already said about covenants. For example, it would seem that God could not be a party to a sovereign-making covenant, because he could not agree to make someone other than himself sovereign. And if there were a sovereign-making covenant, from which God becomes a sovereign over a particular people, it would seem that God could not be a party to it under pain of acquiring duties toward the people with whom he covenants. Unfortunately, Hobbes's discussion of God's role in covenants does not seem to satisfy our expectation. I shall discuss this issue further in Chapter 10.

Part III

Religion within the limits of science and politics

Chapter 7

God

I argued in Chapters 3 and 4 that Hobbes uses the idea of God in his divine command theory of morality, and in Chapters 5 and 6 I asserted that he uses many theological concepts in his theory of politics. In this chapter, I want to discuss what Hobbes says about three related topics: human knowledge of God; the Trinity; and the relation between faith and reason.[1]

THE LIMITS OF KNOWLEDGE OF GOD

It is important to distinguish among three claims:

(1) People have no idea of God.
(2) People have no knowledge of God's nature or essence.
(3) People have no knowledge of God.

Hobbes asserts propositions (1) and (2), but denies (3). Some medieval and early modern theologians asserted (1); most would have denied it, but largely because their criterion of having an idea of something was looser than Hobbes's. It is a matter of conjecture, but I think that if they accepted Hobbes's stringent condition on what counts as an idea of something, they too would have asserted it. Proposition (2) has been a standard claim within Christian theology from the Middle Ages to the present. Virtually all theologians denied (3). In short, Hobbes's position on the three propositions is quite in line with the tradition of Christian theology.

Let's consider these propositions more closely, beginning with (1).

No idea of God

Hobbes says,

> Whatsoever we imagine is *finite*. Therefore there is no idea, or conception of any thing we call *infinite*. No man can have in his mind an image of infinite magnitude; nor conceive infinite swiftness, infinite time, or infinite force, or infinite power. When we say any thing is infinite, we signify only, that we are not able to conceive the ends, and bounds of the thing named; having no conception of the thing, but of our own inability. (EW, 3:17)

The reason Hobbes thinks that humans can have no idea of God is that all human ideas are analyzable or reducible to sensations and that God cannot be sensed. There is nothing radical in this view. Hobbes inherited it indirectly from the dominant medieval tradition. Anselm of Canterbury, who was the most optimistic theologian about the prospects for proving things about God, begins his *Proslogion* with a long, prayful lament that seems to say the same thing Hobbes said. Only a small part of it needs to be quoted here:

> Speak now, my whole heart; speak now to God; I seek your countenance; Your countenance, O Lord, do I seek. So come now, Lord my God, teach, my heart where and how to seek You, where and how to find You. If you are not here, Lord, where shall I seek You in Your absence? But if You are everywhere, why do I not behold You in Your presence? Surely You dwell in light inaccessible. Yet, where is this inaccessible light? O how shall I approach unto a light inaccessible? Or who will lead me to and into this light so that in it I may behold You? Again, in what signs or appearances shall I seek You? Never have I seen You, O Lord my God; I am not acquainted with Your countenance. What shall this Your distant exile do? . . . He pants to see You, but Your face is too far removed from him. He desires to approach You, but Your

dwelling place is inaccessible. He desires to find You but does not know Your abode. He longs to seek for You but does not know Your countenance. O Lord, You are my God and my Lord; yet never have I seen You. (Anselm of Canterbury, 1077, chapter 1)

Anselm's point is the same as the one I attributed to Hobbes: since all knowledge arises from the senses and since God cannot be an object of sensation, it seems that there cannot be any knowledge of God at all. Anselm's own answer to this difficult problem is to claim that a great deal of information about God can be deduced from the definition of God that he has discovered in the Bible, namely, that God is "that than which a greater cannot be conceived." It is from this nonsensory description of God that Anselm purports to prove his existence and all the standard properties that God is thought to possess, such as omnipotence, omniscience, and omnibenevolence.

Anselm tells us that soon after the distribution of the *Proslogion*, a monk named "Gaunilo" criticized Anselm's ontological argument on the ground that no human has an idea of God. Gaunilo said,

I also cannot think of God Himself. . . . For neither am I acquainted with God Himself nor am I able to infer [what God is like] by reference to some other similar being, since, as even you maintain, God is such that there cannot be anything similar to Him. . . . I cannot at all think of God except only with respect to the word. (Quoted from Anselm, 1077, p. 117)

Anselm contested the point. He thought it must be true that Christians have some concept of God and that the description "that than which a greater cannot be conceived" expressed what Bertrand Russell would have called "knowledge by description." What is at issue between Anselm and Gaunilo is how broadly or narrowly the word "idea" should be used. Anselm wants it to be used broadly, in order to ensure that humans can be said to have an idea of God, even though this idea is nonsensory. Gaunilo wanted to restrict the use of the word "idea" to those mental entities that have sensory content and thus thought that humans have no idea of God.

Hobbes's use of the term "idea" is similar to Gaunilo's, and hence they both hold that humans have no idea of God. Anselm's view differs only verbally from theirs. For all three would agree that there is no idea of God, in the sense of having sensory knowledge of him.

Many philosophers and theologians thought that Anselm had engineered a theology upon too thin a foundation, and after his death he was all but forgotten until the early thirteenth century. Many theologians, including Aquinas, argued that the ontological argument and the subsequent deductions are not cogent, because Anselm illicitly used the description "that than which a greater cannot be conceived" to extend human knowledge about God. They held that that description could not even be the basis for proving that God exists. Aquinas was as sensitive to the problem of explaining how humans can have knowledge of God as Anselm and Hobbes were, and for the same reason. All human knowledge begins from the senses, and there cannot be any sensory knowledge of God.

Sometime after the fourteenth century, skeptical concerns were added to the traditional reasons for claiming that humans have relatively little knowledge of God. These skeptical elements were used by both Roman Catholic and Protestant thinkers, each for their own purposes against the other. Of the Catholic thinkers who contributed to this tradition, Montaigne and Charron are two of the most important. Charron, for example, says,

> [I]t is an error to think of finding any reasons which are sufficient and demonstrative enough to prove and establish evidently and necessarily what deity is. We ought not to be surprised at this, but we should rather be surprised if such reasons could be found. For it is not possible that the powers of human nature or the capacities of creatures can go that far. . . . Deity is that which cannot be known or even per-

ceived. From the finite to the infinite there is no comparison, no transition. Infinity is totally inaccessible, even imperceptible. God is the one, true, and only infinite.[2] (Quoted from Bayle, 1702, p. 284)

Hobbes was not trying to follow any Roman Catholic tradition, either medieval or modern. He was committed to the Calvinist tradition, which, ironically, is a continuation of an important strand of medieval theology. Calvin held that a human being "has no power to be able to comprehend the true knowledge of God as is proper. . . . But on the contrary, if he is left by God to what he is by nature, he is only able to live in ignorance" (Calvin, 1536, p. 27; see also Calvin, 1559, II.2.20–1). So far as knowing God is concerned, "[T]he greatest geniuses are blinder than moles" (Calvin, 1559, II.2.18). The biblical basis for Calvin's denial that humans have anything more than a few "droplets of truth" about God are the opening words of John's Gospel: "Life was in God from the beginning and that life was the light of men; this light shines in the darkness, but the darkness comprehends it not" (quoted from Calvin, 1559, II.2.19). Thus, when Bramhall begins his attack on Hobbes with the claim that "The image of God is not altogether defaced by the fall of man, but that there will remain some practical notions of God and goodness," he attacks an entire Reformation tradition, even though he gives the impression that Hobbes is espousing an idiosyncratic view (EW, 4:283).[3]

In addition to theologians, seventeenth-century philosophers agreed that in a strict sense God cannot be conceived. Even Descartes, who used some sort of conception of God to prove his existence, conceded to Hobbes that it is a Christian doctrine that God "cannot be conceived of" (Hobbes, 1641, p. 133). Since both Hobbes and Descartes have been suspected of secret irreligion, it is worth mentioning that the religiously unimpeachable Bishop Berkeley, writing in the eighteenth century, also held that all knowledge arises from sensation and that consequently there can be no idea of God. Berkeley says,

No idea therefore can be like unto, or represent the nature of God. . . . I have properly no idea, either of God or any other spirit. . . . [H]is nature therefore is incomprehensible to finite spirits. It is not therefore to be expected, that any man, whether *materialist* or *immaterialist*, should have exactly just notions of the Diety, his attributes, and ways of operation. (Berkeley, 1713, pp. 65, 86; cf. Berkeley, 1732, pp. 163–70; see also Hume, 1751, p. 152)

No knowledge of the nature of God

Let's now consider proposition (2), namely, that people have no knowledge of the nature of God. To know the nature of an object is to know what that object is in itself or what it is necessarily. To know something about an object, but not its nature, is to know what is accidental and extraneous to its essence or to know it in relation to other things. This distinction between knowing the nature of a thing and knowing extraneous properties of a thing is related to Locke's distinction between "real" and "nominal" essences. The distinction can be illustrated using a contemporary example. Having an atomic number of 2 and being composed of two atoms of hydrogen and one of oxygen are properties relevant to knowing the nature of things. But being odorless and colorless are properties relevant to the nominal essence of things. No human can know the real essence of God, because no one can be acquainted with him.[4] Virtually every medieval and modern theologian affirmed proposition (2). For example, Aquinas says that God's essence cannot be known (e.g., *Summa Theologiae* I, 12, articles 3–4, 12). Among English theologians contemporary with Hobbes, William Ames says in *The Marrow of Theology* that God cannot be understood as he is in himself by anyone except himself (Ames, 1629, p. 83; see also Cavendish, 1664, p. 139).

One consequence of holding that humans can have no knowledge of God's nature or essence is that they are also incapable of defining him. John Preston, in *Life Eternall, or, A Treatise of the Knowledge of the Divine Essence and Attributes*, says that God's nature "is capable properly of no definition" (Preston, 1634, part 1, p. 94). The idea that God is indefinable so pervades the Reformation tradition that Heinrich Heppe, one of its classic expositors, says, "Of course, man cannot discern the nature of this single God. . . . Whence also no real definition of God is possible" (Heppe, 1950, p. 52).[5]

Knowledge of God without an idea of God

Let's now consider proposition (3). To hold either that humans cannot know the nature of God or that they do not have an idea of God because they do not have a sense-based image that is proper to God is not to hold that it is impossible to understand and to assert true propositions about him. Having a proper idea of something is not a necessary condition for asserting things about it. For example, Hobbes points out that it is impossible to conceive of infinite division and to have an image of a quantity that is infinitely small; yet it is certain that there are such entities, and mathematics and physics are filled with talk of such entities (Hobbes, 1643, pp. 29–30). In general, Hobbes believes that it is a mistake to think that "infinity ought to be represented in mind by means of an image as though it were something positive" (ibid., p. 340). Hobbes makes this comment in the context of a discussion of motion, but it applies equally well to God. In short, to say that God is infinite is not to hold that nothing true can be said about him.

To say that God is infinite is to make an ontological claim. To make the corresponding epistemological claim is to say that God is incomprehensible, as Hobbes occasionally does (EW, 3:17, 97, 420). The import of saying that God is incomprehensible is to say that human knowledge does not adequately represent the nature of God. On another level, it is partially to affirm one's creatureliness and subordinateness to God. For a human to claim to comprehend God would not only be false, it would be blasphemous. Thus, to affirm the incomprehensibility of God was standard among both medieval and modern Christian thinkers: cases in point are Hugh, archbishop of Rouen (McGrath, 1986, 1:68); John Preston (Preston, 1634, part 1, p. 94); Robert Vilvain (Vilvain, 1654, p. 230); Margaret Cavendish (1664, pp. 140–1); and Berkeley (Berkeley, 1713, pp. 65, 86; cf. Berkeley, 1732, pp. 163–70; see also Hume, 1751, p. 152). In short, it is spurious to use Hobbes's claim that God is incomprehensible as evidence that Hobbes was in some way irreligious.

THE EXISTENCE OF GOD

If it is certain that humans cannot have any knowledge of God's essence and certain that they cannot have any sense-based idea that is proper to God, one might wonder what reason there is to believe that God exists at all. This question can be understood in two, related ways. In one way, it asks whether there can be a proof for the existence of God. In another way, it asks less formally for the basis upon which one can confidently believe that there is a God.

Let's consider the latter first. According to Hobbes, the basis for believing in God is strictly analogous to the basis for believing in bodies. He says that people who inquire into natural causes are led to believe in God

> though they cannot have any idea of him in their mind, answerable to his nature. For as a man that is born blind, hearing men talk of warming themselves by the fire, and being brought to warm himself by the same, may easily conceive, and assure himself, there is somewhat there, which men call *fire*, and is the cause of the heat he feels; but cannot imagine what it is like; nor have an idea of it in his mind, such as they have that see it: so also by the visible things in this world, and their admirable order, a man may conceive there is a cause of them, which men call God; and yet not have an idea, or image of him in his mind. (EW, 3:93)

Since the only things to which humans have direct cognitive access are their own ideas, belief in bodies must be an inference, but one that is completely justified. One cannot imagine the opposite (Hobbes, 1640, p. 7). Hobbes is not willing to allow a genuine agnosticism about the nature of God to deteriorate into atheism. Our limited knowledge about God is similar to our limited knowledge of the nature of bodies: "[T]he principles of natural science . . . are so far from teaching us anything of God's nature, as they cannot teach us our own nature, nor the nature of the smallest creature living" (EW, 3:354; see also 7:81, and Hobbes, 1639, p. 150).

What I have described as the informal basis for belief in God is similar to, but perhaps not exactly the same as, a proof for the existence of God. Hobbes believes that there is such a proof, and again his belief fits into a long and honorable tradition. Since God's nature cannot be known and there is no proper idea of God, all human knowledge about God derives from the effects of his actions. Aquinas says that God can be known only through "his relationship with creatures, that is, that he is the cause of all things."[6] Reformed theologians followed medieval ones in this matter. Cocceius (Johannes Koch) says the only possible way that humans can know God is "by His effects, and by His name by which He Himself willed to manifest His excellences to us" (quoted from Heppe, 1950, p. 54). Hobbes uses the cause–effect relation as the basis for one of his proofs for the existence of God:

> For the effects we acknowledge naturally, do necessarily include a power of their producing, before they were produced; and that power presupposeth something existent that hath such power; and the thing so existing with power to produce, if it were not eternal, must needs have been produced by somewhat before it; and that again by something else before that: till we come to an eternal, that is to say, to the first power of all powers, and first cause of all causes. And this is it which all men call by the name of GOD: implying eternity, incomprehensibility, and omnipotency. And thus all men that will consider, may naturally know that God is, though not what he is; even as a man though born blind, though it be not possible for him to have any imagination what kind of thing is

fire; yet he cannot but know that something there is that men call fire, because it warmeth him. (Hobbes, 1640, p. 54; Hobbes, 1641, p. 127)

The hunt for the end of the chain of causes and effects is characteristic, not of the superstitious person, but of the scientific mind:

Curiosity, or love of the knowledge of causes, draws a man from the consideration of the effect, to seek the cause; and again, the cause of that cause; till of necessity he must come to this thought at last, that there is some cause, whereof there is no former cause, but is eternal; which is it men call God. So that it is impossible to make any profound inquiry into natural causes, without being inclined thereby to believe there is one God eternal. (EW, 3:93; see also 4:59–60, and Hobbes, 1641, p. 127)

Here is another version of the same argument:

But the acknowledging of one God, eternal, infinite, and omnipotent, may more easily be derived, from the desire men have to know the causes of natural bodies, and their several virtues, and operations; than from the fear of what was to befall them in time to come. For he that from any effect he seeth come to pass, should reason to the next and immediate cause thereof, and from thence to the cause of that cause, and plunge himself profoundly in the pursuit of causes; shall at last come to this, that there must be, as even the heathen philosophers confessed, one first mover; that is, a first and an eternal cause of all things; which is that which men mean by the name of God. (EW, 3:96, 4:59–60)

This proof is similar to one of Aquinas's Five Ways. The major difference is that Hobbes has stripped away its Aristotelian trappings.

Hobbes's proof is not sophisticated or especially interesting philosophically. He is content to rehearse a standard argument. However, one additional comment is required. It may appear that Hobbes's proof entails that the universe has been in existence a finite period of time. But Hobbes thinks it does not. He, like Aquinas, denies that the creation of the world in time can be proven. John Wallis attacked Hobbes for holding this position but never mentions that Hobbes is in complete accord with Aquinas. In *De Corpore* Hobbes says,

> [T]hough from this, that nothing can move itself, it may right-ly be inferred that there was some first eternal movent; yet it can never be inferred, though some used to make such in-ference, that that movent was eternally immoveable, but rather eternally moved. For as it is true, that nothing is moved by itself; so it is true also, that nothing is moved but by that which is already moved. The questions therefore about the magnitude and beginning of the world, are not to be deter-mined by philosophers, but by those that are lawfully autho-rized to order the worship of God.[7] (EW, 1:412, 414, 4:427–8; cf. 3:351; Aquinas, *Summa Theologiae*, I, 46, 2, c)

THE NATURE AND LIMITS OF TALK ABOUT GOD

The limits of cognitive talk about God

We began this chapter by considering the rather stringent limits on human knowledge of God: humans have no proper idea of God based upon sensation, and humans have no knowledge of the nature of God. We have recently come to see that there are some significant things that can be known about God. Hobbes thinks that humans can know that God exists and that his existence implies that he is infinite, eter-nal, incomprehensible, and omnipotent. Hobbes sometimes gives the impression that nothing more can be said about God. But other views that he espouses seem to commit him to holding that much more can be said about God, such as, that he is the author of the laws of nature and that he revealed himself to various people in the Bible. These are obviously relational predications, and less central within Judeo-Christian theology than the predicates already men-tioned. In any case, Hobbes must hold that at least some talk about God is both cognitively meaningful and true.

It might seem that Hobbes did not always speak unambiguously about what can be truly said about God. For example, in a relatively early philosophical work he wrote,

Personally, while I hold that the nature of God is unfathomable, and that propositions are a kind of language by which we express our concepts of the nature of things, I incline to the view that no proposition about the nature of God can be true save this one: God exists, and that no title correctly describes the nature of God other than the word "being" [*ens*]. (Hobbes 1643, p. 434)

Although the general thrust of this passage is clear, it may seem to include some oddity or imprecision. It was unusual in the seventeenth century to call an assertion of God's existence a "proposition about the nature of God." Usually a contrast was drawn between two issues: *whether* something is, and *what* it is. And it was conventional to say that people know that God exists, but not what he is. Hobbes said this in other places (EW, 3:383), as did some of his conservative critics, who were too obtuse to recognize that they and Hobbes held the same doctrine (Vilvain, 1654, p. 230). Only the issue of what an object is concerns its nature.

Also, Hobbes's remark that "no title correctly describes the nature of God other than the word 'being'" may seem odd. To attribute being to an object is tantamount to saying that it exists, so it may seem pleonastic for Hobbes to assert both that God exists and that he is being. Also, why should "being" be called a "title," and, given that it is a title, why say that it "describes" God? The oddity and apparent imprecision disappear if one assumes that Hobbes is a devout, biblically rooted Christian. In this passage Hobbes is alluding to the revelation given to Moses on Mount Sinai. When Moses asked which god was speaking to him, God replied, "I am Yahweh." "Yahweh" is often taken as a proper name, but it is not strictly a proper name. The name "Yahweh" in Hebrew literally means "what is," and when the Hebrew Bible was translated into Greek, the word "Yahweh" was not transliterated; it was translated. Thus, "I am Yahweh" was often understood to mean "I am what is" or "I am being."[8] This is the import of Hobbes's remark. He is alluding to the biblical designation of God. This designation is not a proper name, because it is descriptive. In contrast, "Sitting Bull" is a genuine proper name, because that term was not meant to be literally true of Sitting Bull. But "Yahweh" is not merely a description, because God uses it as a term to refer to himself alone. The linguistic category that is logically halfway between being a proper name and a description is a title. Thus, "Being" or "Yahweh" is similar to "The President of the United States" or "The Prime Minister of England." On the one hand, it is proper to an individual; on the other hand, it correctly describes the titleholder.

Nonliteral talk about God

Granted that some talk about God is cognitively meaningful and true, the scope of literal truths about God is quite limited, according to Hobbes. Again, in holding this position, Hobbes is not an innovator but merely one member of a long tradition of Christian philosophers and theologians. For example, William Ames, who was mentioned earlier, held that human discourse about God is anthropomorphic (Ames, 1629, p. 83). William Perkins, fellow of Christ College and a leading exponent of Puritan theology, claimed that nothing that human beings predicate of God is literally true: "[E]ven the virtues of reasonableness or justice, as human beings conceive them, could not be predicated of God" (quoted from Miller, 1935, p. 52).[9] Without trying to diminish the important break between Reformation and medieval theology, I want to show that Hobbes, Ames, and Perkins are similar to Anselm of Canterbury and Aquinas in their views about the limits of literal talk concerning God.

Anselm of Canterbury denies that God is literally merciful, on the grounds that to be merciful entails that a person feels sad, whereas God, being perfect, cannot feel sad. God is said to be merciful figuratively, because he does good things for humans. God is also not literally perceptive, because being perceptive entails having a body and God has none. He is said to be perceptive as a courtesy, for he has a power greater than perception. Furthermore, God is not literally everywhere, again because only material objects can be in a place. God is said to be everywhere only because he causes everything everywhere to exist. Anselm says that God has his properties "ineffably," because human beings have no direct cognitive access to him (Anselm of Canterbury, 1077, chapters 8, 6, 17, 19; cf. EW, 3:351, 647). The limits that the cognitive inaccessibility of God impose on literal talk about God are recognized by Hobbes and Anselm equally, and they offer similar explanations as to why ordinary talk about God is justified.

The difference between Anselm and Hobbes is that Anselm thinks that God is immaterial and Hobbes does not.[10] While this is an important difference with regard to their beliefs about the nature of God, it is relatively unimportant with regard to their beliefs about the limits of human discourse about God; for Anselm and Hobbes agree about the connection between various aspects of God and the restrictions on human cognition. Hobbes says that no passion that involves grief, such as mercy, can be literally attributed to God, for everything that can suffer is limited in power. Similarly, God does not literally have knowledge in the same sense that humans do, because human knowledge is a "tumult of the mind, raised by external things that press the organical parts of man's body" (EW, 3:352; see also 5:213), and God is not affected by natural causes (Anselm, 1077, chapters 6, 8–9). Also, like Anselm, Hobbes is willing to allow the propriety of saying such things as that God "sees" even though he has no eyes or "speaks" even though he has no tongue, on the same grounds that King David did:

> The prophet David argueth thus, (*Psalm xciv.9*) *Shall he that had made the eye, not see? or he that made the ear, not hear?* But this may be spoken not as usually, to signify God's nature, but to signify our intention to honour him. For to *see*, and *hear* are

honourable attributes, and may be given to God, to declare, as
far as our capacity can conceive, his almighty power. (EW,
3:415, 4:60)

Like Anselm, Aquinas also severely restricts the scope of
what truths can be literally said of God. Although humans
can speak truly about God because their language succeeds
in referring to him, their words "do not properly and strictly
apply to God; for their mode of signification befits creatures"
(*Summa Theologiae*, I, 13, 3, c). Aquinas, however, differs
from Anselm in his theory about what nonliteral talk about
God means. He says that when humans talk about God their
words do not mean the same as they do when the words are
used in their ordinary senses. Not thinking about his earlier
claims concerning the existence and power of God, Aquinas
says that talk about God is not purely equivocal but that it is
analogical (*Summa Theologiae*, I, 13, 5, c).[11]

Anselm and Aquinas have been chosen for special attention both because of their own philosophical acuity and because of their theological respectability. Many other medieval thinkers could have been selected. Alan of Lille denied
that predicates applied literally to God, and William of
Ockham denied that human predicates correspond to anything in God (McGrath, 1986, 1:67–9). Thus, Hobbes's position that literal truths about God are limited is well within
the scope of the orthodox Christian tradition. Hobbes differs
from it, not as regards how much can be truly said about
God, but in his theory about the nature of the talk that is not
literally true, just as Aquinas and Anselm differ from each
other.

Honorific talk about God

According to Hobbes, most talk about God is honorific:
"[T]he attributes we give him [God], are not to tell one another, *what he is*, nor to signify our opinion of his nature, but
our desire to honour him with such names as we conceive

most honourably amongst ourselves" (EW, 3:383; see also p. 17, and 4:60).[12] My guess is that Hobbes was inspired to make this claim by Calvin. In *The Catechism of the Church of Geneva*, Calvin wrote that people should never speak or think "about God and his works except to honour him" (Calvin, 1954, p. 111; see also p. 124). This is in line with what he said in the *Institutes:* "[T]he knowledge of God does not rest in cold speculation, but carries with it the honouring of him" (Calvin, 1559, I.12.1; see also Berkeley, 1732, pp. 163–5, and Miller, 1935, p. 51).

One of the worst excesses of the speculative theological mind that leads to dishonoring God, according to Hobbes and Calvin, is the doctrine of transubstantiation. Hobbes thinks it is incoherent because it claims to explain how one and the same body could be in many places at once. Hobbes concludes his diatribe against the theologians by describing them as intellectual bumblers:

> And these are but a small part of the incongruities they are forced to, from their disputing philosophically, instead of admiring, and adoring of the divine and incomprehensible nature; whose attributes cannot signify what he is, but ought to signify our desire to honour him, with the best appellations we can think on. For they that venture to reason of his nature, from these attributes of honour, losing their understanding in the very first attempt, fall from one inconvenience into another, without end, and without number; in the same manner, as when a man ignorant of ceremonies of court, coming into the presence of a greater person than he is used to speak to, and stumbling at his entrance, to save himself from falling, lets slip his cloak; to recover his cloak, lets fall his hat; and with one disorder after another, discovers his astonishment and rusticity. (EW, 3:678)

I sense in this passage the quiet fury of a person outraged that God should be dishonored by impertinent speculations about the deity (cf. Milner, 1988, p. 412–13).

A contemporary religious thinker (whose name I no longer recall) once said, in criticism of theology, that the problem with humans is that they talk *about* God instead of *to* God. Hobbes had made the same complaint three centuries earlier: "[W]hen men out of the principles of natural reason, dispute of the attributes of God, they but dishonour him: for in the attributes which we give to God, we are not to consider the signification of philosophic truth; but the signification of pious intention, to do him the greatest honour we are able" (EW, 3:354).

Hobbes may have given the mistaken impression that the line between literally true language about God and honorific language about God is sharper than it really is. In fact, there is a coincidence between much of it. Hobbes's own justification for much talk about God seems to blur the line between honor and truth. Because Hobbes is often thought to have suspiciously little to say about God, it is important to quote a large part of Hobbes's summary of what can be said about God and why:

> That we may know what worship of God is taught us by the light of nature, I will begin with his attributes. Where, first, it is manifest, we ought to attribute to him *existence*. For no man can have the will to honour that, which he thinks not to have any being.
>
> Secondly, that those philosophers, who said the world, or the soul of the world was God, spake unworthily of him; and denied his existence. For by God, is understood the cause of the world; and to say the world is God, is to say there is no cause of it, that is, no God.
>
> Thirdly, to say the world was not created, but eternal, seeing that which is eternal has no cause, is to deny there is a God.
>
> Fourthly, that they who attributing, as they think, ease to God, take from him the care of mankind; take from him his honour; for it takes away men's love, and fear of him; which is the root of honour.
>
> Fifthly, in those things that signify greatness, and power; to say he is *finite*, is not to honour him: for it is not a sign of the will to honour God, to attribute to him less than we can; because to finite, it is easy to add more.

Therefore, to attribute *figure* to him, is not honour; for all figure is finite;

Nor to say we conceive, and imagine, or have an *idea* of him, in our mind: for whatsoever we conceive is finite:

Nor to attribute to him *parts,* or *totality;* which are the attributes only of things finite:

Nor to say he is in this, or that *place:* for whatsoever is in place, is bounded, and finite:

Nor that he is *moved,* or *resteth:* for both these attributes ascribe to him place.

Nor that there be more Gods than one; because it implies them all finite: for there cannot be more than one infinite:

Nor to ascribe to him, (unless metaphorically, meaning not the passion but the effect,) passions that partake of grief; as *repentance, anger, mercy* or of want; as *appetite, hope desire;* or of any passive faculty: for passion, is power limited by somewhat else.

And therefore when we ascribe to God a *will,* it is not to be understood, as that of man, for a *rational appetite;* but as the power, by which he effecteth everything. (EW, 3:350-2)

This passage continues for another page and concludes with the most striking biblical characterization of God: the way God revealed himself to Moses: "For there is but one name to signify our conception of his nature, and that is, I AM: and but one name of his relation to us, and that is, *God;* in which is contained Father, King, and Lord" (EW, 3:353; see also pp. 383-4).

Hobbes, like Anselm, knew that most ordinary talk about God is not literally true; and he, like Anselm, devised various explanations that would justify preserving the ordinary talk without being misled about its ultimate logical character. Hobbes is unlike Anselm in that he places almost all religious language outside the category of empirical or scientific language. In this regard, Hobbes is like Ian T. Ramsey, late Nolloth Professor of the Philosophy of the Christian Religion at Oxford, who argued that religious language is not empirical language but the language of "discernment" and "commitment." He, like Hobbes, sees religious language as essentially worshipful and not committed to occult entities. Ramsey says,

> The one "factual" reference it [theology] preserves is the one which alone matters, the one which is given in worship. God and his worship. . . . Need we trouble if we discover meanwhile that a whole heap of metaphysical furniture – underlying "substances," "indelible characteristics," and so on – which some might have supposed to be indispensable, has in fact belonged only to a confusing dream?
>
> I hope I have made it plain, then, that in theology we talk about a situation which, from the point of view of "what is seen," is empirically odd; a situation known best perhaps in what can be called compactly "worship"; a situation which is one of "discernment" and "commitment." (Ramsey, 1957, p. 216)

Both Hobbes and Ramsey were trying to reconcile Christian doctrine with the best science and philosophy of their day.

In short, Hobbes's explanation of what can be said about God is a sophisticated and astute defense of traditionally approved talk about the Judeo-Christian God. There would have been no purpose in his going to such length if his goal had been to undermine religion. And it is impossible that he should be insinuating that he does not believe in God at all. When he tries to rein in unbridled talk about God, it is because he correctly believes that such talk is not merely intellectually unjustified but is inclined to slander God: "To say God spake or appeared as he is in his own nature, is to deny his infiniteness, invisibility, incomprehensibility" (EW, 3: 419–20).

THE TRINITY

The secularist interpretation would have more force if Hobbes never said anything constructive about religious issues other than what has already been discussed. But just the opposite is true. He has constructive discussions of many such issues, several of which will be examined in later chapters. I shall discuss two of them in the remainder of this chapter: the doctrine of the Trinity, and the relation between faith and reason. In none of these discussions is there any indication that he intended to overthrow Christianity, even though his views in fact did have the consequence of undermining Christian belief. His intent, I shall argue, was to reconcile the content of religion with science and to have religion serve the interests of peace, not war.

In Chapter 6, we saw that Hobbes used his views about the nature of a person as a basis for his theory of the nature of sovereignty. In short, the sovereign "beareth the person" of the citizens insofar as the sovereign represents them (EW, 3:151). Even though the citizens are many, the sovereign makes them into one unit in virtue of the unity of his person. Immediately after defining what a person is and explaining the relationships among authors, actors, and authority, but before he explains the origin of the commonwealth – that is, in the thick of developing his political theory – Hobbes applies his theory of person to the doctrine of the Trinity.

The doctrine of the Trinity can be summarized in these propositions:

(1) There is one and only one God.
(2) The Father is God.
(3) The Son is God.
(4) The Holy Spirit is God.
(5) The Father is not identical with the Son.
(6) The Son is not identical with the Holy Spirit.
(7) The Father is not identical with the Holy Spirit.

It is easy to prove within first-order predicate calculus that propositions (1) through (7) are inconsistent several times over. For example, (1), (2), and (3) entail that the Father is identical with the Son, but this is contradicted by (5). And (1), (2), and (4) entail that the Father is identical with the Holy Spirit, but this is contradicted by (7). The history of trinitarian heresies is the history of attempts to eliminate these apparent inconsistencies. Usually a heretic ends up denying at least one of the propositions. Arius denied (3); he argued that the Son is not God but the first and greatest of God's creatures. Sabellius, in the opinion of the church leaders, denied (5) through (7). Tritheism is the denial of (1). The point here is that the doctrine of the Trinity appears to be inconsistent, and even if it is not inconsistent, it is difficult to show that it is consistent (see Martinich, 1978; Martinich, 1979). So, if someone tries to construct a theory that will render the doctrine consistent but fails, this is no evidence of disbelief in the doctrine itself. Not even Aquinas succeeded. He holds the patently inconsistent views that God is absolutely one and that there are three persons in God. But Aquinas was lucky in not running afoul of the church authorities on this matter, because of the studied piety of his language.

Secular interpreters of Hobbes often cast doubt on the sincerity of his religious views by charging that his doctrine of the Trinity is heretical, a version of Sabellianism. Even if we grant that his views are Sabellian, the concession works in his favor. None of the distinguished heretics of Christianity was antireligious. To the contrary, they were ardently religious and were struggling to make the apparently illogical doctrines of Christianity logical. Far from being evidence that they lacked religious faith, their heretical views are evidence of deep religious faith; they merely lost the theological war. In this regard, it should be mentioned that many of the doctrines of Aquinas were condemned by church officials soon after his death; it was only with some luck that his followers won the war for him after several centuries. To be a Sabellian is to have a false theory about the doctrine of the Trinity, but to have a false theory about a doctrine entails that one believes that doctrine. Many, perhaps most, self-professed Christian philosophers of the twentieth century are not even Sabellians in the sense that they do not accept the doctrine of the Trinity at all. So it is absurd to accuse Hobbes of some lukewarm theism when he struggled to save the doctrine of the Trinity. In short, if Hobbes were a Sabellian, then he believed in the Trinity; and if he believed in the Trinity, he was a sincere Christian.

Hobbes begins his discussion of the Trinity by contrasting false idols with the true God. He says that although idols can be personated, that is, some human can represent them, idols cannot be authors, since they do not genuinely exist (EW, 3:150). The true God, however, can be an author. Further, there are three persons who are God. The first person who is God, namely, the Father, is made a distinct person because he was represented by Moses. The second person who is God, namely, the Son, is made a person distinct from the Father, because he was represented by a distinct human, namely, Jesus. Finally, the third person who is God, namely, the Holy Spirit, is made a person distinct from the Father and the Son, because he is represented by a person distinct from Moses and Jesus, namely, the apostles (EW, 3:150–1; see also pp. 376–7, 486–9).

One of the impressive features of this account of the Trinity is that it relies upon concepts that Hobbes developed for purely nonreligious purposes. He did not devise some ad hoc concepts in order to explain the Trinity. Rather, he believes that a coherent account of the Trinity is available through the resources of his political theory, and he is not reluctant to present that account in the middle of presenting his political theory. Further, Hobbes draws an analogy that depends upon politics: just as the unity of the sovereign, who represents many people, makes a person, so the unity of the thing that represents God makes him into a person: "For it is the *unity* of the repres;enter, not the *unity* of the represented, that maketh the person *one*. And it is the representer that beareth the person, and but one person; and *unity*, cannot otherwise be understood in multitude" (EW, 3:151; see also pp. 377, 522–4; Halliday, Kenyon, and Reeve, 1983, pp. 422–3).

One might try to object that Hobbes's account of the Trinity is cynical, in that it reduces Jesus to the same level as Moses and the apostles. That is, Jesus constitutes the Second Person of the Trinity in exactly the same way that Moses constitutes the First Person of the Trinity and the apostles constitute the Third Person. Thus, since Jesus does not occupy any special or elevated role in Christianity, Christianity is undermined. This objection does not succeed. Insofar as the persons of the Trinity are constituted by persons that represent them, Jesus is the equal of Moses and the apostles. The church has never condemned a doctrine because it asserted that Jesus is equal to some other human beings in some respect. Indeed, the doctrine of the Incarnation entails that Jesus, insofar as he is human, is equal to all other humans. In addition, Jesus can be compared to Moses and the apostles in other ways that make clear his superiority. Insofar as Jesus is God and insofar as God is bodily in Jesus, Jesus is incomparably greater than either Moses or the apostles. Jesus is the only person representing God that Hobbes also says is God (EW, 3:420, 422). God is not just bodily in Jesus. Jesus is God and hence omnipotent (ibid., p. 481). In short, Hobbes insists that Jesus is not the equal of Moses (ibid., p. 420; cf. Warner, 1968–9).

I am not arguing that Hobbes's account of the Trinity is free from problems. It is not. For example, when the human who represents a multitude dies, that person ceases to exist unless someone else take up his person. So after Moses died, either the person who is the Father ceased to exist, which is heretical, or someone else bore the person of the Father. Even though Hobbes says that the high priests assumed the office of Moses, he also holds that no one represented the Father after the election of Saul to the kingship of Israel. So the person of the Father would have ceased to exist at that moment. Another problem concerns the ability of the apostles to represent anyone as a group. Since the unity of the thing represented depends upon the unity of the person representing them, the apostles would need to be a unity. But they can be unified only by a sovereign-making covenant, and they clearly are not so unified according to Hobbes's views. Thus, the apostles do not have the kind of unity that Hobbes normally requires of a person representing something. These criticisms do not render Hobbes's religious sincerity suspect to any degree. Due to the logical difficulties that the doctrine of the Trinity presents, almost any theory will be either inconsistent or heretical. What Hobbes has offered is a sophisticated attempt to render the doctrine both consistent and orthodox, and nothing more could be asked of either a philosopher or a dogmatic theologian. But Hobbes offers even more. He uses a central concept from his political theory as the key concept in his theory of the Trinity, and he presents his theory of the Trinity in the context of developing his political theory. It is clear that Hobbes did not see any reason to divorce theology from his general philosophical projects.

FAITH AND REASON

Historical background

So far I have been emphasizing Hobbes's continuity with the medieval and Reformation traditions of theology and arguing that Hobbes's own contribution to these traditions does not contain anything new that should tend to erode religious belief.[13] In the next topic that I want to consider, namely, the relation between faith and reason, Hobbes's views do contribute to an erosion of the credibility of religion.

Nevertheless, this fact does not constitute serious evidence to support the charge that Hobbes himself intended his theory to undermine religious belief. For his views are a plausible next step in a tradition of intellectuals trying to defend religion against the assault of secularizing reason. From at least the fourteenth century on, there arose in theological circles an attempt to separate faith from reason in order to save religion. Hobbes is part of this tradition of trying to save religious belief by immunizing it against the deadly arguments of reason.

As I said earlier, what characterizes medieval philosophy is the project of proving that the dogmas of Christianity are rational, either in the sense of being provable or at least of not being irrational. Anselm of Canterbury, the most optimistic of the medieval thinkers, believed that he could persuade any intelligent, fair-minded person, not only that God exists, is omnipotent, omniscient, and omnibenevolent, but also that three persons are one God and that God became a human being. After Anselm, medieval optimism began to shrink with each succeeding generation. Aquinas believed that the existence of God can be proven, but not the Trinity or the Incarnation. And William of Ockham did not believe that the God of Christianity can be proven to exist, although he did believe that a certain kind of God sought by philosophers can be proven to exist. It is difficult to be certain, but Hobbes's view may have been closer to Ockham's than to Aquinas's on this point.

The diminishing optimism that intellectuals had with respect to the ability of reason to prove the propositions of religion influenced their views about the relation between science (*scientia*) and religion. Aquinas had argued not only that theology is a science but that it is the highest science, because science requires certitude and nothing can be more certain than the propositions that God revealed. However, in the fourteenth century theologians began to argue that there is a difference between theology and science and that theology contains the higher and superior kind of knowledge. This is ironic, since the standard historical view is that science divorced theology.

The theologians involved here, typically nominalists and Ockhamists, argued that human knowledge about God is much more narrowly circumscribed than people often believe. Further, God in his omnipotence is able to make people believe that something is the case when in fact it is not. The motive of these theologians was to undercut the arrogance and pretension of human reason, which was moving toward modern science. The strategy was that if rationality could be subverted, then it could not overthrow religion, and people would need to fall back on faith as the only viable alternative. Thus, in place of rationalism in theology, these theologians advocated fideism. A good example of an advocate of theology divorcing science is Ockham's student Gregory of Rimini (1300–c.1358), according to whom science is restricted to the data it receives through the

senses, while theology has access to supernatural information. Thus, theology is not scientific but is above science. The
purpose of theology is to explain the Bible, and since belief in
the Bible rests upon divine revelation, theology has no rational foundation. (For more about this issue in the fourteenth and fifteenth centuries, see Leff, 1976; Oberman,
1967; and Oakeshott, 1957, pp. xx–xxvii.)

The movement to separate faith and reason (religion and
science) continued in the sixteenth century among both Reformers and Roman Catholics. We have already seen that
Calvin denigrated the ability of human reason to know anything about God's nature, owing to human sinfulness. He
was merely following, in his own way, Luther's refusal to
acknowledge any authority in religion other than the Bible. It
should be recalled that Luther either rejected or had serious
doubts about Copernicanism. On the Catholic side, Erasmus
castigated reason in order to save his religion. According to
Erasmus, reason can be no guide to religion. Humans must
rely upon an authority to specify what religious beliefs ought
to be held, and Erasmus opts for the authority of the Catholic
Church into which he was born. How can Hobbes be faulted
for preferring the church into which he was born, the
Church of England, especially when he also urges it in the
interests of domestic harmony?[14]

Erasmus has sometimes been accused of insincerity, precisely because he is willing to accept whatever the Catholic
church says, whether he understands the doctrines or not
(Erasmus, 1524, p. 6). But this is unfair to Erasmus and also
irrelevant, because of an important difference between Erasmus and Hobbes. It is unfair to Erasmus because there is
substantial evidence that he was trying to promote a simple
Christian piety to replace the arid and nonreligious speculations of scholastic thinkers. It is irrelevant because Erasmus
was reluctant to write anything about theology and avoided
debating Luther as long as he could. In contrast, Hobbes has
extensive, and often original, treatments of theological topics, all of which, as I shall be showing, are designed to save
the content of orthodox Christianity, no matter how things

turned out historically. Although Luther condemned the skepticism of Erasmus, Luther did not seek religious certainty in reason but in the Bible. So Luther and Erasmus agree in separating faith from reason.

As indicated earlier, Hobbes's own reservations about the power of reason alone to determine religious doctrines stem from his Calvinist background, inculcated both by his family and by his education at Magdalen Hall. As Eldon Eisenach has written,

> It was not Hobbes, but Reformation theology which so strictly bounded and separated the realms of faith and reason. Hobbes' critique of claims which mingled faith and reason – claims essential for the institutional church – do rest on a deep skepticism, but certainly this scepticism was matched and often exceeded first by the Anglican and then by the Puritan clergy. And to doubt Hobbes' reliance on revelation as the ground of this scepticism would be to doubt the sincerity of almost the entire body of Reformation churchmen in England from the late sixteenth century onward. (Eisenach, 1982, p. 223; see also Pocock, 1971, pp. 192–4)

In addition to the Reformation context, there is another reason why Hobbes wanted to circumscribe carefully the limits of reason in the realm of religion. He saw that the discoveries of modern science, proceeding solely on the basis of reason, were contradicting biblical doctrines. The most obvious example of this is Copernicus's theory that the earth, contrary to the Bible, goes around the sun, not vice versa. Since Hobbes was committed to both science and religion, he had no choice but to stake out separate areas for each. I shall attempt to substantiate this claim *in extenso* in the following chapters. But first we need to see what precisely he says about the relation between faith and reason.

Hobbes on faith and reason

Hobbes introduces the ideas of faith and belief in chapter 7 of *Leviathan*, "Of the Ends, or Resolutions of Discourse." Judgment, science, and faith (or belief) are the three ends of discourse. A judgment is the content of speech or thought about some matter of fact. It can never be certain, because humans cannot be certain about the way things are. Science is certain, but that is because it does not consist of categorical assertions. Rather, it consists of conditional assertions, based upon the definition of words. Thus "If a plane figure has three sides, then its internal angles contain 180 degrees" and "If a continuous, unbroken line is drawn equidistant from a point, then the resulting figure is a circle" are scientific statements because they are conditional and provable from the definitions of such words and phrases as "plane figure" and "three sides." These conditional propositions are necessarily true because they are analytic propositions. A proposition such as "All triangles have three sides" may appear to be categorical – and indeed is categorical in its surface form – but it is necessary and scientific in virtue of the proposition "If something is a triangle, then it has three sides."

Faith and belief are both similar to and different from both judgment and science. Like judgment, faith is not conditional but categorical; like science, it is certain. However, unlike science, faith is not based upon the definitions of words but upon the trust or authority of the person from whom the faith is received. Unfortunately, Hobbes does not unambiguously indicate whether faith is about things or about nothing. He says that a proposition of faith "is not so much concerning the thing, as the person" (EW, 3:54). One would like to know how little or how much, or whether anything at all, is contained in the phrase "not so much." In any case, faith and belief differ from both judgment and science in that they have a dual aspect. Implicit in any belief is both a reference to the content of the belief, that is, the proposition believed, and a reference to the person upon whom the proposition rests. Thus, according to Hobbes, belief should be viewed as a three-term relation: a person P_1 believes the proposition that p because of trust in a person P_2.

According to Hobbes, there is a serious confusion about the nature of religious faith, because theologians have not observed the distinction between the content of a belief and the authority for a belief. Hobbes bases his argument on dubious claims about grammar. He says that the object of the phrase "belief of" can be a phrase that refers to either the content of the belief or the authority who underpins that content. In effect, he is claiming that it is as correct to say, "I believe John," as it is to say, "I believe Secretariat will win the race," even though logically two different kinds of things are being expressed. But he claims that the same does not apply to faith. First, the word "faith" is not properly used in the phrase "faith of" but only "faith in"; and second, the grammatical object of the phrase "faith in" refers only to the authority for a belief. In effect, Hobbes would claim that one could say, "I have faith in John," but neither "I have faith that Secretariat will win the race" nor "I have faith in Secretariat winning."

The dubiousness of Hobbes's linguistic analysis aside, his substantive point is that by conflating the phrase, "I have belief of" with the phrase "I have faith in" theologians have constructed the misleading phrase "I have belief in" and have given the mistaken impression that people put their faith in the words of the creed rather than in the person in whose authority they trust. Thus, according to Hobbes, every Christian has the same faith, in the sense that each Christian has faith in God, but not every Christian "has belief of" the same doctrines (EW, 3:54). Implicit in this account is the view that the creedal formulation of religion is less important than belief in God:

> From whence we may infer, that when we believe any saying whatsoever it be, to be true, from arguments taken, not from the thing itself, or from the principles of natural reason, but from the authority and good opinion we have, of him that hath said it; then is the speaker, or person we believe in, or trust in, and whose word we take, the object of our faith; and the honour done in believing, is done to him only.[15] (EW, 3:54–5)

Most of the consequences that Hobbes wants to draw from this account of faith and belief are not drawn until the beginning of Part III, "Of a Christian Commonwealth."

Near the beginning of that part, Hobbes says that in matters of religion "we are not to renounce our senses, and experience; nor, that which is the undoubted word of God, our natural reason" (EW, 3:359). The Puritan theologian John Preston had said the same thing: "Of all demonstrations of reason that we have to prove things, nothing is so firme as that which is taken from sense: to prove the fire is hot, we feele it hot, or honey to be sweet, when we taste it to be sweet: There is no reason in the world makes it so firme as sense: As it is true in these cases, so it is an undoubted truth in Divinity, that in all matters of sense, sense is a competent judge" (Preston, 1633, p. 10). Alluding to the story of the talents in the Bible, Hobbes points out that reason is to be used "in the purchase of justice, peace, and true religion" (EW, 3:360). Since God has given humans reason as a tool for discovering true religion, there cannot be any contradiction between the propositions of faith and the propositions of reason.

Neither Preston nor Hobbes, however, said that all the propositions of faith can be proven by reason or even completely understood. Hobbes holds, just as Aquinas had, that "there be many things in God's word above reason" but "there is nothing contrary to it" (EW, 3:360). Preston had said the same thing a few years before, in almost the same words: "But, you will say, faith is beyond sense and reason, it is true, it is beyond both, but it is not contrary to both; faith teacheth nothing contrary to reason" (Preston, 1633, pp. 12–13; see also Miller, 1935, p. 76). Whenever there appears to be a conflict between faith and reason, the source of the apparent problem is either "our unskilful interpretation, or erroneous ratiocination" (EW, 3:360). William Chillingworth, in *The Religion of Protestants a Safe Way to Salvation*, committed himself to believing biblical doctrines that reason could not comprehend, "but nothing which reason can comprehend that it cannot be." This was part of the way he explicated his view that he would "believe many mysteries, but no impossibilities; many things above reason, but nothing against it" (Chillingworth, 1638, p. 377). Later, the respectable religious thinker and scientist Robert Boyle wrote a book with the title *A Discourse of Things above Reason*. Hobbes's view was one standard seventeenth-century position.

Some critics have claimed that Hobbes's occasionally indelicate language about religion is evidence of his disbelief in revealed religion. They cite his remark "For it is with the mysteries of religion, as with wholesome pills for the sick; which swallowed whole, have the virtue to cure; but chewed, are for the most part cast up again without effect" (EW, 3:360; see also 3:712 and 2:305). But "sensibilities change," as has been aptly said (Johnson, 1974, p. 104), and Hobbes's remark was well within the limits of good taste in seventeenth-century religious discourse. Lord Clarendon, who liked little of *Leviathan*, nonetheless approves of Hobbes's words and even quotes them (Clarendon, 1676, p. 202). Metaphors of mastication were quite common, and Clarendon himself employed them (ibid., p. 113). Perhaps the most famous example is Francis Bacon's remark that many books are to be tasted, some to be swallowed, and a few to be digested. Other Christian thinkers were even more explicit in their use of the metaphor. John Cotton says, "And as it was with Christ the head, so it is with all his members, what ever cup the Father mixes for us to drinke, when wee have drunke of it, it passeth from us, it does not make us drunken as the cuppe given to *Babylon* did" (Cotton, 1641, p. 31). Notice, in addition to the gastronomic similarity, that the structure of the analogies of Cotton and Hobbes is the same: taken in the right way, faith does not cause any physiological upset, but taken in the wrong way, it does. Cotton's metaphors are often cast in much stronger language; for example, he describes "the garments of our Sanctification, the best whereof is like *filthy raggs, and menstruous cloathes, Esa 64.6.* so bespotted and besmeared with much filthinesse" (ibid., p. 41).

Although I have been trying to show that Hobbes's views and the way he expresses them are consonant with other seventeenth-century English theologians, I think that they are also more than that. A large portion of Parts III and IV of *Leviathan* involves Hobbes's reinterpretation of the Bible. He tries to show that the standard interpretations that either conflict with modern science or are used to destabilize existing governments are not justified by the text and hence are the result of "unskilful interpretation." Also, he tries to show that many of the standard doctrines that have been adopted on the grounds that they follow from some biblical doctrine in fact do not follow and hence are the result of "erroneous ratiocination." In the next few chapters I will deal with this point extensively, but one minor example can be mentioned here. Hobbes points out that the fact that the fires of hell are eternal does not entail that any one person will suffer eternally: the fires may burn forever, even though each damned person will be consumed by the fires in a mercifully short time. This, I think, is a rather nice illustration of Hobbes's attempt to save the literal meaning of the Bible, and hence its doctrine, without succumbing to its moral harshness.

So far I have has been discussing those propositions of religion to which Hobbes thinks the canons of reason can be applied. There is another class of propositions, however, which simply exceed reason. Concerning this class, Hobbes takes the sensible line that they are to be accepted without "sifting out a philosophical truth by logic, of such mysteries as are not comprehensible, nor fall under any rule of natural science" (EW, 3:360).[16] Earlier Hobbes had said that everyone who believes in God believes everything that God says, "whether they understand it or not" (ibid., p. 54). While secularists will claim that Hobbes is being sarcastic, this interpretation is belied by the fact that Chillingworth had espoused essentially the same view twenty years before: "Propose me anything out of this book [the Bible], and require whether I believe it or not, and seeme it never so incomprehensible to humane reason, I will subscribe it with hand and heart" (Chillingworth, 1638, p. 377). Since the propositions of religion that exceed reason cannot, by definition, belong to the understanding, they must be assigned to some other cognitive faculty. Hobbes assigns them to the will. This raises the question of how a person should direct his will in matters of religion. It will turn out that people ought to obey their sovereign in these matters, since this is reasonable and, as such, God's own command (EW, 3:359). There is no legitimate alternative, because the propositions under discussion are those that are beyond the bounds of reason. It is important to remember that Hobbes considers these propositions as only a subset of the entire set of religious propositions.

Hobbes's explicit relegation of certain propositions of religion to the will was an attempt to protect them from an unjustified encroachment or assault by reason. By removing these propositions from the arena of reason, they cannot be overthrown by reason. This tactic was pursued by later religiously oriented thinkers, the most distinguished of whom is Søren Kierkegaard. He goes much farther than Hobbes by holding that not just some but all propositions of faith are outside the purview of reason. This strategy of defending religion by taking it off the battlefield of reason did not succeed with most intellectuals, because reason, through modern science, became too successful and eventually claimed to explain everything, at least in principle.

Locke on faith and reason

More important than Hobbes in the history of the downfall of religious faith among intellectuals is Locke, who, like Hobbes, Gregory of Rimini, and Kierkegaard, was trying to save religion in the face of challenges by modern science. In the *Essay Concerning Human Understanding*, Locke eroded the intellectual status of religious propositions by making all of them subordinate to reason in several ways (Locke, 1689, IV.18). First, reason can dictate what the possible content of an allegedly revealed proposition is. No revelation can be a contradiction, and none can communicate an idea that is not based upon sense experience. Thus, Saint Paul's experience of things such "as eye hath not seen, nor ear heard, nor hath it entered into the heart of man to conceive" are things in which there can be no faith by other people. Also, all direct sense experience is more certain than any alleged revelation. Thus, someone who sees a person soaking in water cannot receive a revelation that that person is completely dry. Proofs in mathematics and science also cannot be contradicted by divine revelation. The interior angles of a rectangle equal 360 degrees, and no alleged revelation to the contrary is credible. In short, "Nothing that is contrary to, and inconsistent with the clear and self-evident Dictates of Reason, has a Right to be urged, or assented to, as a Matter of Faith" (ibid., IV.18.10).

The strongest blow against faith comes when Locke declares that "*Reason* must judge" whether something is a revelation or not (ibid.) and more generally that "*Reason* must be our last Judge and Guide in Every Thing" (ibid., par. 14). For this totally subordinates faith to reason; and if reason should come to judge that only reason is to be our judge and guide, then faith has no recourse at all. This is in effect what happened in the development of modern science. The crucial difference between Hobbes and Locke is that, while Hobbes believes that people need to apply natural reason to the criteria that the Bible has laid down for such things as prophets (EW, 3:362, 423, 425), Locke makes reason the judge of everything, including what criteria proffered by the Bible ought to be accepted.

Locke, of course, did not want to undermine religious belief. He, like Hobbes, was trying to accommodate religion to the new science. While part of his goal was to outlaw "enthusiasm," the religious belief that the Holy Spirit speaks to individuals on a fairly regular basis, his fundamental intention was to reconcile reason and revelation. Indeed, he calls reason "natural revelation" and revelation "natural reason explained by information communicated by God" (Locke, 1689, IV.19.4).

However, Locke's position on the relation between faith and reason is much more likely to subvert religion than Hobbes's. For Locke subordinates faith to reason, whereas Hobbes preserves a sanctuary for some propositions of faith. Locke's position leads to deism. His friend John Toland, in *Christianity Not Mysterious*, argued that Locke's philosophy leads to the view that Christianity is nothing more than common sense. Toland opposed the view that there are mysteries of divine revelation that humans cannot comprehend. He attributed this view to the church fathers, but it is also Hobbes's view, as we have seen.

I had two purposes for discussing Locke's view about the relation between faith and reason: First, I wanted to show that some mainstream theories about the relation between faith and reason presented immediately after Hobbes's were more subversive than his own. Second, I wanted to show that the subversive consequences of Hobbes and Locke's views were contrary to their intentions. If Hobbes is judged according to the same criteria as such undoubtedly sincere Christians as Calvin, Preston, and Locke, then the genuineness of his religious beliefs cannot be doubted, even though he unwittingly contributed to the decline of religion's intellectual standing (cf. Wootton, 1989).

Chapter 8

Revelation, prophets, and miracles

According to Hobbes, there are two classes of religious propositions: those that are amenable to scrutiny by reason and those that are not. The proposition that God exists belongs to the first class. This class is not especially important for the philosophy of religion, since its members also belong to the general class of true propositions. It is issues relating to the second class that will concern us in this chapter.

It is not clear which propositions belong to the second class, which Hobbes calls "the Christian mysteries." One might expect the doctrine of the Trinity to be a paradigmatic member of this class; it certainly is not provable. However, Hobbes has a theory about the Trinity, which purports to show that it is consistent. That would seem to make the Trinity amenable to scrutiny by reason in a nontrivial sense, and hence a member of the first class. Perhaps he would count propositions such as "The Father generates the Son, and the Holy Spirit proceeds from the Father and the Son" as belonging to the second class. However, the latter proposition is a theoretical statement, dependent upon the scholastic Aristotelianism that Hobbes consistently opposed. Whatever one says about this, there are two points to be made about the Christian mysteries. First, even though they are not demonstrable and may not be comprehensible, nonetheless they do not contradict reason: "For though there be many things in God's word above reason; that is to say, which cannot be either demonstrated or confuted; yet there is nothing contrary to it; but when it seemeth so, the fault is either in our unskilful interpretation or erroneous ratiocination" (EW, 3:360). In religion, as in all other matters, "we are not to renounce our senses, and experience, nor . . . our natural reason. . . ." (ibid., p. 359).

Second, whether intelligible or not, the Christian mysteries can be believed because belief is under the control of the will, not the understanding. It is easy to be confused about Hobbes's position here, because sometimes he says that people have no control over what they believe. The problem is that he uses the term "belief" in two different ways. When he is thinking about ordinary, typically nonreligious beliefs as objects of the intellect, he contrasts what people believe with what they profess or how they worship. In this sense of "believe," he holds that what people believe is not within their control. This is not the sense that is operative in the current context. Here Hobbes is thinking about religious beliefs, and he assigns them to the will. He says that what beliefs a person has is both under his control and subject to the authority of the sovereign. In these contexts, he is thinking of beliefs as embodied in the verbal formulas expressed in creeds or in authorized religious services. Thus, the formulas "Jesus is true God and true man" and "Three persons are one God" embody religious beliefs. For people within a Christian commonwealth, the Christian mysteries, in addition to being a matter of belief, are a matter of obedience. When professing a religious belief, one need not even understand the words:

> [W]e are bidden to captivate our understanding to the words; and not to labour in sifting out a philosophical rule by logic, of such mysteries as are not comprehensible, nor fall under any rule of natural science. . . . But by the captivity of the understanding, is not meant a submission of the intellectual faculty to the opinion of any other man; but of the will to obedience, where obedience is due. . . . We then captivate our understanding and reason, when we forbear contradiction; when we so speak, as by lawful authority we are commanded. . . .

Difficult questions can be asked about the basis or origin of the Christian mysteries. How can God reveal propositions by means other than natural reason? Are prophets a means of supernatural revelation from God? And are miracles a source of supernatural revelation? In short, we need to discuss three key issues in this chapter: revelation, prophets, and miracles.

Hobbes's principal goal in discussing these three topics was to ensure that religion was not used to subvert governments (Sherlock, 1982, pp. 47, 49). In the seventeenth century, many self-professed prophets claimed to have received revelations that justified overthrowing the existing government. Hobbes thinks that such use of religion is a perversion of it; God intended religion to bring peace, not war, to the world. As regards miracles, Hobbes is equally concerned with reconciling their existence with the modern scientific view, according to which all phenomena can be explained in terms of natural laws that would brook no exception.

REVELATION

Mediate revelation

There are two kinds of revelation: mediate and immediate. Immediate revelation occurs when God communicates with a human being without any intervening person. Mediate revelation is not immediate revelation; that is, it occurs when God communicates with a human being through one or more other human beings (EW, 3:361).

Let's begin with mediate revelation, because that is the sort that most people experience, whether they realize it or not. In mediate revelation, there is some chain, beginning with God, proceeding through one or more intermediary persons or things, and ending with a person who is the recipient of the mediated communication. Receiving the word of God through the Bible is a kind of mediate revelation, since the Bible was not written by God but by some person or series of persons. So the word of God is received through the mediation of at least the primary biblical authors. The transmission of the Bible itself was, however, more indirect. God spoke to Moses about three thousand years before Hobbes's contemporaries were born; even worse, seventeenth-century Christians did not possess the autograph copy of Moses's account of the revelation. His account was copied by many generations of scribes; consequently, what has come down through the Bible to the seventeenth century, far from being an immediate revelation of God's word, is a highly mediated one.

Thus, to put one's faith in the Bible is not to put one's faith in God, according to Hobbes, since the Bible does not come directly from God to us. It is also not to put our faith in Moses, for he is also removed from us by many generations. To put one's faith in the Bible is to put one's faith in the person who vouches for the authenticity of the Bible (EW, 3:55). Who is this? It must be someone either with authority or without authority. It cannot be someone who does not have authority, because by that very fact there is no reason to believe in him. Thus, it must be someone who does have authority. The person with authority will either be only a religious authority, such as a pope or religious assembly, or it will be someone who also have civil authority. Since the beginning of the Hebrew monarchy, every person with purely religious authority has been subordinate to some secular authority. The only secular authority to which one owes obedience is one's own sovereign. Thus, faith in the Bible can be justified only by one's obligation to the sovereign. This same result can be arrived at more briefly. If anyone other than the secular sovereign had authority to determine what religious books were canonical, then a person would owe allegiance to more than one authority, which would result in conflict. As the Bible says, no one can serve two masters. Thus, citizens must put their religious faith in the same person who guarantees their physical safety. The civil sovereign is also a religious authority.

The problem posed by mediate revelation is an epistemological problem. Hobbes is not arguing that revelation is impossible; he is arguing that it is difficult or impossible for humans to know when a revelation has occurred. This problem first received intensive discussion at the beginning of the Reformation.[1] Hobbes's solution to the problem occupies a middle ground between the two standard answers that were given by Reformers, on the one side, and Roman Catholics on the other. Luther, for example, argued that the pope does not have the right to decide matters of revelation. Rather, each person has the right to interpret Scripture for himself. This was a scandal to many conservative thinkers, who believed that if every person were free to interpret the Bible as he wished, there would be religious chaos, and (because of the close ties between religion and politics) there would be political chaos as well. Hobbes understands this too and does not accept Luther's solution, which he would consider anarchistic. The standard alternative to Luther's position was the Roman Catholic response, given initially by Erasmus and later by various Counter-Reformation propagandists in the latter part of the sixteenth century. The response was that the pope should settle questions of revelation. Erasmus argued, on skeptical grounds, that human beings do not know much of anything and hence must rely upon authority. Since the pope has been the unquestioned authority on such matters from the beginning of Christianity, he should continue in that position.[2] The Reformers typically opposed Erasmus's solution, on the grounds that many popes had been corrupt and hence unreliable judges of spiritual matters. This does not bother Hobbes especially. His objection to Erasmus's solution is that the pope has no authority outside of the Papal States and thus is no authority at all, insofar as Englishmen are concerned.

Hobbes's solution to the problem of choosing a criterion for what counts as genuine mediated revelation is a compromise between those of Luther and Erasmus. With Erasmus, Hobbes sees that some authority is needed to settle religious disputes; and with Luther, he sees that the pope cannot be the authority. The only proper authority is one's own sovereign (EW, 4:330). His solution is in fact not especially novel but is a generalization of a long English tradition: the sovereign is the final authority in matters of religion. This answer was formally adopted in England in 1534, when Henry VIII issued the Act of Supremacy, according to which the sovereign had always been the head of the church. Hooker later gave a theoretical defense of this view within a scholastic philosophy (Hooker, 1593, VIII.1.2). In other words, Hobbes is simply adding philosophical weight to the official position of England. His solution to this vexing problem of the Reformation is moderate and unoriginal, but it also makes sense to anyone taking the longer view of the vagaries of English history. In the twenty-five years between 1533 and 1558, English citizens were required by law to be successively Roman Catholics; English Catholics; Protestants; Roman Catholics; and Protestants. It is not even possible to catalog briefly all of the changes and attempted changes in the prescribed religion that occurred in the middle of the seventeenth century. Hobbes's view that all citizens, including the clergy, need to be ruled by the civil authorities in every aspect of their lives is the same as Luther's, set out in his *Appeal to the German Nobility*.

The political upshot of Hobbes's analysis of mediate revelation is that the position of the sovereign is solidified; his authority is not threatened by any religious authority, either outside the boundaries of the country, as the Roman Catholics advocated, or inside the boundaries of the country, as the Presbyterians did. This is the positive consequence of Hobbes's view. The negative consequence is that it deprives individuals, not licensed by the sovereign, of the right to demand belief in their alleged revelations. A standard tactic of a self-professed prophet is to coerce belief, on the grounds that if people deny his revelation, then they are denying God. Hobbes makes the astute point that if someone claims to have a revelation from God and that person is not believed, the people are rejecting only that human person, not God: "If *Livy* says the Gods made once a cow speak, and we believe it not; we distrust not God therein, but *Livy*" (EW, 3:55). Hobbes's view was, in effect, adopted by members of the Royal Society. Thomas Sprat says, "But to reject the sense, which any privat man shall fasten to it [an alleged revelation] is not to disdain the word of *God*, but the opinions of men like our selves" (Sprat, 1667, p. 359). Since many people in the seventeenth century claimed that God had spoken to them, Hobbes's point had practical consequences.

Immediate revelation

One might think that mediate revelation obviously offers less certainty than immediate revelation. It is appealing to think that one could achieve infallible knowledge of God's will through a direct revelation. In fact, the problems with this view are as serious as those with mediate revelation.

One of the most devastating arguments in the philosophy of religion is only two lines long: "To say he [God] hath spoken to him [some person] in a dream, is no more than to say he dreamed that God spake to him" (EW, 3:361). Just as the truth of the statement "Cleopatra appeared to me in a dream" does not have an evidential force, neither does the statement "God appeared to me in a dream." People who are inclined to believe in immediate revelation might object that God often speaks to humans when they are not asleep. To this Hobbes replies that humans do not know when they are asleep (ibid., pp. 361–2).[3] Which is more plausible: that God is appearing to someone in a dream, or that a person is not aware that he is asleep and is dreaming that God is appearing to him (cf. Hume, 1748, p. 123; see also Wootton, 1990, pp. 200, 203, 205, 215)? In short, no human has sufficient rational grounds for thinking that God has spoken to him.

All of this notwithstanding, Hobbes argues that God may still cause a person to correctly believe that God has revealed himself to that person. Thus, Hobbes's position does not entail that God has never spoken to any human being. It means only that humans cannot know when this occurs and that there is no compelling evidence for it. Hobbes repeatedly affirms that God has revealed himself to humans (EW,

3:361–2), and, given the Reformation tradition and the seventeenth-century milieu that tended to separate faith from reason, there is no justification for doubting his word, unless we find other evidence that Hobbes is intellectually dishonest. I submit that there is little or none.

So far, we have been discussing the epistemological problems with holding that humans have any supernatural revelation from God. There is also an ontological problem, insofar as a supernatural revelation might come through an actual appearance of God. It would be impossible, Hobbes says, for God to appear "as he is in his own nature" (EW, 3:420), for this would be inconsistent with his infinity, invisibility, and incomprehensibility. When the Bible speaks of God as appearing to humans, this must be figurative talk, because God does not have a shape or a color.

In general, humans can have no idea of how God reveals himself immediately to human beings except by reading the accounts of such revelations in the Bible itself (EW, 3:415–16). The usual way for God to communicate with humans in the Bible is through an apparition, vision, or dream, as he did with Abraham, Isaac, Jacob, Gideon, Samuel, Eliah, Elisha, Isaiah, Ezekiel, and the other prophets in the Old Testament, and to Saints Joseph, Peter, Paul, and John in the New Testament (ibid., pp. 416–17, 423). God communicated in a more extraordinary way than this only with Moses, with whom God made a covenant, and even in this case there was some sort of mediation by an angel or angels (ibid., p. 417). So the passage from Numbers 12:6–8 in which God says, "I will speak mouth to mouth, even apparently, not in dark speech; and the similitude of the Lord shall he behold," and the one in Exodus 33:11 which says, "The Lord spake to Moses, face to face, as a man speaketh to his friend," must be interpreted figuratively (ibid.).

Hobbes's purpose in showing that all the Old and New Testament prophets received their divine messages in "dreams, or vision" is to demonstrate how hard it is to differentiate between true and false prophets (ibid., 423). Alluding to his earlier point that to say that God appeared to someone in a dream is to say that the person dreamed that God appeared to him, Hobbes says, "[G]enerally the prophets extraordinary in the Old Testament took notice of the word of God no otherwise than from their dreams, or visions; that is to say, from the imaginations which they had in their sleep, or in an extasy: which imaginations in every true prophet were supernatural; but in false prophets were either natural or feigned" (ibid., p. 418). As the last two clauses indicate, Hobbes is not denying the existence of true prophets; he simply thinks that they are difficult to identify. Some criteria for identifying them are needed. In his discussion of the prophets, he adopts two criteria, one from the Old Testament and one from the New.

PROPHETS

Revelations come through prophets. Consequently, it is important to know what a true prophet is. Hobbes commits himself to the criteria that the Bible lays down for determining when a person is a true prophet. This satisfies his desire to preserve orthodoxy. He also wants to show that the existence of these criteria does not mean that true prophets appear often or that dissidents can use latter-day prophets to justify their machinations. This constitutes another part of his strategy of making religion an instrument of peace, not rebellion. I shall first consider Hobbes's criteria for true prophets and then the difficulties of identifying true prophets.[4]

Criteria for true prophets

The Bible has two different sets of criteria for discovering who is a true prophet and who is not. One comes from the Old Testament and one from the New. According to the Old Testament, there are two conditions for a true prophet, each necessary and jointly sufficient. One is the performance of miracles; the other is support of the established religion (Deut. 13:1–5, discussed by Hobbes at EW, 3:362–3).[5] Each

228

of these conditions serves Hobbes's political purposes. The first condition makes it virtually impossible for anyone in the seventeenth century to have even a claim to being a prophet. For, according to the philosophically oriented Reformation theologians, either virtually no miracles were performed after the death of the apostles, or such miracles had no doctrinal import.[6] The Puritan preacher John Cotton preached that religious hypocrites required miracles in order to attain true faith (Cotton, 1641, pp. 95–9; see the section "Miracles" later in this chapter).

In the event that someone should satisfy the first condition, his prophecies are guaranteed not to threaten the civil sovereign by the second condition. For no true prophet will preach anything against the established church, and the established church is the one of which the sovereign is the head.[7] There seems to be an obvious objection to this condition, an objection related to one raised against Hobbes's definition of "true religion."[8] Bramhall presents the objection by expressing what he takes to be the consequences of Hobbes's view. Bramhall says, "[H]e that teacheth transubstantiation in France, is a true prophet; he that teacheth it in England, a false prophet; he that blasphemeth Christ in Constantinople, a true prophet; he that doth the same in Italy, a false prophet" (EW, 4:325). Hobbes might have responded at least in part by saying that if there are untoward consequences of this criterion it is not his fault but the fault of the Bible, since he is merely articulating the biblical view. But he does not.

Instead, Hobbes replies to Bramhall by making a distinction between people who claim to be true prophets because they perform miracles, and those who claim to be true prophets because of the doctrine they preach (EW, 4:326–7). The condition being discussed is meant to apply only to the first group. About them, Hobbes says that God would never allow two people who were preaching contradictory doctrines to perform miracles. Only one of them would be associated with a true miracle, because only God performs miracles, and he could not endorse contradictory doctrines (ibid., 328). Concerning the second group, those who preach contradictory doctrines in different countries without the accompaniment of miracles, Hobbes says that the issue here is not who is a true prophet but who has the right to decide what will be preached in a territory. Only the sovereign is competent, for reasons already discussed (pp. 329–30). Hobbes refers to the street rioting that resulted from citizens taking sides on the theological dispute between Gomar, who defended Calvin's view, and Arminius (p. 329).

Hobbes skewers Bramhall, the Arminian and Restoration royalist, by asking him who he would have decide the issue.[9] Hobbes says, "There must therefore be a judge of controverted doctrines. But, says the Bishop [Bramhall], not the king" (p. 329), thereby implying that Bramhall's view is treasonous. Hobbes rhetorically considers other possibilities by naming specific groups. "Shall it be given to a Presbyterian minister? No; it is unreasonable. Shall a synod of Presbyterians have it? No; for most of the Presbyters in the primitive church were undoubtedly subordinate to bishops, and the rest were bishops" (pp. 329–30). Hobbes knows that Bramhall will not support the presbyterian theory. Hobbes then considers the possibility that a synod of bishops should decide the matter. He insinuates that this would be a self-serving position for Bramhall to take. Hobbes says acidly, "A synod of bishops? Very well. His Lordship being too modest to undertake the whole power, would have been contented with the six-and-twentieth part" (because there were twenty-six bishops in England). But the episcopal solution will not work. Drawing upon a standard Reformation argument against the ultimate authority of ecumenical councils, Hobbes points out that only a sovereign could call the bishops into session. He concludes by saying, "The power of the clergy, unless it be upheld by the king, or illegally by the multitude, amounts to nothing" (p. 330). This seems to be a variation on a theme of King James I, who often said, "No bishop, no king," meaning not only that the presbyterian system undermined his authority but also that the authority of bishops depended upon him.

Bramhall had also claimed that by Hobbes's criterion Jesus

was a false prophet, because no sovereign had approved of Christ's mission. Hobbes replied that Christ had the approval of God, who was "king of the Jews, and consequently supreme prophet, and judge of all prophets." More bluntly, he says, "What other princes thought of his prophesies, is nothing to the purpose" (p. 329). Hobbes in effect makes Jesus an exception. In *Leviathan*, he realized that the Erastian views that he and many of his countrymen held were not consonant with the behavior of the early martyrs. Hobbes simply considers them exceptions to the rule: "[S]ome have received a calling to preach, and profess the kingdom of Christ openly. . . . [I]f they have been put to death, for bearing witness to this point, that Jesus Christ is risen from the dead, [they] were true martyrs" (EW, 3:494–5). If this answer is theoretically unsatisfactory, it is nonetheless the answer of a Christian. There is nothing about Hobbes's language or the context to suggest that Hobbes was being sarcastic or implying some secret doctrine.

The marks of a true prophet laid down in the Old Testament are reiterated in the New. Concerning the ability of false prophets to perform miracles, Hobbes cites the Gospel of Matthew:

> In like manner, after our Saviour Christ had made his disciples acknowledge him for the Messiah, (that is to say, for God's anointed, whom the nation of the Jews daily expected for their king, but refused when he came,) he omitted not to advertise them of the danger of miracles. *There shall arise*, saith he, *false Christs, and false prophets, and shall do great wonders and miracles, even to the seducing, if it were possible, of the very elect.* (Matt. xxiv. 24.) By which it appears, that false prophets may have the power of miracles; yet we are not to take their doctrine for God's word. (EW, 3:363–4)

Hobbes also quotes Deuteronomy 13:1–5, which recommends killing any self-professed or alleged prophet who preaches revolution, and Saint Paul's Epistle to the Galatians, 1:8, which declares that anyone who preaches a gospel other than Christ's is "accursed." Since Christ's gospel includes the instruction for people to obey their king, Hobbes infers that Saint Paul meant that anyone who preaches a gospel of revolution is accursed (EW, 3:363–4).

In addition to endorsing the Old Testament criteria for true prophets, the New Testament presents its own: a true prophet is anyone who preaches the doctrine that "Jesus is the Christ" (EW, 3:425). Anyone who preaches anything beyond this message in postapostolic times is a false prophet. This condition on true prophets, like the two in the Old Testament, neutralizes the political aspect of prophecy in Christian countries. Anyone preaching something other than that Jesus is the Christ is preaching a prophetic content that exceeds the bounds of the true prophet, according to this criterion. Consequently, anyone preaching that there are other doctrines to be believed or that citizens should revolt against their sovereign is obviously a false prophet.

Hobbes has in mind three groups of religious and political dissidents: various self-appointed prophets, the Presbyterians, and the Roman Catholics. Each group represented an extreme. The self-appointed prophets, who based their authority upon their private religious experiences, were a constant annoyance in seventeenth-century England. Presbyterians, who were actively engaged against Charles I in the late 1630s and early 1640s, wanted citizens to set religious policy independently of their sovereign. Catholics, who had a long history of opposition to the English monarchy, wanted a foreign sovereign (the pope) to set it. Hobbes's goal was to steer a course through these three extreme views. Alluding to each of them, Hobbes says,

> For when Christian men, take not their Christian sovereign, for God's prophet; they must either take their own dreams, for the prophesy they mean to be governed by, and the tumor of their own hearts for the Spirit of God; or they must suffer themselves to be led by some strange prince; or by some of their fellow-subjects, that can bewitch them, by slander of the government, into rebellion, without other miracle to confirm their calling, than sometimes an extraordinary success and impunity; and by this means destroying all laws, both divine

and human, reduce all order, government, and society, to the first chaos of violence and civil war. (EW, 3:427)

According to the New Testament criterion for a true prophet (that is, anyone who preaches that Jesus is the Christ), any good Christian is a true prophet. Although this may seem to trivialize the notion, this use is consistent with Hobbes's variegated uses of the word "prophet." At the beginning of his discussion of prophets in chapter 36 of *Leviathan*, Hobbes runs through all of the ordinary uses of the term "prophet" in the Bible, as he customarily does for other religiously loaded terms, such as "word of God," "heaven," and "kingdom of God." Hobbes shows that "prophet" is used in many senses: it sometimes means a person who speaks to God and sometimes a person to whom God speaks; sometimes a person who formulates doctrine and sometimes a person who predicts an event. Sometimes being a prophet means nothing more than being a person who prays or praises God. In this sense even poets and heathens can be prophets, and Saint Paul mentions Epimenides, the Cretan prophet, who said that all Cretans were liars (EW, 3:412–14). Also, being a prophet is typically a temporary or part-time job. God sometimes uses a person to prophesy and then allows that person to return to his normal life.

Hobbes's purpose in going through all of these uses of the word "prophet" is clearly deflationary. Because most people immediately think that anyone who is a prophet is a full-time, specially graced agent of God, it is important for Hobbes, relying upon the Bible for his evidence, to show that that is not so. Most prophets are false; of those that are true, most are only part-time.

Although most are part-time help, some prophets had "a perpetual calling." Of these, there are two types: supreme and subordinate. In the Old Testament, Moses and the high priests who succeeded him were supreme, because they, in accordance with Hobbes's view about the structure of history, were God's vice-regents on earth. Other supreme prophets were the kings who "submitted themselves to God's government," such as Saul, David, and Solomon (EW, 3:419; see also pp. 525, 426).[10] In the New Testament, there is only one supreme prophet, "our Saviour, who was both God that spake and the prophet to whom he spake" (ibid., p. 420). The difference between supreme and subordinate prophets is that while God spoke to the subordinate prophets in the usual mode of dreams and visions, he spoke to the supreme prophets in some way "not intelligible" to us (ibid.).

The most likely reason why Hobbes draws this distinction between supreme and subordinate prophets is to limit the number of occasions for which it is necessary to say that something supernatural occurred. He wants to make belief in genuine prophets as plausible as possible by acknowledging supernatural intervention only when the text of the Bible absolutely demands it. Hobbes's view is similar to that of the Roman Catholic Church today, which refuses to recognize promiscuous appearances of the Virgin Mary, whether it be in Yugoslavia or Amarillo, Texas, and denies the similarity between the visage of Christ and either burns on tortillas or rusty patches on water towers. It is easier to believe that some miraculous appearances have occurred in the distant past if those in charge of certifying things in the present show low gullibility and high discretion.

Hobbes's view also puts him in the mainstream of seventeenth-century science, which was willing to admit some cases of miraculous intervention. This view was held by virtually all members of the Royal Society. It was only in the nineteenth century that scientists closed the door to miracles completely. So Hobbes's distinction between the select group of supreme prophets, who were supernaturally inspired, and the large group of subordinate prophets, who merely spoke "according to God's will" (EW, 3:421), is consonant with the piety of seventeenth-century scientists.

Problems with prophets

We have just seen that Hobbes affirms the existence of prophets and cites criteria for identifying them. Lest anyone become sanguine about prophets, Hobbes points out that there are many practical problems surrounding them. First, God says that many prophets lie in his name. Second, there are more false prophets than true ones. Third, they contradict each other. Fourth, one prophet can be deceived, even by another prophet. Fifth, the practical benefit of a true prophet is nil, because one can only determine who he is when it is too late: that is, after the prediction, almost invariably dire, comes true.

Concerning the first point, Hobbes quotes from the prophet Jeremiah: "*The prophets,* (saith the Lord, by *Jeremiah,* chapter xiv.14) *prophecy lies in my name. I sent them not, neither have I commanded them, nor spake unto them; they prophecy to you a false vision, a thing of nought, and the deceit of their heart*" (EW, 3:424). Second, there are more false prophets than true ones. Hobbes points out that when Ahab, king of Israel, was trying to decide whether to attack Ramoth Gilead, he asked four hundred prophets what he should do. All four hundred urged him to make war. Only one prophet, Micaiah, prophesied correctly that Ahab would be defeated and warned him not to attack, and Micaiah did so under duress. For when he was first brought to Ahab, Micaiah had said, "Attack and win the day; the Lord will deliver it into your hands" (1 Kings 22:15; EW, 3:424–5; see also pp. 362–3, and 4:332–3). It was only when Ahab threatened him that Micaiah told the truth and predicted disaster, whereupon Ahab criticized Micaiah. Hobbes misses his chance to point out that not only are true prophets rare, but they must be coaxed or coerced to tell the truth. The prophets most inclined to prophesy are those who are most likely to be frauds.

This story about Micaiah is also evidence for the third problem with prophets: they contradict each other. Concerning the fourth problem, Hobbes rehearses another story from the Book of Kings. There was a certain "man of God from Judah" (1 Kings 13:1), who, after truly prophesying about an altar at Bethel, made his way home, under the divine command not to eat or drink anything along the way. But he met another prophet, who told the man of God that

God had spoken to him and changed the command. Unfortunately for the man of God, he believed the lie, and he ate and drank with the false prophet. When he resumed his journey, he was devoured by a lion, as a punishment from God for disobeying him, albeit unwittingly. Hobbes asks rhetorically, "If one prophet deceive another, what certainty is there of knowing the will of God, by other way than that of reason?" (EW, 3:362).

This brings us to the fifth practical problem with prophets: they are virtually never useful in making decisions. One knows who a true prophet is only after his prophecies have come true, and then it is too late to act on them. The king of Israel followed the seemingly sensible procedure of taking the advice of the four hundred prophets. He attacked Ramoth Gilead and was killed. The term "true prophet" is retrospective. One applies the term only after the prophesied event has occurred. Related to this is the problem that prophecies are often vague, or that the predicted events do not come true, or that they fail to come true until long after both the prophet and his witnesses are dead. For example, the numerous prophets who prophesied the coming of the Messiah were looking many centuries into the future. The term "true prophet" is usually bestowed only posthumously. Hobbes's point is not to discredit all prophecy but to discredit prophets who set themselves up against the sovereign.

MIRACLES

Why Hobbes discusses miracles

We have seen that one of the marks of a true prophet is the performance of miracles. We now need to consider what a miracle is. Roughly, Hobbes holds that a miracle is (1) an "admirable" work; (2) done by God; (3) for the purpose of showing people what he commands or of proving that some person is his special minister. This rendition of Hobbes's understanding of miracles ignores some tensions in his treat-

236

ment. He in effect has two, inconsistent discussions of miracles in chapter 37 of *Leviathan*. He begins the chapter with a quasi-definition of "miracle" and discusses it (EW, 3:427–32). He then seems to begin again: he presents an explicit definition of "miracle" and discusses it (ibid., pp. 432–7). But the two discussions differ in interesting ways: one religious, one scientific.

Who performs miracles?

The religious difference concerns who can perform miracles. Earlier in *Leviathan*, Hobbes had said that the pharaoh's magicians were able to perform miracles (EW, 3:363). The biblical account in Exodus seems to commit one to this view. However, in his second discussion of miracles, Hobbes asserts that only God can perform miracles. Hobbes's intention is to safeguard the sovereignty of God against the pretensions of humans: "[T]he work done, is not the effect of any virtue in the prophet; because it is the effect of the immediate hand of God; that is to say God hath done it, without using the prophet therein, as a subordinate cause" (ibid., p. 432).

If one wanted to reconcile this latter view with the text of the Bible, one could claim that the biblical author meant to be reporting nothing more than what superficially appeared to be miracles. When the author says that the magicians performed miracles, he is simply using imprecise language. Instead, Hobbes says that what the pharaoh's magicians did was "imposture and delusion, wrought by ordinary means" (ibid., p. 433). The alleged miracle is nothing but a deception, "which is no miracle, but a very easy matter to do" (p. 434).

It is easy for people who are generally ignorant, especially if they are ignorant of natural causes, to think that what magicians and other frauds perform are miracles (pp. 433–5) when the phenomenon is simply an eclipse, an instance of ventriloquism, or a prearranged swindle. Hobbes cannot resist repeating his earlier point that the Bible warns people against being taken in by such frauds and specifically warns against believing anyone who preaches against the established religion or the sovereign (p. 435). Hobbes accuses the Roman Catholics of perpetrating such a fraud in their doctrine of transubstantiation. The principal reason that Reformers such as Luther and Calvin downplayed miracles was to counteract the Catholic claim that one of the marks of the true church was the performance of the kinds of miracles that the Catholic church claimed for itself. Neither Luther, Calvin, nor Hobbes thought that miracles occur with anything like the frequency claimed for them (e.g., Luther, 1520, p. 457; Calvin, 1559, vol. 1, "Prefatory Address," sec. 3; Eire, 1986, pp. 221–4). Although he is not consistent, Luther sometimes denies that miracles occurred after the coming of Christ. In a sermon preached in 1537, Luther said, "We should learn to believe no miracle after the revelation of Christ, even though a person who had been dead for ten days were called back to life. If I should now see a priest or a monk raise a dead person in the name of St. Ann, I would say that it was the work of the devil" (quoted from Plass, 1959, p. 957).[11] If one wants to see miracles, one should recognize that grain growing from the earth is miraculous, according to Luther (Plass, 1959, p. 954). Miracles are "the least significant works" for him, because they are merely physical and are observed by relatively few people (Luther, 1537–8, p. 79). Hobbes's remark that "miracles now cease" (EW, 3:365)[12] was not original with him. There seems to have been a Protestant tradition that espoused the view. James I is reported to have said it, and Luther had said that "the day of miracles is past" (Luther, 1537–8, p. 79, and see Thomas, 1971, pp. 197, 203, 256, 485, 570; Locke, 1664, p. 95). Far from being good evidence that Hobbes does not believe in miracles, the phrase presupposes that miracles once occurred, just as the question "Have you stopped beating your wife?" presupposes that the addressee once did.

Calvin and Hobbes are particularly exercised over the Catholic view that a priest performs a miracle at each Mass, when bread and wine are allegedly turned into the body and blood of Christ (EW, 3:436). Such claims of miracles are es-

pecially astounding, since gullible Christians commit themselves to believing that they have witnessed miracles that
they have not even observed (EW, 6:20). The situation is
worse than saying that the emperor, who is seen to be
naked, has new clothes; Catholics think they see the body
and blood of Christ when all that they see is bread and
wine.[13] Hobbes's own explanation for the doctrine of transubstantiation is purely ideological. He thinks that the
priests invented it to control believers in a twofold way. If
priests can get people to believe that priests perform miracles, then they can get them to believe that priests are
worthy of absolute obedience. And if they can get people not
to believe their own eyes, then they can get them to believe
anything (ibid., p. 53). In short, it was characteristic of Protestants to deemphasize the existence of miracles and to tend
to relegate them to the past (Hill, 1986, 3:283).

Hobbes thinks that the biblical injunction against believing
in self-styled prophets who are not authorized to speak by
the government is decisive, but for those who are nonetheless intent on seeing God's hand in certain events, he has a
fallback position. A person is always free to believe in his
own mind that some event is miraculous, "because thought
is free" (EW, 3:436): "But when it comes to confession of that
faith, the private reason must submit to the public; that is to
say, to God's lieutenant" (ibid., p. 437). Hobbes later shows
that God's lieutenant is the sovereign.

Miracles and science

Crucial to the religious point that Hobbes is making (namely,
that God is sovereign) is the fact that genuine miracles are
wrought by "the immediate hand of God." This view of
miracles is consonant with a popular religious mentality that
tries to accommodate both science and religion. According to
this view, the career of nature proceeds in a predominantly
regular way unless and until God intervenes to cause some
event that is anomalous. These interventions cause miracles.
On such a view, science could never provide a final descrip-

tion of nature, because miracles fall outside its ken. Let us say that this view compromises science. Hobbes commits himself to this view when he defines a miracle as "a work of God, (besides his operation by the way of nature, ordained in the creation)" (EW, 3:432). That is, in addition to the normal operations of nature, which can be studied by science, there are divine interventions.

There is another view that refuses to compromise science, and Hobbes was one of the first to try to reconcile religion with science without compromising science, even though it brought his two discussions of miracles into conflict. We have been discussing Hobbes's second discussion of miracles, the one in which he emphasizes the sovereignty of God. Let's now consider his first discussion.

According to Hobbes, a miracle is an "admirable" work of God, and two things are required for a work to be admirable: it must be "strange," in the sense that its occurrence is rare or unprecedented; and *"we cannot imagine* it to have been done by natural means" (my italics, EW, 3:428). These two requirements are individually necessary, and jointly sufficient, conditions for an event's being admirable. The first requirement alone excludes consecrations at the Catholic Mass from the realm of the miraculous. The second requirement is the more interesting one. Notice that it does not require that a miracle be caused "by the immediate hand of God" but only that the believers not be able to imagine how natural causes operated to produce it. Consequently, an event can be both miraculous and natural in the strong sense of not violating any physical law. Thus, a miracle can be a purely natural event. For example, Hobbes says that the first rainbow that was seen was a miracle, simply because it was first and thus "strange" (ibid.). Presumably he thinks that Noah was the first one to see a rainbow, because according to the account in Genesis, God put the rainbow in the sky as a covenant sign that he would never again destroy the world by a flood. But one can also, without being inconsistent, view this rainbow as simply a natural event,[14] the physics of which, though not understood by Noah, is now well understood.[15] A natural event can be a miracle so long as the witnesses to it cannot imagine an explanation of it according to the laws of nature that they have available to them. This does not preclude the possibility that later people will have ways of explaining this admirable event according to their more sophisticated laws of nature.

This discussion of miracles is clearly designed to reconcile traditional religious belief without compromising modern science. Hobbes is trying to show how one can accept both, even though science may come to explain every phenomenon naturalistically. His explanation is ingenious but not surprising. He was not simply a determinist but a religious, scientific determinist. That is, he did not merely believe that every event has a cause but that God is the cause of every event and that he acts in accordance with immutable natural laws. This line of thought was pursued by certain later theologians and religious scientists.[16]

Although no simple generalization will describe the attitude of sixteenth- and seventeenth-century Protestants toward miracles (Thomas, 1971, pp. 105–8, 124–8), roughly, the early Reformers, such as Luther and Calvin, downplayed miracles in order to undermine the claims of the Catholic church. Theologians favoring the established Church of England also tended to downplay miracles, since the church's position was secure without them. Some puritans and nonconforming Christians tended to support miraculous claims, since the ability to work miracles would legitimatize their claims (Duffy, 1981, pp. 253–5, 264–5). Among intellectuals generally, there was a strong tendency to downplay, if not to deny, their existence after the early decades of Christianity. This includes the covenant theologians, some of whom, as we have seen, influenced Hobbes. While conceding that God always "*could* interrupt the normal course of nature if He wished to, . . . they said that a God who voluntarily consented to a covenant would generally, as a matter of choice, prefer to work through the prevailing rules" (Miller, 1935, p. 66). John Preston says that "*God* alters no Law of Nature" (Preston, 1629a, p. 46) and that "Nature, it cannot be altered againe, for that is the property of Nature, it still stickes by us, and will not be changed, but, as Aristotle observes, throw a stone up a thousand times, it will returne againe, because it is the nature of it to returne" (Preston, 1633, p. 97). The invariability of the physical laws of nature is a sign of God's providence. It is part of God's omnipotence, omniscience, and omnibenevolence to have arranged the laws of nature and the initial state of the world in such a way that things would come out right, even if they occasionally appear miraculous to humans. John Cotton, in his *Christ the Fountaine of Life*, published in the same year as *Leviathan*, says that God typically guides natural causes for miraculous effects (Cotton, 1651, p. 33). William Ames almost denies miracles altogether; but if they occur, "God only is the author of true miracles" (Ames, 1629, p. 108).[17]

Religious scientists also tried to accommodate miracles without compromising science (Duffy, 1981, pp. 253, 266). Perhaps the most elaborate and infamous attempt to explain a miracle in scientific terms was Thomas Burnet's explanation of the Deluge in *The Sacred Theory of the Earth*. Burnet took seriously the challenge that Copernicus's theory posed for biblical beliefs. If the earth is not the center of the universe, then the sky is not a dome holding back waters ample enough to flood the earth. Where, then, did the waters come from? He eventually reasoned that after the original chaos, the heavier atoms sank to the center of the earth; the lighter liquid atoms, including the water atoms, rose. The top layer of liquid atoms dried and formed a crust, which cracked from the naturally intense heat of the sun, precisely when Noah's ark had been completed. The underground water surged out and flooded the world. After forty days, the broken fragments of crust began to settle, some turning on their sides to form mountains, others sinking to form the current ocean basins. All of this happened 1,656 years after the Creation, according to God's carefully prearranged natural plan for the world (Burnet, 1681).

William Whiston, Newton's successor as Lucasian Professor of Mathematics at Cambridge, tried to reconcile science and the Bible by explaining Noah's Deluge as the result of a comet passing close to the earth, a passing that God had prearranged from all eternity, since he had foreseen the course that human life would take. This coordination of physical events and moral punishment is "the Secret of Divine Providence in the Government of the World, and that whereby the Rewards and Punishments of God's Mercy and Justice are distributed to his Rational Creatures, without any disturbance of the Course of Nature, or a Miraculous interposition on every occasion" (Whiston, 1708, pp. 432–3; see also pp. 435–6; Force, 1985, p. 47). Whiston wanted to eliminate altogether the belief that there were events that were exceptions to the laws of nature. His effort was resisted by some religious scientists. John Keill, another Newtonian and the Savilian Professor of Astronomy at Oxford, believed that some events are ultimately not explainable by science and must be counted miracles because they are anomalous (Force, 1985, pp. 125–6). Newton both committed himself to miracles and undermined the traditional notion of miracles. He thought that gravity was miraculous and that "a continual miracle is needed to prevent the sun and fixed stars from rushing together through gravity" (quoted from Force, 1985, p. 124).

Today many contemporary theologians, trying to be both religious and scientific, as Hobbes was, adopt his way of explaining miracles, even though they never credit him with the tactic. They affirm that the manna that fell from heaven miraculously saved the Hebrews wandering in the desert but explain that this manna was a secretion of insects feeding on the sap of the tamarisk.[18] They affirm that the Hebrews were miraculously saved from the Egyptians by the parting of the Red Sea but explain that the parting was caused by very strong winds that dried up a shallow stretch of the water. They affirm that Jesus fed five thousand men and uncounted numbers of women and children with only a few loaves and fishes by conjecturing that many people had secretly brought food, which they were moved to share when they saw Jesus's willingness to share all he had. Their view in general is that God had arranged the world in such a way that all the natural events from the beginning of time, in accordance with unswerving natural laws, conspired to do the right thing in the right place to make things come out right for the people who interpreted the events as miraculous.

Although Hobbes is certainly trying to make it harder for a person either to claim that he can perform a miracle or to witness one, he does not rule out their possibility completely. Hobbes does not say or imply that humans will have a scientific explanation for every miracle. For example, humans have no scientific explanation for how Jesus could have changed water into wine and may never have one. Hobbes is trying to reconcile science with religion, not to have science gobble up religion. He is open to the possibility that miracles do occur (cf. EW, 3:365). In 1668, he wrote a letter in which he discusses the possibility that the case of a woman who remained alive although she had allegedly not eaten for six months was miraculous. He names several items that ought to be investigated before a decision on this case can be reached. He says that he does not have sufficient evidence to reach a decision himself and that the proper authority to make such a decision is the church: "The examining, whether such a thing as this be a miracle, belongs (I think) to the church" (quoted from Birch, 1756, p. 334; EW, 7:464). The tone of the letter is neither cynical nor sarcastic, as one would expect if he were skeptical of the possibility of miracles.

Let's take stock of my discussion of Hobbes's treatment of miracles. I have claimed that Hobbes contradicts himself on the issue of who performs miracles. Sometimes he says that magicians perform miracles, while sometimes he says that only God can perform them. There is no subversive motive in this contradiction. He is committed to the first view because he is committed to the Bible and that is what the Bible says. He is committed to the second view because he wants to emphasize the sovereignty of God, which is also a biblical view. Hobbes does not flaunt the contradiction, as one would expect him to do if he were irreligious. Rather, he either slides over the contradiction or tries to resolve it.

Concerning the contradiction about whether miracles involve a violation of the laws of nature or not, the forces operating on Hobbes are slightly different. On the one hand, Hobbes was traditional and conservative in his pre-theoretical beliefs. He abandoned common sense or received opinion only if he saw that there was no alternative to doing so. This led him to accept that miracles were performed through the immediate operation of God. On the other hand, he was committed to modern science, which accepts the uniformity of nature. Thus, he tried to explain miracles without compromising science. I conjecture that Hobbes wrote two drafts of the section on miracles and later tacked them together. He gives two definitions of "miracle" in the chapter, each of which receives its own explication; there is thus substantial repetition. He put the later version of the chapter (the one that explains miracles without compromising science) first and put the earlier version (the one that contains the standard view that there is an ordinary and extraordinary way in which God works) second.

Neutralizing the political force of miracles

I have been emphasizing how Hobbes's treatment of miracles fits in with his broader project of reconciling religion and science. But he uses that same treatment to neutralize the political force of miracles. During the seventeenth century, many political subversives claimed to perform miracles in order to establish their credentials as prophets (Thomas, 1971, pp. 133–40). What Hobbes has done is to make it more difficult to claim that some event is miraculous and thereby more difficult for someone to claim that he is a prophet. Thus, although some kinds of healings could have been considered miraculous before the development of modern medicine, those same kinds of healings cannot be considered miraculous today. As science grows, miracles diminish.

Another aspect of politically neutralizing prophets is the

fact that Hobbes also points out that anyone who accepts a miracle confesses to ignorance:

> Furthermore, seeing admiration and wonder are consequent to the knowledge and experience, wherewith men are endued, some more, some less; it followeth, that the same thing may be a miracle to one, and not to another. And thence it is, that ignorant and superstitious men make great wonders of those works, which other men, knowing to proceed from nature, (which is not the immediate, but the ordinary work of God), admire not at all: as when eclipses of the sun and moon have been taken for supernatural works, by the common people; when nevertheless, there were others, who could from their natural causes have foretold the very hour they should arrive. EW, 3:429)

Holding that every admission of witnessing a miracle is also a confession of ignorance was not a novel doctrine. The medieval theologian Andrew of St. Victor, who insisted that a miracle can be declared only after every attempted natural explanation has failed, said that every such declaration is a declaration of ignorance (Chenu, 1968, p. 17). But only Hobbes uses such a declaration of ignorance to shame people into not believing too readily in miracles or prophets.

In this chapter, we have seen that Hobbes circumscribed the concepts of revelation, prophets, and miracles in such a way that genuine religious phenomena would be preserved without conflicting with modern science and without destabilizing established political units. In the next chapter, I will show how Hobbes pursued the same project in eschatology.

Chapter 9

Angels and eschatology

In this chapter, I will continue presenting evidence for my thesis that, in addition to his project of providing a theory that justifies the existence of government, Hobbes had two principal aims: to reconcile traditional religious doctrine with the emerging modern science of Copernicus, Galileo, and Harvey; and to ensure that religion served the purpose of contributing to peace on earth, not anarchy.

Eschatology is the study of the last things: death, heaven, hell, and divine judgment. These topics will be discussed in this chapter. In addition, Hobbes's views about the alleged first creaturely residents of heaven and hell – namely spirits, angels, and demons – will be discussed. The chapter is divided into four sections. The first concerns angels, spirits and devils; the second, hell; the third, heaven and the Antichrist; and the fourth, salvation and redemption.

ANGELS

Spirit

Angels belong to the genus of spirits, in one of the several senses that the word has in the Bible. At the beginning of chapter 34, "Of the Signification of Spirit, Angel, and Inspiration in the Books of Holy Scripture," Hobbes rehearses the way the word is used in the Bible, just as he does for "word of God" and "prophet" in chapter 36, as we saw earlier. Hobbes makes several other points that are equally

247

important. One is that the word "spirit" has many uses and meanings in the Bible and that which meaning the word has on a given occasion can be determined only by intelligent attention to the context in which it occurs. Hobbes demonstrates an impressive literary sensitivity in distinguishing these senses of the term, and many of his interpretations are accepted by biblical scholars today.

Another point is that when "spirit" is used to refer to a substance, what it refers to is a material object, because the phrase "immaterial substance" is *contradictio in adiecto* (EW, 3:381). This means that a spirit in this sense is a body. Further, a body is something that fills or occupies some place in the universe: "For the *universe*, being the aggregate of all bodies, there is no real part thereof that is not also *body*; nor any thing properly a *body*, that is not also part of that aggregate of all *bodies*, the *universe*" (ibid.). Presumably, although each bodily part of the universe occupies a space and is able to change its location, the universe as a whole does not occupy space and is not able to change its location, because space and location are defined in terms of the relative positions of bodies that form proper parts of the universe. Hobbes's views on this matter have inspired some to think that he is a pantheist, since he insists that God is a body and sometimes says that God does not occupy space or change location (ibid., pp. 351–2). If he were a pantheist, then by his own criterion he would be an atheist (ibid., p. 351; EW, 2:213–14). Some are inclined to interpret the possibility of making this inference as grounds for claiming that Hobbes was communicating a secret message of atheism to them.

But there is no compelling reason to conclude on the basis of these passages that Hobbes was a secret atheist. For one thing, Hobbes makes his claim that spirits must be bodies if they are substances, not in the context of talking about God, but as preliminary to talking about angels. Later, when he comes to explain why spirits are bodies, he senses a conflict with his earlier views about God being a body. He admits that there is a problem and retreats to the position that "the nature of God is incomprehensible." He says that "we understand nothing of *what he is,* but only *that he is;* and there-fore the attributes we give him, are not to tell one another, what he is, nor to signify our opinion of his nature, but our desire to honour him with such names as we conceive most honourable amongst ourselves" (EW, 3:383). In other words, Hobbes admits the ultimate logical untenability of his views when they are extended to God. He has no way of explain-ing how a material God fits into the human understanding of the universe. This does not deter him from persisting in holding what he is certain of, namely, that substantial spirits must be bodies. His candid admission of a problem for this version of his philosophy, far from signifying a secret mes-sage of atheism, is most plausibly interpreted as nothing more than a candid admission of a problem that remains to be solved. Later, Hobbes began to see his way toward a solution. In *An Answer to Bishop Bramhall,* he says there is no need to assert that God is indivisible, since the Bible no-where says that he is (EW, 4:302–3).

In fact, Hobbes had in *Leviathan* the materials for con-structing an even better position. He had said that the term "universe" is equivocal. In one sense, the universe is every-thing that exists. Since God exists, he is part of the universe. It would follow from this that God has a location and is not indivisible. But humans cannot know where God is or any-thing else about him. In addition, it is irreverent to speculate further about the nature of God, since it is clear that humans can never attain knowledge of God. This position does not entail that God is identical either with the universe as a whole or with any visible part of it. There is nothing objec-tionable about defining the universe as everything that ex-ists.[1] In another sense, "universe" refers only to those bodies that people can see or feel (EW, 3:381). In this sense, neither God nor many fine substances would be part of the universe. But they could still be spirits – that is, intangi-ble, diaphonous, and rarefied bodies (ibid., p. 382, see also p. 388).

In order to evaluate his views fairly, it is also important to realize that Hobbes's opponents have problems at least as serious as his. He points out that if God is a spirit and spirits do not move because they are immaterial, how is it that Genesis says that the spirit of God moved upon the face of the waters? If "spirit" is being used here to designate a substance, then God is material, just as Hobbes maintains. Hobbes does not unfairly press this point against his opponents. He sensibly says that the passage from Genesis is best interpreted figuratively, as meaning that God sent a wind, just as it does in other places in the Bible (EW, 3:383–4). The point is that it is either difficult or impossible to make all talk about the Christian God consistent without appealing freely to various interpretive devices, such as claiming that a passage is figurative whenever it does not fit the preconceived idea of God.

Some uses of "spirit" are definitely metaphorical. On such occasions, the word may be used to communicate extraordinary understanding, zeal, authority, submission to doctrine, and various bad dispositions (EW, 3:382, 384–8). Hobbes cogently supports all of these interpretations with diverse biblical citations, from such books as Numbers, Joshua, 1 Kings, and 1 Samuel, the four gospels, and various epistles.[2] By interpreting spirit either literally as a certain kind of body or figuratively in various ways, Hobbes makes talk about spirits fit into the scientific view of the world.

Angels

When "spirits" is used literally, it often refers to angels, which are subtle bodies. To those who deny that angels can have bodies, Hobbes replies that there is no other way to make literal sense of the biblical text. For angels move and talk just as humans do, and they burn in hell as only bodies can do (EW, 3:391–3). While it may not have been the standard seventeenth-century view of angels, Hobbes's view was also held by Milton, who thought that angels were composed of "ether" (e.g., Milton, 1674, V.401ff., VI.344ff., and Elledge, 1975, pp. 394–6). Hobbes's justification for believing in the existence of bodily angels is telling. The New Testament must be handled differently from the Old. He says that although there are legitimate ways of reading the Old Testament that would explain away their existence, Jesus' categorical talk about angels demands that they be admitted into the ontology of the universe. That is to say, Hobbes thinks that his commitment to biblical Christianity entails a commitment to angels. He could have simply asserted that every use of the term "angel" in the New Testament was figurative, as almost all Christian intellectuals do today, but Hobbes was not willing to take this easy way out, notwithstanding his additional commitment to science.

Etymologically, an angel is simply a messenger, and in the Bible this is understood more narrowly as a messenger from God (EW, 3:388). Consequently, anything that would make God's presence known counts as an angel. Since God often manifests himself to humans through dreams and visions, which are only events in the brain, some dreams and visions are, strictly speaking, angels – that is, "messengers."

The widespread, though not universal, belief in substantive angels among the Jews was a false notion introduced by Gentiles during the Diaspora. The Old Testament itself does not justify any such belief. All of the Old Testament uses of "angel" are explainable in natural terms, as either dreams, visions, some other expression of the power or presence of God (or even for God himself), or as ordinary humans on a divine mission (EW, 3:389–90). It is not necessary for me to repeat Hobbes's proof of his point through the careful explication of dozens of Old Testament text. It is sufficient to point out that many of them have become the standard interpretations of those passages among modern biblical scholars (Achtemeier, 1985, p. 30).

When he begins his analysis of the New Testament passages, he continues as he left off with the Old. When angels appear in dreams or visions, they need be interpreted as being no more than dreams or visions that reveal the presence or power of God. But then comes a radical change, with disarming candor:

Considering therefore the signification of the word *angel* in the Old Testament, and the nature of dreams and visions that happen to men by the ordinary way of nature; I was inclined to this opinion, that angels were nothing but supernatural apparitions of the fancy, raised by the special and extraordinary operation of God, thereby to make his presence and commandments known to mankind, and chiefly to his own people. But the many places of the New Testament, and our Saviour's own words, and in such texts, wherein is no suspicion of corruption of the Scripture, have extorted from my feeble reason, an acknowledgment and belief, that there be also angels substantial, and permanent. (EW, 3:394)

Thus Hobbes admits that he began with the intention of denying that there were any substantive angels, presumably because they do not fit neatly into the scientific view, but then felt compelled by the text of the New Testament to change his belief and to subscribe to its literal meaning. If he were bent on rejecting religion completely, he could either have dismissed talk about angels out of hand, as mythology, or he could have maintained his subtle demythologizing interpretations throughout the New Testament.[3] But he did not. He yields to the force of the New Testament, as one would hope a good Christian would do.

Demons

Demons are the Gentile analogs of the Judeo-Christian angels. According to pagan demonology, there are good demons and bad demons, just as there are good angels and bad angels. Although he could have tried to accommodate demons by simply identifying them with angels, Hobbes is unswerving in his denial that demons exist. The reason is that Hobbes is always careful to separate biblical doctrines from the corruptions of biblical religion that resulted from mixing in similar pagan doctrines. It is an important part of his Reformation ardor to purify Christianity of the paganism that Roman Catholicism introduced. This explains why Hobbes separates his discussion of angels, which occurs in chapter 34, from his discussion of demons, which occurs in chapter 45. The same tendency is even more marked in his discussion of other topics in which there has been a pagan corruption of some Christian concept. For example, when he comes to discuss hell, he begins by identifying the pagan doctrines of hell; then he shows that they are absurd and therefore should be dismissed. It is only after the pagan accretions have been removed that he thinks it is possible to interpret the Christian view of hell in a way that makes it consistent with modern science. As Pocock said, Hobbes "most rigorously separated the Hellenic from the Hebraic components of his cultural tradition and went further than any major philosopher since Augustine in rejecting the former and relying upon the latter" (Pocock, 1971, p. 200; see also the section entitled "The Kingdom of Darkness" in Chapter 11 of the present volume).

Hobbes begins his chapter "Of Demonology and Other Relics of the Religion of the Gentiles" by reviewing his theory of vision, first adumbrated in chapters 2 and 3 of *Leviathan*. It may initially appear that any account of perception would be impertinent in the context, and a scientific account all the more so. But to think so misses the point. Hobbes is indicating, I believe, that the scientific account of perception must be accepted; that religious beliefs have to be accommodated within the scientific view if they are to be preserved; and that there is no incongruity in discussing scientific issues within the context of religious issues. He follows his discussion of perception with the claim that demon sightings are nothing but the apparitions resulting from "great distemper of the organs" of cognition, the senses, and the brain (EW, 3:637) and thus have no evidential value.

Demonology – that is, the official theory of demons – as opposed to popular belief in them, was the work of pagan poets, especially Hesiod. The theory entered Judaism when the Greeks introduced their colonies and conquests into Asia, Egypt, and Italy, after the Diaspora. Saint Paul warned against believing in these pagan apparitions when he wrote, "Now the spirit speaketh expressly, that in the latter times some shall depart from the faith, giving heed to seducing spirits, and doctrines of devils" (1 Tim. 4:1; EW, 3:639). However, the Jews departed from the pagan use of the term. They restricted the name "demon" to the evil spirits and attributed the work of the good demons to God. This led them to attribute madness, lunacy, and sickness to devils when these conditions were the result of purely natural causes.[4] The Jews who rejected Jesus accepted this kind of superstitious pseudoscience and accused him of being possessed by the devil. So much for those who believe in demonic possession (EW, 3:640, 389).

Hobbes claims that Jesus himself did not believe in demonic possession. When Jesus seems to speak to the devils who possess people, he is speaking figuratively but not inappropriately, just as it was not inappropriate for him to rebuke the wind and sea or for God to command the light, the firmament, the sun, and the stars. These are merely poetic ways of expressing the power of God (EW, 3:640–1).

It is not clear why Jesus did not make a point of proving this to the Jews. "But such questions as these, are more curious, than necessary for a Christian man's salvation" (EW, 3:643). We could just as unprofitably ask why Christ did not give faith and piety to all, or why he wanted humans to discover natural causes and sciences themselves and did not reveal it to them. The best explanation that Hobbes can think of is that if Jesus had tried to argue that demons did not exist, he would have been engaged in natural science and not in the mission for which he was on earth, namely, to preach "that he was the Christ, the Son of the living God, sent into the world to sacrifice himself for our sins, and at his coming again, gloriously to reign over his elect, and to save them from their enemies eternally" (ibid.). When Hobbes rhetorically asks why Christ did not give faith and piety to all, he is not insinuating that Christ should have or that he thinks Christianity morally bankrupt for teaching that Christ does not. Hobbes is simply espousing the standard views associated with the doctrine of double predestination, which was part of the foundation of seventeenth-century Calvinism.

Hobbes summarizes his position on spirits, angels, and demons in this way: "I find in Scripture that there be angels, and spirits, good and evil; but not that they are incorporeal, as are the apparitions men see in the dark, or in a dream, or vision; which the Latins call *specta* and took for *demons*. And I find that there are spirits corporal, though subtle and invisible; but not that any man's body was possessed or inhabited by them; and that the bodies of the saints shall be such, namely, spiritual bodies, as Saint Paul calls them" (EW, 3:644).

Idols

One of the policies of the Reformers was to strip the old churches of the statues and paintings that they believed represented a kind of idolatry (see Calvin, 1559, I.10–11). Like them, Hobbes condemns such practices as "[a]nother relic of Gentilism" (EW, 3:645), which take away from the devotion owed to God. That is the force of the first two Mosaic commandments (ibid., p. 646). Hobbes's principal target in opposing the use of images is Roman Catholicism (p. 657), which encouraged not only paintings, mosaics, and sculpture in its churches but also relics of saints. Hobbes reports that ignorant Christians believe that such items have spoken, bled, or been involved in other alleged miracles (p. 658).

Hobbes thinks that idol worship was introduced into Christianity when the Gentile converts renamed their pagan idols, rather than destroying them, because of their aesthetic value. Thus a statue of Venus became the Virgin Mary, Cupid became Jesus, Jupiter became Barnabas, and Mercury became Paul. The cult of saints is another aspect of this pagan tendency to divinize important human beings. Romulus was the first to be canonized by the Romans, then Julius Caesar. Later, virtually all the emperors were apotheotized at a propitious moment. Thus, while the cult of saints is superficially Christian, its origin and content are pagan. The saints are simply masquerading members of the pagan pantheon. The position of the pope also evolved out of this pagan cult of the gods. The title of the chief religious official of pagan Rome, *pontifex maximus*, was taken over by Augustus Caesar and successive emperors. After Constantine became a Christian, he transferred the title to the pope. So the pope had this title only because he was the agent of the emperor, who was the genuine head of the church (EW, 3:660–1, 6:17). Hobbes sees other pagan / Christian analogs in the pairs *aqua lustralis* / holy water; *bacchanalia* / wakes; *saturnalia* / carnivals; processions to Priapus / decoration of Maypoles. Hobbes is offended that the Catholic church poured the new wine of Christianity into the old skins of pagan ritual but trusts that those skins will break, as the New Testament predicts (EW, 3:663). Thus, when Hobbes describes the Catholic church as the ghost of the Roman Empire sitting on the chair of the Roman Empire, he considers his words only minimally figurative.

The philosophical basis for opposing worship before images is that since every image in the strict sense must resemble what it represents, and no finite image can resemble an infinite God, no image can resemble God (EW, 3:649). Hobbes is objecting to images on the same grounds that Calvin had (Calvin, 1559, I.11.2; also see I.10–12; and Eire, 1986, pp. 197–212). Hobbes's attack on idols and images is standard Calvinism. But Calvin himself had been more virulent in his condemnation of idols and less yielding in permitting the use of images in worship. Calvin had said that anyone who uses an image to worship God "clings to his own speculations, . . . [and that] God's glory is corrupted by an impious falsehood whenever any form is attached to him" (Calvin, 1559, I.11.1, and more generally I.11.1–14). Hobbes is willing to yield to the Old Testament passages in which God commands that certain sculptures are to be used in his worship:

[H]e that worshippeth in an image, or any creature, either the matter thereof, or any fancy of his own, which he thinketh to dwell in it; or both together; or believeth that such things hear his prayers, or see his devotions, without ears or eyes, committeth idolatry: and he that counterfeiteth such worship for fear of punishment, if he be a man whose example hath power amongst his brethren, committeth a sin. But he that worshipeth the Creator of the world before such an image, or in such a place as he hath not made, or chosen of himself, but taken from the commandment of God's word, as the Jews did in worshipping God before the cherubims, and before the brazen serpent for a time, and in, or towards the Temple of Jerusalem, which was also but for a time, committeth not idolatry. (EW, 3:656)

Hobbes also permits a person to worship before graven images if commanded to do so by his sovereign, because such doings are not the actions of the person being obedient but of the person issuing the command (EW, 3:651–2; see also the section entitled "Worship" in Chapter 10 of the present volume).

HELL

Hobbes's purposes in discussing the nature of hell are the same two that we have been considering: one political, one scientific. At the beginning of chapter 38, "Of the Signification in Scripture of Eternal Life, Hell, Salvation, the World to Come, and Redemption," Hobbes says that it is important to understand what the Bible teaches about eternal life and eternal torment, because if some human other than the sovereign has control over dispensing these things the risk of "calamities of confusion and civil war" (EW, 3:437) are very great. Thus, in order to keep the concept of hell from being used for seditious purposes, he is intent on showing that the ultimate fate of human beings depends, according to God's own plan, upon obedience to the sovereign. Concerning his scientific project, Hobbes wants to explain how belief in hell is consistent with the scientific view of the world.

Hobbes begins by separating the pagan accretions from the genuine biblical doctrine of hell. The Greeks had the view that demons occupy some infinitely deep pit in the earth. The Roman doctrine was similar. Hobbes quotes Vergil's *Aeneid:* "Bis patet in praeceps tantum, tenditque sub umbras,/Quantum ad aetherium coeli suspectus Olympum." That is, Vergil claims that Tartarus is twice as deep as heaven is high. Hobbes objects that the actual dimensions of the earth and the heavens cannot support such a claim.[5] So the pagan doctrines of Hades, Tartarus, and Inferno should not be mixed with the biblical doctrine of hell (EW, 3:445).

The biblical evidence about the condition of humans after death is equivocal. All humans go into the earth when they are dead. But the psalm says that the wicked go with the damned giants of Genesis, and they are described as under water. However, the place of the damned is sometimes described as a fiery place, for two reasons. First, God destroyed Sodom and Gomorrha, the biblical paradigm of wickedness, with fire and brimstone. Second, outside of Jerusalem there was a garbage dump, which was periodically set afire to remove the stench and which had been the place where idolatrous Jews had sacrificed their children to Moloch. This place was called the Valley of Hinnon, from which we get the name Gehenna, usually translated "hell." The idea that the flames of hell are eternal comes from this periodic burning. So hell seems to be a place of light. In contradiction to this, other texts say that the damned live in total darkness (EW, 3:447).

Since no one thinks that hell is the Valley of Hinnon, or that the wicked will live either under the ground or underwater, or that the wicked will not be able to see each other, the texts discussed must be metaphorical. The literal truth behind these metaphors is that hell must be a place on earth since the wicked are the enemies of God's kingdom, and his kingdom is on earth. Because Scripture repeatedly indicates that the pains of the wicked are the most horrible possible, they must be burning in a real fire, for only a real fire burns real bodies. Hobbes also takes the Bible at its word when it says that these fires burn eternally. However, he makes the logical point that it does not follow that each wicked person will burn or otherwise suffer eternally (EW, 3:450, 615, 624–7; cf. Pocock, 1971, p. 175). Indeed, there are three reasons why the suffering of the wicked must be finite. First, as already mentioned, since real fire destroys real bodies in a finite period of time, the wicked must be consumed in a finite period of time (EW, 3:597). Second, the mercy of God is inconsistent with eternal suffering, even for the most wicked person. There is no mercy at all involved in letting someone suffer eternally (EW, 3:624, 4:354, 358, 5:214).[6] Third, if the suffering of the wicked were infinite, then no literal sense could be attached to Saint Paul's doctrine that the wicked will suffer a second death (EW, 3:450–1); and Hobbes wants to give a literal interpretation to the Bible whenever it does not conflict with common sense, his metaphysics, or modern science. Hobbes's view is similar to that recently expressed by Richard Swinburne, Nolloth Professor of Philosophy of the Christian Faith at Oxford, who says, "Annihilation, the scrap heap, seems an obvious fate for the corrupt soul. [And] . . . if we take such talk [of hell] literally, and suppose the wicked to be ordinary embodied men, the consequence of putting them in such a fire will be their elimination" (Swinburne, 1989, pp. 182–3). In the seventeenth century, some Christians thought that the doctrine of eternal punishment encouraged atheism and thus adopted a form of limited temporal punishment as a way of defending Christianity (Walker, 1964, pp. 145, 243–4).

While Hobbes's attempt to come up with a plausible, relatively humane, and biblically based doctrine of hell to compete with the cruel standard view is laudable, it is not completely successful. He seems to think that the eternal fires of hell need to be stoked by an inexhaustible, and hence infinite, supply of wicked people. He suggests that since the wicked, unlike the blessed, will have "gross and corruptible bodies," they may procreate "perpetually, after the resurrection, as they did before" (EW, 3:626). Hobbes assumes that these children, or at least a sizable proportion of them, will themselves be corrupt and be sent to hell, but not before they generate more reprobate children: "To the reprobate there remaineth after the resurrection, a *second* and *eternal* death: between which resurrection, and their second and eternal death, is but a time of punishment and torment; and to last by succession of sinners thereunto, as long as the kind of man by propagation shall endure; which is eternally" (ibid., p. 627). The scene that Hobbes paints is quite horrible and out of keeping with his general humaneness. The idea of an infinite number of wicked people tortured for a finite period of time is not much more satisfying than the idea of a finite number tortured for an infinite period of time.

HEAVEN

Eternal life on earth

According to Hobbes, heaven is the place of eternal life. Adam would have enjoyed an eternal life on earth if he had not sinned. However, the story of the first sin does not allow for a completely literal interpretation. For the Bible says that Adam was warned that he would die on the day he ate the fruit from the tree of the knowledge of good and evil; but he did not die. Thus, in order to defend the Bible against the accusation that what it says is false, Hobbes interprets the phrase figuratively. He says it means that on that day, Adam became mortal: that is, from that day, it was certain that Adam would die (EW, 3:438, 613–14). This was a standard way of treating this problem in the biblical text.

As explained in Chapter 5, covenant theologians held that God's covenant of works with Adam was conditional upon his perfect obedience. Also, just as all humans lost eternal life through the sin of Adam, they all regained it through Jesus. Hobbes's language is the very same as that of the covenant theologians (EW, 3:614), but he carries the symmetry between Adam and Christ farther. Just as Adam continued to live for many years after he lost eternal life, Christ has already given eternal life to Christians, even though they will die and will remain dead until the Resurrection (ibid., pp. 440–1). Hobbes, who seems to savor this doctrine (ibid., p. 438), then points out that if Jesus restored what Adam lost, and Adam lost eternal life on earth, then Jesus has restored eternal life on earth. In other words, heaven must be on earth. He then quotes Psalms, Acts, the Book of Revelation (twice), Isaiah (twice), the Epistle to the Romans, and the Gospel of John, not to mention other books, in order to prove the point. Heaven will either be located in or centered on Jerusalem (ibid., pp. 439–40, 453–5). The view that heaven will be on earth also makes sense of the biblical doctrine that after the Resurrection there will be no marriage. For if the blessed were able to reproduce eternally, the earth would eventually be overpopulated: "The Jews that asked our Saviour the question, whose wife the woman that had married many brothers should be in the resurrection, knew not what were the consequences of immortality" (ibid., p. 440). The standard view that heaven will be populated in a presumably infinite space cannot account for the eventual abolition of marriage.

While there is substantial textual evidence that eternal life will be enjoyed on earth, there is no good text that indicates that the blessed will live in the starry heavens after the Resurrection, according to Hobbes (ibid., pp. 441, 455–6).

Heaven and the Kingdom of God

Many seventeenth-century Christians, like many today, distinguish between heaven and the Kingdom of God. They think that the Kingdom of God already exists on earth, whereas heaven is a place to which the elect go after they die. One of the novel features of Hobbes's view is that he thinks that the two concepts overlap. He agrees with the majority view that the Kingdom of God is an earthly kingdom, but not in a way that they would like. He thinks that the Kingdom of God or, what is the same thing, the Kingdom of Heaven, means literally the place or the people over which the King, who lives in the heavens, reigns. Since God reigned over the people of Israel and Israel is on earth, the Kingdom of Heaven must be on earth (EW, 3:441). But it is obvious that it does not exist now. For every kingdom occupies a territory, and there is no territory on earth that has God as its special sovereign. In fact, the term Kingdom of God refers to several things. There has already been a divine kingdom in the past; none exists now; and a second, final kingdom is reserved for the indefinite future. Hobbes identifies heaven with this second kingdom.

There is strong textual support in the Bible for Hobbes's interpretation. He is fond of pointing out that it would have made no sense for Jesus to teach humans to pray "Thy kingdom come" if it were already here (EW, 3:618). And when the apostles ask Jesus when the kingdom will be restored, he answers that no one knows when that will happen and that he promises to send the Holy Spirit in the meantime (ibid.; see also EW, 4:322–3).

There is one strong New Testament passage, interpreted by Theodore Beza, that suggests that the Kingdom of God has already come: "Verily I say unto you, that there be some of them that stand here, which shall not taste of death, till they have seen the kingdom of God come with power" (Mark 9:1; EW, 3:617; see also Luke 9:27 and Matt. 16:28). Hobbes says that the correct interpretation of this passage requires attention to the context. It occurs immediately before the report of the transfiguration of Jesus, which was witnessed by only Peter, James, and John (Mark 9:2–8). So Jesus' words were confirmed immediately by the vision those apostles had of the kingdom that was to come permanently in the future. (Notice how ingeniously Hobbes tries to save the literal truth of the Bible.)

Mortalism

Hobbes was a mortalist; that is, he held that after the sin of Adam it was the natural condition of humans to die, and death means the end of existence. He did not believe that the soul survived in a disembodied form. This required him to explain how several passages in the Bible that are used to support belief in the immortality of the soul actually have a different purpose. For example, the verse that God is not a God of the dead but of the living and that "all live to him" (EW, 3:442, quoting Luke 20:38) means that people have eternal life because God bestows it as a grace to the faithful. For immortality is not "a property consequent to the essence and nature of mankind" (EW, 3:442). By nature, all men are mortal; it is only by the grace of God that the faithful are given eternal life (see also EW, 4:350–4).

Some might object that Hobbes's mortalism, combined with a belief in the resurrection of the dead, presents him with the problem of personal identity. On what basis can a person alive now be identified with some person alive in the indefinite future when there is no intervening spatiotemporal continuity? Hobbes is not disturbed by the question: "For God, that could give a life to a piece of clay, hath the same power to give life again to a dead man, and renew his inanimate, and rotten carcase, into a glorious, spiritual, and immortal body" (EW, 3:631). Although this is not a theory-based reply, Hobbes's explicit treatment of personal identity is consistent with the sentiment just expressed. In *De Corpore*, he indicates that the body at (or perhaps immediately preceding) the moment of death is identical with the body formed from that same matter in the same configuration of parts, even if a very long time has intervened (EW, 1:136–8).

Hobbes's appeal to the Book of Job for evidence of mortalism is completely appropriate: "There is hope of a tree if it be cast down. Though the root thereof wax old, and the stock thereof die, in the ground, yet when it scenteth the water it will bud, and bring forth boughs like a plant. But man dieth and wasteth away, yea, man giveth up the ghost, and where is he? . . . Man lieth down , and riseth not, till the heavens be no more" (EW, 3:443, quoting Job 14:7, 12). If there are other passages from other books that seem to suggest immortality, they are more difficult to interpret than the one from Job (EW, 3:622).

Hobbes is right in holding that there is no doctrine of immortality in the Hebrew Bible. The idea of the immortality of the soul entered Judaism in about the fourth century B.C. from Hellenistic sources. Although Saint Paul seems to speak of an afterlife prior to the Resurrection, he more often talks about the Resurrection itself. Hobbes realizes that his view of heaven is a novelty and consequently twice says that he is willing to yield his opinion if the sovereign dictates a different doctrine. But since the outcome of the Civil War is still not decided and since the issue is so important, he has given his opinion (EW, 3:438, 444).

Hobbes's mortalism is sometimes used as evidence of his allegedly antireligious views. It is certainly not obviously so. For Luther did not believe that the disembodied soul was conscious, and Calvin refused to discuss the matter. The devout Anglican Thomas Browne and the Puritan John Milton were both moralists like Hobbes (see Burns, 1972, pp. 1–3, 26–30, 148–91). The view is fairly common today. Perhaps the most distinguished living proponent of the view that Christianity is philosophically defensible is Richard Swinburne, and he argues for mortalism on largely Hobbesian grounds (Swinburne, 1989, p. 184). Moreover, the discussion earlier in this chapter of Hobbes's views about heaven and hell shows that his mortalism is deeply rooted in his reading of the Bible. The fact that his mortalism was also consistent with his metaphysics is no evidence that he did not also hold it for religious reasons. While mortalism was Christian in spirit for all of the people just mentioned, it was especially so for Hobbes. Although man is naturally mortal, as every student ever exposed to a categorical syllogism knows, the blessed are made immortal by the mercy of God, and the damned are not punished eternally, again due to his mercy.

Mark Johnston has argued that Hobbes did not think that there was any inconsistency in holding that the soul is both material and immortal (Johnston, 1989, p. 654); at least, he says, this is the view Hobbes expressed during the 1640s. It is only in *Leviathan* that Hobbes becomes a mortalist. Hobbes changed his mind on this issue, according to Johnston, because mortalism had a political consequence that Hobbes found desirable. That is, if the soul is mortal, then the threats of religious authorities that eternal suffering will befall those who oppose them will be diminished (ibid., p. 659). Johnston's suggested explanation for Hobbes's change would be plausible except for two things. First, Hobbes subscribes to the view that there will be a resurrection of the dead, at which time the elect will enjoy eternal happiness and the reprobate will suffer and will eventually die a second death. That is, excruciating pain awaits the wicked after death, even if not immediately after death. There is no solace in knowing that the suffering will occur after a period of unexperienced inexistence. Second, even if it were coupled with a denial of resurrection, mortalism would be desirable only if a person thought that he would have to choose between the laws of God and the laws of man. But the whole thrust of Hobbes's political philosophy, especially his doctrine of the Christian commonwealth, is that there is virtually no possibility of a conflict between God and one's sovereign, since the Kingdom of God must await the Second Coming.

Johnston thinks that Hobbes may be speaking to those who are not persuaded that the chance of a conflict is small (Johnston, 1989, p. 659). But this does not affect the point that if severe suffering awaits those who disobey God, disobeying God cannot be recommended. One of the major themes of Hobbes's political philosophy is that humans too often mistakenly choose their short-term immediate good at the expense of their long-term, nonimmediate good. Choosing one's sovereign over God would be an instance of this sort of mistake.

As an alternative to Johnston's explanation, I would suggest that Hobbes adopted mortalism only when he wrote *Leviathan*, for two reasons. First, it takes a long time for a person to understand what all the consequences are of his theory. Second, Hobbes's desire to be conservative in religious doctrine would incline him to espouse the immortality of the soul until he saw that its denial was compatible with other Christian doctrines and with modern science. By the time he wrote *Leviathan*, he saw that mortalism fit better with his materialism and that it was consistent with orthodoxy. The Christian creeds say nothing about the immortality of the soul, only about the resurrection of the dead.

In addition to the reasons just given, Hobbes would have found mortalism attractive because it was not a Roman Catholic view. Mortalism is a Protestant view. The Anabaptist Richard Overton, as well as Milton and Hobbes, all used mortalism to attack the Roman Catholic doctrine of purgatory (Burns, 1972, p. 27 n. 24) and indulgences. If nothing of a human being survives death prior to the Resurrection, then there is nothing to suffer in purgatory, and hence nothing to be gained from the buying of indulgences (EW, 3:627). The cult of the saints also suffers, because there is no longer any point in praying to a saint to intercede for someone in purgatory. Because Hobbes is never satisfied with simply a logical argument against a religious doctrine, he also contests the scriptural interpretations that Robert Bellarmine presented to defend belief in purgatory (ibid., pp. 627–36).

Before proceeding to the doctrines of salvation and redemption, which underlie the hope of heaven, it is worth quoting part of Hobbes's summary of his eschatology:

> I have showed already, that the kingdom of God by Christ beginneth at the day of judgment: that in that day the faithful shall rise again, with glorious and spiritual bodies, and be his subjects in that his kingdom, which shall be eternal: that they shall neither marry nor be given in marriage, nor eat and drink, as they did in their natural bodies; but live for ever in their individual persons, without the specific eternity of generation: and that the reprobates also shall rise again, to receive punishments for their sins: as also, that those of the elect, which shall be alive in their earthly bodies at that day, shall have their bodies suddenly changed, and made spiritual and immortal. (EW, 3:625)

SALVATION AND REDEMPTION

Religious salvation

Salvation is the condition of being removed from various kinds of evil, such as sickness, fear, pain, and worst of all, according to Hobbes, death. Hobbes's Christianity dictates that he hold that humans cannot save themselves from eternal death. Because of sin and their absolute dependence on God, humans can be saved only if they are redeemed. Redemption is the process by which humans are preserved from the evils they incurred as the consequences of sin. The redeemer is Jesus Christ (EW, 3:451–2). All of this is common to Christians of every major sect and tantamount to orthodoxy. Oddly, the church never declared any particular theory of the nature of redemption orthodox. In the course of many centuries several theories were developed. What has never been noted is that Hobbes produces a new theory of Christian redemption which eliminates a serious defect in one of the two most important standard theories.

In the Middle Ages, the two strongest theories of redemption were the ransom theory and the satisfaction theory. According to the ransom theory, which was developed most fully by Saint Augustine, human beings were originally under the control of God. After they sinned, they came under the control of the devil and needed to be redeemed. Since they had been captured by the devil through an injustice – disobedience to God – they could be redeemed only through an injustice. That injustice was the death of Jesus on the cross, because, as a wholly innocent man, he did not deserve to die. While there is some biblical support for this theory, it nonetheless has serious problems, which were exposed by Anselm of Canterbury in the late eleventh century. He pointed out that it is Manichean. If humans are under the control of the devil and God must defeat him in order to reestablish control, then the devil is on the same level as God. But that is heretical. The devil is a creature just like humans and is under the dominion of God.

267

Because of the inadequacies of the ransom theory, Anselm invented the satisfaction theory, according to which humans needed to satisfy the debt they incurred when they sinned against God by disobeying him. This required some kind of repayment or compensation. The difficulty in which humans found themselves was that they had nothing of their own with which to pay God. For everything that humans have they received from God and hence already owe to him. If someone objects that humans could pray to God, make sacrifices to him, or to honor him in some other way, Anselm would point out that God already deserves all of our prayers, honors and everything else we might do, since we are not dependent upon God for just some of the good things we have but are dependent upon him for everything we have, including our existence. Humans are absolutely dependent.

Humans also could not look to any other creature for salvation, because every creature is similarly absolutely dependent on God. In other words, the only kind of being that had the wherewithal to pay a ransom to God is something that was God. Further, since humans owed the debt, only a human could repay it. Thus, the redeemer had to be both God and man. Hence the Incarnation.[7]

Originally, the Reformers did not intend to devise a new theory of redemption.[8] But the invention of a new theory was a natural outcome of their opposition to the practice of indulgences. For the Reformers denied that humans could buy merit for themselves or anyone else. The entire work of redemption was accomplished by Jesus' death. One of the principal issues in this connection is whether Jesus redeemed humans by satisfying God's justice or whether his work essentially drew upon God's mercy. Luther emphasized God's justice. According to him, since Jesus took all the sins of the world upon himself and, by dying, paid the debt that humans owed, justice was done and man was redeemed (Luther, 1535, pp. 278–90; Grensted, 1920, pp. 199–201). Although Calvin conceded that God's justice requires damnation for unredeemed sinners, he emphasized that redemption is wholly the work of the mercy of God (Calvin, 1559, II.17.4–5). Hobbes follows Calvin in this matter. On several occasions he says that redemption depends upon God's mercy, not his justice (EW, 3:457, 476).

Hobbes's language and the content of his theory makes it clear that Hobbes was well informed about traditional theories of redemption. Further, far from either denigrating the possibility of such theories or adopting some generic theory of redemption, Hobbes is committing himself to a specific, and in some ways new, theory. Hobbes advances a revision of a ransom theory of redemption. He implicitly rejects the satisfaction theory in this line: "By this ransom, is not intended a satisfaction for sin" (EW, 3:457). My guess is that he rejects the satisfaction theory, at least, because it had come to be the favored theory of Roman Catholic theologians. He wants to accept some form of the ransom theory, because it was developed by Augustine, Calvin's favorite church father. Since Hobbes was too good a theologian to take over the ransom theory in its standard form, he revised it. He says that a redeemer is someone who pays a ransom to a person holding a captive. Realizing that humans cannot be under the control of the devil, Hobbes says that they are under the control of God and that a ransom must be paid to him for their sins.

The language of "payment" is required by the theory, but Hobbes wants to avoid giving the impression that sin is being traded or sold. Thinking of redemption as involving a repayment is objectionable for several reasons. Hobbes explains that if redemption amounted to a literal repayment, then sin would have a price; it would be a commodity for sale. This is unacceptable, because that would "make liberty to sin, a thing vendible" (EW, 3:457). Thus, Jesus' redemption is not to be considered "recompense" to God. Hobbes does not want people calculating how much a sin costs and ruminating over whether it is worth the price, as Catholics may be thought to do if they think a certain sin is worth three Hail Marys or one hundred days in purgatory, which can be paid off by indulgences. Also if God were being repaid for sin, then he would be in the sin business, a sin-mongerer, and that is not only offensive to pious ears but blasphemous.

Another problem is that if a payment could be made for sin, then human salvation would be a matter of justice, because things bought at an acceptable price belong to the buyer as a matter of justice. But Hobbes refuses to accept the view that redemption is a matter of justice. It cannot be, because God cannot be unjust, since he is subject to no law. Not even the death of Jesus "could make it unjust in God to punish sinners with eternal death" (EW, 3:457).

It is likely that Hobbes was also thinking of and arguing against the covenant theologians, since their theory also made redemption a matter of justice. According to the covenant theologians, once God made the covenant of grace, he was obligated to humans. That is, by the covenant God "bindes himselfe to us" (Bulkeley, 1651, p. 314). John Preston puts the following words into the mouth of God: "I will binde my selfe, I will ingage my selfe, I will enter into bond, as it were, I will not bee at liberty any more, but I am willing even to make a Covenant, a compact and agreement with thee" (Preston, 1629a, p. 316). In other words, a covenant made God and humans equal in this regard (Miller, 1935, p. 63). Hobbes denies that God can be bound. I believe that Hobbes's repetition of "bind" three times in the following sentence must be a reaction to the covenant theologians: "Even amongst men, though the promise of good, bind the promiser; yet threats, that is to say, promises of evil, bind them not; much less shall they bind God, who is infinitely more merciful than men" (EW, 3:457). A defender of covenant theology might suggest that God cannot undo his promise of evil except by making a covenant or promise of good in view of Jesus' death. But that suggestion will not work with Hobbes. For a later promise or covenant can never contradict an earlier one. The only way to negate the first promise of evil is to forgive it, and that requires an act of mercy, not justice, according to Hobbes.

Hobbes would never concede that God could be an equal

to humans but always emphasized the sovereignty of God over all creation. That is why Hobbes says, "Our Saviour Christ therefore to *redeem* us, did not in that sense satisfy for the sins of men, as that his death, of its own virtue, could make it unjust in God to punish sinners with eternal death" (EW, 3:457). He acted wholly out of mercy.[9]

Thus, humans are redeemed because God "was pleased in mercy" to forgive humans their sins if they did something that he demanded. In the Old Testament he demanded oblations and sacrifices. In the New Testament, he demanded the death of Jesus on the Cross, which would suffice for all time (EW, 3:457).

Another aspect of Reformation theories of redemption concerns the relationship between human sin and the person of Jesus insofar as he represents humans beings. As explained in Chapter 6, Hobbes accepted the idea of a representative person; he also felt committed by the Bible and by Reformation theories to use the formula that Jesus takes on himself or "bears upon his own head" the sins of all humans. But he did not accept the view of Luther and the covenant theologians that a consequence of this formula is that Jesus paid off the debt of sin (Luther, 1535, p. 277), because this again would imply that redemption was achieved through justice, not mercy (EW, 3:476). No person, not even a "righteous man can ever be able to make [satisfaction] for another man" (ibid., p. 457).

Secular salvation

Both the language and the content of Hobbes's explanation of redemption makes it clear that he was knowledgeable about the major theories of redemption and that he adhered to a form of Calvinism that was philosophically more viable than at least many of the alternatives. However, there is another side to Hobbes's views about redemption. He transmuted the religious paradigm and applied it to a secular issue.

Human beings in the state of nature are subject to all sorts of evils that endanger their lives. Humans need a redeemer. It is not Christ, because the effects of his salvation will not be experienced until he comes a second time (EW, 3:457). Yet something is needed in the meantime. God has not abandoned humans. Through his laws of nature, humans are able to make a covenant, just as the ancient Jews did. The covenant establishes a sovereign, who is like God in that he is not subject to the laws of justice but guarantees, through his irresistible power, that justice will be done. He is also a redeemer, because he saves humans from the dangers of death in this life. Since "life" and "death" are meant literally when Hobbes applies them in both his political and his religious discussions, salvation here and now is every bit as precious to humans as salvation at the Second Coming will be then.

It is possible to see Hobbes's transmutation of the theological theories of redemption as a subversion of religion. As a matter of fact, I think that it is part of a long process of secularization that has gone on from perhaps as early as the thirteenth century through the twentieth century. However, the leading figures of this history of secularization intended something quite different. In their various ways, these people saw that the medieval theories underpinning Christianity were breaking down and that something was needed to replace it. Each offered some powerful and dramatic alternative. I include among these people Erasmus, Luther, Milton, Locke, Boyle, Newton, and Hobbes. Hobbes's right to a place among these figures has not been recognized, I think, partially because he was more candid than some of them, partially because he was doctrinally more parochial than some, and partially because he was the most acerbic. However, rather than trying to subvert religion through his transmutation of the idea of redemption and others, I believe that he was trying to show how religious ideas pervade all aspects of human experience and how theology can be made relevant to securing peace and happiness in the present world.

Angels and eschatology

Predestination

Since human redemption is wholly the work of God – salvation by faith, not by works – and God is the cause of everything, it would seem that each person is predestined to either salvation or damnation. The Lutherans recoiled from the brutality of that inference. They tried to escape the consequence by distinguishing between God's foreknowledge and predestination. God foreknows who will be saved and who will be damned, but he wills only salvation for everyone (Grensted, 1920, p. 232). Calvin was uncompromising. He held to double predestination. God predestines the elect to salvation and the reprobate to damnation: "[A]ll are not created in equal condition; rather, eternal life is foreordained for some, eternal damnation for others" (Calvin, 1559, III.21.5). Some theologians, who were originally authentic Calvinists, eventually found this doctrine too hard to swallow and tried to soften it in various ways. The most important of these was the Dutch theologian Jacob Arminius (d. 1609). Although his doctrine was condemned at the Synod of Dort in 1619, his view began to flourish in several places, notably England. At least by the Restoration, it was the dominant view among Anglican churchmen. Hobbes, ever at the defense of the traditional Calvinist doctrine, opposed the Arminian innovations and was accused of heresy and atheism for his efforts. To a large extent, this is not surprising. Hobbes found himself in a situation analogous to the one faced in our day by those conservative Roman Catholics who refused to accept the innovations of Vatican II. Hobbes clung to Calvinism and turned his back on Arminianism in the same way that Tridentine Catholics clung to Thomism and turned their backs on phenomenology and process philosophy. As has been said, "Yesterday's orthodoxy is today's heresy" (Moore, 1972, p. 63).

Hobbes's commitment to predestination is for him the logical consequence of orthodox and traditional Christian doctrine. The Christian God is a creator god. God created the world from nothing. What this means is that there is only one principle of all that exists, namely, God. Whatever else exists must come from him and is absolutely dependent on him. Creatures must be absolutely dependent on him, because if there were something that did not depend upon God, then God would not be the source of all being. There would be something other than God from which things came. He would not be the creator. It is not only substances that depend upon God; all of their properties – this includes their actions – depend upon him also (see Leibniz, 1710, p. 139; Ames, 1629, p. 107). For if there were some property that did not depend upon God for its existence, then either there would be some being other than God that it depends upon (which contradicts the idea of a creator), or it would depend upon nothing (which is impossible for a creature).

In short, God causes everything. This is a proposition that Hobbes often asserted (e.g., EW, 5:215, 245, 450). The major objection to this view, an objection that Bramhall pressed against Hobbes, is that it seems to entail that God is also the author of sin. Hobbes denied the inference, on the grounds that merely causing someone to sin does not make one the author of a sin. For example, suppose someone threatens to kill a hostage if a doctor treats a certain patient. If the doctor treats the patient and causes the hostage to be killed, it is, nonetheless, not true that the doctor is responsible for the murder. According to Hobbes, the term "moral causality" does not even make sense. An action is moral if and only if it is in accordance with a law; an action is immoral if and only if it contravenes a law. Whether the action is necessitated is not relevant to its moral character. Although Bramhall, the Arminian, found this view reprehensible, Hobbes was merely following Calvinist theology. Theodore Beza, Calvin's chosen successor, held that God is not the author of sin, even though humans sin out of the necessity that results from God's universal causality (Muller, 1986, pp. 81–2, 84). And William Perkins, a distinguished and perfectly respectable theologian whom Hobbes explicitly praised, claimed that God's will "is a moving cause of the wills of evill men" and that sin is neither a matter of chance nor of God's permission (Perkins, 1596, pp. 86–6; see also pp. 345–7).[10]

As already indicated, since God is the cause of everything, everything that happens is necessary. Hobbes either did not appreciate or did not recognize the distinction between conditional or absolute necessity or the different scopes that the necessity operator might have in a sentence (EW, 5:218–19). That is, he would have denied that there is an important difference between the following sentences:

> If Socrates is sitting, then he is necessarily sitting.
> Necessarily, if Socrates is sitting, then he is sitting.

Most philosophers today would disagree and hold that everyone ought to accept only the second of these propositions. The first is at least dubious. Leibniz thought that Hobbes made a serious mistake in neglecting the distinction (Leibniz, 1710, p. 234).

Foreknowledge

In the end it does not matter that Hobbes never discussed the distinction. Hobbes thinks that God's foreknowledge imposes absolute necessity on things. The Lutherans and the Arminians thought that they could escape from the idea that God necessitates everything by arguing that God's foreknowledge does not necessitate anything. To know something is not thereby to cause it to exist. Hobbes could have pointed out that even though knowing does not ordinarily cause its object of knowledge, God's knowledge does, because God's knowledge is identical with his will. That is, necessarily, God knows that p just in case God wills that p. However, Hobbes focuses his argument on the logic of foreknowledge. He argues that everything that God foreknows necessarily occurs, because if it were possible for it not to occur, then it could not be something that was genuinely known (EW, 5:212). If someone were to try to sidestep this argument by suggesting that God does not have foreknowledge, Hobbes has an argument to show that anyone who gives up foreknowledge also gives up omniscience: if God does not know the future, then there is something that he does not know, and hence he is not omniscient.

One might respond to Hobbes that foreknowledge can be abandoned and omniscience preserved, given the correct definition of "omniscience" and the correct idea about the future. To be omniscient is to know everything that is knowable. But the future is not completely knowable, because the free actions of humans make it indeterminate. Hobbes could at this point return to his argument about what follows from the idea of God the creator. But we need not pursue this line any farther. Hobbes was not familiar with the response just explained, and all the evidence indicates that he was trying to preserve the orthodox view that God causes everything and the authentic Calvinist view that God predestines everything.

Double predestination

Some Christians subscribe to "single predestination," the view that God predestines the elect, those whom he chooses for heaven. God does not predestine the reprobate. They fall by their own acts of disobedience, and God merely damns them at the appropriate time, whether that be when they sin or when they die in sin. Calvin thought that single predestination was an impious refusal to acknowledge the consequences of God's sovereignty and creatorship. Arguing from God's foreknowledge, Hobbes committed himself to "double predestination," the view that God predestines both the elect and the reprobate (Calvin, 1559, III.21.5). God saves the elect out of mercy and punishes the reprobate out of justice. It is no good to say that God is not being just, because God's will is the standard of justice (ibid., III.23.2). Hobbes argues this very same case against Bramhall (e.g., EW, 5:104, 115–17).

One of the apparent consequences of double predestination is the proposition that the effects of redemption extend only to the elect. Calvin may not have drawn the inference, but his successor Beza did, as did the English Calvinists (Kendall, 1979, pp. 13–76). According to this view, Jesus did not die for all humans. For if he had and some humans were not saved, then his work would have been ineffectual or wasted. And that cannot be (Grensted, 1920, pp. 231–2). The doctrine that Christ's work of redemption is limited to the elect (limited atonement) was formulated as a canon at the Synod of Dort (McNeill, 1967, p. 264, and Kendall, 1979, p. 1).[11] In addition to the Lutherans, who never accepted this view but insisted that Jesus died for all humans, the Arminians persisted in the doctrine of universal atonement. Rioting broke out in Holland over this theological dispute, and Grotius had earlier been imprisoned for his Arminian views (McNeill, 1967, p. 265). Hobbes follows the view of standard English Calvinism, in particular, that of Perkins, in holding that Jesus died only for the elect (Perkins, 1596, p. 94, and Kendall, 1979, pp. 51–76, 197–208). Moreover, he appeals to this proposition to explain a difficult passage in the Gospel of Mark (EW, 3:431–2). Hobbes's commitment to the belief that Jesus died for the elect only also explains why he holds that miracles are intended for the elect only. Only they can benefit from them (EW, 3:431; see also p. 626).

Hobbes's commitment to the harsh views of Calvin and his followers on such matters as predestination has sometimes been taken as evidence that Hobbes's words are intended to be taken ironically and that he is conveying a secret message at variance with the literal text. But there is no more reason to interpret Hobbes in this way than any other Calvinist, and Hobbes explicitly denies that he intends "any plotting secretly, or any mockery or derision" in matters of religion, contrary to the suggestion of Bramhall (EW, 5:103). Most theologians recognized that there is a harshness to predestination that is difficult or impossible to reconcile with the idea of either a just or a merciful God. Theologians dealt with the problem in various ways. Calvin himself tried not to talk about it (McNeill, 1967, pp. 211–12). The Arminians simply denied the doctrine. The covenant theologians emphasized a covenant that the reprobate violated. Hobbes had the reprobate destroyed by the flames of hell. This latter solution is surely one of the most interesting. For it is the result of directing conservative premises, namely, the literal interpretation of the flames of hell, to a liberal conclusion, namely, the merciful destruction of the reprobate.

Chapter 10

The church

One of the principal reasons for political instability, according to Hobbes, is that people misunderstand what the Christian church is and how it fits into world history. He devotes a substantial part of *Leviathan* to explaining (1) what a church is; (2) how God's sovereignty imposes a structure on history; (3) what the mission of Jesus was; (4) what worship is; and (5) what the essence of Christianity is. These topics will be discussed in successive sections in this chapter.

THE NATURE OF THE CHRISTIAN CHURCH

Just as he does for "spirit," "angel," and other difficult words, Hobbes begins his discussion of what a church is with a survey of the various uses of the word. "Church" can refer to the building within which people worship God. This use is derived from a more basic one in which "church" refers to the people gathered or assembled for worship in the building. In a related use, "church" refers to all the people who might be assembled but are not. Hobbes points out that in none of these uses does "church" signify something that has a unity. As described thus far, a church is a conglomeration of individuals who lack political organization, because the church is not represented by any person (EW, 3:458–9, 4:337). The only way for a church to attain unity is for its members to institute some kind of leader. There are two possibilities. The leader will either be the civil sovereign or it will not. Hobbes thinks that the leader must be the civil sovereign, for both logical and historical reasons.

Logically, the sovereign must be the head of the church, according to Hobbes, because of the impossibility of the alternative. Suppose that the sovereign is not the head of the church. Then the head is either under the jurisdiction of the sovereign or he is not. If he is, then he is a subject of the sovereign and cannot legally act against his will. This means that the sovereign is the actual and ultimate head of the church. The person originally supposed to be the head of the church is in fact only the titular head. (This line of reasoning is an attack on the Presbyterians.) If, on the other hand, the head of the church is someone not under the jurisdiction of the sovereign, then the head is an enemy of the sovereign, and no citizen can lawfully pledge allegiance to him because of the prior allegiance owed to the sovereign. It does not matter whether the alleged head of the church is inside or outside the territory of the sovereign. In either case, the head of the church would be an enemy of the sovereign, and this is obviously an untenable position to take toward religion. (This line of reasoning is an attack on Roman Catholicism.)

The logic-based objection to thinking that anyone other than the sovereign can be the head of the church can be put in another way. If the secular sovereign is not identical with the head of the church, then there will be two sovereigns (one for religious matters and one for nonreligious matters); but that is absurd. For a sovereign is one to whom all authority has been passed. Thus sovereignty cannot be shared. As the Bible teaches, a man cannot serve two masters. Since the head of the church cannot be anyone other than the sovereign, it must be the sovereign. This line of reasoning was adopted by defenders of the Church of England after the Restoration. Bishop John Stillingfleet, most famous for his extended controversy with Locke, argued that if the sovereign and the head of the church were not identical, then the following absurdities would result: "First, that there are two supreme powers in a Nation at the same time. Secondly, that a man may lie under two different Obligations as to the same thing; he is bound to do it by one power, and not to do it by the other" (Stillingfleet, 1662, p. 49). In short, "the Magistrate then hath power concerning Religion, as owned in a Nation" (ibid., p. 41).

Because he, along with other defenders of the Church of England, thinks that the sovereign must be the head of the church, Hobbes defines a church as "a company of men professing Christian religion, united in the person of one sovereign, at whose command they ought to assemble, and without whose authority they ought not to assemble" (EW, 3:459; see also pp. 379–80). Hobbes's definition should be compared with that of Hooker. Hooker says, "[The church is] divided into a number of distinct Societies, every of which is termed a Church within itself. In this sense the Church is always a visible society of men . . . as the Church of Rome, Corinth, Ephesus, England" (Hooker, 1593, III.1.14). That is, there is not one church that Christ founded, but many. Notice that Hooker's view is just like Hobbes's except that Hobbes makes the principle of church unity explicit. Both Hobbes and Hooker want to make sure that their definitions of "church" undermine the claims of the Roman Catholic Church. Hobbes makes this point when he comments on his definition: "It followeth also [from his definition], that there is on earth, no such universal Church, as all Christians are bound to obey; because there is no power on earth, to which all other commonwealths are subject" (EW, 3:460, 4:337).

People sometimes object that Hobbes's position makes religion subordinate to secular concerns. But the objection is not correct. The sovereign rules equally both secular and religious matters. So there is no subordination of one to the other. This point is so important that Hobbes incorporates it into the famous illustrated title page of *Leviathan*, reproduced as frontispiece to the present volume (Brown, 1978). In the bottom half, the subtitle indicates that *Leviathan* is a study of a commonwealth "Ecclesiastical and Civil." This equality of secular and religous elements is represented by two parallel columns of images, one of which signifies the religious role of the sovereign, the other his nonreligious or secular role. Each secular symbol of power has a religious analog standing at the same level. (See Appendix C.)

In the text of *Leviathan* itself, Hobbes explains that *"Temporal* and *Spiritual* government are but two words brought into the world, to make men see double, and mistake their *lawful sovereign"* (EW, 3:460). There is only one government, which encompasses both religious and nonreligious matters alike. Clarendon, who commended Hobbes for virtually nothing else, completely endorsed his views on this point. As I have indicated earlier, both men supported the traditional English monarchy, which had consistently asserted its supremacy in church matters at least since Henry VIII (Queen Mary being a brief but complicated exception). Clarendon even made the outrageously strong claim that no bishop or priest "pretends to any Power or Jurisdiction, inconsistent with the Kings Supremacy, in Ecclesiastical as well as Temporal matters." He then says, "No man can be made a Bishop, but by his [the sovereign's] appointment and grant" (Clarendon, 1676, p. 249; see also pp. 232–3). For Hobbes, the sovereign is not the head of the church because he is a secular ruler but because there can be only one earthly ruler for humans: "There is therefore no other government in this life, neither of state, nor religion, but temporal" (EW, 3:460). Although the sovereign is instituted out of fear of death in this life, he is instituted in accordance with the laws of nature, which have God as their author. Further, the sovereign is ultimately answerable to God.

In addition to the logical objections against having anyone other than the civil sovereign be the head of the church and the philosophical reasons in favor of it, Hobbes's position is also grounded in his quite conventional understanding of the history of England. William the Conqueror refused to swear fealty to the pope when it was demanded. And his son William II (Rufus) had a long dispute with Anselm of Canterbury about ecclesiastical supremacy. The issue is clearest, however, after the Reformation. By the Act of Supremacy of 1534, Henry VIII declared himself head of the Church of England. Bishop Cranmer reported that he told Henry that the King "was only the supreme governor of this church of England, as well in causes ecclesiastical as temporal, and that the full right and donation of all manner of bishoprics and benefices, as well as of any other temporal dignities and promotions, appertained to his grace, and not to any other foreign authority, whatsoever it was" (Cranmer, 1846, 2:223). Henry was interested and asked whether Cranmer could prove it. Cranmer said he proved it out of the Scriptures. Years later, addressing Edward VI at his coronation, Cranmer said that the king was "God's vicegerent and Christ's vicar within your own dominion" (ibid., p. 126). In 1550, John Hooper, bishop of Gloucester and Worcester, referred to Edward VI as "our most redoubted Sovereign Lord, King of England, France, and Ireland, defender of the faith, and in earth, next and immediately under God, the supreme head of the churches of England and Ireland" (Hooper, 1852, 2:65). In 1559, the Act of Supremacy was renewed by Elizabeth I. Thus, the authority of the English sovereign over the church was the standard view of members of the Church of England against the Roman Catholics and later the Puritans. In the late sixteenth century, John Whitgift, Archbishop of Canterbury, responding to the Presbyterian Thomas Cartwright, said that the civil magistrate is "the head of the commonwealth, next and immediately under God . . . [and] under God also, he is head of the church, that is, chief governor" (Whitgift, 1851, p. 85). The supremacy of the sovereign in religious matters was incorporated into the 1571 version of the Thirty-Nine Articles of the Church of England (Leith, 1982, p. 280). James I, who began his rule over England during Hobbes's formative years as an adolescent and continued to reign through Hobbes's middle years as an adult, also maintained that the civil sovereign was at the same time the head of the church. So, rather than trying to undermine the legitimacy of religion by arguing that the civil sovereign is its supreme governor, Hobbes is trying to provide a theoretical foundation for a conservative English tradition in religion (EW, 4:340).

Decades earlier, others had argued for the same view as Hobbes. The position is summarized by J. P. Sommerville:

> Since natural law, and not revelation, was the basis of the Supremacy it followed that heathen as well as Christian kings were supreme heads of the church within their realms. This implication, which seemed absurd to Catholics and Presbyterians, was accepted by English Protestants. Richard Thomson, defending Andrewes against popish attack in 1611, declared that heathen and Christian kings both had precisely the same powers over the church, though pagans were likely to exercise them badly if they bothered to exercise them at all. "Princes not baptized, nay nor so much as godly minded," said Samuel Collins in 1617, "have the same supreme right to govern the Church that Christian Kings and professing the faith have, though by error and transportation they either neglect it and perish it, or perhaps evil employ it. (Sommerville, 1986, p. 204)

Hobbes's view was later expressed by the respectable latitudinarians. Bishop Stillingfleet held that the civil sovereign has the only authority to dictate what form religion will take within his territory: "The Magistrate . . . is bound to defend, protect and maintain the religion *he* owns to be true, and that by virtue of his office" (Stillingfleet, 1662, p. 40). His justification for the view was this: "[H]e only hath power to oblige who hath power to punish upon disobedience. And it is evident that none hath power to punish but the Civil Magistrate" (ibid., p. 48). Stillingfleet did not restrict the application of his principle only to Christian rulers. He said that even if the religious dissenter actually holds the true view, the sovereign's judgment ought to prevail. The dissenter should take comfort in the fact that his reward will come in the future life, as it did for the early Christian martyrs. An appeal to the rights of conscience provides no additional privilege for a dissenter. For any infidel or idolater could make the same appeal to conscience, and it is obvious that a principle that justifies the infidel or idolater cannot be a good principle (ibid., p. 40). Bishop John Tillotson, a future Archbishop of Canterbury and an associate of Stillingfleet, also rejected privileges for claims of conscience. In *The Protestant Religion Vindicated from the Charge of Singularity and Novelty*, he wrote,

> I cannot think . . . that any pretence of Conscience warrants any man, that is not extraordinarily commision'd . . . to affront the establish'd Religion of a Nation (though it be false) and openly to draw men off from the profession of it in contempt of the Magistrate and the Law: All that persons of such a different Religion can . . . reasonably pretend to, is to enjoy private liberty and exercise of their own Conscience and Religion. (Tillotson, 1680, pp. 11–12)

He holds that the proper governor of religion is "the Civil Magistrate" (ibid., p. 9).

It is significant that both Stillingfleet and Tillotson, like Hobbes, require adherence to the state or public religion even if what it teaches is false and even if it cannot produce miracles as proof of its divine appointment. The similarities were not lost on their contemporaries. Simon Lowth, in *On the Subject of Church Power*, convicted both Stillingfleet and Tillotson of "Hobism" (Lowth, 1685; Marshall, 1985). Whether they were actually influenced by Hobbes is not important; what is important is that this Hobbesian view appeared to be compatible with genuine Christianity, according to Hobbes's contemporaries.

THE THEOCRATIC STRUCTURE OF HISTORY

In addition to the national history of England, Hobbes thinks that world history, which is divinely directed, supports the view that the secular sovereign is the true head of the church.

Some Christian views of history

Christianity is often described as a historical religion. To Christians, time is linear, not cyclical. Notwithstanding the claim of Ecclesiastes that there is nothing new under the sun, new things happen in time, and events are not repeatable. History had a beginning and has an end toward which all is moving. The events most important to Christianity allegedly occurred in an ordered sequence in time.

In addition to these quasi-dogmatic aspects, there have been many attempts to attribute either a finer-grained structure to history or to overlay this structure with another. Indeed, a philosophy of history[1] is inherent in the distinction between the Old and New Testaments. God entered into history in a special way when he appeared to Moses and again when Jesus died on the Cross. Saint Augustine distinguished six ages in biblical history: from Adam to Noah; from Noah to Abraham; from Abraham to David; from David to the Babylonian exile; from the exile to the preaching of John the Baptist; and from John until the end of the world, which is imminent (Augustine of Hippo, 1964, p. 224). Eight centuries later, Joachim of Fiore (Flora) (c.1132–1202) argued that there were three ages of the world, corresponding to the three persons of the Trinity. The Father ruled during the first age, which ran from the creation of the world to the birth of Jesus. The Son ruled during the second age, which Joachim thought was soon coming to an end. The Holy Spirit was to rule during the third age, at which time the Eastern and Western Christian churches would be reunited, the Jews converted, and the world (as he and his audience knew it) would end. His work was supported by the popes during his life, and the first condemnation issued against him did not occur until 1215. In the middle of the thirteenth century, his teachings attracted a substantial, destabilizing following and both his followers and his doctrine came to be condemned.

In the seventeenth century, covenant theologians put their own spin on redemption history.[2] They held that God first made a covenant with Adam, called "the covenant of works." After Adam sinned, God made a new covenant, "the covenant of grace." Depending upon the theologian, the covenant was instituted with either Noah, Abraham, or Moses. If it was made with Noah, then God renewed it with Abraham, Isaac, Jacob, Moses, and Jesus. The covenant with Jesus is the same as the covenant with the Old Testament prophets; the only difference is the way the covenant is dispensed or administered.[3] Jesus is superior to the Old Testament prophets and patriarchs in that he is the fulfillment of the promise of salvation that God made to them.

Hobbes on the structure of history

While Hobbes's version of the structure of history is novel, it is biblically based and theocentric; indeed, he has a theocratic view of the structure of history, in the sense that history gets divided on the basis of whether God is or is not a sovereign over a particular people.[4] World history consists of four epochs (EW, 3:605–6, 616–17).

1. The first epoch begins with Adam, but it is not clear where it ends. Sometimes Hobbes says that it extends from Adam to Abraham, but in other places he seems to say that it extends from Adam to Moses, and Moses does get much more attention from Hobbes than Abraham. In either case, this is the period when God is supposedly sovereign over all humans in virtue of his omnipotence but not sovereign over any particular nation, although even here Hobbes is not always consistent, because sometimes he says that God reigned over Adam as a peculiar subject and that God gave Adam the commandment not to eat from the tree of good and evil. Also, Hobbes sometimes includes Noah in this kingdom of God (EW, 3:397). These passages notwithstanding, Hobbes's preferred account is that God's kingdom begins properly with either Abraham or Moses.

2. The second epoch, whether it begins with Abraham or Moses, is the first time that God establishes in a special way his sovereignty over a particular people. (My guess is that Hobbes subliminally recognized that neither Adam's nor

Noah's family constituted a large enough population to count as a kingdom; cf. EW, 2:227–8.) Clarendon criticized Hobbes for saying that God could have a "special sovereignty," but Hobbes's view is clearly the more traditional and standard one. At the beginning of chapter 40, "Of the Rights of the Kingdom of God, in Abraham, Moses, the High-Priests, and the Kings of Judah," Hobbes suggests that the epoch begins with Abraham. He says that with Abraham God becomes for the first time a sovereign over a particular people. For it was by this covenant with God that Abraham "obliged himself, and his seed after him, to acknowledge and obey the commands of God; not only such as he could take notice of, (as moral laws,) by light of nature; but also such, as God should in special manner deliver to him by dreams and visions" (EW, 3:461; cf.2:230). The fact that Abraham commits himself to obeying God's commands and that these commands are laws seems to me to make it clear that a sovereign-making covenant is being enacted.[5]

In other places, Hobbes says that the Kingdom of God begins with Moses (e.g., EW, 3:605, 617, 645–6). His account of God's sovereignty and Moses' lieutenancy is similar to the one concerning Abraham. The major point that Hobbes wants to make is that God's lieutenant is the head of religious matters. In a theocracy, this may be obvious, but when God is not the sovereign of a special people, it is his will that citizens defer to the secular sovereign for their religion.

Moses differs from Abraham insofar as he was not a sovereign prior to the sovereign-making covenant enacted with God. He acquired the lieutenancy of God's sovereignty only after the people agreed among themselves to obey him (EW, 3:464). When the people say, "*[S]peak thou with us, and we will hear, but let not God speak with us lest we die* . . . they obliged themselves to obey whatsoever he [Moses] should deliver unto them for the commandment of God" (ibid., pp. 464, 514). Thus Moses alone exercises authority over the Israelites. He was the ultimate authority in both religious and nonreligious matters. He destroyed the golden calf that

Aaron, who was a priest, had made; he determined who would be a prophet and when the prophet would speak to the people; and he transmitted God's laws to them (ibid., pp. 466–8, 513–14). Another difference is that the lieutenancy that Moses acquired in virtue of the sovereign-making covenant was hereditary through the high priests, while Abraham's sovereignty or lieutenancy, whichever term may be correct, was not.[6] Thus, the secular and religious authority was united in the same person, just as God wanted.

It is not surprising that Hobbes should want Moses to have a special role to play in his theocratic view of history. For that is the standard Judeo-Christian view. Although God makes covenants with Noah, Abraham, and others under the Old Covenant, the central covenant and the one that gives its name to the Old Covenant is the one between the Israelites, through the mediation of Moses, and God. It is only the Israelites or Jews who are God's chosen people, not all of Abraham's descendants. For Abraham was the ancestor, not only of the Jews through Isaac, but also of the Bedouins, through Ishmael (Gen. 16:11).

After the death of Moses, "[T]he kingdom, as being a sacerdotal kingdom, descended by virtue of the covenant" to Aaron and then to each succeeding high priest until the time of Samuel (EW, 3:468–70). Even Joshua, who seemingly took command after the death of Moses, was subordinate to the high priest, according to Hobbes. However, after Joshua died the government of Israel fell into disarray. Although the high priest was still the sovereign under the covenant, he did not exercise his power, and the Israelites followed the judges, not out of duty, for the judges had no legal authority, but out of respect. Samuel was the last of the judges, and, like the others, he had no legal authority but was respected by the Israelites because of his charisma.[7] The second epoch ends with him, and he plays a role in ushering in the third epoch of history.

3. The third epoch begins with the accession of Saul as the king of the Israelites and will continue until the Second Coming of Jesus. During the judgeship of Samuel, the Jews de-

cided to throw off theocracy in order to embrace a human monarchy and be like other nations. Hobbes quotes God, consoling Samuel: "Hearken unto the voice of the people, in all that they shall say unto thee; for they have not rejected thee, but they have rejected me, that I should not reign over them" (EW, 3:471, quoting 1 Sam. 8:7). Hobbes says that God consents to the change of governmental structure but does not comment on the fact that the action of the Jews is a revolution and that the most powerful sovereign conceivable permits it. There was a moral here that Hobbes did not recognize. Since God did not interfere with the Israelites' decision to change their government, it is clear that the people who form a government and institute a sovereign retain the right to change the government and depose the sovereign, and a good sovereign will step aside gracefully.

Theologians in the seventeenth century did not realize that the Book of Samuel contains two parallel accounts of Samuel's attitude toward the institution of the monarchy. On one account, Samuel approves of the change and anoints Saul. On the other account, Samuel is opposed to the change. I once thought it was ironic that Hobbes quotes only from the negative account, on the grounds that Hobbes favors the governmental structure that overthrew God. But now I think I was mistaken. Hobbes is merely describing how world history is structured, not endorsing or condemning any particular epoch. In describing the overthrow of theocracy in favor of mundane monarchy, Hobbes is not expressing any negative attitude toward religion. Every commonwealth has a religion, and the only issue is whom God wants to lead it.

4. The fourth epoch consists of the return of theocratic rule to the earth. Hobbes claims it will occur when Jesus returns to rule as God's lieutenant for the rest of time. Unlike many millenarian thinkers of the seventeenth century, Hobbes does not suggest that this final age is imminent. Hobbes thought that all millenarians were seditious, and he would have none of that.[8]

Setting aside Hobbes's belief in its truth, we can say that

the political purpose of his interpretation of history is two-fold: first, to preserve the facts about the literal kingdom of God and biblical history; and second, to use that interpretation to make it impossible to use religion in general and Christianity in particular to destabilize governments. For if the next kingdom of God must follow the Second Coming of Jesus, then there is no kingdom of God in existence now, and the civil sovereign is the only sovereign people have.

There are several problems with Hobbes's treatment of the structure of history, and two of them will be discussed in the next two sections.

Abraham, Moses, and sovereignty

One of these problems concerns Abraham and Moses. First, although a special feature of Hobbes's theory of sovereign-making covenants is that the sovereign is not himself a party to it, Hobbes either says or seems to presuppose that God is a party to the covenants with Abraham and Moses. He says, "[I]t pleased God to speak to Abraham, and (*Gen. xvii. 7, 8*) to make a covenant with him" (EW, 3:397; see also p. 398), and it is a covenant in which "God on his part promiseth to Abraham the land of Canaan for an everlasting possession" (ibid., p. 398). It would seem that since God is a party to the covenant, he would incur some obligation, according to Hobbes's theory of covenants, even though this seems to conflict with his omnipotence. It is striking, however, that while Hobbes does say that Abraham obligates himself to God by this covenant, he never says that God obligates himself. Consonant with much seventeenth-century usage, Hobbes often uses the noun "promise" to mean simply "expression of intention." Thus, making a promise did not impose an obligation, and for that reason people could not be sued for breaking a promise. However, the covenant theologians emphasized that God did incur an obligation in making covenants. I suspect that Hobbes felt the tension between his own understanding of sovereignty (and in particular, God's sovereignty), which denied that a sovereign could have obligations to his subjects, and the idea of a covenant, which he believed imposed obligations on both parties.

It is unfortunate that Hobbes did not have one of the fruits of recent biblical scholarship at his disposal, for then he might have found a way around his dilemma. Many contemporary biblical scholars distinguish between two kinds of covenants: suzerainty and parity (see Nicholson, 1986, pp. 83–117). Parity covenants are covenants by which equal parties enter into a personal relationship with each other by taking on mutual responsibilities and obligations. Parity covenants can be enacted by individual people, families, tribes, or nations. Hobbes's notion of a covenant is virtually identical with the idea of a parity covenant, and I believe that is because he was inspired by much of the biblical talk about covenants. The other kind of covenants are suzerainty covenants. Suzerainty covenants are covenants by which two unequal parties establish a personal relationship with each other. In such cases, only the inferior party actually incurs an obligation toward the superior party. The superior party expresses his intention to perform some good action for the inferior party, but this action is supposed to proceed from the power and goodness of the superior party, not because of any obligation to the inferior one. As its name suggests, one party to the covenant either is or becomes the "suzerain," or sovereign. The other party is subject to the suzerain. Hobbes's idea of a sovereign-making covenant is similar, insofar as the sovereign does not incur an obligation from such a covenant. It diverges from the idea of a suzerainty covenant insofar as the sovereign is not a party to it.

Contemporary Bible scholars hold that there are two different versions of God's covenant with Abraham. In one version, a parity covenant is enacted (Gen. 15; Nicholson, 1986, pp. 106, 112). God is depicted as nothing more than the equal of Abraham. But in the other covenant, a suzerainty covenant is enacted (Gen. 17). In it, Abraham is told by God what he *must* do, while God says what he *will* do. Hobbes discusses only the suzerainty version.

Having the distinction between parity and suzerainty covenants, however, does not provide one with an answer to the question of why Hobbes said that God is a party to the covenant with Abraham. One might suggest that the covenant between God and Abraham is not a sovereign-making covenant. But that suggestion will not stand up to the text. Hobbes says that even though "the name of *King* be not yet given to God, nor of *kingdom* to Abraham and his seed; yet the thing is the same; namely, an institution by pact, of God's peculiar sovereignty over the seed of Abraham" (EW, 3:398). It is also not acceptable to say that an exception must be made in the case of God because he is God: just the opposite. There is less justification for making God a party to a sovereign-making covenant than there is for making a human sovereign a party to one. For the whole point of excluding the sovereign from the covenant is to guarantee that he has no duties whatsoever toward his citizens, and no one could be more free from duties than the omnipotent creator of the universe.

The second problem with Hobbes's discussion of God's covenant with Abraham is that Abraham is himself a sovereign (EW, 3:462). For, if a sovereign-making covenant is being enacted with a nation that already has a sovereign, then an existent government is destroyed. Consequently, the institution of the new government ought to be a case of sovereignty by acquisition. There are two problems here. First, such cases are always supposed to involve a threat of immediate death by the person specifying the terms of the covenant. But God does not threaten Abraham at all. Second, as quoted earlier, the covenant with Abraham was "an institution by pact," which suggests that God becomes sovereign by institution, not by acquisition.

There is a related problem. Hobbes draws the moral that since Abraham is a sovereign, none of his subjects is permitted to speak with God without Abraham's permission and also that "in every commonwealth, they who have no supernatural revelation to the contrary, ought to obey the laws of their own sovereign" (EW, 3:462). But if God were made sovereign by this covenant, Abraham would lose his own authority unless God makes him his lieutenant. But Hobbes never says that Abraham is God's lieutenant, even though he often says this about Moses.

All of this notwithstanding, the covenant between God and Abraham does seem to have been of the sovereign-making kind. In addition to the evidence already adduced, when Hobbes makes the transition from Abraham to Moses he says that the "same covenant was renewed with Isaac; and afterwards with Jacob . . . and then it was renewed by Moses" (EW, 3:463). Since it is "the same covenant" and since it is being "renewed," it seems that Moses merely continued what was instituted with Abraham.

The role of Jesus in theocratic history

Someone is sure to object to Hobbes's philosophy of history in the following way: although Jesus is supposed to be a king, he is not a king according to Hobbes's theory. Hobbes in effect replies to this objection in chapter 41, "Of the Office of Our Blessed Saviour." There are three parts to Jesus' mission: redeemer, counselor, and king (EW, 3:475–82). In holding this, Hobbes was following Calvin, who was the first one to make this treatment of Christ's threefold office an explicit aspect of Christology (Calvin, 1559, II.15; Jansen, 1956, 20–38). During his life on earth, Jesus' purpose was to redeem humanity. He achieved this by paying the ransom that God demanded for human sin; that ransom was his death. Hobbes continues to follow Calvin in holding that Jesus redeemed humans by relying upon God's mercy, not his justice (EW, 3:476). After his death, Jesus' first mission was finished; thus, he rose from the dead and ascended into heaven. His presence on earth was no longer needed.

Jesus's second mission was to counsel humans about the best way to gain eternal life. It ran concurrently with his mission as redeemer but it continued after his ascension and will continue until he comes again. Hobbes promotes the Reformation view that Jesus counseled through his preaching, which Bishop Hugh Latimer had called "God's instrument of salvation" (Latimer, 1552, p. 349). The apostles were commissioned to preach, not to legislate; preaching is a ministerial, not a magisterial office (EW, 3:497). This time of preaching is also called "the *regeneration;* which is not properly a kingdom" (ibid., pp. 479, 490). As counsels, Jesus' teachings are not commands and hence cannot be laws in themselves. Jesus taught that people were to obey their civil sovereigns in all matters until Jesus returns to reign as king in person (ibid., p. 480). The doctrines of religion, then, are in themselves merely counsels, although they can be turned into commands if a sovereign so chooses.

Jesus' third mission will begin when he returns to earth at some unspecified time in the future. It is then that he will become king. And Hobbes quotes several passages that imply that Jesus will be king when he comes in glory at the end of time (p. 481). It is clear that Jesus is not now king and was not king during his first time on earth. For when he first came, humans needed to be ransomed from God the Father. Jesus, as the person who was to pay the ransom, did not yet have sovereignty over the human race, which was to be ransomed (p. 477). Nonetheless, in baptism, Christians obligate themselves to take Jesus as king, "under his Father," whenever he should return and restore the kingdom that was abolished with Saul (p. 479; see also pp. 484–5).

If Jesus had been king over the earth, he could not truthfully have said, "My kingdom is not of this world" (p. 478); he could not have recommended that people render unto Caesar the things that are Caesar's or that they obey those who sit in Moses' chair without seriously misleading them (pp. 479–80). The Bible often talks of two worlds, the one in existence now and the one to come. In that future world, Jesus will reward and punish people as appropriate in accordance with the office of a king. But he refused to judge while he was on earth: "How then could his words or actions be seditious, or tend to the overthrow of their then civil government?" (p. 480). In other words, if Jesus did not try to destabilize the existing government, even when it was preparing to put him to death, what right do his followers today have to do it?

It is clear that Hobbes is using his interpretation of the mission of Jesus to prevent people from using Christianity to destabilize governments. But there is no evidence that Hobbes does not sincerely believe that he has accurately rendered the mission of Jesus, independently of his own immediate political motivations.

THE MISSION OF THE CHURCH

Command and counsel

The mission of the church is to continue the work that Jesus began on earth, namely, to counsel humans about how to attain eternal life. Just as Jesus did not command, the ministers of the church do not have the authority to command or make laws. Religious propositions can, however, be made into laws by a civil sovereign. Hobbes illustrates this distinction between the time when Christian propositions are counsels and when they are laws by elaborating his views about the theocratic structure of history.

Christian history, which occupies a segment of the third part of Hobbes's theocratic view of history, is divided into two parts. The first goes from A.D. 30, when Jesus was executed, to A.D. 300, when Constantine became the first emperor to convert to Christianity. The second period runs from A.D. 300 until the Second Coming of Jesus (EW, 3:485). The principle of division is the status of Christianity in relation to the civil sovereign. Before its formal adoption as the official religion of the Roman Empire, the propositions of the Christian faith were in no way commanded and were counsels only. After its adoption by Constantine, the same propositions acquired the force of commands. The distinction between a proposition and the force it may have is absolutely essential for understanding Hobbes's point. In order to understand the structure of communication, one must know that the same proposition or thought can be expressed with very different forces, depending upon the intentions of the speaker, his status, and several other features or circumstances of the speech act. If one friend says to another, "Close the door," the friend may be making a request, or giving advice, or something similar, but he cannot be making a command. But if a sergeant says, "Close the door," to a private, the sergeant is, in normal circumstances, giving a command. So the same utterance, expressing the same proposition, can have different forces.

As explained in Chapter 4, the sentence "That bull is about to charge" may have the weight of a conjecture uttered with one intention in one situation, or a warning uttered with another intention in another situation. In the two examples just given, the force of the utterance is more or less implicit, but it can be made explicit by prefixing the sentence with an explicit illocutionary-act verb in performative form: "I ask whether John is in Peking"; "I state that John is in Peking"; "I conjecture that that bull is about to charge"; "I warn you that that bull is about to charge." Hobbes's claim about the propositions of Christianity is that they had one illocutionary force before it became a state religion, namely, the force of counsel or advice, and a different force afterward, namely, the force of command.

Faith and obedience

Counseling belongs to ministers, and their purpose is to instill faith in Christ, "but faith hath no relation to, nor dependence at all upon compulsion or commandment" (EW, 3:491). It follows that the ministers of the church do not have the power to punish anyone for either not believing or for contradicting what they say. As usual, Hobbes supports his view with quotations from the Bible, for example, Saint Paul, saying, "We have no dominion over your faith, but are helpers of your joy" (ibid.). The civil sovereign, in contrast, has both the authority and the power to punish people. He demands not faith but obedience.

The difference between faith and obedience is that faith is

an interior condition of belief in matters of religion, while obedience is a matter of external behavior. Faith is inaccessible to any human other than the person who has it: "Faith is a gift of God, which man can neither give, nor take away by promise of rewards, or menaces of torture" (EW, 3:493, 518). Further, "faith hath no relation to, nor dependence at all upon compulsion or commandment" (ibid., p. 491), because faith is internal. So no sovereign can command a person to have some faith contrary to the faith that that person has by himself. Behavior, in contrast, is properly within the control of a sovereign. Even if a sovereign commands someone to say, "I deny Christ," a Christian subject is required to obey the command, because "[p]rofession with the tongue is but an external thing, and no more than any other gesture whereby we signify our obedience" (ibid., p. 493). Hobbes mentions that there is precedent for this in the Old Testament when the prophet Elisha allows Naaman to worship the idol Rimmon. That is, worship is a kind of obedient behavior. Hearkening back to his view of authorization, Hobbes says that the worship commanded by a sovereign is not the act of the person performing the behavior but of the sovereign himself. Thus, if a Christian utters the words "I deny Christ" in response to the command of his sovereign, it is not the Christian but the sovereign who denies Christ (p. 494; see also p. 601).[9]

There are many places in which the Bible supports the idea that Christians ought not to challenge the secular authorities, and Hobbes knows them all. Saint Paul says, "Servants, obey in all things your masters according to the flesh," and Hobbes underscores that Paul says "in all things" (p. 492, quoting Col. 3:22). Saint Peter says, "Submit yourselves to every ordinance of man, for the Lord's sake, whether it be to the king, as supreme; or unto governors; . . . for so is the will of God" (p. 492, quoting 1 Peter 2:13–15). If the Apostles urged Christians to obey infidel rulers, how much more should Christians obey Christian rulers?

WORSHIP

Worship is the human expression of reverence for God. The position Hobbes takes on worship in *Leviathan* can easily be mistaken if certain distinctions relevant to the issue are ignored. Hobbes distinguishes between private and public worship. This distinction corresponds to John Preston's distinction between internal and external worship (Preston, 1629b, p. 43). Private worship is the method a person has of indicating reverence for God out of the view of other people. Public worship is what is commanded by the sovereign to be the method of expressing reverence for God (EW, 3:350, 647). Thus, citizens must participate in public worship as required by the sovereign as a matter of obedience to him.

Underlying worship is what Hobbes sometimes calls "honor." To honor a person is to "value highly the power" of that person (ibid., p. 647). Since God's power is infinite, any expression of that honor is going to be inadequate. Thus, "[H]onour is properly of its own nature, secret, and internal in the heart" (ibid.). These views are in the spirit of Calvin:

> Calvin's principal concern in worship . . . was to defend the glory of God who is 'entirely other,' . . . and whose reality is inaccessible. Calvin's attack on idolatry was an effort to restore God's primary dignity among human beings. Calvin forcefully asserted God's transcendence through the principle *finitum non est capax infiniti.* . . . Calvin maintains that the only correct form of worship that can be offered to God is 'spiritual worship.' (Eire, 1986, pp. 197, 200)

Hobbes also thought that reason can tell us relatively little about the most appropriate way of worshiping God. Nonetheless, the guiding principle should be that, whatever form worship takes, it should "best expresseth our desire to honour" God (EW, 3:672). Certainly, prayers of various sorts – for example, prayers of thanksgiving or petitions – are appropriate: "not sudden, nor light, nor plebian; but beautiful, and well composed" (ibid., p. 354; see also p. 98; 4:67; Calvin, 1559, IV.10.29). But most religious ritual is a matter of convention and subject to local preferences. Hobbes's view is consonant with a long tradition within the Church of England. William Alley, future bishop of Exeter, preached during Elizabeth's reign that a Christian should worship according to whatever ceremonies are prescribed by the church "to which he shall happen to come" (quoted from Collinson, 1979, p. 171). Edmund Grindal, a future Archibishop of Canterbury, was similarly unconcerned about ceremonies so long as they did not involve the "superstitions" of the Roman Catholics. The reason for this tolerance is that ceremonies were considered "things indifferent" (ibid.).

Hobbes thinks that his view of worship leaves the integrity of what is most important to religion intact, namely, private belief. To bow down or to burn incense in front of an idol is not an expression of one's own belief, which is a private, unobservable thing: "Faith is a gift of God, which man can neither give, nor take way by promise of rewards, or menaces of torture. . . . Profession with the tongue is but an external thing, and no more than any other gesture whereby we signify our obedience" (EW, 3:493). Hobbes's views are not irreligious. They are based upon his Reformation Christianity, according to which people are saved by faith alone rather than by works. The exact relation between good works and justification is disputed by Christian theologians, and in many who treat the topic explicitly it is not clear what they hold. But Hobbes's view about worship is a plausible application of the Lutheran doctrine of *sola gratia, sola fide.*

What has been said so far does not deal directly with the hard case. What is one to do if the sovereign is an infidel and commands non-Christian worship? Hobbes's view about this matter changed between the time he wrote *De Cive* and *Leviathan.* In *De Cive*, the requirement to worship as the sovereign commands is restricted. Hobbes says that a citizen is not to worship in any way that implies that the sovereign has properties that apply only to God. Thus a citizen may not participate in worship that implies that the sovereign is immortal or of infinite power, or requires him to pray to the sovereign for rain or fair weather, or to offer to the sovereign what only God can accept (EW, 2:224). One of the interesting aspects of this view is the reason Hobbes gives for imposing the restriction. To worship a sovereign as if he had the attributes of God implies that God may not be the ruler of the universe, but this consequence contradicts what was "supposed from the beginning" (ibid., p. 225), namely, that God is the sovereign from whom the earthly sovereign derives his authority. That is, no one may represent that any human has "a sovereignty independent from God" (ibid., p. 224). The most plausible explanation for Hobbes's insistence on this point is the one I argued for in Chapters 3 through 6, namely, that all positive law and obligation depend upon the omnipotence of God, which is the basis of human sovereignty.

The religious and political environment of England changed dramatically between 1640 and 1650. Some of these changes are reflected in Hobbes's new view about a citizen's requirement to worship as the sovereign commands even when the sovereign is an infidel. In *De Cive*, the citizen's obligation to obey the sovereign was limited. In *Leviathan*, the requirement is unlimited.

Hobbes knew that his Erastian position on worship would be objectionable to most people. So, he tried to get them to see the evenhandedness that underlay his view. Hobbes asked his objectors whether they thought that a Muslim ought to obey a Christian sovereign who commands him to worship in a Christian service. If the objectors were to say the Muslim ought to disobey, then they are justifying civil disobedience. If the objectors were to say the Muslim ought to obey, then they are requiring of the Muslim something that they do not require of themselves, in contradiction to both the law of nature and to Jesus' own words, "Whatsoever you would that men should do unto you, that do ye unto them" (EW, 3:494, quoting Luke 6:31). However unpopular Hobbes's view might have been, he was not alone in the view. In 1651, a group of Independent and Baptist ministers wrote, "[A]ll people in every Nation as well Members of

Churches, as others . . . are to submit to the Civill Commands, not onely of such Rulers as are faithfull, but even to Infidels" (quoted from Capp, 1972, p. 58).

The agreement of Hobbes's view and that of the Independent and Baptist ministers should not be shocking. It reflects a sensible reaction to the diversification that resulted from the Reformation. With the numerous changes in the established religion in the sixteenth century and the proliferation of religious sects in the seventeenth, one could have expected the eventual development of a more relaxed attitude about how one must worship. Further, political pressures applied by one religious group to another engendered a more liberal attitude about how one may appear to worship in public. In England, many Christians were known as "church papists," that is, people who attended the services required by the Elizabethan settlement but remained Roman Catholic in belief. Within Judaism there is a long tradition that allows one to adopt the manners of one religion in public and to practice another in private. The case of the Spanish Marranos, who were baptized as Catholics but practiced Judaism in private, is the best-known example. This is not to say that most religious people were relatively relaxed about how people worshiped. The point is that Hobbes's emphasis on the internal character of faith and his lack of emphasis on a rubric for worship was rooted in the Reformation tradition and was one legitimate stance to take.

Some might accuse Hobbes of Nicodemism, that is, the view that a person may dissemble about his religious beliefs, especially when it concerns how he worships. Most, if not all, Nicodemites were motivated by the fear of persecution, especially at the hands of Roman Catholic princes. Perhaps some justified this view because they believed that whether or how one worshiped was not important for spirituality. Hobbes, however, does not seem to me to be a Nicodemite. As has been explained, he thinks that people should accept the religion of the sovereign because citizens owe him obedience concerning all public behavior, religious ritual included. Hobbes also thinks that God commands such behavior, because the sovereign derives his authority from the consent of the people, who act in accordance with the laws of nature, which are the commands of God.[10]

To say that Hobbes deemphasizes a rubric for worship is also not meant to suggest that he thought that any form of worship was appropriate to God. After receiving the Eucharist and making his confession on what he thought was his deathbed, he said that "he liked the religion of the church of England best of all other" (Aubrey, 1680, 1:353). He found many practices within other Christian churches highly objectionable. He did not mince words in condemning ancient Greek and Roman religion (EW, 3:101–5). He was especially offended by it because many of these elements had been imported into Roman Christianity under a vague disguise. So, he liked the reformed Church of England and despised superstition in all its forms. But he realized that these personal preferences were independent of the issue of what citizens owe their sovereigns in obedience. On this matter, he held a view that he thought did not compromise private religious belief. He held that the integrity of belief is preserved, because although obedience can be commanded, belief cannot (ibid., p. 493).

Hobbes does have a problem with regard to worship. By his theory of authority, the behavior of citizens in acts of public worship are not their own acts but the acts of the sovereign. But by his theory of authorization, the commands of the sovereign are not his own acts but those of the citizens. Hence, the behavior of citizens in acts of public worship are their own acts. So there is a contradiction here. But it is a contradiction that arises from the conflict between his theories of authority and authorization and not specifically from his views about worship. He wants only his theory of authority to determine what he says about worship.

Martyrs

Because humans owe their sovereigns obedience and are not generally required to worship in a distinctively Christian manner, there is virtually no danger that a person will have to die for his faith. Nonetheless, there are exceptions. Hobbes thinks that martyrs, who have been called by God to preach the Kingdom of Christ openly, are required by God's special revelation to do so and to suffer whatever adverse consequences may come of it. However, since "martyr" means "witness"; since Saint Peter considered only witnesses to the resurrection of Christ to be Christian martyrs; and since no one today fits this category, it follows that no one today can claim the distinction of being a martyr.[11] So it is not the death but the witnessing of Jesus' Resurrection that makes a person a martyr. Latter-day "martyrs" disobey the message of Jesus already articulated earlier (EW, 3:494–6).

More generally, Hobbes holds that only people with a special mission from God need to die for their beliefs. In the Book of Daniel, the three brothers Shadrach, Meshach, and Abednego refuse to worship a golden idol constructed by Nebuchadnezzar and are tossed into a fiery furnace as a consequence. Hobbes praises them for their behavior, as "worthy champions of the true religion" (EW, 4:361). In *De Cive*, Hobbes was rather sanguine about the prospects of martyrdom for Christians. If a Christian finds that he cannot obey his sovereign in good conscience, then Hobbes's advice is "Go to Christ by martyrdom; which if it seem to any man to be a hard saying, most certain it is that he believes not with his whole heart, *that Jesus is the Christ, the Son of the living God*" (EW, 2:316).

Forgiveness of sins

Since the apostles did not have legislative power, they also could not have judicial power. This means that contrary to the claims of the Catholic church, pastors do not have an absolute ability to forgive sins. Rather, they do so conditionally. If a person repents in his heart, then he is absolved of his sins, and not otherwise (EW, 3:500).

Excommunication during apostolic times also involved no coercive force; it was merely a counsel not to associate with

Christians who had sinned (ibid., pp. 502–6). Also, only publicly scandalous offenses were cause for excommunication, not differences of opinion concerning matters of doctrine. To be a Christian it was enough to believe that Jesus is the Christ. Since the Catholic church had used excommunication as a weapon against civil sovereigns, Hobbes takes care to show that such a use of it makes no sense. Not only is a sovereign not subject to the pope, but all citizens have an obligation to associate with their sovereign if he desires it: "Excommunication therefore, when it wanteth the assistance of the civil power, as it doth, when a Christian state or prince is excommunicate by a foreign authority, is without effect; and consequently ought to be without terror" (p. 508). The popes are benighted in trying to excommunicate civil sovereigns. Their delusion is built upon two mistakes: the belief that the Kingdom of Christ already exists on earth, and the belief that the pope is Christ's vicar (p. 509).

THE ESSENCE OF CHRISTIANITY

Christianity and obedience

If a choice has to be made between obeying God and obeying a human, it would be the height of absurdity to obey the human, since to disobey God means "being damned to eternal death" (EW, 3:585). Hobbes's earlier discussion of revelation may seem to make it virtually impossible for a person to know when God is speaking to him. If this were correct, Hobbes's philosophy might instill as much anxiety as Calvin's view of predestination. But since Hobbes knows that Christ's yoke is easy and his burden light, there is no conflict between obeying God and obeying man. For it is God's command that citizens obey their sovereign. Hobbes derives this reassuring conclusion from his views about the essence of Christianity.

He says, "All that is NECESSARY *to salvation*, is contained in two virtues, *faith in Christ*, and *obedience to laws*" (EW, 3:585). Hobbes's choice of these two so-called virtues is not arbitrary. It was part of Hobbes's religious and political upbringing to pin salvation on obedience. More particularly, it is Calvinistic and Jacobean. Similarly, Chillingworth, in his defense of Protestantism, had claimed that people are saved "only by obedience" and damned only for disobedience (Chillingworth, 1638, p. 393). For Hobbes, the paradigm case of obedience is Christ's redemption of all mankind through obedience. Calvin says, "Now someone asks, How has Christ abolished sin, banished the separation between us and God, and acquired righteousness to render God favorable and kindly toward us? To this we can in general reply that he has achieved this for us by the whole course of his obedience" (Calvin, 1559, II.16.5).

A more immediate influence on Hobbes's specific treatment of obedience is covenant theology. Recall that according to that theory, God made two covenants with humans: a covenant of works and a covenant of grace. The terms of the covenant of works was that if Adam and his posterity obeyed God, then they would have eternal life. But Adam disobeyed, and thus sin and all its attendant miseries came into the world. Hobbes's "virtue" of "obedience to laws" is an allusion to the covenant of works. For he says that "[t]he latter of these, if it were perfect, were enough to use. But because we are all guilty of disobedience to God's law, not only originally in Adam, but also actually by our own transgressions, there is required at our hands now, not only *obedience* for the rest of our time, but also a *remission of sins* for the time past" (EW, 3:585).

Since God in his mercy could not leave humans foundering in their misery, he took the initiative and enacted a second covenant, the covenant of grace, according to which God will give humans eternal life if they believe in Jesus Christ. Hobbes says the same thing. For the remission of sins that he referred to is "the reward of our faith in Christ" (ibid.). He goes on to say, "That nothing else is necessarily required to salvation, is manifest from this, that the kingdom of heaven is shut to none but to sinners; that is to say, to the disobedient, or transgressors of the law; nor to them, in case they repent, and believe all the articles of Christian faith necessary to salvation" (pp. 585–6).

Actual and complete obedience cannot be required of humans, according to the covenant of grace, because then it would not differ at all from the covenant of works and because, as the name suggests, humans are saved not by works but by grace (p. 599). Thus, Hobbes says,

> The obedience required at our hands by God, that accepteth in all our actions the will for the deed, is a serious endeavor to obey him; and is called also by such names as signify that endeavor. And therefore obedience is sometimes called by the names of *charity* and *love*, because they imply a will to obey; and our Saviour himself maketh our love to God; and to one another, a fulfilling of the whole law: and sometimes by the name of *repentance;* because to repent, implieth a turning away from sin, which is the same with the return of the will to obedience. Whosoever therefore unfeignedly desireth to fulfil the commandments of God, or repenteth him truly of his transgressions, or that loveth God with all his heart, and his neighbor as himself, hath all the obedience necessary to his reception into the kingdom of God. For if God should require perfect innocence, there could no flesh be saved. (p. 586)

The laws that humans are supposed to obey are the laws of nature and, what is the same thing, the law of Moses. The most important of these laws of nature is that people should not break their covenants. And since the chief covenant is to obey the sovereign, the essence of Christianity entails obedience to the sovereign.

Not only is Hobbes's express connection between Christianity and political loyalty striking, but his derivation of it is plausible, especially when seen from the perspective of traditional accounts of the fall of humankind and its redemption. The standard description of the first or original sin is that the sin was disobedience and the source of that sin was pride. Hobbes is simply following the covenant theologians in specifying obedience as the remedy for human woe.

Hobbes's idea of obedience is of course not a purely religious idea. It is seemingly consubstantial with politics. It is quite likely that Hobbes was to some degree inspired by the views prevailing when James I assumed the throne in England. In "An Homily against Disobedience and Wylful Rebellion" (1570), one of the sermons commanded to be read in the churches, obedience is described as "the principal virtue of all virtues." Further, the sermon explains that God had wanted perfect obedience from his creatures and that if he had been obeyed, then "there had been no poverty, no diseases, no sickness, no death, nor other miseries wherewith mankind is now infinitely and most miserably afflicted and oppressed" (quoted from Wootton, 1986, p. 94). The world was repaired in two ways. First, God set up rulers to whom people were to be obedient; second, he sent his son Jesus, who repaid the debt owed to God through his own perfect obedience (ibid., p. 95).

Jesus is the Christ

We have just discussed the second of the two "virtues" of Christianity, namely, obedience to laws. The first is "faith in Christ." When Hobbes analyzes belief, in chapter 7 of *Leviathan*, he says that it has two aspects. One is its content, that is, what is believed; the second is its source, that is, who is believed. For one difference between belief and knowledge is that belief *in* or trust of someone, substitutes for evidence. It would be pious but false to say that the primary object of Christian belief is Jesus or God. It is false because the object of such belief must be someone "that we have heard speak" (EW, 3:587). And neither God nor Jesus is accessible to humans today. Rather,

> the faith of Christians ever since our Saviour's time, hath had for foundation, first, the reputation of their pastors, and afterward, the authority of those that made the Old and New Testament to be received for the rule of faith; which none could do but Christian sovereigns; who are therefore supreme

pastors; and the only persons whom Christians now hear speak from God; except such as God speaketh to in these days supernaturally. (ibid., p. 588)

Of course, because there are many false prophets roaming the world, as the Bible tells us there would be, only the sovereign himself is qualified to judge which prophets are the true ones.

While it is not Jesus in whom Christians believe, Jesus is at the center of the content of religious belief. Hobbes says that the one article of faith necessary to salvation is that "JESUS IS THE CHRIST" (p. 590). Hobbes derives this content of Christianity from the New Testament itself. He presents a fair précis of Saint Matthew's Gospel, which is intended to show that its purpose is to establish that one proposition. He then quotes the last line of Saint John's Gospel to the same effect: "These things are written, that you may know that Jesus is the Christ, the Son of the living God" (p. 591). Other scriptural arguments extending over several pages are also developed. Hobbes's position is in line with seventeenth-century Protestant views. Hooker says that "[t]he main drift of the whole New Testament is that which St. John setteth down" and then quotes the end of that gospel, just as Hobbes did (Hooker, 1593, I.14.4).

Christianity may seem to be pretty thin soup if the proposition that Jesus is the Christ is its only ingredient. In one sense it is supposed to be, for Jesus himself had said that his yoke is easy and his burden light (EW, 3:592–3, referring to Matt. 11:30). The essence of Christianity needs to be easy, in order to give everyone a chance at salvation. To believe in Jesus is "sufficient to eternal life: but more than sufficient is not necessary; and consequently no other article is required" (EW, 3:593). Christianity is not solely for, and not even primarily for, intellectuals. Its message and its means of salvation need to be available to people of every station in life. However, in another sense, the one necessary article of faith is not thin at all. For from this one proposition, many others can be inferred. Hobbes begins by pointing out that as the

Christ, Jesus is "the king, which God had before promised by the prophets of the Old Testament, to send into the world, to reign . . . under himself eternally; and to give them eternal life, which was lost by the sin of Adam" (ibid., p. 590). Later, he says it follows that God is the omnipotent creator of all things, because such was the king of the Jews. And Jesus must have risen from the dead, otherwise he could not be a king with an eternal reign. All of these doctrines are implicit in the proposition that Jesus is the Messiah, even though not everyone who believes that proposition is intelligent enough to derive them (pp. 597–8).

Chapter 11

Scripture

Since Christianity is built upon the Bible, it is crucial to understand what the Bible is, who authored it, and where it gets its authority. These topics will be discussed in two sections, "The Authorship of the Bible" and "The Canon of the Bible." Three additional sections discuss certain mistakes and abuses of Scripture: "The Kingdom of Darkness," "The Beneficiaries of the Kingdom of Darkness," and "The Catholic Church and the Kingdom of Fairies."

THE AUTHORSHIP OF THE BIBLE

The Christian church would not exist if it were not for the Bible. The foundation for the belief that Jesus is the Christ is the fact that that is the message of the Bible and that the latter has regulative force. Given its importance, it is worth asking who the authors of the Bible are and what makes some books canonical and others not. The Bible was written over many centuries by many authors. Since the external evidence for who these authors were is rather meager, the best basis for determining authorship must come from internal evidence, that is, from studying features of the texts themselves.

The Pentateuch

The question of who wrote the various books of the Bible has a long history. At various times, several of the books that now are an established part of the canon were considered dubious by distinguished theologians of the patristic and medieval eras. Some theologians thought that the Book of Revelation was not authored by John the Apostle and thus should not be considered canonical, and some thought that the Epistle to the Hebrews was not authored by Saint Paul and thus was not canonical. According to the leading authority on the issue, "It was not until the Council of Florence (1439–43) that the See of Rome delivered for the first time a categorical opinion on the Scriptural canon" (Metzger, 1987, p. 240). This council did not settle the question of authorship. The distinguished Thomist theologian Thomas de Vio ("Cajetan") (1469–1534) argued that Saint Paul was not the author of Hebrews and doubted that Saints James and Jude were the authors of the epistles attributed to them; he similarly doubted whether Saint John was the author of the second and third epistles attributed to him. Erasmus also doubted that all of the works attributed to Saints Paul, James, Peter, John, and Jude were by them. In the Reformation tradition, Andreas Bodenstein of Karlstadt (1480–1541) and Luther also cast doubt on the authorship of some of the New Testament books (Metzger, 1987, p. 240). So to question the authorship of some books of the Bible was neither unprecedented nor proof of heterodoxy.

Hobbes fits into this tradition of studying the Bible with an open and critical eye. He is especially noteworthy for being the first European to argue in print that Moses could not have been the author of the entire Pentateuch. Although the Bible nowhere says that Moses was the author of the Pentateuch, tradition ascribed the first five books to him. Yet the arguments propping up this tradition are unsound. It is no good to argue that Moses must be the author because the Pentateuch is called "the five books of Moses." For the phrase "of Moses" may be an instance of the objective genitive, not the subjective genitive. That is, the phrase may mean books *about* Moses, rather than books authored *by* Moses. Indeed, it is uncontroversial that the titles of other books of the Bible should be understood in just this way. The

Book of Joshua means the book about Joshua, not the book by Joshua; the Book of Judges means the book about judges, not the book by judges; and the Books of Kings mean the books about kings, not the books by kings (EW, 3:368).

There are many verses in the Pentateuch itself that show that Moses was not its author.[1] Hobbes points out that near the end of Deuteronomy, it says that "no man knoweth of his [Moses'] sepulchre to this day" (EW, 3:368, quoting Deut. 34:6). There are two reasons this passage could not sensibly have been written by Moses. First, a person cannot write with certainty about where he is buried until after he is dead, and then he is unable to write. Second and more important, the phrase "to this day" only makes sense if it is written by someone long after the event has occurred. Phrases similar to this supply further evidence of passages that Moses did not write. For example, Genesis 12:6 reads, "And Abraham passed through the land to the place of Sichem, unto the plain of Moreh, and the Canaanite was then in the land" (ibid., pp. 368–9).[2] The phrase "was then in the land" is only sensibly used by someone who is writing when the Canaanites no longer are in the land. Thus, General George Custer would not have written "the Indian was then in the land" the day before the Little Big Horn massacre, although a late twentieth-century historian may.[3] But the Canaanites were in the land when Moses was alive; indeed, since Moses never reached Canaan, he could hardly have known (except, of course, through supernatural revelation) who was in the Promised Land. Although the biblical account is not unequivocal about when the Canaanites disappeared, it is certain that the Canaanites were in Canaan after Moses died.

As compelling as these arguments are, they convinced few of Hobbes's contemporaries. Defenders of the Mosaic tradition had various responses. Alexander Ross said that Moses spoke of his own death and burial "by anticipation, which is an usual way of writing, amongst some" (Ross, 1653, p. 35). As for the talk about the Canaanites, Ross makes the logical, though irrelevant, point that Moses spoke truly. He reasons:

since the sentence "The Canaanite was *not* in the land" was false when Moses wrote, the sentence "The Canaanite was *then* in the land" (my italics) was true, just as Moses reported it (ibid.). The problem with Ross's point is that the truth of Moses' statement is not sufficient to explain why Moses would have included the word "then" when he could have more simply said, "The Canaanite was in the land." John Whitehall takes a different tack. The statement about the Canaanites must be read with contrastive stress, thus: "The *Canaanite* was then in the land," as opposed to the Philistines or someone else (Whitehall, 1679, p. 94). The problem with Whitehall's point is that neither the Philistines nor any other nation is mentioned in the passage, so they cannot sensibly be considered the contrasted member.

Let's now turn to another point of authorship. Whoever wrote the Book of Numbers relied upon other, more ancient, sources – for example, one called *The Book of the Wars of the Lord* (EW, 3:369, referring to Num. 21:14).[4] Although Moses did not write everything attributed to him by tradition, he did write part of the Pentateuch, namely, those passages that are specifically assigned to him – for example, Deuteronomy 12–25, which contains legal prescriptions that were to be read every seventh year (cf. note 1). Hobbes astutely identifies these chapters as the long-lost material found by Hilkiah and given to King Josiah (EW, 3:369, referring to 2 Kings 23). Later he says that the first writings put into the Bible are what Moses wrote (ibid., p. 515).

Authorship of other Old Testament books

Hobbes uses the same techniques he applied to the Pentateuch when he discusses who did or did not write certain other books of the Old Testament. For example, Joshua did not write the book of which he is the title character, because the phrase, "They are there unto this day" (EW, 3:370, quoting Joshua 4:9), is sensibly used only by an author reporting events long past. Other passages indicate either that some place has the same name or that some monument exists "unto this day," which again is only sensibly used of an event in the distant past. Hobbes uses other passages to show that Judges, Ruth, and the two books of Samuel were written long after the events recorded in them. Hobbes reasons that the books of Kings and Chronicles also were written after the Babylonian Captivity, that is, after 539 B.C., because they contain a record of those events. Hobbes is on much less firm ground here. He is not entertaining the hypothesis, accepted by contemporary biblical scholars, that these books, like other books of the Bible, are composites from several sources, some of which may be roughly contemporaneous with the events reported and some of which may be much later.

He is on firmer ground when he reasons that the books of Ezra and Nehemiah "were written after their [the Israelites'] return from captivity; because their return, the re-edification of the walls and houses of Jerusalem, the renovation of the covenant, and ordination of their policy, are therein contained" (EW, 3:371). He also discusses other books in the same vein. He observes that while Job was probably a real person, the book about him is not a history, since he, like his friends, converses in verse, which is unusual for a person in pain but not unusual for a work of philosophy, especially ancient moral philosophy (ibid., p. 372).

Authorship of the New Testament

Unlike the Old Testament, the New Testament was written relatively soon after the events reported occurred and by eyewitnesses (EW, 3:374). Further, there is no reason to fear that the text has been corrupted in the process of the centuries. It was in the care of priests, and

> yet I am persuaded they did not therefore falsify the Scriptures, though the copies of the books of the New Testament, were in the hands only of the ecclesiastics; because if they had had an intention so to do, they would surely have made them more favourable to their power over Christian princes, and

civil sovereignty, than they are. I see not therefore any reason to doubt that the Old and New Testament, as we have them now, are the true registers of those things, which were done and said by the prophets and apostles. (EW, 3:375–6)

Given that Hobbes thinks that the New Testament was written within a generation after Jesus and that it was composed by eyewitnesses to the works of Jesus, it is plausible that Hobbes was a sincere Christian.

THE CANON OF THE BIBLE

Hobbes was one of the few intellectuals in the seventeenth century to appreciate the consequence of the fact that the Bible was many centuries in the making and that there were many other ancient books of the Hebrews that had some claim to canonicity. What should be the principle of selection in order to establish the canon?

Its age cannot be the criterion, because there are many books as ancient as the Bible, and some that are older. Subject matter cannot be the criterion, because there are many nonbiblical books that deal with the Jews or Christians. Age and subject matter jointly cannot be the criterion, because some apocryphal books are as old as and deal with the same subject matter as some biblical books. Adding "high moral content" also does not solve the problem, because some noncanonical books are spiritually more valuable than some of the canonical ones. Thus, the question recurs: Given that many books talk about God and his people, what principle of selection should be used to establish the canon?

Hobbes's answer is that the sovereign must decide. He would defend this answer in both a positive and negative way. On the positive side, the sovereign must decide because the citizens have agreed to allow him to decide all issues that bear upon their well-being, as religion surely does. The negative side is that there is no one other than the sovereign who is a plausible source for the decision.

Hobbes's answer that the sovereign must decide the canon

is a middle way between the disastrously subjective view of the dominant strand of the Reformation and the mistakenly objective view of Roman Catholicism. Many Protestants thought that each person should decide religious issues for himself. Calvin claimed that the authority of the Bible comes, not from the church, but from "the interior witness of the Holy Spirit (*testimonium Spiritus sancti internum*)" (Metzger, 1987, p. 245). This is perhaps the most important point on which Hobbes departs from Calvin. But, as the sad history of Christianity has shown, trusting religious decisions to each person's individual conscience is the straightest path to anarchy or war. The only alternative to this unacceptable eventuality is to have some authority make the decision. According to Roman Catholicism, the pope ought to be the authority on such matters. But Hobbes argued that if a sovereign deferred to an authority outside of his own control, the same threat to political stability existed. The pope cannot have sovereignty over religious matters, because the civil sovereign is sovereign over all matters. As the Bible teaches, no one can serve two masters. Hobbes's view does not exclude the possibility of a sovereign's using the decisions of the pope as the basis for the religion within his realm, as the Spanish sovereign does. But in such a case, the pope is a counselor to the sovereign, not his commander. Some English bishops thought that while neither the pope nor each individual could make decisions on religious matters, a distinctively religious authority needed to be supreme in such matters, and they had themselves in mind. But this position solves nothing. There can be no genuine "religious authority" within the realm of the sovereign, because all citizens are subject to the sovereign in all matters.

I have suggested that the question of who is to decide the canon of the Bible arises from an awareness of the historical character of that book, and much of this awareness is due to the work of Christian Renaissance thinkers such as Erasmus and John Colet, who were among the first to originate critical, historical, and literary investigations of the Bible. Hobbes is an heir to that tradition. But that is not the only source for the question. When Luther challenged the authority of the pope, he in effect raised the question, because traditionally the canonicity of the Bible was established, if not by the pope himself, then by church councils, which were ultimately subject to the pope. In short, according to the standard pre-Reformation view, the Bible consisted of certain books because the pope declared those books, and no others, to be the word of God. But when the pope's authority was abolished, or at least undermined, by the Reformation, a religious crisis arose that dovetailed with more broadly skeptical issues that were resurrected in the sixteenth century (Popkin, 1979, pp. 1–17).

Hobbes's view about the canon of the Bible, then, was inspired by Reformation concerns and was designed to silence not just practical objections but skeptical ones also. Since nothing in sense experience is infallible, the only way to eliminate controversies about the Bible canon is to let an authority decide it. The pope's authority, as already mentioned, has been overthrown, so there is only one alternative. The civil sovereign must decide the canon. This solution to the canon of the Bible is just a special case of Hobbes's views about religious controversy in general. There will always be controversy unless some authority settles the matter, and the sovereign is that authority: "Seeing therefore I have already proved, that sovereigns in their own dominions are the sole legislators; those books only are canonical, that is, law, in every nation, which are established for such by the sovereign authority" (EW, 3:366) For, as Hobbes says, "it is not the writer, but the authority of the church, that maketh the book canonical," and that authority has resided in the sovereign, since the time of King Saul (ibid., p. 376; see also pp. 377–8).

If someone finds it hard to understand why the sovereign ought to decide what is canonical and what is not, it may be because he mistakenly thinks that the issue concerns obedience to God. But the real issue is *"when* and *what* God hath said" (ibid., p. 366; see also pp. 378–80). Now since no citizen has an immediate revelation from God, he must use his natural reason to determine what method is appropriate for settling when and what God said, a method that will maintain peace and justice. The only such method is to defer to the sovereign, since it is his job alone to maintain peace and justice.

Hobbes thinks his theoretical view about the proper procedure for deciding the canon is confirmed by history. Nothing other than Moses' rather small number of writings was "received amongst the Jews for the laws of God" until after the Babylonian Captivity (approximately 539 B.C.). From the time of Rehoboam (c. 922 B.C.) until Josiah rediscovered them, not even Moses' writings were held to be canonical (EW, 3:516). Each king ruled according to his own discretion. Many of the writings of the men who were later accepted as true prophets were condemned in their own time and before the canon of the Old Testament was fixed: "The Scriptures of the Old Testament, which we have at this day, were not canonical nor a law unto the Jews till the renovation of their covenant with God at their return from the captivity, and restoration of their commonwealth under Esdras" (ibid., pp. 373–4, 517).[5] In short, the Old Testament canon was established by Esdras, sovereign and high priest, about the year 400 B.C.[6] These books are the ones "commanded to be acknowledged for such, by the authority of the Church of England" (p. 367) and are listed in the Thirty-Nine Articles.

Although some suppose that Clement, successor to Peter as head of the Christian church in Rome, enumerated all the books of the Old and New Testaments, there is no firm evidence of such an enumeration until A.D. 364, as the result of the Council of Laodicea (EW, 3:375, 522–3).[7] This action was made possible by the conversion of Constantine to Christianity about A.D. 300 (ibid., pp. 375, 517). Prior to that, no Christian had the authority to make any writings canonical. Each Christian decided for himself what writings would be honored by him: "[T]he books of the New Testament, which contain that doctrine [of salvation], until obedience to them was commanded by them that God had given power to on earth to be legislators, were not obligatory canons, that is, laws, but only good and safe advice, for the direction of sinners in the way of salvation, which every man might take and refuse at his own peril, without injustice" (p. 519). Neither the apostles nor their successors had any authority to institute laws (pp. 519–22).

No text is self-interpreting. Luther held that the Bible is clear enough in the passages that are essential to salvation, but he conceded that others were difficult to interpret. Who, then, ought to interpret the Bible? According to Hobbes, the answer depends roughly upon whether the interpreter lives before the conversion of Constantine or after.[8] Before the conversion, Christian propositions, when they were allowed to be preached, were not regulated by anyone as to their interpretation. Thus, when Saint Paul preached to the Thessalonians, some converted and some did not, because each was free to decide what the preaching meant and whether it was persuasive (EW, 3:509). In general, the apostles had to rely upon reason and their own testimony of the life and resurrection of Jesus (ibid., p. 510; see also p. 511).

THE KINGDOM OF DARKNESS

Hobbes's concern with the canon of the Bible and its proper interpretation is rooted in his allegiance to Reformation Christianity. His concern includes a deep abhorrence for the enemy of the true church, namely, the Kingdom of Darkness. This kingdom is a "confederacy of deceivers, that to obtain dominion over men in this present world, endeavor by dark and erroneous doctrines, to extinguish in them the light, both of nature, and of the gospel; and so to disprepare them for the kingdom of God to come" (EW, 3:604). The head of the kingdom was usually thought to be the Antichrist, whom seventeenth-century Protestants commonly identified with the pope. This identification was codified in England in the Westminster Confession of 1646: "[T]he Pope of Rome . . . is that Antichrist, that man of sin and son of perdition, that exalteth himself in the Church against Christ, and all that is called God" (Leith, 1982, p. 222). Hobbes resists this parochial condemnation. Although he detests the political theory and the Aristotelian theology of the Catholic church, he denies that the pope is the Antichrist. Incidentally, his theoretical objections to Catholicism did not prevent him from having many Catholics as close friends, including Marin Mersenne and Thomas White. His ability to have friendships with some intellectual opponents was made easier by his Pauline belief that Christians will be saved so long as they are sincere, even though they believe pernicious and false doctrines (EW, 3:597, 631, alluding to 1 Cor. 3). It also suggests that the enmity of some of his opponents was based upon something other than a difference over theoretical arguments.

Although the pope is not the Antichrist, he cannot be the sovereign of the kingdom of God, because there are many sovereigns, each of which has the elusive power over the church within his domain. The pope's word is ultimately authoritative only for subjects of the Papal States.

Hobbes identifies four causes of spiritual darkness. The first is the misinterpretation of Scripture. The second is the introduction of pagan mythology. The third is the mixture of pagan practices and philosophy, such as that of Aristotle. The fourth is the mixture of any other false tradition or history (EW, 3:605; McGrath, 1988, pp. 120–1).

The abuse of Scripture

The worst mistake that has been made in reading Scripture is the misinterpretation of what the Kingdom of God is. Most people think that it is made up either of living Christians or of the dead Christians who will rise from the dead (EW, 3:605). One reason why this interpretation cannot be correct is that it does not account for the fact that the Bible speaks about a functioning kingdom of God in the Old Testament. Another problem is that it gives a needlessly figurative sense to the phrase. For it is obvious that God is not now reigning on earth.

Hobbes's insistence that the Kingdom of God is a literal

kingdom, which once existed and will exist again at the Second Coming of Jesus, satisfies two of his goals at once. On the one hand, it keeps him true to the Reformation rule of giving a literal interpretation to the Bible whenever possible, and on the other hand it relegates politically disruptive religious claims to the indefinite future. It surprises me that Hobbes never explicitly tries to prove that the Second Coming is destined for the remote future, given the extent of millenarianism in the seventeenth century. His demeaning references to the Fifth Monarchy men, however, make it clear that he was cognizant of such movements. Hobbes rather sanguinely implies that the Second Coming is remote: "Which second coming not yet being, the kingdom of God is not yet come, and we are not now under any other kings by pact, but our civil sovereigns; saving only, that Christian men are already in the kingdom of grace, in as much as they have already the promise of being received at his coming again" (EW, 3:606). In *Human Nature*, he gives short shrift to the generally respectable seventeenth-century project of calculating the date of the end of the world: "We have had also divers examples of learned madness, in which men have manifestly been distracted upon any occasion that hath put them in remembrance of their own ability. Amongst the learned men, may be remembered, I think also, those that determine of the time of the world's end, and other such points of prophecy" (EW, 4:57-8).

The correct interpretation, according to Hobbes, is that the Kingdom of God is a literal kingdom, which was once on earth and will come again in the indefinite future. In order to understand this fully, one must understand the theocratic structure of history. (See the section entitled "The Theocratic Structure of History" in Chapter 10.)

The second general abuse of the Bible is "turning consecration into conjuration, or enchantment" (EW, 3:610). To consecrate something is to make it holy, and humans make things holy by offering things to God through the use of "pious and decent language and gesture" (ibid., p. 610). The consequence of consecrating something is that it is removed from its ordinary, mundane use. Thus, a cow that is made sacred is one from which milk is no longer extracted for ordinary nutritional purposes; a sheep that is made sacred is one that is not slaughtered to be eaten but burned to signify that it is being raised to the heavens for God's use. Thus, while consecrating something may as a matter of fact involve some change in its character, such a change is not essential to the act of consecration. Essentially, to consecrate something changes only the *use* a thing has "from being profane and common, to be holy, and peculiar to God's service" (ibid.).

In contrast, conjuration or incantation is essentially a way of changing the nature or properties of something through words. It is a kind of magic, not in the sense of legerdemain, but in the sense of being the work of a magus, such as Merlin the Magician. According to Hobbes, the paradigmatic case of pseudo-Christian conjuration is the Roman Catholic Church's theory of transubstantiation, namely, the view that when the priest speaks the words of consecration, the bread and wine are changed, contrary to all appearances, into the body and blood of Jesus.[9] The Catholic claims of what the priest accomplishes according to the doctrine of transubstantiation compares unfavorably with what was achieved by the Egyptian sorcerers of the pharaoh who kept the Hebrews as slaves. At least the sorcerers were able to make it appear that their rods turned into serpents, whereas the Catholic priests are not able even to create an illusion.

Hobbes's language about consecration closely tracks that of Calvin, who also claimed that the sorcerers did not turn their rods into serpents but only created an illusion (Calvin, 1559, IV.17.15), even though Exodus does not say or imply that it was only an illusion. Likewise, Calvin claims that Catholic priests compare unfavorably with the sorcerers: "But what likeness or nearness do they find between that glorious miracle [of Moses' changing his rod into a serpent] and their trumped-up illusion, to which no eye is a witness? Magicians by playing tricks persuaded the Egyptians that they were able by divine power beyond the order of nature to change the creatures" (Calvin, 1559, IV.17.15). There are also other important congruences of language and doctrine. Calvin, in his discussion of transubstantiation, said that after the consecration of the bread and wine "they now have to be considered of a different class from common foods intended solely to feed the stomach." The Catholic view is "virtually equivalent to magic incantation" (ibid., IV.17.14).

Hobbes is willing to concede that Christ's own words of consecration turned the bread and wine into Christ's own body and blood (EW, 3:612). By his own principles, he should not have, for there is just as much absurdity in Christ's making his whole body to exist in two disjoint spaces as there is in priests' making it exist in disjoint spaces. My conjecture is that Hobbes felt the pull of the literal interpretation of the Bible so strongly that he let it override his standard procedure of figuratively interpreting any biblical passage that contradicted logic or physics.

The Catholic church also practices conjuration in the blessing of the water, salt, and oil used for baptism, and in the surrounding rituals, such as the exorcism of the "unclean spirit" in each unbaptized child (EW, 3:613; cf. Calvin, 1559, IV.17.14). Analogous things could be said of other Catholic rites: marriage, extreme unction (anointing of the sick), visitation of the sick, consecrating churches and graveyards, and so on.

The third general abuse of Scripture that Hobbes mentions is the misinterpretation of eternal life, everlasting death, and the second death, three topics that I have discussed in Chapter 9, "Angels and Eschatology."

Demonology

So far we have been discussing the contribution that misinterpreting Scripture makes to the Kingdom of Darkness. Hobbes next discusses how modern science can eliminate an element of the Kingdom of Darkness. He begins chapter 45, "Of Demonology, and Other Relics of the Religion of the Gentiles," by adumbrating the features of visual perception:

an impression is made on the sense organ by light refracted from opaque bodies, and so on. The point of this little lesson in psychology is that it would have been difficult for the ancient Greeks to have known that the evanescent phantasms they sometimes experienced either in sleep, delirium, or madness were nothing more than the consequences of an abnormally disturbed sense organ, because they did not have an adequate scientific theory (EW, 3:637–8). But seventeenth-century Europeans have no similar excuse available to them. The upshot is that modern science can assist true religion by expurgating nonbiblical theories from standard Christian beliefs. Since the science of Copernicus, Galileo, and Harvey is the true science, there can be no conflict between it and true religion (ibid., p. 687).

There is a further point to be made. Christians would not have been deceived by the abnormal phenomena just mentioned if they had not embraced pagan doctrines. For "demonology" is merely a theory about the perceptual phenomena that occur in dreams, delirium, or insanity. The sense experiences themselves do not require one to believe that there exist demons which are the cause of the bizarre experiences. If Jews and Christians had not embraced Gentile philosophy, their religion would not have been perverted.

As noted earlier, one mark of Protestantism is the rejection of all the cultic practices of the Catholic church, such as the use of pictures and sculptures in church and the veneration of saints. Hobbes contributes to this rejection both by criticizing the excessive use of paintings and sculptures in Catholic churches and by giving a historical diagnosis of how the corruption originated. Concerning the latter, he argues that after the Greeks and Romans were converted, instead of abandoning their religious practices they merely transformed them into a Christian guise. As I mentioned in the first section of Chapter 9, he notes that Jupiter became the apostle Barnabas, Mercury became Paul, and Venus and Cupid became the Virgin Mary and the infant Jesus respectively (EW, 3:659–60; 656–7). Saints are nothing but pagan gods in masquerade. The canonization of saints is another aspect of this institution. Romulus was the first person to be canonized, because Julius Proculus testified that Romulus, after his death, appeared to Julius and assured him that he (Romulus) was in heaven (ibid., p. 660). Hobbes's history of the corruption of Christianity is similar to Calvin's history of idolatry in his *Inventory of Relics*. For example, Calvin says, "So the priests of Gaul gave rise to the sacrifice of Great Cybele's celibacy. Nuns came in place of vestal virgins. The Church of All Saints to succeed the Pantheon; against ceremonies were set ceremonies not much unlike" (quoted from Eire, 1986, p. 211).

The Greeks and Romans worshiped the phantasms of their brains as gods and represented them with idols. But, as Saint Paul said, "[W]e know that an idol is nothing," and the worship of idols was condemned in the first of God's laws, "Thou shalt not have strange gods before Me" (EW, 3:645–6). Evidence that ignorant Catholics believe images to be divine is the fact that they believe that some paintings and sculptures "have spoken; and have bled; and that miracles have been done by them" (ibid., 658). Hobbes's criticisms here are reminiscent of Calvin's *Inventory of Relics*, in which he listed and then critiqued the numerous alleged relics claimed by the Catholic church. Eire comments,

> Calvin says over and over in the *Inventory* that what one sees, or observes as real, *is* real in this material sphere. If something is contrary to experience, or reason, then it must be considered false. This is why he lashed out with such comic fury against "pious frauds," using a keen empirical eye to unmask inconsistencies, and sharp measured descriptions to demolish absurd claims. What fish ever lasted over 1,500 years?, he asks. How, then, is it possible that the fish distributed by Jesus can still be around? This is not the way the world works. What object ever multiplied itself endlessly? How then is it that there are so many duplicated relics? Has any ancient object ever taken on the appearance of something new? How, then, is it that the wine jars from Cana are all in different styles, shapes, and sizes? Or that so many of Jesus' household

items are strikingly contemporary in appearance? (Eire, 1986, pp. 230–1)

Hobbes has no objection to marking out certain places or objects for special religious attention. This is in keeping with the true meaning of "holy," and the Old Testament contains many examples of appropriate behavior toward the holy. Nor does he object to religious pictures, which, like "monuments of friends, or of men worthy," are merely aids to remembering them (EW, 3:659). But keeping a picture as a reminder is altogether different from worshiping an inanimate image or place as a god (ibid., pp. 652, 656). The worst instance of such idolatry is the Catholic belief in the real presence of Jesus in the Eucharist, which is propped up by the scholastic theory of transubstantiation (p. 654).

It would be perverse to interpret Hobbes's scruples against Roman Catholic ritual and what he explicitly identifies as Greek and Roman pagan practices as a general attack on revealed religion. He is merely continuing the Reformation tradition of debunking and excoriating Roman Catholic practices, which the Reformers identified as holdovers from paganism. Hobbes's criticisms, then, are focused against specific religious practices, and there is no more reason to think that he intends the reader to generalize them to all religious practices than there is to think that Calvin and other Reformers so intended. To think that he is attacking revealed religion wholesale but that Calvin and other Reformers are not is to commit the fallacy of special pleading.

Vain philosophy

The presence of pagan rituals in Christianity is objectionable for two reasons. First, it interferes with the proper form of worshiping God. Second, it introduces doctrines that many people mistakenly think are part of the doctrine of Christianity. There is another pagan element that is objectionable because it has been used to provide the theoretical foundations for Christianity. This is Hobbes's point in the following passage from *De Corpore:*

> The first doctors of the Church, . . . whilst they endeavoured to defend the Christian faith against the Gentiles by natural reason, began also to make use of philosophy, and with the decrees of Holy Scripture to mingle the sentences of heathen philosophers; and first some harmless ones of Plato, but afterwards also many foolish and false ones out of the physics and metaphysics of Aristotle; and bringing in the enemies, betrayed unto them the citadels of Christianity. From that time, instead of the worship of God, there entered a thing called *school divinity,* walking on one foot firmly, which is the Holy Scripture, but halted on the other rotten foot, which the Apostle Paul called *vain,* and might have called *pernicious philosophy;* for it hath raised an infinite number of controversies in the Christian world concerning religion, and from these controversies, wars. (EW, 1:x)

Useless wars and religious controversies will not end, according to Hobbes, until Aristotelianism is replaced by an adequate philosophical theory. Thus, it is important for Hobbes to attack the theological use of Aristotelian philosophy, which he identifies as another element of the Kingdom of Darkness.

Hobbes begins chapter 46, "Of Darkness from Vain Philosophy, and Fabulous Traditions," with a definition of philosophy as the knowledge of the relations between causes and effects. He then gives a short history of Greek philosophy, the purpose of which is to show that it hardly deserves the name "philosophy." The natural science of the ancient Greeks is unacceptable because it did not use geometry. Their moral philosophy is unacceptable because it is nothing but a description of their own passions. And their logic is unacceptable because it is nothing but "captions of words." The worst of it all are Aristotle's *Metaphysics, Politics,* and *Ethics* (EW, 3:668–9), which universities during the Middle Ages took up and applied to the Christian religion. Hobbes attacks the idea of abstract essences, incorporeal spirit, and separated essences. He considers these refutations important, because he thinks that these ideas led to political instability. If a separated soul might be "seen by night amongst the graves," then it makes sense to obey the people who have control over such spirits, namely, the priests. Also, if a person can convince people that what has the look, taste, and feel of bread is not bread, he can convince them of anything; for, as Hobbes says, "who will not obey a priest, that can make God, rather than [obeying] his sovereign, nay even God himself" (ibid., p. 675). What is insidious about this whole matter is that if the duped people thought that the whole doctrine rested on Aristotle's philosophy, they would not accept it. But, because they think that it is part of their religion, they believe it.

THE BENEFICIARIES OF THE KINGDOM OF DARKNESS

Whatever else may lie behind the advocacy of the elements of the Kingdom of Darkness, one motive is personal gain. It is self-serving for the pastors of the church to claim that they have the right to govern people independently of the sovereign. Since the pope has the most to gain, he makes the strongest claims for himself. The popes were able to expropriate titles of sovereignty for themselves because of a power vacuum that was created when the Roman Empire fell. Because there was in consequence no emperor, there was no one strong enough to prevent the pope from taking the title *pontifex maximus*, which had previously belonged to the Roman emperor. Unfortunately for Christianity, the pope transmuted his appropriate office of teacher and counselor into the fake office of spiritual sovereign. Hence the doctrine of a spiritual kingdom of God on earth was invented (EW, 3:689–90). What Hobbes wants to insist upon is that a genuine kingdom requires a genuine king; the pope is not a genuine king and is a pretender to the throne that will legitimately be occupied by Jesus.

Although almost all of what Hobbes has said about the

Kingdom of Darkness applies either exclusively or most directly to the Roman Catholic Church, Hobbes thinks that the Presbyterian Church also occupies a place in the Kingdom of Darkness. One would have expected that after the ideology of the Roman Catholic Church had been broken by the Reformation leaders, the proper relation between church and state would have been established. But the Presbyterian Church stepped into the breach and argued "that the kingdom of Christ is already come, and that it began at the resurrection of our Saviour" (EW, 3:690). Thus their leaders made the same claims for themselves as the Catholics had. And the predictable result was the English Civil War.

Showing some signs of exasperation, Hobbes asks himself what the best option is for Christianity in England, given its history and its then current political problems. At this point, he abandons the position he otherwise so ardently advocates. He suggests that perhaps Christianity ought to return to the condition that existed when it was founded. Pastors should be counselors only and make no pretense to having secular authority. In turn, the civil sovereign would exercise no control over Christians, each of whom would be free to formulate his religious beliefs according to his own conscience. That is, *incredibile dictu*, Hobbes comes to recommend what was known in his day as Independency, the separation of church and state: "and so we are reduced to the independency of the primitive Christians, to follow Paul, or Cephas, or Apollos, every man as he liketh best; which, if it be without contention, and without measuring the doctrine of Christ, by our affection to the person of his minister . . . is perhaps the best" (EW, 3:696). Earlier, in a letter that he wrote in 1641 to the earl of Devonshire, Hobbes comments on the popular movement to abolish episcopacy. He thinks it is a mistake to confuse the unworthiness of individual bishops with the institution of episcopacy, which he favors. However, he is willing to accept an alternative church polity if people are unwilling to tolerate episcopacy. (The letter is published in Tonnies, 1904, pp. 302–3.)

As this letter of 1641 and the passage of *Leviathan* just cited indicate, Hobbes was willing to tolerate alternative forms of church polity. His toleration is in keeping with the times. Episcopacy had been abolished by Parliament in 1643, and Independency was the de facto condition of interregnum England. Although Cromwell supported Independency, it is unlikely that this consideration could have influenced Hobbes much. For Cromwell did not become Lord Protector until 1653, two years after Hobbes had written *Leviathan*. Given the volatility of the government in 1651, it would have been foolhardy for Hobbes or anyone else to have taken a political stance merely on the expectation that Cromwell would eventually acquire a dominant, institutional power. Finally, Independency is essentially the solution that Charles II wanted to adopt in preparation for his return to England. In his *Declaration of Breda* of 1660, Charles wrote, "Because the passion and uncharitableness of the times have produced several opinions in religion, by which men are engaged in parties and animosities against each other . . . we do declare a liberty to tender consciences and that no man shall be disquieted or called into question for differences of opinion in matters of religion which do not disturb the peace of the kingdom" (quoted from Moorman, 1972, p. 249).

THE CATHOLIC CHURCH AND THE KINGDOM OF FAIRIES

Hobbes is never more sardonic than when he draws an extended analogy between the Catholic church and the kingdom of fairies of English folk mythology. He says that the papacy is "no other than the *ghost* of the deceased *Roman empire*, sitting crowned upon the grave thereof. For so did the Papacy start up on a sudden out of the ruins of that heathen" (EW, 3:698).[10] Just as the fairies have a mysterious language, the papacy has Latin.[11] The pope is the King Oberon of Catholics. Priests, who are self-professedly spiritual beings, are like the fairies themselves, who inhabit the darkness and graves just as the priests walk in obscure doctrine and inhabit churches and churchyards. Both fairies and priests are immune from civil prosecution. Both fairies and priests have their own monetary system. (The clerical currencies are masses, canonizations, and indulgences.) Perhaps Hobbes's sharpest cut is one in which the reader must infer the punch line: "The *faeries* marry not; but there be amongst them *incubi*, that have copulation with flesh and blood. The *priests* also marry not." As abusive as this passage is, it is within the bounds of acceptable preaching by the seventeenth-century clergy. Thomas Cole, an archdeacon, preached that the head of a Catholic priest is analogous to the buttocks of an ape, for "they be both bald alike, but that the priest be bald before, the apes behind" (quoted from Collinson, 1979, p. 170).

Finally, fairies and the papacy are similar in that neither exists except in the fancies of ignorant people. While belief in fairies is based upon old wives' tales, belief in the papacy "consisteth only in the fear that seduced people stand in, of their excommunication; upon hearing of false miracles, false traditions, and false interpretations of the Scripture" (EW, 3:700).

Conclusion

A historically informed and philosophically sensitive reading of *Leviathan* presents a very different picture of Hobbes's philosophy from the standard one. I have been arguing that Hobbes's political philosophy cannot be separated from his philosophy of religion. His religious views were much more sophisticated than scholars have previously believed. In addition to arguing that he was not an atheist, I have shown that to say no more than that he was a theist or even a Christian is a misleading oversimplification. In order to understand how it is that Hobbes did not intend to subvert religion, it is necessary to appreciate the specific religious and political tradition that Hobbes was trying to uphold. The ordinary religious classifications used by philosophers to categorize seventeenth-century thinkers are not fine-grained enough to represent Hobbes's views fairly. It is important to distinguish between at least three different aspects of religion: (1) doctrine, (2) church government, and (3) theology.[1]

1. In doctrine, he was orthodox. He explicitly subscribes to the dogmatic pronouncements formulated in the Christian creeds of the first four ecumenical councils, as required by the terms of Queen Elizabeth's Act of Supremacy. It is always possible for someone to accuse him of heterodoxy, just as people accused Aquinas of it in the late thirteenth century. Hobbes and Aquinas are alike in that they both tried to reconcile orthodoxy with new philosophical or scientific theories. Ultimately the only body competent to settle the issue

333

would be an ecclesiastical court, if one could be agreed upon. But who has the authority to regulate such a court? This brings us to the issue of church government.

2. Hobbes argued, as earlier monarchs and archbishops of England had, that only the sovereign has the authority to regulate ecclesiastical matters. Hobbes preferred the episcopal system, in part because it was the system preferred by sovereigns in England. He also preferred it in part because it did not suffer from the logical objections that he had raised against the presbyterian and Catholic systems. The presbyterians wanted ultimate religious authority to be vested in the laity, independent of the sovereign. In his own way, he was trying to provide a theoretical foundation for the formula of James I, "No bishop, no king." Two Catholic systems can be distinguished. The Roman Catholics wanted ultimate religious authority to be vested in the pope, who is himself a sovereign, but not the sovereign of English Christians, nor most Christians. The English Catholics (Anglo-Catholics) wanted the ultimate religious authority to be vested in the college of English bishops, operating independently of the sovereign. Much of the animosity against Hobbes in his own time came from proponents of these systems. Because members of influential Christian churches on both the left and the right attacked him, their opposition gives the false impression that Hobbes was anti-Christian, when in fact he occupied a middle ground between these two extremes. This is not the only source of parochial religious opposition to Hobbes.

3. Hobbes also had the historical misfortune to subscribe to a theology that was falling into disfavor. Hobbes was a Calvinist. This fact is crucial for understanding the source of much of the opposition to him by his contemporaries. He was opposed on the right by Protestant scholastic theologians, who had adapted Aristotle to their needs, and on the left by the Arminians, who were avowedly anti-Calvinistic.[2] Hobbes's two most famous critics, Bishop Bramhall and Lord Clarendon, were both Arminians.[3] When Bramhall attacks Hobbes's determinism, he is attacking the

metaphysical manifestation of Hobbes's subscription to predestination. Hobbes's religious views, like his political views to a large extent, were similar to those of James I, the monarch under whom he spent his adolescence and early childhood. It is important to recall that James I sent to the Council of Dort representatives who, like Hobbes, were committed to the doctrine of predestination, against the Arminians. Hobbes's religious views would also have been in the mainstream of those at Oxford University when Hobbes was a student at Magdalen Hall. When Hobbes criticizes universities, it is partially because they had abandoned Calvinism for Arminianism (Tyacke, 1987a, pp. 58–86, and Tyacke, 1987b; see also Trevor-Roper, 1989, pp. 40–119).[4] The term "high Calvinist" has been coined to describe someone who was in favor of the monarchy, the episcopal form of church government, and Calvinist theology (Trevor-Roper, 1989, p. 44). The term applies perfectly to Hobbes.[5]

Let's now consider how his religious views affected his philosophy. Although his religious views did not determine his moral and political views, they did influence them. Hobbes subscribed to a divine command theory of morality. He believed that the basic laws of morality are the laws of nature. Like all laws, these consist of two elements, a form and a content. The form is provided by the command of God, who, in virtue of his overwhelming power, has the authority to issue commands. The content of the first law commanded by God is that each person is to seek peace. The content of the second law specifies the general means of achieving this end, namely, the laying down of the right to all things. The other laws of nature express specific ways of achieving the content of the first two. The laws of nature are deducible by reason because every law must be promulgated, and deducibility is the only natural method of promulgation available to all humans. Hobbes takes it as beyond question that what is deducible by reason as the best means to self-preservation must be the command of God. This has the happy consequence that long-term prudence is incorporated into morality.

To turn to his political theory, Hobbes held that the civil state is a mortal god, who serves under the immortal God. The civil state imitates God in three crucial respects. First, the civil state has overwhelming power to control its citizens. Second, it has no obligations to its citizens, even though they have obligations to it. Third, the civil state saves people from the imminent death lurking in the state of nature, just as God supposedly saves people from the death of sin. The secularizing consequence of Hobbes's thought is most obvious in this third respect. In subsequent political thought, the secular idea of salvation from the observable dangers in this world extinguishes the religious idea of salvation from the unobservable dangers of a dubious otherworld.

Hobbes's religious views make him a transitional figure in the history of philosophy. His thought is an odd combination of traditional and progressive elements. His orthodoxy and Calvinist theology make him a religious conservative, and much of his philosophy of religion is traditional, for example, his proof for the existence of God and his views about the limits of literally true talk about God. Also, his desire to have Christianity serve the cause of peace and not be an instrument of sedition was a biblical and conservative view. Offsetting these elements are his progressive views about science. He was an ardent supporter of Galileo and Harvey. Hobbes recognized, I think, that there was a tension and the appearance of a conflict between religion and science. One of his projects was to reconcile the two. His explanations about how angels exist but are material, how heaven and hell will exist but will be located on earth, and how miracles occurred but did not violate the physical laws of nature are ingenious attempts to accommodate Christianity to modern science. His critical reading of the Bible is another aspect of this project and continues the Renaissance tradition of applying the highest standards of literary science to the Bible, which was considered the greatest literary work, precisely because it was thought to express the word of God.[6] Unfortunately, Hobbes's attempted synthesis failed. His principles had consequences other than the ones he thought they would have. Far from making him unique, his kind of failure is typical of a tradition of thinkers from the fourteenth through the eighteenth century. Despite their best efforts to save the intellectual respectability of Christian doctrine, they contributed to its downfall.

Appendix A

Curley on Hobbes

Edwin Curley has presented the most sustained and well-wrought case that Hobbes was "rather likely . . . an atheist," although Curley also says that "if someone were to insist that we'll never really know what Hobbes's religious beliefs were, I would cheerfully concede the point" (Curley, 1991, p. 57). He is motivated to explore the issue of Hobbes's alleged atheism because of an incident related in John Aubrey's biographical essay on Hobbes. Aubrey writes, "When Spinoza's *Tractatus Theologico-Politicus* first came out [1670], Mr. Edmund Waller sent it to my lord of Devonshire and desired send him word what Hobes said of it. Mr. H. told his lordship: – Ne judicate ne judicemini [Judge not that ye be not judged, Matt. 7:1]. He told me he [Spinoza] had outthrown him [Hobbes] a bar's length, for he durst not write so boldly" (Aubrey, 1680, 1:357).

While admitting that "we cannot infer much from the reported remark," Curley nonetheless asks "what he might have meant by it" (Curley, 1991, p. 10). I think this question is fruitless to ask. First, Hobbes's own remark is so cryptic and vague that we have no idea what specifically he was talking about. Spinoza's *Tractatus Theologico-Politicus* is quite large. Was Hobbes thinking of some specific passages or the entire work? If only some passages, which? Even if Hobbes was thinking of the entire work, notice that Hobbes would perhaps not be remarking on the content of the work but its style. To write "boldly" is to write in a certain way, not necessarily to write about a specific matter or to hold a spe-

339

cific doctrine. Any position can be expressed boldly. Second, if Aubrey is to be counted a reliable reporter in this matter, then he ought to be considered a reliable reporter on other matters, unless there is some special reason not to. But Aubrey explicitly, and – compared with the anecdote just given – extensively, discusses Hobbes's Christianity: "For his being branded with atheisme, his writings and vertuous life testifie against it. . . . And that he was a Christian, 'tis cleare, for he recieved [*sic*] the sacrament of Dr. ⟨John⟩ Pierson, and in his confession to Dr. John Cosins, . . . on his (as he thought) death-bed, declared that he liked the religion of the Church of England best of all other" (Aubrey, 1680, 1:353; see also OL, 1:xvi). So if Aubrey is to be used as a witness, he is a witness for the defense. Aubrey's remarks about Hobbes's Christianity contradict any attempt to construe Hobbes's remark about Spinoza's views as evidence of atheism. Surely Aubrey would have explained Hobbes's remark about Spinoza if he had thought it was in any way inconsistent with his own assertion that Hobbes's "writings and vertuous life testifie against" atheism. But he does not. In this situation, Aubrey's silence is further evidence that Hobbes was not an atheist.

One might object that Aubrey testifies to other things that show that Hobbes was an atheist. For example, Aubrey says, "When Mr T. Hobbes was sick in France, the divines came to him, and tormented him (both Roman Catholic, Church of England and Geneva). Said he to them 'Let me alone, or else I will detect all your cheats from Aaron to yourselves!' I think I have heard him speak something to this purpose" (1:160). Notice that the divines were tormenting, not comforting, him. Again because of the brevity of the report, we do not know who these people were or how they were tormenting him. Of course, Hobbes would have been offended by Roman Catholic priests trying to convert him. The divines from the Church of England may well have been Arminians, who were equally offensive to him. And Hobbes objected to the Genevan church because it was independent of the secular authorities (McNeill, 1967, p. 311; see also pp. 188–9). The fact that the divines are referred to as being from Geneva, rather than as being Calvinist, is significant. It suggests that Hobbes objected to their political views, not their theological ones. So there is nothing surprising or suspicious in his remark. In any case, when he refers to "all your cheats," there is no need to interpret this as implying that every divine cheat is deceptive. It may mean only that he will reveal all the cheats that bad divines committed.

Hobbes certainly held that many priests and ministers abused their legitimate function of preaching the word of God and tried to usurp power. There is nothing extraordinary in this belief. The Catholic church has admitted such, even accusing its own popes. Roman Catholics insist, however, that the human and the divine aspects of the church need to be distinguished. Further, the fact that some priests abuse their legitimate function presupposes that they have a legitimate function, and Hobbes discusses that function extensively in *Leviathan*. Unfortunately, Curley does not comment on this aspect of Hobbes's work at all.

In fact, the passage in question concerns a possible anticlericalism, much more than atheism. But it is not worth arguing over whether Hobbes was anticlerical or not. That would be largely a semantic dispute. Anticlericalism is sometimes an attitude about the people who tend to become clerics and sometimes a view about church government. No matter how the term "anticlerical" should be defined, it would be tendentious to allow "X is anticlerical" to entail "X is an atheist." Indeed, clericalism and theism are logically independent. Being proclerical does not entail being a theist. A person may be an atheist but believe in the desirability of religion, specifically a priestly religion. It was once said of Santayana that he believed that God did not exist and that Mary was his mother. These are logical points. There is also an important historical point to be made, since this question bears more directly and heavily on the issue of how Hobbes's thought ought to be interpreted.

Anticlericalism was a prominent theme in Protestantism. Luther's argument against indulgences was also an attack on an abuse promoted by the clergy. In England, anti-clericalism among reform-minded Christians in the sixteenth century was so pervasive that it was difficult to find suitable candidates for the clergy (Collinson, 1979, p. 112). This religiously inspired anticlericalism persisted among seventeenth-century English Protestants. Far from regarding anticlericalism as good evidence of atheism, many considered it a mark of the truly religious Protestant. Many reform-minded people, including some clergy, were anticlerical. The clergy, or certain types of clergy, were associated with a corruption of original Christianity or with a corruption of government. This is most easily seen in connection with the specific anticlericalism that is antiepiscopal. One historian claims that "no one liked the bishops" (Kenyon, 1985, p. 120). Even some future bishops disliked bishops. John Hooper, future bishop of Gloucester, complained of their "fraud and artifice, by which they promote the kingdom of Antichrist" (Hill, 1971, p. 42). In England, the bishops as a group had long been understood to support absolute monarchy. The monarch often had the same understanding: thus James I's own pronouncement, "No bishop, no king." To oppose the king was to oppose the bishops. In 1637, three distinguished Puritans, William Prynne, John Bastwick, and Henry Burton, were punished by the Star Chamber for criticizing the bishops. For example, Burton had written, "From plague, pestilence and famine, from bishops, priests, and deacons, Good Lord deliver us" (quoted from Gregg, 1981, p. 276).

As part of the attack on Charles I's reign, the Root and Branch petition was introduced into Parliament in December 1640; the substance of this bill was to abolish episcopacy. When Parliament debated the matter, "[N]o one was prepared to defend the present bishops" (Kenyon, 1985, p. 138): "[T]he Root and Branch Bill was no mere charter of destruction; it offered a comprehensive secularization and reorganization of the Church, comparable with the Civil Constitution of the Clergy imposed on France in 1790" (ibid., p. 139; see also p. 153). The episcopacy was in fact dissolved in

September 1642. Fortunately Hobbes expressed himself about the substance of the Root and Branch petition in late July or early August of 1641. After the original petition was submitted to Parliament, many counties submitted their own petitions on the same matter. Writing to the earl of Devonshire about the one submitted by Nottinghamshire, Hobbes concedes that the charges that have been made about specific "[e]cclesiasticall persons and their officers" are well founded. He denies that the episcopacy itself is at fault. However, he thinks that a nonepiscopal form of church government is acceptable (Tonnies, 1904, p. 302; see also Fletcher, 1981, pp. 91–6). Hobbes's view must be judged to be moderate and temperate. The view expressed in this letter is consistent with his published writings. When he criticized priests, he attacked them as being self-serving, or purveyors of paganism, or political malcontents, not because they were men of God. I think he wrote truly when he said in *Leviathan* that he was not writing against the bishops (EW, 7:5). In various contexts he endorses the episcopal system against the papal and presbyterian ones. In his autobiography, written in Latin verse, Hobbes explains that many people confused his attacks on the papacy with attacks on all clergy: "Nam dum Papalis Regni contrecto tumorem, / Hos, licet abscissos, laedere visus eram" [For while I was dealing with the commotion of the papal kingdom / I was viewed as injuring these [the English clergy], although they had been separated] (OL, 1:xciv). Perhaps he was thinking of Henry Hammond (N. Pocock, 1850, p. 295). That Hobbes was not strongly anticlerical is also well attested by his warm friendships with numerous clerics, many of whom were Roman Catholics – Mersenne, Gassendi, and Thomas White being perhaps the most conspicuous.

Curley mentions Mersenne's failed attempt to convert Hobbes to Catholicism on his deathbed, as if this had some special relevance to Hobbes's alleged atheism. Hobbes always spoke against that religion and presbyterianism, not because he was non-Christian, but because he was a member of the Church of England. Hobbes's reply to Mersenne's plea that he convert to Catholicism is worth considering. He said, "Father, I have debated all that with myself long ago; to debate it now will be tiresome" (OL, 1:xvi). This remark recalls a passage in *Behemoth*, where he says, "This controversy between the Papist and the Reformed Churches, could not choose but make every man, to the best of his power, examine by the Scriptures, which of them was in the right" (EW, 6:190). It implies that Hobbes had also chosen. Only two options are mentioned: Catholicism and the Reformed churches. We know what Hobbes thought about Catholicism, and I have argued extensively that Hobbes's positive views are informed by and show an unwavering commitment to either Calvin's own religious views or to some of the seventeenth-century Reformed views. If Hobbes had any covert atheistic inclination, this would have been an excellent opportunity for him to convey that fact. He could have said, "This controversy between the Papist and the Reformed Churches, could not choose but make every man, to the best of his power, examine by the Scriptures, which of them was in the right, *if either*." In this way, Hobbes could have implied, or at least broached the possibility, that careful biblical study undermines religion. But he does not.

Thus, it is not true that Hobbes had "a low view of all the major sects of his time" (Curley, 1991, p. 7). Hobbes promoted the doctrine of the Church of England. He criticized its officials only for abdicating their duty as discernible from Scripture and as defined by the decrees of Henry VIII, Elizabeth I, and James I. Hobbes attacked the theories underlying Roman Catholicism and Presbyterianism; he also disliked Quakers, Fifth Monarchy men, and lesser sects. But these clearly focused attacks, far from being evidence of his alleged atheism, are evidence of his sectarian Christianity. Another example of this is his attack on Robert Bellarmine's *De Summo Pontifice*, the only modern book mentioned in *Leviathan*.[1] The longest discussion in the whole of *Leviathan* is his effort to show that Bellarmine has failed to prove that the pope is the supreme authority in Christianity (EW, 3:547–84).[2] If Curley or any of those who suggest that Hobbes was non-Christian were correct, then Hobbes's attack would be absurdly inapt. It is a maxim of conversation that a person should convey as much as is required by the goals of the conversation. A corollary of this maxim is that a person should not prove a proposition that is weaker than is required. Now if Hobbes thought that he had undermined the intellectual respectability of Christianity, this enormous effort would have been pointless. For if Christianity is untenable, then, *a fortiori*, Catholicism is untenable. And it is not as if Bellarmine had some large following in England. As a Catholic cardinal and theologian, he was *verboten*, notwithstanding some sympathy for the Catholic religion in the Caroline court. Some brief refutation of Bellarmine's work might be compatible with Curley's thesis, but not the extensive refutation in which Hobbes engages, especially since it occurs after Hobbes's critique of religion and the Bible.

Like others before him, Curley thinks that Hobbes's treatment of prophecy, miracles, and the Bible subverts belief in revealed religion. I have already conceded that Hobbes's work, like that of Gregory of Rimini, William of Ockham, Locke, and Newton, is part of a long history of increasing secularization of thought. Yet each of them intended to save religion by his theories, not to undermine it. It is part of the Hegelian cunning of Spirit that their efforts had the opposite of their intended effect. I have also shown how Hobbes's positions are either part of Reformation theology or attempts to make religion compatible with modern science. If there is no way to make revealed religion compatible with modern science, then Hobbes's failure is hardly evidence that he wanted to fail.

Many of the positions that Curley regards as evidence of Hobbes's irreligion are held by most respectable Christian scholars today. An example is Hobbes's argument that Moses was not the author of the Pentateuch; only fundamentalist Christian scholars think that Moses authored all of the Pentateuch.

It is ironic that Curley believes that Hobbes is suspect for holding that it is difficult to discriminate between true and false prophets, yet then refers to the article on prophecy in *Harper's Bible Dictionary*, which says that the early church may have suppressed prophecy altogether because of the difficulty of identifying false prophets (Achtemeier, 1985, p. 830; see also Curley, 1991, p. 29). If the same standards are applied to each, then the faith of the early Christians is as suspect as that of Hobbes. I have indicated earlier that Hobbes has suffered because he has been the victim of a double standard. The same doctrine, considered respectable when held by early Christians or Reformers, is counted as atheistic in Hobbes. Hobbes, like the Reformers, doubts that miracles occurred after the death of the last apostle, because the Catholic church had exploited such claims. Hobbes, like the Calvinists, restricted Christ's redemption to the elect, because of predestination and the impossibility of God's work being ineffective. And Hobbes, like William Ames, attributes miracles only to God, in order to maintain his sovereignty (Ames, 1643; cf. Curley, 1991, p. 34).

The last issue that Curley raises concerns Hobbes's attitude about proofs for the existence of God. In both *Elements of Law* (c. 1640) and *Leviathan*, Hobbes presents a conventional cosmological argument for the existence of God. But according to Curley, Hobbes holds that there is no philosophical proof of the existence of God, both in *De Corpore*, written after *Leviathan*, and in *Thomas White's De Mundo Examined*, written about 1642. His nemesis John Wallis uses the relevant passage from *De Corpore* as evidence of Hobbes's atheism. One might have hoped for a good deal of clarification from the passage, but it provides little. Hobbes's response is perfunctory. Beyond quoting what he said in *De Corpore*, which, he remarks, was "not ill said" (EW, 4:428), Hobbes commits himself to the evidence provided by the Bible and to the creation, the only evidence "from natural reason" that is persuasive (ibid., p. 427).

Even if Curley were correct in holding that there is a conflict, there would be several possible responses. One possibility is that since the biblical evidence was sufficient for Hobbes, he was not concerned with whether there was or

346

was not a rational proof. Another is that since the possibility of atheism in the seventeenth century was so remote and Hobbes was so secure in his Christianity, he could not get exercised about Wallis's academic objection. Still another possibility, which Curley considers, is that Hobbes was some sort of fideist or at least considered fideism at various times. Curley thinks there is evidence of this in *Thomas White's De Mundo Examined*. Speaking in what seems to be an uncharacteristically self-righteous tone, Hobbes says that those who try to "demonstrate" that there does exist and has existed "an omnipotent God, Maker of heaven and Earth, as the Creed of our faith proposes we must believe . . . sin against religion" (Hobbes, 1642, pp. 304, 306). A proposition that has been demonstrated belongs to natural knowledge, not to faith. He says, "Therefore as soon as any proposition is demonstrated it is no longer an article of faith but is a theorem in philosophy" (ibid., p. 306; see also Brown, 1962, p. 340).

I think that none of these possibilities is correct. But the correct answer is historically interesting and does bear upon the texts just quoted. Whether Hobbes was a fideist or not depends upon the definition or the criteria for the term. It is clear that there was a drift toward fideism, beginning in the late thirteenth century and continuing through to the end of the seventeenth, and Hobbes is a part of this drift. However, it is more fruitful not to worry about the semantic issue of how to define a tag such as "fideism" and to deal with the substance of Hobbes's view as it relates to this drift. At least from the time of Duns Scotus, there was a tendency to separate theology from philosophy. At first the goal was to elevate theology above philosophy. In time the trend was reversed, and theology eventually became intellectually disreputable (Martinich, 1990a, pp. 478–9). A distinction was drawn between the God of philosophy and the God of the Christian religion. Both Duns Scotus and William of Ockham claimed to have proofs for the existence of a God, but not the omnipotent God of the Christian faith (Duns Scotus, 1303, 4.71; William of Ockham, 1964, p. 139). Thus when Hobbes denies that there is a demonstration of "an omnipotent God, Maker of Heaven and Earth, as the Creed of our faith proposes," he is not denying that there is a proof for the existence of God. He is denying only that such a proof entails that God has the properties of the Christian God, properties that are revealed only in the Bible. This is in line with Hobbes's remark that "those who worship no god but the one they do understand are not Christians" (Hobbes, 1643, p. 326).

There is another point to be made here. There is a big difference between a demonstration of the existence of God and a proof. The reason is that "demonstration" is a technical term of Aristotelian philosophy, and its meaning is stronger than that of "proof." A demonstration is an argument in which "the meaning of the predicate [of each proposition] must be included [in] that of the subject" (Hobbes, 1643, p. 305). Such propositions are a priori and necessary and thus cannot be used to prove the existence of anything. For proofs of existence require empirical premises. Since Hobbes had been educated at Oxford in the nominalist tradition of scholasticism, and since his opponent was his friend Thomas White, a priest, trained in scholastic philosophy, and since the description of God that Hobbes gives fits the point, there is little room for doubting that he understood the difference between a proof for the existence of a philosophical God and a demonstration of the existence of the Christian God; his denial that the latter can be proved does not affect his own proofs of the former.

It is now easy to deal with Curley's interpretation of a passage in *De Corpore* in which Hobbes says that he will not discuss whether the world is eternal and infinite because humans cannot decide such issues (OL, 1:337; EW, 1:414). Hobbes, like Aquinas, Duns Scotus, and Ockham, does not think that the creation of the world in time is provable. Although Curley is aware of Aquinas' views, he does not think that Hobbes invokes that distinction in *De Corpore* (Curley, 1991, p. 55). I think that Hobbes's awareness of the entire issue has already been proven and that Aquinas' point is implicit in what Hobbes says when he distinguishes between proving that "there was some first eternal movent," which he had done in *Elements of Philosophy* and *Leviathan*, and proving that "that movent was eternally immoveable," which is the Christian God (EW, 1:414). That is why Hobbes then concludes, not that the existence of God cannot be proved, but that the "magnitude and beginning of the world" cannot be proved. The existence of God is provable, but not that the world had a beginning in time.

One reason that Hobbes refrains from proving that the world is not eternal is that any such proof must fail. It is important for a Christian philosopher not to present a bad argument for a seemingly religious proposition, because once the error in reasoning is detected, someone may (incorrectly) infer that if the argument for the conclusion is bad, then the conclusion itself must be false. Another problem is that the offending argument may contain premises that have objectionable consequences. Hobbes makes this charge against White's argument that the world was created in time. After showing that the argument is unsound, Hobbes says that a consequence of White's argument is that "everlastingness" is denied, "not only to motion but to every act in general; to existence; even to God Himself. See how, almost inevitably, those who subject to their own metaphysical speculations Divine matters beyond our understanding come at every step into conflict with the Christian faith!" (Hobbes, 1642, p. 341). Curley is required to interpret this passage as ironic. But there are no clues in the passage that would suggest any irony or sarcasm. There are numerous passages in which Hobbes expresses the same sentiment that the Christian faith needs to be preserved from the inappropriate incursions of reason (Hobbes, 1642, esp. pp. 347, 351, 359, 364). But Curley does not quote any of them.

Curley does not think Hobbes is a fideist. He constructs an argument consisting of six premises to which Hobbes is committed, to prove that Hobbes's view entails atheism. He claims that the "argument is not so abstruse" that Hobbes could not have seen where the argument leads. There are several problems with this. First, the premises come from works written over three decades and from five different works, one of which was never intended for publication. Second, Hobbes's ability to see the consequences of his premises was surely flawed. Ignore the obvious contradictions in *Leviathan*. As the long, unfortunate history of his dispute with John Wallis shows, Hobbes could not see what followed and what did not from perhaps the clearest kind of propositions: geometrical propositions. It is ironic that before his long dispute with Wallis, Hobbes had written, "For who is so stupid, as both to mistake in geometry, and also to persist in it, when another detects his error to him?" (EW, 3:35).[3] In fact, even geniuses sometimes do not see their errors when pointed out to them.

Whatever the correct answer is to Hobbes's views about cosmological arguments, the context of his answer should not be ignored. The context immediately preceding Hobbes's reply shows him embracing the Bible. As in so many other cases, when Hobbes's orthodoxy is attacked, he takes up the Reformers' posture: "I believe what is in the Bible." In answer to Wallis's argument that Hobbes is an atheist because he does not believe in immaterial substances, Hobbes says, "And would you learn Christianity from Plato and Aristotle? But seeing there is no such word [as incorporeal spirit] in the Scripture, how will you warrant it from natural reason?" (EW, 4:427). Any Reformer might have said something similar. This allows Hobbes, speaking of himself in the third person, to conclude: "Is not Mr. Hobbes his way of attributing to God, that only which the Scriptures attribute to him, or what is never any where taken but for honor, much better than this bold undertaking of yours, to consider and decipher God's *nature* to us?" (ibid.). Wallis's boldness is analogous to the sinful pride of humans who aspired to the nature of God, either, like Adam and Eve, by eating of the tree of the knowledge of good and evil or, like the denizens of Babel, by building a tower to heaven.

While there may be many reasons why Curley has misread the evidence about Hobbes's religious beliefs, one especially important one is that Curley operates with a defective idea of how to recognize irony. He says that there is a rhetorical device which he calls "suggestion by disavowal." According to Curley, there are cases in which uttering "I am not suggesting that *p*" conversationally implies "I am suggesting that *p*." Whether a speaker is making a suggestion by disavowal or not depends upon the context. I have tried to show that, by this criterion, Hobbes is not making any suggestions by disavowal that are intended to undermine revealed religion in general. Curley discusses a small number of passages from Hobbes's corpus. The vast amount of what Hobbes wrote about religion is on the face of it favorable to religion or presupposes it. Given this general appearance of approval, a few allegedly dubious passages cannot be used to drive an interpretation.

Curley thinks otherwise. At this point, no further evidence on either side is appropriate. What needs to be pointed out here is that Curley misuses the principle of "suggestion by disavowal" by applying it too broadly. This is evidenced by his attempt to apply it to a philosophically neutral text, which I shall discuss in the next paragraph. Thus, while I am not denying that there is such a rhetorical device, I am insisting that it be applied correctly. Its misuse is characteristic of Inquisitional thinking. Suppose a person being tried for heresy for his views about the Trinity says, "I am not suggesting that each person of the Trinity is nothing but a manifestation of God." The Grand Inquisitor, by the principle of "suggestion by disavowal," rends his cloak and screams, "He is condemned out of his own mouth. He has suggested that each person of the Trinity is nothing but a manifestation of God. He thinks we are so stupid as to take him at his word, when in fact he expects his diabolical followers to understand his true meaning, just as we do." The Grand Inquisitor is not interpreting what the speaker means with an open mind. He has prejudged what the speaker will mean and uses the principle of suggestion by disavowal, whenever it is needed, in order to make the words uttered fit the prejudged meaning. Someone might object that Curley's use of the device is exactly the opposite of the Grand Inquisitor's, for Curley wants to prove that Hobbes is an atheist in order to enhance his reputation as a philosopher, not to condemn him. My reply is that the Grand Inquisitor and Curley are using suggestion by disavowal in the same way: each is illegitimately interpreting the speaker to mean the opposite of what he says, merely in order to get the words uttered to fit their interpretation. They differ only in their attitude toward atheism.

Let's now consider Curley's use of the principle of suggestion by disavowal to interpret a Hobbesian-neutral passage. He uses the example of G. E. M. Anscombe's tract against President Truman's decision to drop the atomic bomb on Japan. She wrote, "I will not suggest, as some would like to do, that there was an exultant itch to use the new weapons, but it seems plausible to think that the consciousness of the possession of such instruments had its effects on the manner in which the Japanese were offered their 'chance'" (Anscombe, 1981, 3:65). Curley claims that Anscombe, in saying, "I will not suggest . . . that there was an exultant itch to use the new weapons," is thereby suggesting that very thing (Curley, 1991, pp. 14–15). I think he is wrong. If she were suggesting that, she would be making her position vulnerable to attack. For to prove that Truman or his advisers had an "exultant itch" to use the atomic bomb would be a difficult thing to do, and she never gives any evidence for that view. (She presents no evidence for it, I maintain, precisely because she is disavowing it.) Further, she has no need for such a strong proposition in order to accomplish her task, namely, to prove that it was wrong to drop the bomb. She says, "I will not suggest . . ." precisely because she wants to dissociate herself from that suggestion. For, if she had not dissociated herself from it, someone might have taken her to have suggested and then failed to prove that strong and virtually unprovable proposition that Truman and his advisers had "an exultant itch to use the new weapons." Her inclusion of the phrase "as some would like to do" is further evidence that she is dissociating herself from the "exultant itch" theory. Indeed, if Curley is correct, then Anscombe's case can be criticized for implausibly holding that the American leaders took joy in wreaking destruction. But that is absurd. Anscombe says that she is resting her case on the "plausible" thought that Truman and his advisers wanted to see whether the atomic bomb would work. She should be taken at her word; and so should Hobbes.

The phrase "I am not suggesting" is usually employed in order to guarantee that the audience does not put a wrong interpretation on what the speaker is saying. The audience may think that what the speaker has said either entails or conversationally implies something stronger than he intends, and the speaker wants to make sure that that false impression does not survive. How else can a speaker protect herself from an unintended implication?

There is one last biographical fact relevant to this issue that has not yet been considered. When he was eighty-four, Hobbes wrote the verse autobiography that I mentioned earlier. In the first line of that poem, Hobbes goes out of his way to indicate the year of his birth in relation to the birth of Christ. He does not assert that he was born, but that "the Man-God, our savior, had been born": "Natus erat noster servator Homo-Deus" (OL, 1:[lxxxv]). It is implausible that an octogenarian atheist would expressly subordinate his own birth to that of Jesus Christ under the title of God and Redeemer.

Appendix B

Skinner on Hobbes

In "The Context of Hobbes's Theory of Political Obligation," Quentin Skinner argues for two theses. The first is that Hobbes had many followers in England, France, and Holland during the seventeenth century. I agree with this thesis. Skinner's efforts to set the historical record straight put Hobbes scholars greatly in his debt. His second thesis is twofold. One is that Hobbes believed that "the obligation to obey a given government derived not from any religious sanction, but merely from a self-interested calculation made by each individual citizen"; the second is that human nature is "basically anti-social" (Skinner, 1972, pp. 116, 118). I accept the second as a brief statement of Hobbes's view and shall not discuss it further. I shall discuss the first, for I think it is mistaken. I shall not rehearse the evidence I have presented in Chapters 3 through 6 for my own interpretation but only discuss the quality of the evidence that Skinner presents for his.

What is partially at stake in this matter is the proper method for determining an interpretation.[1] In the Introduction and Chapter 2, I indicated that the basis for a good interpretation of what a speaker means is a function of what he intends to communicate, and that what he intends to communicate is constrained by what his words mean and the context within which he utters them. That is to say, a proper interpretation of *what an author means* must focus on the meaning of the words he uses and the context in which he uses them. I did this by analyzing Hobbes's own texts and the immediate religious, political, and historical context within which he was writing. Skinner does not follow this procedure. He does not argue from Hobbes's text at all. Rather, he argues that what Hobbes means is what his contemporaries interpreted him as meaning. In other words, Skinner's interpretation of what Hobbes meant is, if not dictated, then constrained by the interpretation of Hobbes's contemporaries. The most obvious problem with this method of interpretation is that it assumes that Hobbes's critics are easier to understand than Hobbes himself. But nothing justifies that assumption.

There are other problems with such an approach. An author's own contemporaries are often not in the best position to interpret what he or she means. Aristotle is not the best interpreter of Plato. Hobbes is not the best interpreter of Descartes. Russell is not the best interpreter of Bradley. Contemporary interpreters lack perspective. Because they are typically closer in their opinions to each other than they are to philosophers of another age, they tend to exaggerate their differences. Also, they have not had the benefit of centuries of reflection and scholarship to assist them in their interpretation. This is not to suggest that contemporary interpreters cannot provide valuable information about the correct interpretation of an author. The point is that they are not in a superior position to interpret an author simply in virtue of their temporal proximity, and any interpretation must be measured against the author's own text. More generally, if the contemporaries of great philosophers were as reliable in their interpretations as Skinner implies, there would be no need for new interpretations, which are represented almost always as being better, in the sense of "closer to what the author meant," than earlier ones. My interpretation is predicated on the belief that what Hobbes meant must be determined, not by what his contemporaries claimed he meant, but by what he actually said, understood within the historical, political, religious, scientific, and philosophical context that influenced him.

There are two other problems with taking Hobbes's contemporaries as reliable interpreters. First, none of them is anywhere near his equal in philosophical ability. Marchamont Nedham was a journalist who changed his views with every change in the political winds; Alexander Ross, an anti-Copernican, authored potboilers on whatever topic was popular at the time. Even Bramhall and Clarendon, who occasionally score points against Hobbes, were at best second-rate philosophers. When they interpret or criticize Hobbes, it is not at all like Aristotle interpreting Plato, or Russell Bradley. Hobbes often complains about the philosophical incompetence of his critics. For example, he writes that Bramhall "had but a weak attention in reading, and little skill in examining the force of an argument" (EW, 4:291). Often he thinks his critics are so incompetent that he does not consider them worthy a reply – for example, Ross, whom Skinner nonetheless treats as an unimpeachable commentator (EW, 4:237; Skinner, 1966, pp. 112–13). Hobbes was also generally aloof and did not pay a great deal of attention to what was being published, as evidenced by his not learning of Bramhall's *Catching of Leviathan* until ten years after its publication (EW, 4:281).

Second, virtually all of those who interpreted Hobbes's philosophy at any length were enemies, not friends. One simply cannot assume that Hobbes is getting a fair presentation of his views. Hobbes's complaints against Bramhall and Wallis are again relevant here.

Let's now turn from the general dubiousness of Skinner's case to its details. Immediately after asserting his thesis that, according to Hobbes, religion plays no role in political obligation, Skinner says, "God had left it 'arbitrary to men (as the Hobbeans vainly fancy)' to establish political societies 'upon the principles of equality and self-preservation agreed to by the Hobbists'" (Skinner, 1972, pp. 116–17). Skinner is here quoting two anonymous pamphlets. The language "God had left it" is tendentious and misrepresents what Hobbes said by making his point much weaker than it is. Hobbes had said that God "commanded" the laws of nature, and the fact that God commanded something that would benefit humans "upon the principles of equality and self-preservation" does not change the fact that Hobbes is asserting that God's commands underlie human political institutions.

It is also important to notice that the anonymous authors that Skinner quotes attack "Hobbeans" and "Hobbists." Perhaps their claims are valid against such monsters, but that does not settle the question of whether they are valid against Hobbes. One might refute Augustinianism without thereby refuting Augustine, or refute scholastic Aristotelianism without thereby refuting Aristotle. Although Skinner knows that "Hobbism" was little more than a term of abuse, he nonetheless equates it in this article with Hobbes's own views (ibid., p. 116).

Skinner assimilates Hobbes to the *"de facto* theorists" who justified obedience to the interregnum government on the grounds that overwhelming power is a sufficient condition for legitimate government.[2] He treats Hobbes's position as if it were an instance of the view that the existing government ought to be obeyed "even if it could not be shown either to reflect the will of the people or to have been rightfully acquired" (p. 119). Skinner's interpretation is clearly wrong. Hobbes holds that overwhelming power is a necessary, not a sufficient, condition for legitimate government. In addition to power, legitimate government requires the consent of the governed. The victor in a civil war establishes dominion "when the vanquished, to avoid the present stroke of death, covenanteth either in express words, or by other sufficient signs of the will. . . . It is not therefore the victory, that giveth the right of dominion over the vanquished, but his own covenant" (EW, 3:189). According to Hobbes, the antiroyalist forces did not acquire sovereignty over Englishmen by the mere fact that they had power but because Englishmen covenanted with the forces that had the power (and because the royalists lacked the requisite power). Hobbes says that a person is not sovereign unless he is designated as such by someone who covenants to transfer his power to that person and that by virtue of such an act the government does reflect the will of the people. That is Hobbes's unequivocal meaning, no matter what his contemporary interpreters believed. Skinner quotes one of these interpreters as saying, "Mr. Hobbes makes power and nothing else give right to dominion" (p. 122). What such a quotation tends to confirm is the position that Hobbes's contemporaries are not reliable interpreters.

In trying to prove that Hobbes did not hold a deontological view of obligation, Skinner typically quotes works that were published after Hobbes was dead and to which he had no opportunity to respond. Further, most of the quoted books were published soon after the Glorious Revolution of 1688, when the political motivation for justifying the reign of William and Mary further complicates the problem of interpretation.[3] Virtually all of the books and pamphlets published before Hobbes's death and quoted by Skinner concern the fact that Hobbes's philosophy was influential or disliked. But virtually none indicates that Hobbes's moral theory is not deontological. It is easy to miss this fact, because Skinner is concerned with several different issues, as I have explained. And I think that Skinner is correct about all but one of these issues. He is correct that Hobbes's views were influential; correct that his interpreters were impressed or disturbed by his account of the nature of humans or the condition of the state of nature; and correct that *some* of his interpreters did not take him to be a deontologist. But he is wrong to conclude that "the deontological interpretations of Hobbes's theory of political obligation . . . must for this reason be regarded at least as very doubtful" (p. 142), because he has not provided enough evidence for that particular thesis.

One problem is that Skinner's own interpretation of some of the alleged Hobbesians is questionable.[4] For example, Skinner says that Anthony Ascham, in *Of the Confusions and Revolutions of Governments*, comes to the "Hobbesian conclusion . . . that the will of a power 'absolute without redress or appeal,' and the virtues of passive obedience, provided the sole means of escape from the mutability of things" (p.

130). Skinner claims that Ascham argues from the Hobbesian premises that self-preservation is the sole and essential right in the state of nature and that anarchy is the alternative to political order. However, these are not the only premises upon which Ascham relies. In addition to those just mentioned, Ascham uses a premise that depends upon a divine command theory of obligation. Ascham justifies his view that citizens should obey the person in power on the grounds that God himself has commanded it, either directly or as the creator. The obligation to obey the person in power arises from God's own "Sanctity, Wisedom, and Justice, as he is a Creator and a Governour; or else they flow from Nature," of which God is the author (Ascham, 1649a, p. 6). The "originall and Primary force of obliging" does not arise from human laws. The ground of obligation is "the state of Gods and of Natures fixt Lawes, to which we are all equally obliged" (ibid., p. 7). Thus, if Ascham is a Hobbesian, then Hobbes held a divine command theory, as I argued in Chapter 4.

Although interpreting Ascham as a Hobbesian provides evidence for my interpretation, I think that there are so many differences between them that at most Hobbes should be said only to have influenced Ascham. I shall mention four of the important differences between them.

First, Ascham holds that property rights exist in the state of nature. He says that immediately after the Deluge and before a government had been established, no one could legitimately take an object from someone "without doing them manifest wrong." He goes on to say, "Possession therefore is the greatest Title" (Ascham, 1649a, pp. 9–10; see also pp. 12–13). About Hobbes, he says that "this gentleman hath much injured, yea, committed an *intellectuall rape upon nature*" in holding that there was no division of property prior to government (ibid., p. 15).

Second, in contrast with Hobbes, Ascham casts his lot with the theorists of patriarchy. Sovereigns are the moral descendants of the patriarchs, according to Ascham. Thus, citizens are like children, not slaves, and "he who rules

. . . hath obligations of care and tenderness over us" (ibid., p. 107). These are extremely un-Hobbesian sentiments.

Third, Ascham explicitly criticizes Hobbes for holding that people give up all their rights to the sovereign and thinks it is "one of our morall impossibilities" (p. 121). Ascham thinks that people can depose a sovereign whenever he acts against their interests or consent "as lawfully . . . as it was imposed" (p. 108; see also Ascham, 1649b, p. 5). Ascham has no appreciation for Hobbes's ambivalence about whether people give up all their rights or not. (See Chapter 4 of the present volume.)

Fourth, according to Ascham, it is only power, not consent, that makes someone a sovereign. Skinner quotes Ascham as saying, "So that Mr. *Hobbs* his supposition (if there were two Omnipotents, neither would be oblig'd to obey the other) is very pertinent and conclusive to this subject" (Skinner, 1966, p. 132). But Skinner does not quote or indicate the context for Ascham's remark. What Ascham says immediately before is, "Omnipotency or Supreme irresistability is the primary reason for the obedience which all things owe to God" (Ascham, 1649a, p. 108). A bit later he says, "Allegiance is due to those who immediately protect us, and plenarily possesse us, but in and above all to God, the Universall Eternal Magistrate, under whose Jurisdiction we are to live eternally in another world" (ibid., p. 131). In other words, the legitimacy of political power is exactly like the legitimacy of divine power. This is not Hobbes's view. Although Hobbes compares divine and human sovereignty, there are important differences. God's sovereignty is absolute and does not depend upon consent; human sovereignty, however, is made possible by God's commands in the laws of nature and also requires the consent of the governed. The passage from Ascham that has just been discussed is particularly important because it clearly shows how one of Hobbes's contemporaries began with a premise from Hobbes and drew a conclusion inconsistent with Hobbes's view. This demonstrates how dubious a policy it is to draw an inference about what Hobbes's views are on the basis of his contemporaries' understanding of his philosophy.[5]

Hobbes was often misinterpreted by his contemporaries, sometimes because his readers were unsympathetic to him, often because they were relatively untalented interpreters. But there is a more important reason why he was often misinterpreted. His contemporaries could not understand his doctrine because they could not see that he was trying to do something for the modern era that had not been tried on such a grand scale.[6] He was trying to marry orthodox Christian doctrine to modern science, just as Aquinas had tried to marry Christian doctrine to Aristotelianism. And he was also trying to prevent Christianity from being used as an instrument of dissension and rebellion.

Appendix C

The frontispiece to *Leviathan*

The most conspicuous evidence for the kind of interpretation I have developed in this book is the dramatic frontispiece[1] to *Leviathan*,[2] reproduced at the front of the present volume. Frontispieces were an important component of books in the sixteenth and seventeenth centuries, when society was still in transition to a print culture. They were intended to be studied at some length and not given a cursory perusal, and they amounted to something between an introduction to and summary of the entire book. The frontispiece to *Leviathan* is especially significant, since Hobbes probably designed it himself and included a hand-drawn copy of it in the manuscript copy of *Leviathan* that he presented to Charles II (Brown, 1978).

What first catches the eye on this engraving is the image at the top of the page of the sovereign, the mortal god who rules under the immortal God. His most prominent feature is his face. Scholars have argued whether this is a stylized representation of either Cromwell or Charles I. It has even been suggested that it is a composite of both. On this hypothesis, Hobbes must be imagined to have lacked the foresight to anticipate that Cromwell might recognize only Charles's features and Charles recognize only Cromwell's, or, perhaps worse, that they would recognize the duplicity of representing both. (See also Goldsmith, 1981, p. 237 n. 25.) Anyone tempted to think that both are represented should also try to imagine Hobbes instructing the artist about how to draw Leviathan. Hobbes says, "I want Leviathan to incorporate features of both Cromwell and Charles." The artist looks at him quizically. Hobbes says, "Well, I need to hedge my bets, you see." The artist turns away and begins to draw. A similarity has even been recognized between the image of Leviathan and William Cavendish, third earl of Devonshire (Rogow, 1986, p. 115). It is just as plausible that the sovereign resembles Hobbes himself.[3]

Since no one knows what Christ looked like, it would be pointless to claim that Leviathan resembles him. But Leviathan does have the mien of the Christ of judgment in Renaissance paintings. Certainly the size of Leviathan is consonant with a divine figure. His two outstretched arms indicate both divine, or quasi-divine, judicial judgment and universal jurisdiction. In the right hand Leviathan wields the sword of secular power; in his left hand he wields a baroque-style bishop's crozier. The point of the figure would appear to be that both secular and spiritual power are united in the same authority; not just the generalized spiritual power of any religion, but also the power of an episcopal system such as that of the Church of England before it was abolished by Parliament. Someone might object that if the figure of Leviathan is meant in any way to suggest the Christ of judgment, then the fact that he holds the bishop's crozier in his left hand must be an allusion to the damned being relegated to the left hand of God on Judgment Day. That is, Hobbes may be surreptitiously revealing an antireligious message. There are several reasons for not accepting this interpretation. The sword and crozier, for example, are not placed in opposition to each other but are pointed in such a way that they would converge above Leviathan's head if they were extended. Further, both hands have a similar orientation; they are balanced, rather than positioned so as to contrast with each other. Were Hobbes trying to indicate that the left hand is the side of the damned, then the hand and crozier should have pointed down. Also, it would have been unnatural for Leviathan not to have the sword in his right hand, since most people are right-handed. Further, a bishop carries his crozier in his left hand in order to leave his other hand free to bless people. This means that there is no other plausible place for the crozier except Leviathan's left hand. It would not do to have the crozier in his mouth or hooked around his neck; and if no religious symbol were held at all, then someone would use this fact as evidence that Hobbes had no genuine religious interests. In short, the presence of the crozier is strong evidence that a major feature of *Leviathan* is the significance of religion as practiced by the Church of England.

Leviathan's body is composed of the bodies of his subjects. Far from being original with Hobbes, the idea was stereotypical in late medieval and early modern thought. In the Plowden *Reports*, presented to Queen Elizabeth, we find clear expression of the claim that the "body politic" has the sovereign as its head and the subjects as its limbs (Kantorowicz, 1957, pp. 13, 15).

The figure of Leviathan oversees a landscape that is composed of two parts. The first, which is immediately in front of him, is a rural scene consisting of several scattered clusters of buildings. No fewer than three of them are churches, and no fewer than two are fortresses. Evidently the rough equality between secular and religious institutions, visually stated in the sword and crozier, is continued into the realm over which Leviathan rules. The second part of the landscape portrays a city with buildings arranged in an orderly fashion. To the left is a fortress, which is vertically in line with Leviathan's sword-wielding arm. To the right is a cathedral, which is likewise vertically in line with Leviathan's crozier-bearing arm. The cathedral is by far the larger and more dominant edifice in this segment of the frontispiece.

While Western books are read in one way – from left to right, and from the top down – a frontispiece, like other pictures, may be read in several different ways, and those ways are dictated in large part by the composition. Our frontispiece in general should be interpreted from top to bottom and from left to right, not from the bottom up, as has sometimes been suggested (Brown, 1978). The dominance of Leviathan focuses attention immediately to the top of the page. It has also been most natural to investigate the surrounding details from higher to lower and from left to right. This same procedure is appropriate for the bottom half of the frontispiece, which repeats much of the same information as in the top half, but in more detail.

Beginning at the top and center of this segment and stretching down is a curtain with "Leviathan" printed in large letters. To the left and right of the curtain are two parallel columns, each of which consists of five panels. Immediately to the left of the word "Leviathan" is a fortress, built upon a hill. This image continues the theme of representing the secular aspect of the commonwealth along the left-hand side of the page. Opposite the fortress is a cathedral. The standard cruciform shape of cathedrals is minimized and thus suggests a Protestant design.

Beneath "Leviathan" on the curtain is the word "Or," and beneath the latter is the phrase "The Matter, Forme." Immediately to the left of the words "The Matter" is a crown. Immediately to the right of the word "Forme" is a bishop's miter. If any correlation is suggested by this arrangement – and it is difficult not to think there is – then the secular power signifies the "matter" and the religious power signifies the "form" of a commonwealth. The crown and miter are visual instances of synecdoche. It has been suggested that in *Leviathan* Hobbes abandoned his support for monarchy and the episcopal form of government for Independency (Tuck, 1989, pp. 28–30). Leviathan's crown and the crown beneath the fortress are prima facie evidence against the first part of this claim. The bishop's crozier, the cathedral, and the miter are even stronger evidence against the second part of this claim. Hobbes preferred episcopacy, although he was willing to accept Independency if that was the choice of the people (as I explained in Chapter 11).

Beneath the crown and miter are a cannon and the thunderbolts of Zeus, respectively. The cannon represents secular power unambiguously; the thunderbolts, however, signify both spiritual power and sovereignty (de Vries, 1976, p. 466; Cirlot, 1972, 342). Thus, not only are secular and spiritual power coordinate and equal, but secular power cannot be divorced from spiritual power. Between the cannon and the thunderbolts is the middle of the curtain, on which is written "and Power of A Common- / Wealth Ecclesiastical / and Civil." The placement of these words does not appear to be accidental. "Power" is closer to the cannon than to the thunderbolts; "Ecclesiastical" is adjacent to the thunder-bolts; and "Civil" is midway between each. That is, the civil state is composed of equal parts of secular and religious power.

Beneath the cannon is the paraphernalia of battle: crossed muskets, drum and drumsticks, flags, fasces, and pikes. Beneath the thunderbolts are the weapons of intellectual disputation, as it is practiced by the clergy-dominated universities. At the left is a trident, labeled "Syllogism." In the middle is a two-pronged fork, with one prong labeled "Spiritual" and the other "Temporal." Crossing behind this fork is another, which also has two prongs, one of which is straight and labeled "Directe"; the other is curved and labeled "Indirecte." These probably refer to the distinction between direct and indirect moods of the syllogism, since that distinction was controversial in the sixteenth and early seventeenth century (Ashworth, 1988, 170–1), and the terms "direct" and "indirect" had not yet been applied to proofs, to my knowledge. To the right is a two-pronged fork, of which one is labeled "Real" and the other "Intentional." These prongs represent the two classes of real beings, according to late scholastic ontology. The term "real being" is self-explanatory. "Intentional beings" refers to the objects of thought alone. In the foreground of this panel is a pair of horns that encompasses the instruments just described; the horns are labeled "Dilemma." Between these panels containing the images of the physical and intellectual weapons is the phrase "By Thomas Hobbes of Malmesbury." Perhaps there is some self-deprecating whimsy in this placement of the author's name.

In the bottom panel on the left side (beneath the paraphernalia of battle) is a battle scene. In the middle segment of the bottom of the frontispiece is a plate with the words "London / Printed for Andrew Crooke / 1651." Are we to infer from the juxtaposition of the date and battle scene that the Civil War was ongoing in 1651? In the bottom panel on the right side is what appears to be some formal but nonecclesiastical proceeding. It appears to me to be a university disputation. At the top of the panel a presiding officer sits alone. At the bottom, nine figures, whom I take to be judges, sit with their backs to the reader. On each side of the panel sits a pair of individuals, whom I interpret as two teams of disputants. These disputants would be using the weapons depicted in the panel above them, just as the soldiers in the battlefield scene on the opposite side of the page are using the weapons depicted in the panel above them.

I do not detect any skepticism or cynicism toward religion in this frontispiece. If Hobbes had some secret message he wished to convey in *Leviathan*, he should have given some indication of it here. Instead, the frontispiece gives the message that the civil and religious elements of a commonwealth have an equal standing and must be coordinated. More, religion should take the episcopal form of the Reformed Church of England, not Roman Catholicism and not Presbyterianism.[4]

Notes

1 Scholars often mistakenly think that Hobbes did not believe in hell (Johnston, 1986, p. 187; Warrender in Hobbes, 1983, p. 39 n. 1).

2 David Johnston says that some scholars "have noted that the theology of *Leviathan* complements its political doctrines, and some have even claimed that theology is the foundation of his politics. Surprisingly, however, these claims have almost never been supported by any systematic examination of the relevant portions of his work. With one or two notable exceptions those few interpreters who have taken the trouble to examine his metaphysics and theology have accepted the prevailing orthodoxy that a rigid wall separates his treatment of these topics from his political philosophy as such" (Johnston, 1986, pp. xvi–xvii; see also p. 117). To a large extent the present book is intended to rectify this situation.

3 On Perkins, see Kendall, 1979.

4 Here are some other examples: "[A]ll human works, if judged according to their own worth, are nothing but filth and defilement. And what is commonly reckoned righteousness is before God sheer iniquity; what is adjudged uprightness, pollution; what is accounted glory, ignominy" (Calvin, 1559, III.12.4). In the "Confession of Faith which all the citizens and Inhabitants of Geneva and the Subjects of the Country Must Promise to Keep and Hold" ("The First Helvetic Confession" of 1536), Calvin says, "We acknowledge man by nature to be blind, darkened in understanding, and full of corruption and perversity of heart. . . . [I]f he is left by God to what he is by

nature, he is only able to live in ignorance and to be abandoned to all iniquity" (quoted from Calvin, 1954, p. 27; see also Calvin, 1537, p. 22).

5 Other friends of Hobbes were engaged in a similar enterprise, notably Marin Mersenne (Zagorin, 1990b, p. 319 n. 74) and Thomas White (Johnston, 1989, p. 654).

6 Although there are good reasons for replacing the traditional terms "Old Testament" and "New Testament" with the terms "Hebrew Bible" and "Christian Bible," I shall retain the older terms because Hobbes uses them and because I do not want to multiply terminology.

7 Such a theory is sometimes called a "theology," as in "Augustinian theology" or "Thomistic theology."

8 "Fact" and "theory" may be relative terms. Whether something is a fact or part of a theory may depend upon what the speakers presuppose. Possibly all propositions have some theoretical content. Nonetheless, it is still possible to distinguish between more and less theoretical sentences; that is, propositions that are more or less explanatory but less basic to the belief system. Thus my claim that the propositions of the creeds are nontheoretical can be understood to mean that they are more basic or central than other propositions.

9 The metaphor can be extended farther. He thought that the Catholic church had also mixed the new wine of Christianity with the old wine of Greek and Roman mythology.

10 Hobbes uses the same metaphor. He says that it is his intention "to offer new wine, to be put into new casks, that both may be preserved together" (EW, 3:711). But he means something different by the metaphor. For him, the new casks are new theories; the new wine is not new religious doctrine but new political doctrines "that manifestly tend to peace and loyalty" (EW, 3:711).

11 Other historians have made the same or a similar point. Leszek Kolakowski has made the same point: "Every established ideology occasionally has to make headway against unexpected circumstances and new dangers. When existing and proven means will not suffice, it takes people with a more imaginative faculty than the common ideological warrior to forge new intellectual weapons: it takes intellectuals. Usually they attempt to beat the enemy with his own weapons, to appropriate to themselves various components of a doctrine in

order to render it innocuous within the transmitted ideology. The independent force of the word, however, carries them almost inevitably further than the defense requires; and for all their good intentions, they become destroyers of what they were determined to defend" (Kolakowski, 1990, p. 29). He mentions both Aquinas and Calvin as examples. See also Tierney, 1982, p. 49, and Kors, 1990, pp. ix–xii.

12 In the first edition of *The Political Philosophy of Hobbes*, Leo Strauss called Hobbes the first modern political philosopher (Strauss, 1952b, p. 1).

13 I do not have a general theory of interpretation. But I do think that a good interpretation tries to establish an equilibrium between the text and its context. The meaning of a text is not fully conveyed by the words of the text alone. What the text means can be determined only by considering the context, both linguistic and nonlinguistic, in which it occurs. The context alone, however, does not determine any meaning at all for a text, since it is not part of the text. These brief remarks help explain why "textualists" and "contextualists" are both mistaken. For a criticism of the textualists, see Skinner, 1988a, pp. 29–67. Ashcraft, 1986, pp. 3–16, argues that a historical investigation of political works is indispensable in a very strong sense. My view is not as strong as his.

14 For an extended discussion of this point, see Popkin, 1987b.

15 Dionysius of Helicarnassus said that history is the way philosophy teaches by example.

16 I am speaking only of influence. There are several excellent treatments of Hobbes's religious views: e.g., Glover, 1965, and Hepburn, 1972.

CHAPTER 1

1 The seventeenth-century use of the term "atheist" was similar to the Elizabethan use. For a detailed discussion of the latter, see Strathmann, 1951, pp. 61–97. For its use in France, which is similar to that in England, see Kors, 1990, pp. 3–43. David Wootton thinks that "atheist" had a "clear signification in the sixteenth and early seventeenth century." He says an atheist was a person "who denied God's providence" (Wootton, 1988, p. 704; see also Wootton, 1983a, p. 1). For example, Pufendorf defines an atheist as someone who denies God's

providence (Pufendorf, 1688, pp. 381–2; see also EW, 3:344). Wootton also says, "Atheist . . . meant primarily not someone who denied God's existence, but someone who denied his justice, someone who denied the existence of divine retribution" (Wootton, 1983b, p. 62). By this definition, atheism is consistent with belief in a God. I am using "atheist" in its current sense of "one who does not believe that God exists." It is important not to confuse the various senses of the term.

2 Vorst was also accused of the heresy of Socinianism, precisely because of his Arminianism (Milward, 1978, p. 34; Walker, 1964, p. 188; cf. Wootton, 1983a, pp. 90–3). Ironically, Hobbes has also been called a Socinian, even though he was anti-Arminian.

3 Strathmann, 1951, p. 61. See also Eisenach, 1982, p. 224 n. 23, and Redwood, 1976, pp. 70–91, for other distinguished Christians whom someone or other accused of atheism.

4 Raleigh was accused of atheism by the Jesuit Robert Parsons; Raleigh was acquitted at an inquiry into his atheism at Cerne Abbas, but the accusation of atheism was again raised at his trial for treason, which proved fatal to him. I accept this judgment: "In brief, Ralegh's reputation as an 'atheist' is traceable in large part to the Catholic polemics against him, especially Parsons' widely circulated attack, and to the casual usage of 'atheist' in moral censure. . . . Yet sober accounts of his table talk . . . in no wise support the charge of 'atheism' against him; and his conversations on religious topics, as reported, are consistent with the orthodoxy of his published writings" (Strathmann, 1951, p. 271; see also Lacey, 1973).

5 See Adamson, 1960, p. 60, and Trevor-Roper, 1989, pp. 186–92. It is also worth mentioning in this context that Milton was an Arian heretic: that is, he held that Jesus is not equal to God the Father, but is the first and greatest creature. This belief was condemned at the Council of Nicea in A.D. 325. Milton prudently kept his views to himself (cf. Hunter et al., 1971, pp. 29–70).

6 Jacobus Arminius (1560–1609) was the founder of an anti-predestination Reformed church in Holland. He affirmed free will. Arminianism was condemned as heretical at the Synod of Dort in 1618–19 but gained acceptance among Anglican theologians, who tended to favor more Catholic-like ritual than

the Puritans did. Hobbes mentions Arminius in a number of places (e.g., EW, 4:329, 5:2, 6:241).

7 My guess is that at least some of his contemporaries would not have found this epithet paradoxical.

8 The problem could be put more sharply by drawing upon the so-called paradox of the preface. It is provable that every person who is not an extreme dogmatist has inconsistent beliefs. To put the proof briefly, every nondogmatist believes each of his (first-order) beliefs; but, in addition, he believes that at least one of his beliefs is false (because he believes he is not infallible). Thus each nondogmatist believes that the conjunction of his beliefs is true and believes that the entire conjunction is not true. Since every proposition follows from an inconsistency, every nondogmatist is logically committed to every proposition.

9 Later, I shall argue that Hobbes's views did tend to undermine religious belief, in a sense to be explained. So I agree with those who see Hobbes's thought as playing an important role in the drift toward atheism in modern philosophy.

10 In his history of heresy, Hobbes gives an analogous definition of "heresy by consequence" (EW, 4:397).

11 Of course, Hobbes's critics thought that his materialism entailed atheism, e.g., Rust, 1661, p. 129.

12 I shall use the term "scholastic philosopher" and its cognates to refer to a person who follows the Aristotelian/Christian philosophy that began in the thirteenth century with Albert the Great and Aquinas. Hobbes often uses the term "School philosopher."

13 Bramhall's case is even weaker than I have been suggesting thus far. I have been assuming, for the sake of discussion, that Hobbes himself did not clarify his principles in reply to Bramhall's accusations. But that is not correct. Hobbes explains at some length where he thinks Bramhall's reasoning goes awry and why his own principles do not entail any irreligious sentiment. This point is discussed in more detail later in this section.

14 Clarendon thinks that every human life is "owned" by God. Hobbes may well have agreed with this.

15 Although being well-informed about theological theories is consistent with atheism, it is at least worth mentioning that

Hobbes was quite knowledgeable about both church history and theology. In addition to the Bible, he knew the Apocrypha, the church fathers, the history of the church, Reformation theology, and quite a bit about such Catholic apologists as Bellarmine and Suarez (see, e.g., EW, 4:387–408).

16 See, for example, Appendix B.

17 There are more subtle and, I think, more plausible explanations; see, e.g., Sherlock, 1982.

18 Fifth Monarchy men were so-called because they thought that the everlasting "fifth monarchy" mentioned in the Book of Daniel was about to be established under the kingship of Jesus (Dan. 2:44; see also Capp, 1972).

19 For the history of the Arminian conquest of the English episcopacy before 1640, see Tyacke, 1987a, esp. pp. 100, 157, 162, and Tyacke, 1987b.

20 As mentioned in the Introduction to the present volume, Hobbes was also accused of being a "Papist" (Whitehall, 1679, p. 147).

21 The text of the condemnation is in Wootton, 1986, pp. 120–6. The parenthetical descriptions following the names in my text are simply intended to identify the persons, not to describe the charges cited in the condemnation.

22 The political dimension is even more elaborate than I can indicate in these introductory remarks and will be addressed in the main body of the book. The Puritans held that the Kingdom of God was already in existence in the heart or soul of the elect in order to justify acting against the king and without providing any additional justification for those actions. The non-Puritan clergy thought that if the Kingdom of God was already in existence, then they were the obvious ministers of it.

CHAPTER 2

1 I am not denying that there were atheists in the seventeenth century. However, atheism seems to have been more prevalent among the lower than among the upper classes (Thomas, 1971; Hill, 1984b).

2 David Wootton has proven that the Renaissance intellectual Paolo Sarpi (1552–1630) was probably a genuine theoretical atheist (Wootton, 1983b). But there are several significant dif-

ferences between Sarpi and Hobbes that help lead to different judgments about their religious beliefs. Sarpi left a private document that expressed irreligious views; and Wootton says that without that document "it would be impossible to guess his true motives" (Wootton, 1983, p. 133). None of Hobbes's private documents indicates anything religiously amiss. His private life seems consonant with his public life, as he declared in his Latin verse autobiography, written when he was eighty-four: "Nam mea vita meis non est incongrua scriptis" [For my life is consonant with my writings] (OL, 1:xcix). Also, Sarpi wrote that one should "conceal one's true beliefs at all times" (ibid., p. 37; see also p. 119). On the general issue of atheism in the early modern period, see Febvre, 1942; Wootton, 1988; and Hunter, 1981, pp. 162–87. I think the case against other early modern intellectuals, such as the theologian Pierre Charron (1541–1603), is much weaker. I side with those who think Charron was a sincere Christian. See Popkin, 1979, pp. 55–60; Jean Charron 1961; Kogel, 1972; cf. Grendler, 1963, and Gregory, 1991.

3 Transubstantiation is the Catholic theory that explains the doctrine of the Real Presence, that is, the belief that the consecrated eucharist is the body and blood of Jesus Christ. According to the theory of transubstantiation, at the consecration of the Mass, three things happen: the substance of the bread is annihilated; the physical properties are unchanged; and Jesus comes to be present where the bread had been.

4 I distinguish between the Modern Age (and hence modern man) and the Postmodern Age. The first can be taken to begin with Luther's posting of his ninety-five theses in 1517; the second can be taken to begin with Nietzsche's declaration in 1882 that God is dead.

5 In fact, some medieval thinkers in the twelfth century had developed the idea that nature is God's art (Chenu, 1968, pp. xvii, 19; Seung, 1982, p. 121). The idea is also present in Plato's *Timaeus* insofar as the Demiurge fashions the cosmos; however, the cosmos is natural insofar as it has a World-Soul.

6 The seventeenth-century dramatist John Ford has a character in one of his plays say, "But Kings are earthly gods" (quoted from Sommerville, 1986, p. 40.)

7 Hobbes's divinization of government is picked up by other

modern philosophers, though usually not so explicitly. An exception is Hegel, who says, "Man must therefore venerate the state as a secular deity" (Hegel, 1821, p. 285).

8   On the significance of the concept of Leviathan, see also Mintz, 1989.

9   Ironically, Hobbes's assertion of the equality of mankind, which became a cornerstone of later political institutions from the United States to the United Nations, was one of the features of his philosophy that his contemporaries objected to. Lord Clarendon, in particular, was offended that Hobbes should hold such a view when he had lived off the generosity of aristocrats for his entire adult life (Clarendon, 1676, p. 181). So, when one uses the opposition of his contemporaries as evidence of his irreligion, one should also consider the content of that opposition.

10   Although he lists curiosity as the first of three causes of religion, it is obvious that the second cause (the search for origins) and the third cause (observing the fixed sequence of things) are consequences of the first, and hence reducible to it.

11   Paul Johnson supplied me with this reference.

12   It is more plausible that Hobbes uses "power imagined" because he wanted a phrase that would apply quite broadly to whatever mental activity occurs when a person is thinking about religious entities. It is hard to find a word more general or vague than "imagine," and the term thus seems to be a fairly good choice, even though it may appear to be inconsistent with his semitechnical use of it. He is not thinking exclusively, and perhaps not even consciously, about the Christian God when he is concerned with defining "religion" and related terms. The phrase "power imagined" is not essential and could easily be replaced by another phrase that would do the same job, such as "power referred to." The fact that Hobbes uses a phrase that is not essential does not mean that he is implying anything special by it.

13   I think that Berman's interpretation also assumes that intolerant theists were not smart enough to understand the surreptitious message but that atheists or candidates for atheism were. Reading between the lines, I surmise that Strauss also meant this when he wrote, "[T]houghtless men are careless readers and only thoughtful men are careful readers" (Strauss, 1952a, p. 25). In my experience, intelligence is distributed fair-

ly evenly between tolerant and intolerant people, between theists and atheists.

14 Among Hobbes's contemporaries, the suspicious minds of insecure clerics might interpret him in this way. But this is the audience with whom Hobbes would be least likely to intend to communicate in a surreptitious way and to whom he would least want to convey that he was an atheist.

15 Since all geometrical theorems are necessarily true, to deny a geometrical theorem is to subscribe to a contradiction. Thus, Hobbes subscribed to some contradictory propositions.

16 I am not suggesting that Anglicans called Presbyterians "superstitious."

17 The sentiment survives to this day. The author of the standard work on Anglicanism writes that although he is not perfectly happy with the Church of England, "[i]n this part of the people of Christ I am content to live and to die" (Neill, 1976, p. 7).

18 Calvin says, "[E]veryone has a certain seed of religion implanted in him" (Calvin, 1958, p. 132). Calvin and Hobbes use the same term, *religionis semen* (OL, 1:85).

19 Hobbes is offering an inchoate performative theory of religious discourse.

20 The premise is that any philosopher will see that the conception, birth, and life of Jesus are just like those of many pagan gods who had one divine and one human parent. The inference is that Jesus is a mongrel god.

21 Some people think that Hobbes's reference to "unpleasing priests" is evidence of an antireligious sentiment. This is not so. In February 1991 the forty-five-year sentence of convicted swindler Jim Bakker, a minister and television evangelist, was overturned as too harsh, on the grounds that the presiding judge in his trial had been prejudiced against Bakker. The judge had said, "Those of us who do have a religion are ridiculed as being saps for money-grubbing preachers or priests." The judge's attack on "money-grubbing preachers or priests" was interpreted as an expression of "religiosity" by the Court of Appeals. See also Hosea 4:5–11.

22 In *Human Nature*, Hobbes's examples run from Saint Andrew through Saint Peter to tumult (EW, 4:15). Clarendon completely misunderstands the import of Hobbes's example (Clarendon, 1676, p. 61).

23 The comparison between Charles I and Jesus was popular

with royalists after the king's execution; see Wedgewood, 1964, pp. 196–7.

CHAPTER 3

1   The phrase "if and only if" in this section should be understood as expressing something like logical equivalence, not material equivalence. Better, any phrase of the form "*p* if and only if *q*" should be understood in this section as meaning "What makes it the case that *p* is the fact that *q*." Any phrase of the form "*p* only if *q*" should be understood as meaning "What makes it the case that *p* is in part the fact that *q*."

2   Warrender thinks that Hobbes could have detached God from his system but as a matter of fact did not; see Warrender, 1979, p. 932.

3   Clarendon realizes that Hobbes needs only the weaker claim (Clarendon, 1676, p. 29).

4   Hobbes's example may have been inspired by something he had heard at church during his childhood. One of the sermons appointed to be read in churches in the time of Queen Elizabeth says, "Take away kings, princes, rulers, magistrates, judges and such estates of God's order, no man shall ride or go by the way unrobbed, no man shall sleep in his own house or bed unkilled, no man shall keep his wife, children and possessions in quietness, all things shall be common" ("An Exhortation concerning Good Order and Obedience to Rulers and Magistrates," quoted by Hill, 1986, 2:11).

5   As in the passage discussed earlier, Hobbes seems to be implying here that unilateral transfer of right is impossible. That is, every transfer of right presupposes that some covenant has been made. Perhaps Hobbes is thinking at this moment that the very first transfer of right must involve a sovereign-making covenant. But I do not see why he should hold such a view. In other places, he says or implies that other kinds of covenants can be made in the state of nature.

6   I realize that standardly justice was understood to be an absolute, not a relative, term, but it is a relative term for Hobbes.

7   See also EW, 2:55–6: "[T]he institution of eternal punishment was before sin, and had regard to this only, that men might dread to commit sin. . . ."

8   It should be noted that Hobbes uses "promise" the way we

would use the term "statement of intention." In seventeenth-century usage, a promise did not necessarily entail a moral obligation.

9 Something like this interpretation can be used to explain what Hobbes means when he says the laws of nature "oblige *in foro interno*" but not always *"in foro externo"* (EW, 3:145; see also the next section "Obligation.")

10 Barry lists five key propositions over which Hobbes scholars disagree:

(a) there can be obligations in the state of nature;
(b) no new kind of obligation is added with the formation of a state;
(c) the laws of nature do not rest on individual self-interest either for their demonstration or for their effectiveness;
(d) the laws of nature oblige (in the primary Hobbesian sense of the word "obligation") in the state of nature and *a fortiori* under a sovereign; and
(e) the obligation to keep the covenant by which a sovereign is set up (or equally any other covenant) depends on, and is merely a special case of, the obligation to obey the law. (Barry, 1968, p. 47)

Warrender and Hood accept (a) through (e); Watkins accepts none; Barry accepts only (a) and (b); I accept (a), (b), (d), and (e).

11 Of course many contemporary scholars also accept this interpretation of Hobbes (e.g., Plamenatz, 1957, p. 75).

12 I agree with the proposition that "omnipotence is to serve as the origin of obligation and the basis of God's dominating relationship to man" (Kodalle, 1987, p. 223).

CHAPTER 4

1 Suarez is relevant here because he was a distinguished early seventeenth-century philosopher who influenced Grotius. Hobbes read Suarez both on metaphysics and politics and may have been substantially influenced by him, though often negatively. (See, e.g., EW, 6:23; also EW, 5:11, 18, 37.) Suarez was the author of *A Defence of the Catholic and Apostolic Faith: In Refutation of the Errors of the Anglican Sect with a Reply to the Apologies for the Oath of Allegiance and to the Admonitory Preface of*

His Most Serene Majesty James, King of England. In this work, Suarez argues that regicide, discussed under the rubric of "tyrannicide," is sometimes justifiable. He was no doubt influenced to reach this purely philosophical conclusion by James I's requirement that all Englishmen swear to accept the monarch as their head of the Christian church. Part of Suarez's argument is Hobbesian: "[I]f one acts in defence of his very life, which the king is attempting to take violently away from him, then to be sure, it will ordinarily be permissible for the subject to defend himself, even though the death of the prince result from such defence. For the right to preserve one's own life is the greatest right" (Suarez, 1613, p. 709).

2 An example of a scholar who confuses the normativity of "right" with a deontic sense is Zagorin, when he calls the right of nature "an original claim" (1954, p. 170). The right of nature does not involve a claim against anyone, in the sense in which claims depend upon some authority or title. Claims between people arise only as the result of covenants enacted in accordance with the laws of nature.

3 They make it possible for humans to institute a government, which will establish peace. (See Chapters 5 and 6 of the present volume for a complete discussion of this issue.)

4 In *Elements of Law*, Hobbes holds the very different view that the law of nature is nothing more than reason (EW, 4:87).

5 Even some religionists, e.g., Hood, believe that the law of nature is not a genuine law but a "philosophic fiction" (Hood, 1964, pp. viii, 4, 85).

6 It is a basic principle of interpretation that a sentence should not be given a metaphorical interpretation unless a literal interpretation is absurd (Martinich, 1984, pp. 81, 89–90; Searle, 1979, p. 105). But there is nothing absurd about a literal interpretation. An example of a secularist who thinks that Hobbes uses the phrase "law of nature" metaphorically and that such a use is misleading is Zagorin, 1954, p. 175.

7 Hood, like the secularists, thinks that "forbidden" is a metaphor (Hood, 1964, p. 86).

8 Cicero talks about the commands of reason, but Cicero was not a Christian, and there is no reason to think that he influenced Hobbes in this regard.

9 Hood, like many secularists, mistakenly identifies laws with precepts (Hood, 1964, p. 85).

10 Hobbes's views are identical, or virtually identical, with those of John Selden on this point. Selden says, "I cannot fancy to myself what the law of nature means, but the law of God. How should I know I ought not to steal, ought not to commit adultery, unless somebody had told me, or why are these things against nature? Surely, 'tis because I have been told so. 'Tis not because I think I ought not to do them, nor whether you think I ought not. If so, our minds might change. When then comes the restraint? From a higher power. Nothing else can bind. I cannot bind myself, for I may untie myself again; nor an equal cannot bind me: we may untie one another. It must be a superior, even God Almighty. If two of us make a bargain, why should either of us stand to it? What need you care what you say, or what need I care what I say? Certainly because there is something above me, tells me *fides est servanda*. And if we after alter our minds and make a new bargain, there's *fides servanda* there too" (Selden, 1696, pp. 90–1; cf. p. 45; cf. Zagorin, 1985). Richard Cumberland held the same view as Selden (Tuck, 1979, pp. 165–6). The precise connections between Hobbes and Selden have not been worked out (Sommerville, 1984; Tuck, 1979). What is known is that both were members of the circle of scholars who met at Great Tew and that Hobbes greatly admired Selden.

11 This objection is directed against Hobbes's views, not against my interpretation of him.

12 What Hobbes and Grotius call the "law of nature," Hooker prefers to call the "Law of Reason or human Nature" and defines it as "that which men by discourse of natural Reason have rightly found out themselves to be all forever bound unto in their actions" (Hooker, 1593, I.8.8). Mentioning that it is also called the "Law of Nature," he says it comprehends "all those things which men by the light of their natural understanding evidently know, or at leastwise may know, to be beseeming or unbeseeming, virtuous or vicious, good or evil for them to do" (ibid., I.8.9). Explaining that following the law of nature naturally benefits humans and violating it naturally injures them, Hooker says that God is the "author" of the law of nature (I.9.2).

13 Stanley Moore coined the term "rule egoism" for Hobbes's theory. But Moore denies that there is any theological aspect to Hobbes's moral theory. (See Moore, 1971.)

14 A final one is derived in the Review and Conclusion (EW, 3:703). The final law is *"that every man is bound by nature, as much as in him lieth, to protect in war the authority, by which he is himself protected in time of peace"* (ibid.). So the criticism of Clarendon and others that Leviathan is "a rebel's catechism" at least goes against Hobbes's explicit intention.

15 My guess is that by "eternal" Hobbes means "not made." Thus, he can assert the conventional wisdom that the laws of nature are eternal.

16 Performative form is first person, singular, present perfect, active, and indicative.

17 John Searle thinks that every speech act has an illocutionary force indicating device. I have explained why I think that is mistaken in Martinich, 1984, pp. 72–6, and Martinich, 1990c, pp. 94–8.

18 In the Latin version, Hobbes uses different words for "pretendeth" in discussing a command and a counsel: *postulat* ("he demands") and *praetendere* ("to present in front" or "to pretend"), respectively.

19 Hobbes would not agree. He stubbornly thinks that the parent aims primarily at her own good (EW, 3:244).

20 I suspect that Hobbes was also outlining his views about an issue that had been actively debated for decades before the Civil War, namely, the proper relationship between the King and Parliament. Hobbes is implying here, I believe, that it was the King's role to command and Parliament's role to counsel.

21 Secularists would argue that Hobbes never changed his view. I hold that he did. If my view is correct, one can conjecture that he came to realize that his earlier view yielded only a theory of prudence, not a theory of morality, and that adding God to the theory was essential to give him what he wanted, namely a genuine theory of morality. However, I admit that this explanation of the difference between *De Cive* and *Leviathan* is only a conjecture.

22 Locke holds the same view; cf. Wootton, 1986, pp. 61–2.

CHAPTER 5

1 Cf. Kodalle, 1972, pp. 70–87, 94–7, 100–4, and Kodalle, 1987. For an interesting discussion of a probable influence on Hobbes, see Grover, 1980.

2 Hill quotes Tyndale as saying, "Without a promise there can be no faith" (Hill, 1986, 3:302).

3 For example, see Aquinas, *Summa Theologiae*, I-II, 114, and Robert Bellarmine, *De Iustificatione*.

4 Curiously, this section is omitted from the Latin version of *Leviathan*. One would expect Hobbes's Latin readers to have had more interest in and familiarity with these terms than his English readers.

5 Later Hobbes says, "[M]erit . . . is not due by justice; but is rewarded of grace only" (EW, 3:137; see also p. 476).

6 Other evidence of the same nature is Hobbes's discussion of the Catholic scholastic distinction between *dulia* and *latria* (EW, 3:647) and his extensive discussion of Bellarmine's book *De Summo Pontifice*; see also Calvin, 1559, I.12.2. On the concept of merit, see McGrath, 1986, 1:109–19.

7 The term "covenant" for these agreements was not used until after 1590 (Burrell, 1958, pp. 340–1; Henderson, 1957, p. 61).

8 There was nothing lunatic about such discoveries at the time. Manasseh ben Israel, chief rabbi of Amsterdam, also discovered England mentioned in the Bible. As part of his argument urging the readmission of the Jews into England, he wrote in 1656, "As also, that this our scattering, by little, and little, should be amongst all people, from the *one end of the earth even unto the other*, even as it is written *Deut.* 28,64: I conceived that by the *end of the earth* might be understood this *Island*" (quoted from Wolf, 1901, p. xvi). Many Englishmen, including Cromwell, either believed Manasseh or were inclined to, and it was through Cromwell's efforts that Jews were allowed de facto readmission to England. (See, for example, Hill, 1986, 2:269–300.)

9 Hobbes also must have had in mind the Solemn League and Covenant of 1643 when he wrote *Leviathan*.

10 The importance of these English theologians notwithstanding, the classic treatment of covenant theology is attributed to Cocceius (Johannes Koch, 1603–69).

11 The term "federal theology" also comes from the fact that *foedum* is a Latin word for "covenant."

12 Covenant theology is based in large part on 1 Cor. 15 and Rom. 5:15–21.

13 Reventlow recognizes that Hobbes was influenced by covenant theology but does not develop the theme: "The use of the

idea of covenant itself shows the influence of federal theology on Hobbes, though because of its wide dissemination we should not think in terms of any specific model" (Reventlow, 1984, p. 535 n. 122).

14 Theologians hedged on whether justice or mercy was the operative concept in God's covenants. Recall also Tyndale's remark, quoted earlier, that "God hath bound himself unto us to keep and make good all the mercies promised in Christ" (Tyndale, 1534, p. 4).

15 While Christopher Hill recognizes the influence of covenant theology on Hobbes, he thinks that Hobbes wholly opposed it (1986, 3:317–19). I have explained my reasons for thinking he was somewhat more favorably disposed toward it.

16 I do not know why we speak of "exercising" a right but not of "using" one.

17 This section summarizes various themes discussed in this and the preceding two chapters.

18 Hobbes does not mention that there is another tradition in the Bible, the so-called Deuteronomic view, according to which there is a perfect correlation between merit and deserts in this life. It is a mark of his decency that he does not embrace this view.

CHAPTER 6

1 Since God warrants the sovereign, Hobbes feels able to say that the civil laws are God's laws (e.g., EW, 6:236).

2 Since this passage occurs near the beginning of the chapter, "Of the Kingdom of God by Nature," Hobbes must mean that God governs by his word, known through natural reason.

3 Gauthier misinterprets a related passage (EW, 3:342–3; Gauthier, 1969, pp. 184–5). Hobbes says that the laws of nature are not merely natural but, "in respect of God, as he is King of kings, are *laws*" (EW, 3:343).

4 Brian Tierney claims that certain theories about representative persons and kings derive from Roman law and from the idea of a corporation in the Middle Ages. I do not see that these ideas had any impact on Hobbes, nor does Tierney claim that they did. But see Tierney, 1982, pp. 70, 98, 101.

5 It is a bit more complicated than this. Hobbes, and most English Calvinists, thought that the merit Christ earned extended

only to the elect. The Arminians thought that the merit extended to all humans.

6　God is also the only one who can save them.

7　"Authorize" in this context cannot mean "set up to make final decisions." To make the decisions of someone final is not to take that person's decisions as one's own. An umpire's decisions are final, but they are not the players' own decisions. There is a difference between making a decision and following the decision of another.

8　The conflict between the two theories comes out in various places when Hobbes discusses punishment and worship. Concerning punishment, each person is the author of his own punishment, according to the theory of authorization; but the sovereign alone is the author of the punishment, according to the theory of authority (EW, 3:160, 163). Concerning worship, each person should be worshiping for himself, according to the theory of authorization. But this is an unacceptable consequence of the theory. For it would mean that if a Christian were to offer sacrifices to Baal, then he himself would be worshiping Baal. Hobbes knows that this is unacceptable. That is why, in his explicit treatment of worship, he appeals to his theory of authority and claims that such seeming worship of Baal is not the Christian's own worship but that of the pagan sovereign. The Christian is merely obeying the legitimate commands of the sovereign (EW, 3:350, 647, 651, 2:225). For more about Hobbes's views on worship, see the section entitled "Worship" in Chapter 10 of the present volume.

9　I am not denying that (1) if a group of people, $P_1, P_2, \ldots, P_n$, authorizes a person S to govern them, then S acquires greater power than any person P_i; nor (2) that P_i will be coerced by S's power not to withdraw his authorization of S. The issue in general is whether Hobbes's account of authorization is correct and compatible with his theory of absolute sovereignty. Further, with regard to (1), S acquires this power, not because he is authorized, but because $P_1, P_2, \ldots, P_n$ transfer their power to him. With regard to (2), logically, any P_i can withdraw his authorization from S even though it would be extremely imprudent to do so since S retains the overwhelming power contributed by $P_1, P_2, \ldots, P_{n-1}$.

10　One final problem may be mentioned. Whatever "governing myself" might mean, Hobbes should have recognized that the phrase is incoherent, because "*x* governs *y*" is an asymmetric relation for him. No one can govern himself, because the person governed is subordinate to the governor (EW, 3:252). For an interesting account of Hobbes's view of authorization that complements mine, see Wootton, 1986, pp. 56–8.

11 Since the institution of punishment is important for defending all those who seek peace in society, transferring the right to defend everyone else also involves assisting the sovereign in punishing others (EW, 3:297). When Hobbes says, "[T]he subjects did not give the sovereign that right [to punish]; but only in laying down theirs, strengthened him to use his own" (ibid., p. 298), he means that the sovereign exercises his own natural *right* to punish by using the *power* contributed by citizens.

12 James I wrote, "So in the first original of kings, whereof some had their beginning by conquest, and some by election of the people, their wills at that time served for law" (James I, 1610, p. 108).

13 Hobbes was not the only Englishman who thought that the consent of the conquered was necessary for a legitimate government: "Sir Edwin Sandys and John Floyd did indeed claim that even in a case of conquest, the victor gained no power over the defeated population until they consented to his rule" (Sommerville, 1986, p. 66). Hobbes was not a de facto theorist (cf. Skinner, 1972). See also Appendix B in the present volume.

14 The Glorious Revolution is not a good example. William of Orange was only titular sovereign over Orange when he entered England. Also, he was invited to England by English nobles, who considered him the rightful sovereign.

CHAPTER 7

1 Hobbes's views about God are widely misunderstood. Two notable exceptions are Taylor, 1938, and Glover, 1965. I shall not repeat their evidence, which in my opinion has never been refuted.

2 Whether Montaigne and Charron were fideistic Roman Catholics or dissembling atheists is disputed. Although I think they were fideists, it is outside the scope of this book to argue the issue; see, however, Bayle, 1738, 2:448–56, 5:145–6; Charron,

1961; Popkin, 1979, pp. 56–62; Zagorin, 1990, pp. 319–22; and Gregory, 1991.

3 It is not surprising that the Arminian Bramhall should insist that God is knowable. One reason Calvinists asserted that God was unknowable was the hope of making the doctrine of predestination more palatable by forestalling the question of why some people were among the elect and others not. If God is unknowable, then no answer is available to humans, and thus the question is pointless. Even though many people who are certain that they have been divinely chosen for heaven accept the doctrine with equanimity, many other people are disturbed by the apparent injustice, arbitrariness, and irrationality of the doctrine. Calvin thinks that Christians ought to believe the doctrine because it is taught in the Bible. He also urges them not to try to understand it, because it exceeds human knowledge (Calvin, 1559, III.21.2). Arminians, however, and most of the early modern intellectuals who tried to wed science and religion (e.g., Locke and Boyle) wanted not only to make God and his judgments accessible to reason but also to make them sound reasonable. Since predestination and determinism do not sound reasonable, they were rejected by many seventeenth-century intellectuals. Hobbes seems to be rather an odd case in England, insofar as he wants to preserve both Calvinist doctrine, because he thought it was biblical, and science, because he thought it was intellectually compelling. He succeeded in offending both the religious conservatives, who did not like his science and metaphysics, and the religious liberals, who did not like his Calvinism. He was not antireligious. He was a member of a Christian tradition that lost the theologicopolitical battle to the people who would come to write the history of who and what were orthodox in the seventeenth century.

4 This discussion is restricted to natural knowledge of God, not mystical experience, which would fall under the general topic of revelation. See Chapter 8 of the present volume.

5 Heppe quotes many Reformation thinkers to the same effect (Heppe, 1950, pp. 52–3). This was also a medieval view (McGrath, 1986, 1:67–9).

6 *Summa Theologiae*, I, 12, 12, c.: "Unde cognoscimus de ipso habitudinem ipsius ad creaturas, quod scilicet omnium est causa."

7 For more on this issue, see Appendix A.

8 "Yahweh" was also translated "I am." See EW, 3:353, and the section "Honorific Talk about God" in the present chapter.

9 Hobbes admired Perkins; see EW, 5:64–5, 266.

10 Concerning the materiality of God, Hobbes aligns himself with the great third-century theologian Tertullian against the dominant tradition (EW, 3:307, 383, 429). Milner, 1988, p. 411, acknowledges that Hobbes's view is not unbiblical. Also, Mormons see no contradiction in holding that God is material.

11 It is difficult to say what Aquinas means by "analogical language," but it is at least clear that it is not strictly literal language.

12 Bramhall was displeased with this. Even if propositions about God are largely honorific, Bramhall asks, "[A]re they not likewise truths?" (Bramhall, 1655, 4:228). We have already seen that Hobbes would agree that some propositions about God are literally true. Hobbes's remark is hyperbolic. He should have said something like "The *primary* purpose of the attributes we give God are to honor Him."

13 I think the materials for this erosion were already in the tradition.

14 Some scholars think that Hobbes's aphoristic remark that atheism is "opinion of right reason without fear" implies that a purely rational person (as surely Hobbes was) must be an atheist (Milner, 1988, p. 414). There are two serious problems with this interpretation of Hobbes's aphorism. First, it ignores the qualifying word "opinion" in the phrase "opinion of right reason." An atheist is one who *thinks* he has right reason, not one who in fact has right reason. Second, the interpretation ignores the extent to which the Reformation tradition required faith or grace to have any knowledge of God. Calvin says, "[W]e shall not say that, properly speaking, God is known where there is no religion or piety" (Calvin, 1559, I.2.1). Hobbes's view that religion is right combined with fear of invisible things may be an echo of the biblical adage "The beginning of wisdom is fear of the Lord" (Glover, 1965, p. 162). In the text under consideration, as in so many others, if Hobbes's words are considered within the tradition of Reformation religion, his views are quite conventional.

15 In *Behemoth*, the focus is different; there, he says that everyone

believes the same doctrines, namely, the Trinity, Incarnation, and so on; but each puts his faith in different people. He wants citizens to put their faith in the sovereign, while the Presbyterians want citizens to put their faith in their preachers (EW, 6:226).

16 Notice here Hobbes's explicit concern with natural science.

CHAPTER 8

1 See Popkin, 1979, pp. 1–17, on this matter of the epistemological problem surrounding mediate revelation.

2 Erasmus's view of the authority of the pope is analogous to Edward Coke's view of the authority of common law: authority comes from custom. Hobbes rejects this move in both the religious and the legal domain. He is equally a critic of papal authority and of Coke's theory of common law.

3 One of my students has reported that there was a philosophy professor who dreamed that he was lecturing to his class and found, when he woke up, that he was. Nonetheless, the link between dreams and reality remains unreliable.

4 Hobbes has two main discussions of prophets. These occur in the second half of chapter 32, "Of the Principles of Christian Politics," and the latter two-thirds of chapter 36, "Of the Word of God, and of Prophets."

5 Thomas Sprat also requires that the credentials of an alleged prophet be supported by miracles and is skeptical of most such claims (Sprat, 1667, p. 359).

6 This is also Hobbes's view (EW, 4:327). On the complicated issue of belief in miracles in sixteenth- and seventeenth-century England, see Thomas, 1971, esp. pp. 105–8; 124–5; 490. See also the section entitled "Miracles" in the present chapter.

7 Luther said that no genuine miracle could be used to contradict the Bible but should reaffirm faith in it (Luther, 1537–8, pp. 74–7; see also Plass, 1959, pp. 955–7).

8 See Chapter 2 of the present volume.

9 Since Bramhall was already dead when Hobbes wrote this in about 1668, Hobbes's question was rhetorical; but since the criticism does apply to Bramhall's own views, Hobbes was also speaking ill of the dead.

10 As we shall see in Chapter 10, calling Saul, David, and Sol-
    omon God's "vice-regents" does not fit neatly into Hobbes's
    view of the structure of history.

11 Given Luther's words, Hobbes should not have been criticized
    by Clarendon for emphasizing the importance of the doctrine
    that Jesus is the Christ, when Hobbes says, "Here we see this
    article, *Jesus is the Christ*, must be held, though he that shall
    teach the contrary should do great miracles" (EW, 3:595).

12 The Latin version is stronger: "Cessantibus autem jam pridem
    miraculis" [Miracles having ceased long ago] (OL, 3:269).

13 Kurt Vonnegut makes an analogous point in his novel *Cat's
    Cradle*. In reply to the question "See the cat? See the cradle?"
    in a few strands of string, Vonnegut's character eventually
    screams "No damn cat, and no damn cradle."

14 Hobbes shares this view with Saint Augustine, who wrote in
    De Civitate Dei that a miracle is "not contrary to nature, but
    contrary to what is known of nature" (Augustine of Hippo,
    1964, 21.8).

15 Hobbes's sometime nemesis Descartes discovered the laws of
    the rainbow.

16 It is now well known that Hobbes's views also had a direct
    influence on deistic thinkers who, unlike him, did not want to
    preserve orthodox Christian doctrine: e.g., Charles Blount, in
    Miracles No Violations of the Laws of Nature. This is another
    example of how the consequences of Hobbes's effort to pre-
    serve orthodoxy were different from the ones he intended. See
    Jacob, 1983, pp. 147–60.

17 For more about English views on miracles, see the references
    from Thomas, 1971, just cited. Some Protestants continued to
    see miracles, but, Thomas says, "Miracles as such had been
    relegated by most Protestants to the days of the early Church"
    (p. 107; see also pp. 80, 128, 485).

18 See Achtemeier, 1985, s.v. "manna," for a fuller description of
    the natural explanation of this miracle.

CHAPTER 9

1 In the ninth century, John Scotus Eriugena defined the universe as God and creation: "[U]niversitatem dico Deum et

creaturam" (Eriugena, 850, p. 524). Unfortunately, Eriugena was accused of pantheism.

2   Chapter 34 gives a good sense of the breadth and depth of Hobbes's biblical understanding; it is implausible that Hobbes would have written so knowledgeably and sympathetically about Christianity if he had been either an atheist or an agnostic.

3   Later, Hobbes employs this strategy in order to deny that Jesus believed in demons (EW, 3:641–2). The reason for this is that he wants to oppose, not the Judeo-Christian idea of angels, but the pagan doctrine of demons. (See the next subsection, "Demons," and EW, 3:640–1.)

4   Hobbes follows his contemporary, the distinguished biblical scholar Joseph Mede, who held that demoniacs are simply madmen (EW, 4:327). See also Thomas, 1971, p. 490.

5   Hobbes may have had Alexander Ross, one of his first critics, in mind as his specific target here, for Ross had quoted the very same lines of Vergil approvingly (Ross, 1646, p. 60).

6   It also does not seem consistent with his justice. The evil for which the wicked are guilty is only finite, no matter how horrendous. Even if Hitler were to burn for 1 million years for each person he wrongfully caused to die and we suppose that he is culpable for the deaths of 20 million people, he would burn for 20 trillion years, which, though a very long time, would still be finite.

7   The satisfaction theory has many other features that are not pertinent here. For example, the Incarnation was necessary because if no humans were redeemed then God's purpose in creating humans, namely, for humans to be happy with him, would have been frustrated, and God's purposes cannot be frustrated.

8   These are sometimes called "theories of the Atonement." I shall simply speak of theories of redemption.

9   The Westminster Confession, insensitive to the logical problems, wanted to have it both ways, a matter of God's justice and mercy (Leith, 1982, p. 207).

10   On Hobbes as a Reformation theologian, with special reference to the issue of whether the will is free, see Damrosch, 1979.

11   Hobbes comments on the Synod of Dort and its effect on En-

glish theology and politics in *Behemoth*. Oddly, he says that the synod "came to nothing" (EW, 6:241). Perhaps he means that the canons passed at the synod were never ratified by convocation in England.

CHAPTER 10

1 I shall use the term "philosophy of history" to designate any theory that attributes a structure to history.

2 For Renaissance views about the structure of history, see Kelley, 1988, pp. 746–62; for more on the sixteenth and the seventeenth century, see Firth, 1979, pp. 193, 209–10.

3 This idea is even in Calvin (Calvin, 1559, II.10.2).

4 For a general discussion of Christian views about the structure of history, see also Eisenach, 1982, pp. 217–21, and Lamont, 1969.

5 The Latin text gives the same impression: "[P]er quod pactum seipsum . . . obedire mandatis Dei obligavit, non solum naturalibus, sed etiam illis mandatis quae Deus supernaturaliter manifesta faceret per somnia et visiones" (OL, 3:338; also EW, 2:228–30).

6 Whereas God becomes the sovereign over the Jews, Moses acquires the sovereign power in virtue of his lieutenancy; that is, he holds the place of God (EW, 3:465).

7 Hobbes is not always consistent. In *An Answer to Bishop Bramhall*, he calls Samuel "the sovereign prince in Israel" (EW, 4:331).

8 A "millenarian" may be defined as a person who believes that Jesus will rule on earth. By this definition, Hobbes is a millenarian. But the term may be defined more narrowly as referring to a person who believes that the reign of Jesus is imminent. I shall use the term in this narrower sense (Pocock, 1971, pp. 175–6).

9 For various sixteenth- and seventeenth-century interpretations of Naaman, see Zagorin, 1990b.

10 On Nicodemism, see Eire, 1986, pp. 234–75; Ginzburg, 1970; and Zagorin, 1990b, esp. pp. 102, 138–51, 237, 244, 327.

11 Hobbes, no doubt working with a Greek New Testament, alters the King James translation of Acts 1:22. He puts the word "martyr" for "witness" (EW, 3:495).

CHAPTER 11

1 Hobbes thinks that Moses transmitted the Ten Commandments to the Jews and was the author of Deuteronomy 12–25
(EW, 3:515).

2 Contemporary biblical scholars assign this text to about the
tenth century B.C. Abraham lived about nine hundred years
earlier.

3 Clarendon does not understand Hobbes's point (1676, p. 210).

4 The gloss for the Geneva Bible on this text says, "Which
seemeth to be the boke of the Iudges, or as some thinke, a
boke which is lost."

5 Although the covenant with God is renewed, the terms presumably are different. God does not resume his position as the
particular sovereign of the Jews. Hobbes plays rather loose
with history at this point, both brute historical fact and his
own philosophy of history. He claims that Esdras was both the
high priest and the civil sovereign of the Jews. But as a matter
of brute fact, the Persians, who allowed the Jews to return to
Palestine, thus ending the Babylonian Captivity, retained their
sovereignty over the Jews. Also, it was part of Hobbes's structure of history that the Jewish theocracy ended with the accession of Saul and would not be restored until the Second Coming of Christ. But Hobbes is so intent on uniting religious and
secular authority that he may falsify history and contradict
what he has said elsewhere.

6 Contemporary biblical scholars typically use A.D. 90 as the
date when the Old Testament canon was established by a
gathering of rabbis at Jamnia.

7 Hobbes himself gives this date. See also Metzger, 1987, pp.
210, 216.

8 If a person lives after the conversion of Constantine but in a
country where no religion is prescribed, he is in effect living
before the conversion of Constantine.

9 Hobbes identifies the doctrine of transubstantiation as origi-
nating with Innocent III in the late twelfth and early thirteenth
centuries. (The doctrine is actually older than this, but Hobbes
could not have known it.)

10 Hobbes is embellishing on a standard theme of the Reformed
churches. Thus, a marginal note in the Geneva Bible for Reve-

lation 13:14 says that the papacy is the "image and shadowe" of the Roman Empire (Geneva Bible, 1560, p. 119 of the New Testament).

11 A language in which Hobbes was proficient.

CONCLUSION

1 A fourth aspect, liturgy, is not important in this context. It may seem surprising that Hobbes preferred the Anglican ceremonies of the Book of Common Prayer to the Puritan liturgies. But this is consonant with his "high Calvinism," discussed later in this chapter.

2 The logical space of theological theory is such that it is possible to be both an Aristotelian and an Arminian.

3 They also corresponded; the letters are in Huntington Library Manuscripts HA 14984–6.

4 The universities also opposed Hobbes for more purely political reasons. He had described them as hotbeds of sedition and wanted them under state control.

5 I have tried to prove that the claim that Hobbes had no doctrinal preferences is false (see Strauss, 1952b, pp. 75–6).

6 I believe that Hobbes's thought failed to attract a larger, more mainstream following in his own time in part because of the discordant blend of the conceptual elements just described. The intellectual conservatives were by and large willing to abandon their Aristotelianism for materialism and modern science. Many of them did not accept the Copernican theory of the heavens and were offended by Hobbes's allegiance to it (Whitehall, 1679, p. 162; see also Ross, 1653, pp. 93, 101). In contrast, the intellectual progressives accepted Copernicanism in science and rejected absolutism in politics and Calvinism in theology. The progressives won the battle. Their strategy was to reconcile religion and science by placing religion wholly within the limits of reason. This required a severe contraction of dogma. Locke, Boyle, and the Latitudinarians, all of whom believed in the rationality of Christianity, contributed to this withering away of doctrine and thereby fostered the decline of orthodoxy and the rise of deism.

APPENDIX A

1 Hobbes alludes to a book by John Selden (EW, 3:84).
2 Hobbes may also single out Bellarmine because the latter had defended English Roman Catholics during the reign of James I and had also played a role in Galileo's condemnation by the Inquisition.
3 Clarendon noticed the irony also (Clarendon, 1676, p. 298).

APPENDIX B

1 Skinner has a very specific theory of historical interpretation. I am concerned only with his interpretation of Hobbes, not with the general issue of the adequacy of his historical theory. For his various statements of the theory, articles by his critics, and his replies, see Skinner, 1988a.
2 Skinner has since abandoned this position, but he does not explain how it went wrong (Skinner, 1990, p. 145 n. 155).
3 One exception is John Heydon's *The Idea of the Law*, published in 1660. But Heydon is not reliable. He was an astrologer and wrote extensively about Rosicrucianism. He also had extensive legal problems, due to dubious financial dealings, and spent time in jail as a result. Elias Ashmole called him "an ignoramus and a cheat" (quoted in Stephen and Lee, 1917, 9:796).
4 See State, 1985, for more extensive evidence on this matter.
5 *The Original & End of Civil Power or a Discourse* is a pseudonymous work by "Eutactus Philodemius." Skinner and others say the authorship of this work is undetermined. However, it has been attributed to Ascham by, e.g., the Union Catalog; Stephen and Lee, 1917, 8:1129a, and Halkett and Laing, 1926, 2:365. (For more about Ascham, see Wallace, 1968.) Whoever the author may be, he argues from very un-Hobbesian premises to un-Hobbesian conclusions. He holds that humans are by nature sociable; that a person cannot irreversibly transfer his power; that no form of government is preferable to any other; that the sovereign is subject to the laws as much as any citizen; and that a sovereign should be deposed if he habitually opposes the will of the people (Ascham, 1649b, pp. 4–5, 14, 21). An anonymous work that might also be mentioned here is *Bounds and Bonds of Publique Obedience* (1650), which, though

often attributed to Francis Rous (e.g., by Zagorin, 1954, n. 2) has more recently been attributed to Ascham; see Wallace, 1964, p. 391.

6 Descartes had a similar project, but its scope was more limited. His work did not have either the political or the theological depth and breadth of Hobbes's.

APPENDIX C

1 The page I am referring to is technically an illustrated title page. I refer to it as a frontispiece for the sake of brevity and because it serves the same function as a frontispiece, in the strict sense.

2 The frontispieces for the first and second editions of *De Cive* supply similar evidence.

3 Since writing this, I have seen it reported that M. M. Goldsmith has suggested this in a lecture.

4 Norman Farmer helped me interpret this frontispiece. For an extensive discussion of the importance of frontispieces for early modern books, see Farmer, 1979.

Bibliography

Scholarship on Thomas Hobbes has flourished in the last quarter-century. It is impossible to include all of the works that merit inclusion. I therefore list here virtually all of the seventeenth-century books that I consulted but only those post–seventeenth-century books that are either cited in the text or important for the study of Hobbes's historical and intellectual context. I consulted various manuscripts in the British Library in London, the Huntington Library in San Marino, California, and the Newberry Library in Chicago, including the handwritten copy of *Leviathan* presented to Charles II, but these are not included in the bibliography.

CLASSICAL TEXTS

Allestree, Richard. 1659. *The Whole Duty of Man.* London, 1706.
Ames, William. 1629. *The Marrow of Theology*, tr. John Dykstra Eusden. Durham, N.C.: Labyrinth Press, 1983.
  1633. *Technometry*, tr. Lee W. Gibbs. Philadelphia: University of Pennsylvania Press, 1979.
Anselm of Canterbury. 1077. *Proslogion*, tr. Jasper Hopkins and Herbert Richardson. Toronto: Mellen Press, 1974.
Ascham, Anthony. 1649a. *Of the Confusions and Revolutions of Governments.* London.
  [Eutactus Philodemius, pseud.]. 1649b. *The Original and End of Civil Power or a Discourse.* London.
Aubrey, John. 1680. *Brief Lives*, ed. Andrew Clark. 2 vol. Oxford: Clarendon Press, 1898.

Bibliography

Augustine of Hippo. 1964. *The Essential Augustine*, ed. Vernon Bourke. New York: New American Library.

Ball, John. 1632. *A Treatise of Faith*. London.

Bayle, Pierre. 1702. *Historical and Critical Dictionary: Selections*, tr. Richard H. Popkin. Indianapolis: Library of Liberal Arts, 1965.

  1735. *The Dictionary Historical and Critical of Mr. Peter Bayle*. 2nd ed. London: 1738.

Berkeley, George. 1713. *Three Dialogues between Hylas and Philonous*, ed. Robert Adams. Indianapolis: Hackett, 1979.

  1732. *Alciphron or the Minute Philosopher*. In *The Works of George Berkeley*, ed. A. A. Luce and T. E. Jessop. Vol. 3. London: Nelson, 1950.

Birch, Thomas. 1756. *The History of the Royal Society of London for Improving of Natural Knowledge*. 4 vol. London.

Blount, Charles. 1693. *Oracles of Reason*. London.

  1695. *The Miscellaneous Works of Charles Blount, Esq.*, ed. Charles Gildon. London.

The Bounds and Bonds of Publique Obedience, or a Vindication of Our Lawful Submission to the Present Government, Or to a Government Supposed Unlawfull, but Commanding Lawfull Things. London, 1650.

Boyle, Robert. 1690. *The Christian Virtuoso*. In Boyle, 1772, 5:508–40.

  1772. *Works*. 2nd ed., ed. Thomas Birch. 6 vol. London.

Bramhall, John. 1655. *Works*. 4 vol. Oxford: Parker, 1844.

Bulkeley, Peter. 1651. *The Gospel-Covenant, or the Covenant of Grace Opened*. 2nd ed. London.

Burnet, Thomas. 1681. *The Sacred Theory of the Earth*. London.

Calvin, John. 1536. "The Genevan Confession." In Calvin, 1954, pp. 26–33.

  1537. *Instruction in Faith*, tr. Paul T. Fuhrmann. Philadelphia: Westminster.

  1559. *Institutes of the Christian Religion*, ed. John T. McNeill. 2 vols. Philadelphia: Westminster, 1960.

  1954. *Calvin: Theological Treatises*, ed. J. K. S. Reid. Philadelphia: Westminster.

  1958. *Calvin: Commentaries*, ed. Joseph Haroutunian. Philadelphia: Westminster.

Cavendish, Margaret. 1664. *Philosophical Letters: or, Modest Reflections upon Some Opinions in Natural Philosophy*. London.

Bibliography

Charron, Pierre. 1595. *Les Trois Veritez*. Paris.

    1612. *Of Wisdome*, tr. Samson Lennard. London.

Chillingworth, William. 1638. *The Religion of Protestants, A Safe Way to Salvation*. Oxford.

    1742. *Works*. London.

Clarendon, Edward, earl of. [Edward Hyde]. 1676. *Brief View and Survey of thee Dangerous and Pernicious Errors to Church and State, In Mr. Hobbes's Book, Entitled Leviathan*. Oxford.

Cobbett, Thomas. 1648. *A Just Vindication of the Covenant*. London.

Coke, Roger. 1660. *Justice Vindicated*. London.

    1662. *Survey of the Politics of Mr. Thomas White, Thomas Hobbes, and Hugo Grotius*. London.

"Confession of Faith." 1679. Boston Synod.

Cotton, John. 1641. *Gods Mercie Mixed with His Justice*. London.

    1651. *Christ the Fountaine of Life*. London.

    1655. *The Covenant of Grace*. London.

Cranmer, Thomas. 1846. *Miscellaneous Writings and Letters of Thomas Cranmer*, ed. John Edmund Cox. 2 vols. Cambridge: Cambridge University Press.

Cudworth, Ralph. 1678. *True Intellectual System of the Universe*. London.

Dell, William. 1646. *Right Reformation: Or, The Reformation of the Church of the New Testament*. London.

    1666. *The Trial of Spirits*. London.

Descartes, René. 1984. *The Philosophical Writings of Descartes*, tr. John Cottingham et al. Cambridge: Cambridge University Press.

Duns Scotus, John. 1303. *A Treatise on God as First Principle*, tr. and ed. Allan B. Wolter. Chicago: Franciscan Herald Press, 1966.

Erasmus, Desiderius. 1524. *On Free Will*. In *Erasmus-Luther: Discourse on Free Will*, tr. and ed. Ernst Winter. New York: Ungar, 1961.

Eriugena, John Scotus. 850. *De Divisione Naturae*. In *Patrologiae Latinae*, ed. J. P. Migne, 122:439–1022. Paris, 1865.

Evelyn, John. 1669. *Diary and Correspondence of John Evelyn, F.R.S.*, ed. E. S. De Beer. 6 vols. Oxford: Clarendon Press, 1955.

Fiennes, Nathaniel. 1641. *A Second Speech . . . in the Commons House of Parliament*. London.

Filmer, Robert. 1655. *Patriarcha, and Other Political Works*, ed. Peter Laslett. Oxford: Blackwell, 1949.

Bibliography

Geneva Bible. 1560. Madison: University of Wisconsin Press, 1969.

Goodwin, Thomas. 1654. *A Sermon of the Fifth Monarchy. Proving by Invincible Arguments, That the Saints Shall have a Kingdom Here on Earth, Which is yet to come after the Fourth Monarchy is destroyed by the Sword of the Saints, the Followers of the Lamb*. London.

Gordon, John. 1604. *England and Scotlands Happinesse*. London.

Grotius, Hugo. 1646. *De Jure Belli ac Pacis Libri Tres*. Oxford: Clarendon Press, 1925.

Hammond, Henry. 1650a. *Of the Reasonableness of Christian Religion*. 3rd ed. London.

1650b. *A Vindication of Dr. Hammond's Addresse, &c. From the Exceptions of Eutactus Philodemius, in Two Particulars, The Power Supposed in the Jew Over his own Freedom. The No-power over a Mans Own Life*. London.

Hariot, Thomas. 1588. *A Brief and True Relation of the New Found Land of Virginia*. In *The New World*, ed. S. Lorant, pp. 227–77. New York: Duell, Sloan & Pearce, 1946.

Harris, Robert. 1635. *Treatise of the New Covenant*. In *The Works of Robert Harris*, London.

Hegel, G. F. W. 1821. *Hegel's Philosophy of Right*, tr. T. M. Knox. London: Oxford University Press, 1952.

Heydon, John. 1660. *The Idea of the Law Charactered from Moses to King Charles. Whereunto is Added the Idea of Government and Tyrany*. London.

Hobbes, Thomas. 1639. "Tractatus Opticus," ed. Franco Alessio. *Rivista Critica di Storia Della Filosofia* 18 (1963):147–228.

1640. *Elements of Law*, ed. F. Tonnies. Oxford: Thornton, 1888.

1641. "Third Set of Objections." In Descartes, 1984, pp. 121–37.

1643. *Thomas White's De Mundo Examined*, tr. Harold Whitmore Jones. London: Bradford University Press, 1976.

1655. *Computatio sive Logica*, tr. Aloysius Martinich. New York: Abaris, 1981.

1839. *English Works*, ed. William Molesworth. 11 vols. London: Longman, Brown, Green, & Longmans, 1839. [Cited in text as EW.]

1839. *Opera Latina*, ed. William Molesworth. 5 vols. London: Longman, Brown, Green, & Longmans, 1839. [Cited in text as OL.]

1983. *De Cive*, ed. Howard Warrender. Oxford: Clarendon Press.

Bibliography

Hooker, Richard. 1593. *Of the Laws of Ecclesiastical Polity*, ed. John Keble. New York: Appleton, 1844.

Hooker, Thomas. 1638a. *The Soules Exhaltation*. London.

1638b. *The Soules Humiliation*. London.

1651. *The Saintes Dignitie*. London.

1656. *Application of Redemption*. London.

Hooper, John. 1852. *Later Writings of Bishop Hooper*, ed. Charles Nevinson. Cambridge: Cambridge University Press.

Hume, David. 1748. *An Inquiry Concerning Human Understanding*. Indianapolis: Bobbs-Merrill, 1955.

1751. *Dialogues Concerning Natural Religion*, ed. Norman Kemp Smith. Indianapolis: Bobbs-Merrill, 1955.

1754. *The History of England*. In *David Hume: Philosophical Historian*, ed. Richard Popkin and David Fate Norton, pp. 111–376. Indianapolis: Bobbs-Merrill, 1965.

James I. 1603. *Basilikon Doron*, ed. James Craigie. 2 vols. Edinburgh: Blackwood, 1944.

1610. "A Speech to the Lords and Commons of the Parliament at White-Hall." In Wootton, 1986, pp. 107–9.

1616. *The Workes of the Most High and Mightie Prince, James, by the Grace of God, King of Britaine, France and Ireland*. London.

Johnston, Archibald. [See Wariston, Archibald Johnston.]

Journals of the House of Commons. Vol. 8.

Latimer, Hugh. 1552. *The Second Sermon upon the Lord's Prayer*. In Latimer, 1844, pp. 341–53.

1844. *Sermons*, ed. George Elwes Corrie. Cambridge: Cambridge University Press.

Leibniz, G. 1710. *Theodicy*, tr. E. M. Huggard. La Salle, Ill.: Open Court, 1985.

Locke, John. 1660. *Essays on the Law of Nature*, ed. W. von Leyden. Oxford: Clarendon Press, 1954.

1664. *Questions Concerning the Law of Nature*, ed. and tr. Robert Horowitz, Jenny Strauss Clay, and Diskin Clay. Ithaca: Cornell University Press, 1990.

1689. *Essay Concerning Human Understanding*, ed. Peter Nidditch. Oxford: Clarendon Press, 1975.

1690. *Two Treatises of Government*, ed. Peter Laslett. Cambridge: Cambridge University Press, 1988.

Lowth, Simon. 1685. *Of the Subject of Church Power*. London.

Luther, Martin. 1520. *An Appeal to the Ruling Class*. In *Martin Luther:*

Selections from His Writings, ed. John Dillenberger, pp. 403–85. Garden City, N.Y.: Doubleday [Anchor Books], 1961.

1535. *Lectures on Galatians*, tr. Jaroslav Pelikan. Vol. 26 in Luther 1961.

1537. *Lectures on the Gospel of St. John, Chapters 1–4*, tr. Martin Bertram. Vol. 22 in Luther, 1961.

1537–8. *Sermons on the Gospel of St. John, Chapters 14–16*, tr. Martin Bertram. Vol. 24 in Luther, 1961.

1961. *Luther's Works*, ed. Jaroslav Pelikan. St. Louis: Concordia.

Manwaring, Roger. 1627. *Religion and Allegiance*. In Sacheverell, 1710.

1628. *Proceedings of the Lords and Commons in the Year 1628 against Roger Manwaring*. In Sacheverell, 1710.

Margaret, Duchess of Newcastle. [1667.] *The Life of William Cavendish, Duke of Newcastle*, ed. C. H. Firth. 2nd ed. London: Routledge, n. d.

Marvell, Andrew. 1672. *The Rehearsal Transpros'd and the Rehearsal Transpros'd: The Second Part*, ed. D. I. B. Smith. Oxford: Clarendon Press, 1971.

Milton, John. 1674. *Paradise Lost*, ed. Scott Elledge. New York: Norton, 1975.

Montaigne, Michel de. 1588. *The Complete Essays of Montaigne*, ed. and tr. Donald Frame. Stanford: Stanford University Press, 1957.

Nedham, Marchamont. 1650. *The Case of the Commonwealth of England, Stated*, ed. Philip A. Knachel. Charlottesville: University of Virginia Press, 1969.

Ockham, William. 1964. *Philosophical Writings*, tr. Philotheus Boehner. Indianapolis: Bobbs-Merrill.

Paine, Thomas. 1795. *The Age of Reason*. Buffalo: Prometheus Books, 1984.

Perkins, William. 1596. *Exposition of the Symbole of Creede of the Apostles, According to the Tenour of the Scriptures*. Cambridge.

1597a. *The Foundation of the Christian Religion: Gathered into Sixe Principles*. London.

1597b. *A Goldene Chaine, or the Description of the Theologie, Containing the Order of the Causes of Salvation and Damnation*. Cambridge.

Philodemius, Eutactus. 1649. *The Original and End of Civil Power: or a Discourse*. London. [See Ascham, 1649b.]

Pike, William. 1656. *Examinations, Censures, and Confutations of Di-*

vers Errours in the Two First Chapters of Mr Hobbes His Leviathan.
London.

Preston, John. 1629a. *The New Covenant, or the Saints Portion.*
London.

1629b. *The Saints Daily Exercise.* London.

1633. *The Cuppe of Blessing.* London.

1634. *Life Eternall, or A Treatise of the Knowledge of the Divine Essence and Attributes.* 4th ed. London.

Pufendorf, Samuel. 1688. *De Jure Naturae et Centium Libri Octo,* tr.
C. H. Oldfather and W. A. Oldfather. Oxford: Clarendon
Press, 1934.

Ross, Alexander. 1643. *The Rebells Catechism.* N.p.

1646. *New Planet, No Planet; or, the Earth No Wandering Star; Except in the Wandering Heads of Galileans.* London.

1653. *Leviathan Drawn Out with a Hook, or Animadversions Upon Mr. Hobbs His Leviathan.* London.

1656. *View of the Jewish Religion.* London.

Rust, George. 1661. *A Letter of Resolution Concerning Origen and the Chief of His Opinions.* London.

Sacheverell, Henry. 1710. *An Impartial Account of . . . Dr. Henry Sacheverell.* London.

Scot, Philip. 1650. *A Treatise of the Schism of England. Wherein Particularly Mr Hales and Mr Hobbs are Modestly Accosted.* Amsterdam.

Selden, John. 1614. *Titles of Honor.* London.

1618. *The Historie of Tithes.* London.

1696. *Table Talk.* London.

Sibbes, Richard. 1862. *The Works of Richard Sibbes,* ed. Alexander
Balloch Grosart. Edinburgh: Nichol.

Simon, Richard. 1682. *Critical History of the Old Testament.* London.

Sprat, Thomas. 1667. *The History of the Royal Society.* London.

Stanley, Thomas. 1701. *The History of Philosophy.* 3rd ed. London.

Stillingfleet, John. 1662. *Irenicum, a Weapon-Salve for the Churches Wounds.* 2nd ed. London.

Suarez, Francisco. 1612. *De Legibus.* In *Selections from Three Works,*
pp. 2–646. Oxford: Clarendon Press, 1944.

1613. *A Defence of the Catholic and Apostolic Faith.* In *Selections from Three Works,* pp. 647–865. Oxford: Clarendon Press, 1944.

Tenison, Thomas. 1670. *The Creed of Mr. Hobbes Examined; in a Feigned Conference between Him, and A Student in Divinity.*
London.

Thomas Aquinas. 1267–73. *Summa Theologiae.*

Tillotson, John. 1680. *The Protestant Religion Vindicated from the Charge of Singularity and Novelty.*

Tyndale, William. 1526. *The Works of William Tyndale*, ed. G. E. Duffield. Appleford, UK: Sutton Courtenay, 1964.

    1528. *The Obedience of a Christian Man.* In Tyndale, 1848, pp. 127–344.

    1534. *Tyndale's New Testament*, ed. David Daniell. New Haven: Yale University Press, 1989.

    1536. "Prologue upon the Gospel of St. Matthew." In Tyndale, 1848, pp. 468–79.

    1848. *Doctrinal Treatises*, ed. Henry Walter. Cambridge: Cambridge University Press.

Vilvain, Robert. 1654. *Theoremata Theologica: Theological Theses.* London.

Walton, Izaak. 1662. *The Lives of John Donne, Sir Henry Wotton, Richard Hooker, George Herbert, and Robert Sanderson.* London, 1927.

Ward, Seth. 1654. *Vindiciae Academiarum.* Oxford.

Wariston, Archibald Johnston. 1632–9. *The Diary of Sir Archibald Johnston of Wariston, 1632–39.* Edinburgh: Scottish History Society, 1911.

Webster, John. 1654. *Academiarum Examen.* London.

Whiston, William. 1696. *A New Theory of the Earth.* London.

    1708. *A New Theory of the Earth.* 2nd ed. London.

White, Thomas. 1659a. *Catechism of Christian Doctrine.* Paris.

    1659b. *The Middle State of Souls from the Hour of Death to the Day of Judgment.* N.p.

Whitehall, John. 1679. *The Leviathan Found out: or the Answer to Mr. Hobbes's Leviathan, in that which my Lord of Clarendon hath Past Over.* London.

    1680. *Behemoth Arraign'd: Or, A Vindication of Property Against an Fanatical Pamphlet Stiled Beneath Behemoth.* London.

Whitgift, John. 1851. *Works*, ed. John Ayre. 3 vols. Cambridge: Cambridge University Press.

CONTEMPORARY TEXTS

Achtemeier, Paul J., ed. 1985. *Harper's Bible Dictionary.* San Francisco: Harper & Row.

Adamson, J. H. 1960. "Milton's 'Arianism.'" In Hunter, Patrides, and Adamson, 1971, pp. 53–62.

Bibliography

Allen, Don Cameron. 1949. *The Legend of Noah: Renaissance Rationalism in Art, Science, and Letters*. Urbana: University of Illinois Press, 1963.

Allen, J. W. 1938. *English Political Thought: 1603–1644*. London: Methuen.

Anscombe, G. E. M. 1981. *Collected Philosophical Papers*. 3 vol. Minneapolis: University of Minnesota Press.

Archer, Stanley. 1983. *Richard Hooker*. Boston: Twayne.

Armstrong, A. H. 1970. *The Cambridge History of Later Greek and Early Medieval Philosophy*, ed. A. H. Armstrong. Cambridge: Cambridge University Press.

Ashcraft, Richard. 1986. *Revolutionary Politics and Locke's Two Treatises of Government*. Princeton: Princeton University Press.

Ashton, Robert. 1978. *The English Civil War*. London: Weidenfeld & Nicolson.

1985. *Reformation and Revolution, 1558–1660*. London: Paladin.

Ashworth, E. J. 1988. "Traditional Logic." In Schmitt and Skinner, 1988, pp. 143–72.

Aylmer, G. E. 1978. "Unbelief in Seventeenth Century England." In Pennington and Thomas, 1978, pp. 22–46.

1986. *Rebellion or Revolution?: England, 1640–1660*. Oxford: Oxford University Press.

Aylmer, G. E., ed. 1972. *The Interregnum*. London: Macmillan.

Axtell, James L. 1965. "The Mechanics of Opposition: Restoration Cambridge v. Daniel Scargill." *Bulletin of the Institute of Historical Research* 38:102–11.

Barry, Brian. 1968. "Warrender and His Critics." In *Hobbes and Rousseau*, pp. 37–65. Garden City, N.Y.: Doubleday, 1972.

Baumgold, Deborah. 1988. *Hobbes's Political Theory*. Cambridge: Cambridge University Press.

Berman, David. 1988. *A History of Atheism in England: From Hobbes to Russell*. London: Croom Helm.

Bettenson, Henry. 1963. *Documents of the Christian Church*. 2nd ed. Oxford: Oxford University Press.

Brodrick, James. 1961. *Robert Bellarmine: Saint and Scholar*. Westminster: Newman Press.

Brown, Keith. 1962. "Hobbes's Grounds for Belief in a Deity." *Philosophy* 37:336–44.

1978. "The Artist of the *Leviathan* Title-Page." *British Library Journal* 4:24–36.

Brown, Keith, ed. 1965. *Hobbes Studies*. Oxford: Blackwell.

Bibliography

Burns, Norman T. 1972. *Christian Mortalism from Tyndale to Milton.* Cambridge, Mass.: Harvard University Press.

Burrell, S. A. 1958. "The Covenant Idea as a Revolutionary Symbol: Scotland, 1596–1637." *Church History* 27:338–50.

——— 1964. "The Apocalyptic Vision of the Early Covenanters." *Scottish Historical Review* 43:1–24.

Capp, B. S. 1972. *The Fifth Monarchy Men.* London: Faber & Faber.

——— 1984. "The Fifth Monarchists and Popular Millenarianism." In McGregor and Reay, 1984, pp. 165–90.

Charron, Jean Daniel. 1961. *The "Wisdom" of Pierre Charron: An Original and Orthodox Code of Morality.* Chapel Hill: University of North Carolina Press.

Chenu, M.-D. 1968. *Nature, Man, and Society in the Twelfth Century.* Chicago: University of Chicago Press.

Christianson, Paul. 1978. *Reformers and Babylon: English Apocalyptic Visions from the Reformation to the Eve of the Civil War.* Toronto: University of Toronto Press.

Cirlot, Juan. 1972. *Dictionary of Symbols.* 2nd ed. New York: Philosophical Library.

Collinson, Patrick. 1979. *Archbishop Grindal, 1519–1583: The Struggle for a Reformed Church.* Berkeley and Los Angeles: University of California Press.

Cowan, Ian B. 1976. *The Scottish Covenanters.* London: Gollancz.

Coward, Barry. 1980. *The Stuart Age.* London: Longmans.

Cranston, Maurice. 1957. *John Locke.* 2nd ed. Oxford: Oxford University Press, 1985.

Cranston, Maurice, and Richard S. Peters, eds. 1972. *Hobbes and Rousseau.* Garden City, N.Y.: Doubleday [Anchor Books].

Crimmins, James E., ed. 1989. *Religion, Secularization and Political Thought: Thomas Hobbes to J. S. Mill.* London: Routledge.

Curley, Edwin. 1991. "'I Durst Not Write So Boldly,' or How to Read Hobbes' Theological-Political Treatise." In *Hobbes e Spinoza,* ed. Emilia Giancotti. Naples: Bibliopolis, forthcoming. [Page references are to the typescript. This work is discussed with permission of the author.]

Daly, James. 1979. *Sir Robert Filmer and English Political Thought.* Toronto: University of Toronto Press.

Damrosch, Leopold, Jr. 1979. "Hobbes as Reformation Theologian." *Journal of the History of Ideas* 40:339–52.

Davidson, Donald. 1984. *Inquiries into Truth and Interpretation.* Cambridge: Cambridge University Press.

Bibliography

Debus, Allen. 1970. *Science and Education in the Seventeenth Century.* New York: American Elsevier.

De Vries, Ad. 1976. *Dictionary of Symbols and Imagery.* 2nd ed. Amsterdam: North-Holland.

Dickinson, William Croft, and Gordon Donaldson. 1954. *A Source Book of Scottish History.* Vol. 3. London: Nelson.

Dietz, Mary, ed. 1990. *Thomas Hobbes and Political Theory.* Lawrence: University of Kansas Press.

Dillenberger, John. 1960. *Protestant Thought and Natural Science.* New York, Doubleday.

Duffy, Eamon. 1981. "Valentine Greatrakes, the Irish Stroker: Miracle, Science and Orthodoxy in Restoration England." In *Religion and Humanism*, ed. Keith Robbins, pp. 251–73. Oxford: Blackwell.

Edwards, Charles S. 1981. *Hugo Grotius: The Miracle of Holland.* Chicago: Nelson-Hall.

Eire, Carlos. 1986. *War against the Idols: The Reformation of Worship from Erasmus to Calvin.* Cambridge: Cambridge University Press.

Eisenach, Eldon J. 1982. "Hobbes on Church, State and Religion." *History of Political Thought* 3:215–43.

Elledge, Scott. 1975. "Angels." In John Milton, *Paradise Lost*, ed. Elledge, pp. 394–6. New York: Norton.

Emerson, E. H. 1956. "Calvin and Covenant Theology." *Church History* 25:136–44.

Farmer, Norman. 1979. "Renaissance English Title-Pages and Frontispieces: Visual Introductions to Verbal Texts." In *Proceedings of the Ninth Congress of the International Comparative Literature Association*, pp. 61–5. Innsbruck: AMOE, 1981.

———. 1984. *Poets and the Visual Arts in Renaissance England.* Austin: University of Texas Press.

Farr, James. 1990. "Atomes of Scripture: Hobbes and the Politics of Biblical Interpretation." In Dietz, 1990, pp. 172–96.

Febvre, Lucien. 1942. *The Problem of Unbelief in the Sixteenth Century: The Religion of Rabelais*, tr. Beatrice Gottlieb. Cambridge, Mass., Harvard University Press, 1982.

Feingold, Mordechai. 1985. "A Friend of Hobbes and an Early Translator of Galileo: Robert Payne of Oxford." In North and Roche, 1985, pp. 265–80.

Firth, Katharine R. 1979. *The Apocalyptic Tradition in Reformation Britain: 1530–1645.* Oxford: Oxford University Press.

Fletcher, Anthony. 1981. *The Outbreak of the English Civil War*. London: Arnold.

Flew, Antony. 1964. "Hobbes." In *A Critical History of Western Philosophy*, pp. 153–69. London: Collier-Macmillan.

Flinker, Noam. 1989. "The View from the 'Devil's Mountain': Dramatic Tension in Hobbes's *Behemoth*." *Hobbes Studies* 2:10–22.

Force, James E. 1985. *William Whiston: Honest Newtonian*. Cambridge: Cambridge University Press.

Forster, Winfried. 1969. *Thomas Hobbes und der Puritanismus*. Berlin: Duncker & Humblot.

Fuller, Thomas. 1990. "Compatibilities on the Idea of Law in Thomas Aquinas and Thomas Hobbes." *Hobbes Studies* 3:112–34.

Funkenstein, Amos. 1988. "The Body of God in Seventeenth Century Theology and Science." In Popkin, 1988, pp. 149–75.

Gardiner, Samuel R. 1884. *History of England*. 10 vols. London: Longmans, Green.

Gardiner, Samuel R., ed. 1889. *The Constitutional Documents of the Puritan Revolution: 1625–1660*. Oxford: Clarendon Press.

Gauthier, David P. 1969. *The Logic of Leviathan*. Oxford: Clarendon Press.

1977. "Why Ought One Obey God? Reflections on Hobbes and Locke." *Canadian Journal of Philosophy* 7:425–46.

Geach, Peter. 1981. "The Religion of Thomas Hobbes." *Religious Studies* 17:549–58.

Gert, Bernard. 1965. "Hobbes, Mechanism, and Egoism." *Philosophical Quarterly* 15:341–9.

1967. "Hobbes and Psychological Egoism." *Journal of the History of Ideas* 28:503–20.

Gierke, Otto. 1958. *Political Theories of the Middle Age*. Cambridge: Cambridge University Press.

Ginzburg, Carlo. 1970. *Il Nicodemismo: Simulazione e Dissimulazione Religiosa nell'Europa del'500*. Turin: Einaudi.

Glover, Willis. 1965. "God and Thomas Hobbes." In Brown, 1965, pp. 141–68.

Goldsmith, M. M. 1966. *Hobbes's Science of Politics*. New York: Columbia University Press.

1981. "Picturing Hobbes's Politics?" *Journal of the Warburg and Courtauld Institutes* 44:232–7.

1991. "The Hobbes Industry." *Political Studies* 39:135–47.

Greaves, Richard. 1967. "John Bunyan and Covenant Thought in the Seventeenth Century." *Church History* 36:151–69.

Bibliography

Green, V. H. H. 1964. *Religion at Oxford and Cambridge.* London: SCM Press.

Greenleaf, W. H. "A Note on Hobbes and the Book of Job." *Anales de la Catedra Francisco Suarez* 14:11–34.

Gregg, Pauline. 1981. *King Charles I.* Berkeley and Los Angeles: University of California Press.

Gregory, Tullio. 1991. "Pierre Charron's 'Scandalous' Book." In Hunter and Wootton, 1991.

Grendler, P. F. 1963. "Pierre Charron: Precursor to Hobbes." *Review of Politics* 25:212–24.

Grensted, L. W. 1920. *A Short History of the Atonement.* Manchester: Manchester University Press.

Grenville, George Nugent [Lord Nugent]. 1832. *Some Memorials of John Hampden, His Party and His Times.* 2 vols. London: Murray.

Grover, Robinson. 1980. "The Legal Origins of Thomas Hobbes's Doctrine of Contract." *Journal of the History of Philosophy* 18:177–94.

———. 1990. "Individualism, Absolutism, and Contract in Thomas Hobbes' Political Theory." *Hobbes Studies* 3:89–111.

Halliday R. J., Timothy Kenyon, and Andrew Reeve. 1983. "Hobbes's Belief in God." *Political Studies* 31:418–33.

Halkett, Samuel, and John Laing. 1926. *Dictionary of Anonymous and Pseudonymous English Literature,* 2nd ed. James Kennedy, W. A. Smith, and A. F. Johnson. 8 vols. Edinburgh: Tweeddale Court.

Hamilton, Anthony. 1846. *Memoirs of the Court of Charles the Second by Count Grammont,* ed. Sir Walter Scott. London: Bohn.

Hamilton, J. J. 1978. "Hobbes's Study and the Hardwick Library." *Journal of the History of Philosophy* 16:445–53.

Hampton, Jean. 1986. *Hobbes and the Social Contract Tradition.* Cambridge: Cambridge University Press.

Hart, H. L. A. 1961. *The Concept of Law.* Oxford: Clarendon Press.

Henderson, G. D. 1957. "The Idea of the Covenant in Scotland." In *The Burning Bush: Studies in Scottish Church History,* pp. 61–74. Edinburgh: St. Andrews Press.

Henry, Nathaniel. 1951. "Milton and Hobbes: Mortalism and the Intermediate State." *Studies in Philology* 48:241–4.

Hepburn, Ronald. 1972. "Hobbes on the Knowledge of God." In Cranston and Peters, 1972, pp. 85–108.

Heppe, Heinrich. 1950. *Reformed Dogmatics.* London: Allen & Unwin.

Bibliography

Herbert, Gary. 1989. *Thomas Hobbes: The Unity of Scientific and Moral Wisdom*. Vancouver: University of British Columbia Press.

Hill, Christopher. 1961. *The Century of Revolution, 1603–1714*. New York: Norton.

1970. *Oliver Cromwell and the English Revolution*. New York: Harper & Row [Harper Torchbooks].

1971. *Antichrist in Seventeenth Century England*. London: Oxford University Press.

1972. *The World Turned Upside Down*. Harmondsworth: Penguin Books, 1975.

1977. *Milton and the English Revolution*. Harmondsworth: Penguin Books.

1984a. *The Experience of Defeat: Milton and Some Contemporaries*. New York: Viking.

1984b. "Irreligion in the Puritan Revolution." In McGregor and Reay, 1984, pp. 191–211.

1986. *Collected Essays*. 3 vols. Amherst: University of Massachusetts Press.

Historical Commission Reports. Thirteenth Report, Appendix, Part II: *The Manuscripts of His Grace, the Duke of Portland, Preserved at Welbeck Abbey*. Volume 2 (London: 1893), pp. 124–5, 128–31. [Contains letters by and about Hobbes.]

Holmes, Stephen. 1989. "Truths for Philosophers Alone?" *Times Literary Supplement*, December 1–7, pp. 1319–25.

Hood, F. C. 1964. *The Divine Politics of Thomas Hobbes: An Interpretation of "Leviathan."* Oxford: Clarendon Press.

Hughes, Philip. 1965. *Theology of the English Reformers*. Grand Rapids: Eerdmans.

Hunter, Michael. 1981. *Science and Society in Restoration England*. Cambridge: Cambridge University Press.

1985. "The Problem of 'Atheism' in Early Modern England." *Transactions of the Royal Historical Society*, 5th ser., 35:135–57.

Hunter, Michael, and David Wootton. 1991. *Atheism from the Reformation to the Enlightenment*. Oxford: Clarendon, forthcoming.

Hunter, W. B., C. A. Patrides, and J. H. Adamson. 1971. *Bright Essence: Studies in Milton's Theology*. Salt Lake City: University of Utah Press.

Idziak, Janine Marie. 1979. *Divine Command Morality: Historical and Contemporary Readings*. New York: Mellen Press.

Jacob, J. R. 1977. *Robert Boyle and the English Revolution*. New York: Franklin.

410

Bibliography

1983. *Henry Stubbe, Radical Protestantism and the Early Enlightenment.* Cambridge: Cambridge University Press.

Jacob, Margaret. 1976. *The Newtonians and the English Revolution.* Ithaca: Cornell University Press.

1981. *The Radical Enlightenment: Pantheists, Freemasons and Republicans.* London: Allen & Unwin.

Jansen, John F. 1956. *Calvin's Doctrine of the Work of Christ.* London: Clarke.

Johnson, Paul J. 1974. "Hobbes's Anglican Doctrine of Salvation." In Ross, Schneider, and Waldman, 1974, pp. 102–28.

1989. "*Leviathan's* Audience." In *Thomas Hobbes: De la Metaphysique à la Politique,* ed. Martin Bertman and M. Malherbe, pp. 221–36. Paris: Vrin.

Johnston, David. 1986. *The Rhetoric of Leviathan.* Princeton: Princeton University Press.

1989. "Hobbes's Mortalism." *History of Political Thought* 10: 647–63.

Jones, H. W. "Thomas White (or Blacklo), 1593–1679: New Data." *Notes and Queries,* n.s. 10:381–8.

Jordan, W. K. 1932. *The Development of Religious Toleration in England: From the Beginning of the English Reformation to the Death of Queen Elizabeth.* Gloucester, Mass.: Smith, 1965.

1938. *The Development of Religious Toleration in England: From the Convention of the Long Parliament to the Restoration, 1640–1660.* Gloucester, Mass.: Smith, 1965.

1940. *The Development of Religious Toleration in England: Attainment of the Theory and Accommodations in Thought and Institutions (1640–1660).* Gloucester, Mass.: Smith, 1965.

Kantorowicz, Ernst. 1957. *The King's Two Bodies.* Princeton: Princeton University Press.

Kaplan, Lawrence. 1976. *Politics and Religion during the English Revolution: The Scots and the Long Parliament, 1643–1645.* New York: New York University Press.

Kavka, Gregory S. 1986. *Hobbesian Moral and Political Theory.* Princeton: Princeton University Press.

Kelley, Donald. 1988. "The Theory of History." In Schmitt and Skinner, 1988, pp. 746–62.

Kendall, R. T. 1979. *Calvin and English Calvinism to 1649.* Oxford: Clarendon Press.

Kenyon, J. P. 1985. *Stuart England.* 2nd ed. London: Penguin Books.

Kenyon, J. P., ed. 1986. *The Stuart Constitution*. Cambridge: Cambridge University Press.

King, Preston. 1974. *The Ideology of Order: A Comparative Analysis of Jean Bodin and Thomas Hobbes*. London: Allen & Unwin.

Kirk, K. E. 1931. *The Vision of God*. London: Longmans.

Knappen, M. M. 1939. *Tutor Puritanism*. Chicago: University of Chicago Press.

Kodalle, Klaus-Michael. 1972. *Thomas Hobbes: Logik der Herrschraft und Vernunft des Friedens*. Munich: Beck.

    1987. "Covenant: Hobbes's Philosophy of Religion and His Political System 'More Geometrico.'" In Walton and Johnson, 1987, pp. 223–38.

Kogel, Renee. 1972. *Pierre Charron*. Geneva: Droz.

Kolakowski, Leszek. 1990. "What Are Intellectuals, Anyway?" *New Republic*, October 29, pp. 28–32.

Kors, Alan Charles. 1990. *Atheism in France, 1650–1729*. Princeton: Princeton University Press.

Kraynak, Robert P. 1990. *History and Modernity in the Thought of Thomas Hobbes*. Ithaca: Cornell University Press.

Kristeller, Paul Oskar. 1968. "The Myth of Renaissance Atheism and the French Tradition of Free Thought." *Journal of the History of Philosophy* 6:233–43.

Lacey, Robert. 1973. *Sir Walter Ralegh*. London: Weidenfeld & Nicolson.

Laird, John. 1934. *Hobbes*. New York: Russell & Russell, 1968.

Lake, P. G. 1987. "Calvinism and the English Church: 1570–1635." *Past and Present* 114:32–76.

Lamont, William. 1963. *Marginal Prynne*. London: Routledge & Kegan Paul.

    1969. *Godly Rule: Politics and Religion, 1603–1660*. London: Macmillan.

Leff, Gordon. 1976. *The Dissolution of the Medieval Outlook*. New York: Harper & Row [Harper Torchbooks], 1976.

Leites, Edmund, ed. 1988. *Conscience and Casuistry*. Cambridge: Cambridge University Press.

Leith, John H. 1982. *Creeds of the Churches*. 3rd ed. Atlanta: Knox.

Letwin, Shirley. 1976. "Hobbes and Christianity." *Daedalus* 105: 1–21.

Levack, Brian. 1973. *The Civil Lawyers in England, 1603–1641: A Political Study*. Oxford: Clarendon Press.

1987. *The Formation of the British State: England, Scotland, and the Union, 1603–1707.* Oxford: Clarendon Press.

Levin, Michael. 1973. *Dictionary of the History of Ideas,* ed. Philip P. Wiener, s.v. "Social Contract." New York: Scribners.

Lieb, Michael. 1981. *Poetics of the Holy: A Reading of Paradise Lost.* Chapel Hill: University of North Carolina Press.

Lievsay, John L. 1973. *Venetian Phoenix: Paolo Sarpi and Some of His English Friends.* Lawrence: University Press of Kansas.

Lyons, Henry. 1944. *The Royal Society, 1660–1940.* Cambridge: Cambridge University Press.

McGee, J. Sears. 1976. *Godly Man in Stuart England: Anglicans, Puritans and the Two Tables: 1620–1670.* New Haven: Yale University Press.

McGrath, Alister. 1986. *Iustitia Dei.* 2 vols. Cambridge: Cambridge University Press.

1988. *Reformation Thought.* Oxford: Blackwell.

McGregor, J. F., and B. Reay. 1984. *Radical Religion in the English Revolution.* Oxford: Oxford University Press.

McNeill, John T. 1967. *The History and Character of Calvinism.* Oxford: Oxford University Press.

Macpherson, C. B. 1962. *The Political Theory of Possessive Individualism: Hobbes to Locke.* Oxford: Clarendon Press.

Makey, Walter. 1979. *The Church of the Covenant: 1637–1651: Revolution and Social Change in Scotland.* Edinburgh: Donald.

Mallet, Charles Edward. 1924. *A History of the University of Oxford.* 2 vols. London: Methuen.

Manning, Brian. 1973. "Religion and Politics: The Godly People." In *Politics, Religion and the Civil War,* ed. Brian Manning, pp. 83–123. London: Arnold.

Manuel, F. E. 1974. *The Religion of Isaac Newton.* Oxford: Oxford University Press.

Marshall, John. 1985. "The Ecclesiology of the Latitude-Men, 1660–1689: Stillingfleet, Tillotson and 'Hobbism.'" *Journal of Ecclesiastical History* 36:407–27.

Martinich, A. P. 1978. "Identity and Trinity." *Journal of Religion* 58:169–81.

1979. "God, Emperor, and Relative Identity." *Franciscan Studies* 39:180–91.

1980. "Infallibility." *Religious Studies* 16:15–27.

1981. "Commentary." In Hobbes, 1981, pp. 335–440.

1982. "In Defence of Infallibility." *Religious Studies* 18:81–6.

1984. *Communication and Reference.* Berlin: De Gruyter.

1990a. "The History of Epistemology." *Encyclopaedia Britannica,* 15th ed., s.v. "Epistemology."

1990b. *The Philosophy of Language.* 2nd ed. New York: Oxford University Press.

1990c. "Meaning and Intention: Black versus Grice." *Dialectica* 44:79–98.

May, Larry. 1980. "Hobbes's Contract Theory." *Journal of the History of Philosophy* 18:195–207.

Metzger, Bruce M. 1987. *The Canon of the New Testament: Its Origin, Development, and Significance.* Oxford: Clarendon Press.

Mijuskovic, Ben. 1974. *The Achilles of Rationalist Arguments.* The Hague: Nijhoff.

Miller, Perry. 1935. "The Marrow of Puritan Divinity." In *Errand into the Wilderness,* pp. 48–98. New York: Harper & Row [Harper Torchbooks], 1964.

Milner, Benjamin. 1988. "Hobbes: On Religion." *Political Theory* 16:400–25.

Milward, Peter. 1978. *Religious Controversies of the Jacobean Age: A Survey of Printed Sources.* Lincoln: University of Nebraska Press.

Mintz, Samuel. 1962. *The Hunting of Leviathan.* Cambridge: Cambridge University Press.

1968. "Hobbes on the Law of Heresy: A New Manuscript." *Journal of the History of Ideas* 29:409–14.

1989. "Leviathan as Metaphor." *Hobbes Studies* 2:3–9.

Moore, Brian. 1972. *Catholics.* Toronto: McClelland & Stewart.

Moore, Stanley. 1971. "Hobbes on Obligation: Moral and Political: Part 1." *Journal of the History of Philosophy* 9:43–62.

1972. "Hobbes on Obligation: Moral and Political: Part 2." *Journal of the History of Philosophy* 10:29–41.

Moorman, J. R. 1972. *A History of the Church in England.* 3rd ed. London: Black.

Morrill, John. 1984. "The Religious Context of the English Civil War." *Transactions of the Royal Historical Society,* 5th ser., 34:155–78.

Morrill, John, ed. 1982. *Reactions to the English Civil War.* London: Macmillan.

Mullan, David George. 1986. *Episcopacy in Scotland: The History of an Idea, 1560–1638.* Edinburgh: Donald.

Bibliography

Muller, Richard A. 1986. *Christ and the Decree*. Durham, N.C.: Labyrinth Press.

Nagel, Thomas. 1959. "Hobbes's Concept of Obligation." *Philosophical Review* 68:68–83.

Neill, Stephen. 1976. *Anglicanism*. 2nd ed. London: Oxford University Press.

Nethenus, Matthew. 1965. *William Ames*. Cambridge, Mass.: Harvard Divinity School.

New, John. 1964. *Anglican and Puritan: The Basis of Their Opposition*. Stanford: Stanford University Press.

Nicholson, Ernest. 1986. *God and His People*. Oxford: Oxford University Press.

Norman, Edward. 1985. *Roman Catholicism in England from the Elizabethan Settlement to the Second Vatican Council*. Oxford: Oxford University Press.

North, J. D., and J. J. Roche, eds. 1985. *The Light of Nature: Essays in the History and Philosophy of Science, Presented to A. C. Crombie*. Dordrecht: Nijhoff.

Oakeshott, Michael. 1957. "Introduction." In Hobbes, *Leviathan*, ed. Michael Oakeshott, pp. vii–lxvi. Oxford: Blackwell.

Oberman, Heike. 1967. *The Harvest of Medieval Theology: Gabriel Biel and Late Medieval Nominalism*. Grand Rapids: Eerdmans.

Ollard, Richard. 1988. *Clarendon and His Friends*. New York: Atheneum.

Pacchi, Arrigo. 1988. "Hobbes and the Problem of God." In Rogers and Ryan, 1988, pp. 171–88.

Packer, John W. 1969. *The Transformation of Anglicanism, 1643–1660*. Manchester: Manchester University Press.

Parry, G. J. R. 1987. *A Protestant Vision: William Harrison and the Reformation of Elizabethan England*. Cambridge: Cambridge University Press.

Passmore, John. 1951. *Ralph Cudworth*. Cambridge: Cambridge University Press.

Patrides, C. A. 1966. *Milton and the Christian Tradition*. Oxford: Clarendon Press.

Patterson, Annabel. 1984. *Censorship and Interpretation*. Madison: University of Wisconsin Press.

Pennington, Donald, and Keith Thomas, eds. 1978. *Puritans and Revolutionaries*. Oxford: Clarendon Press.

Plamenatz, John. 1957. "Mr. Warrender's Hobbes." In *Hobbes Studies*, ed. K. C. Brown, pp. 73–87. Oxford: Blackwell.

Plass, Ewald. 1959. *What Luther Said: An Anthology*. St. Louis: Concordia.

Pocock, John G. A. 1971. "Time, History, and Eschatology in the Thought of Thomas Hobbes." In *Politics, Language, and Time*, pp. 148–201. New York: Athenaeum.

[Pocock, Nicholas]. 1848. "Illustrations of the State of the Church during the Great Rebellion." *Theologian and Ecclesiastic* 7:1–12, 65–80, 161–75, 212–26, 297–310.

——— 1849. "Illustrations of the State of the Church during the Great Rebellion." *Theologian and Ecclesiastic* 8:47–64, 118–29, 137–52, 158–68, 276–93, 373–85.

——— 1850. "Illustrations of the State of the Church during the Great Rebellion." *Theologian and Ecclesiastic* 9:113–25, 288–98.

Pohle, Joseph. 1911–24. *Dogmatic Theology*, ed. Arthur Preuss. 12 vols. St. Louis: Herder.

——— 1923. *Soteriology*, ed. Arthur Preuss. St. Louis: Herder, 1947.

Popkin, Richard H. 1971. "The Philosophy of Edward Stillingfleet." *Journal of the History of Philosophy* 9:303–20.

——— 1979. *The History of Scepticism: from Erasmus to Spinoza*. Berkeley and Los Angeles: University of California Press.

——— 1980. "Jewish Messianism and Christian Millenarianism." In Zagorin, 1980, pp. 67–90.

——— 1987a. *Isaac La Peyrere (1596–1676)*. Leiden: Brill.

——— 1987b. "The Religious Background of Seventeenth Century Philosophy." *Journal of the History of Philosophy* 25:35–50.

Popkin, Richard H., ed. 1988. *Millenarianism and Messianism in English Literature and Thought: 1650–1800*. Leiden: Brill.

Pritchard, Arnold. 1979. *Catholic Loyalism in Elizabethan England*. Chapel Hill: University of North Carolina Press.

Raab, Felix. 1964. *The English Face of Machiavelli*. London: Routledge & Kegan Paul.

Ramsey, Ian T. 1957. *Religious Language*. New York: Macmillan.

Rashdall, Hastings. 1919. *The Idea of Atonement in Christian Theology*. London: Macmillan.

Reardon, Bernard. 1981. *Religious Thought in the Reformation*. London: Longmans.

Redwood, John. 1976. *Reason, Ridicule and Religion: The Age of Enlightenment in England, 1660–1750*. London: Thames & Hudson.

Reik, Miriam. 1977. *The Golden Lands of Thomas Hobbes*. Detroit: Wayne State University Press.

Bibliography

Reith, Herman R. 1986. *René Descartes: The Story of a Soul*. Lanham, Md.: University Press of America.

Reventlow, Henning Graf. 1984. *The Authority of the Bible and the Rise of the Modern World*. Philadelphia: Fortress.

Rogers, G. A. J. 1985. "Descartes and the English." In North and Roche, 1985, pp. 281–302.

Rogers, G. A. J., and Alan Ryan, eds. 1988. *Perspectives on Thomas Hobbes*. Oxford: Clarendon Press.

Rogers, Jack. 1985. *Presbyterian Creeds: A Guide to The Book of Confessions*. Philadelphia: Westminster.

Rogow, Arnold. 1986. *Thomas Hobbes: Radical in the Service of Reaction*. New York: Norton.

Ross, Ralph, Herbert Schneider, and Theodore Waldman. 1974. *Thomas Hobbes in His Time*. Minneapolis: University of Minnesota Press.

Roth, Leon. 1934. *A Life of Menasseh Ben Israel*. Philadelphia: Jewish Publication Society of America.

Ryan, Alan. 1983. "Hobbes, Toleration, and the Inner Life." In *The Nature of Political Theory*, ed. David Miller and Larry Siedentop, pp. 197–218. Oxford: Clarendon Press.

Schmitt, Charles, and Quentin Skinner, eds. 1988. *The Cambridge History of Renaissance Philosophy*. Cambridge: Cambridge University Press.

Schneider, Herbert. 1974. "The Piety of Hobbes." In Ross, Schneider, and Waldman, 1974, pp. 84–101.

Scott, James Brown. 1944. "Introduction." In Suarez, 1612, pp. 3a–41a.

Searle, John. 1979. *Expression and Meaning*. Cambridge: Cambridge University Press.

Seaward, Paul. 1989. *The Cavalier Parliament and the Reconstruction of the Old Regime, 1661–1667*. Cambridge: Cambridge University Press.

Seung, T. K. 1982. *Semiotics and Thematics in Hermeneutics*. New York: Columbia University Press.

Shapin, Steven, and Simon Schaeffer. 1985. *Leviathan and the Airpump: Hobbes, Boyle, and the Experimental Life*. Princeton: Princeton University Press.

Shapiro, Barbara. 1983. *Probability and Certainty in Seventeenth Century England*. Princeton: Princeton University Press.

Sherlock, Richard. 1982. "The Theology of *Leviathan*: Hobbes on Religion." *Interpretation* 10:43–60.

Shulman, George. 1988. "Hobbes, Puritans, and Promethean Politics." *Political Theory* 16:426–43.

Skinner, Quentin. 1964. "Hobbes's *Leviathan*." *Historical Journal* 7:321–33.

1965a. "History and Ideology in the English Revolution." *Historical Journal* 8:151–78.

1965b. "Hobbes on Sovereignty: An Unknown Discussion." *Political Studies* 13:213–8.

1965c. "Thomas Hobbes and His Disciples in France and England." *Comparative Studies in Society and History* 8:153–67.

1966. "The Context of Hobbes's Theory of Political Obligation." In Cranston and Peters, 1972, pp. 109–42.

1972. "Conquest and Consent: Thomas Hobbes and the Engagement Controversy." In Aylmer, 1972, 79–98.

1980. "The Origins of the Calvinist Theory of Revolution." In *After the Reformation*, ed. Barbara Malament, pp. 309–30. Philadelphia: University of Pennsylvania Press.

1988a. *Meaning and Context*, ed. James Tully. Princeton: Princeton University Press.

1988b. "Political Philosophy." In Schmitt and Skinner, 1988, pp. 389–452.

1990. "Thomas Hobbes on the Proper Signification of Liberty." *Transactions of the Royal Historical Society*, 5th ser., 40:121–51.

Slaughter, Thomas. 1984. *Ideology and Politics on the Eve of the Restoration: Newcastle's Advice to Charles II.* Philadelphia: American Philosophical Society.

Smith, Norman Kemp. 1952. *New Studies in the Philosophy of Descartes.* London: Macmillan.

Snyder, David C. 1986. "Faith and Reason in Locke's *Essay*." *Journal of the History of Ideas* 47:197–213.

Solt, Leo. 1958. "Revolutionary Calvinist Parties in England under Elizabeth I and Charles I." *Church History* 27:234–9.

1990. *Church and State in Early Modern England, 1509–1640.* New York: Oxford University Press.

Sommerville, J. P. 1984. "John Selden, the Law of Nature, and the Origins of Government." *Historical Journal* 27:437–47.

1986. *Politics and Ideology in England, 1603–1640.* London: Longmans.

Sorell, Tom. 1986. *Hobbes.* London: Routledge & Kegan Paul.

Spragens, Thomas, Jr. 1973. *The Politics of Motion: The World of Thomas Hobbes.* Lexington: University Press of Kentucky.

Bibliography

State, Stephen A. 1985. "Text and Context: Skinner, Hobbes, and Theistic Natural Law." *Historical Journal* 28:27–50.

1989. "The Religious and the Secular in the Work of Thomas Hobbes." In Crimmins, 1989, pp. 17–38.

Stephen, Leslie. 1904. *Hobbes*. Ann Arbor: University of Michigan Press, 1961.

Stephen, Leslie, and Sidney Lee, eds. 1917. *Dictionary of National Biography*. 22 vols. London: Oxford University Press.

Stone, Lawrence. 1967. *The Crisis of the Aristocracy*. Abridged ed. New York: Oxford University Press.

Strathmann, Ernest. 1951. *Sir Walter Ralegh: A Study in Elizabethan Skepticism*. New York: Columbia University Press.

Strauss, Leo. 1930. *Spinoza's Critique of Religion*. New York: Schocken, 1965.

1952a. *Persecution and the Art of Writing*. Glencoe, Ill.: Free Press.

1952b. *The Political Philosophy of Hobbes*. Chicago: University of Chicago Press.

1953. *Natural Right and History*. Chicago: University of Chicago Press.

Swinburne, Richard. 1989. *Responsibility and Atonement*. Oxford: Clarendon Press.

Sykes, Norman. 1956. *Old Priest and New Presbyter*. Cambridge: Cambridge University Press.

Tavard, George. 1964. "Scripture and Tradition among Seventeenth Century Recusants." *Theological Studies* 25:343–85.

Taylor, A. E. 1938. "The Ethical Doctrine of Hobbes." In *Hobbes Studies*, ed. Keith Brown, pp. 35–56. Oxford: Blackwell, 1965.

Thomas, Keith. 1971. *Religion and the Decline of Magic*. New York: Scribner.

Thompson, Martyn. 1987. *Ideas of Contract in English Political Thought in the Age of John Locke*. New York: Garland.

Tierney, Brian. 1982. *Religion, Law and the Growth of Constitutional Thought, 1150–1650*. Cambridge: Cambridge University Press.

Tönnies, Ferdinand. 1904. "Hobbes-Analekten." *Archiv für Geschichte der Philosophie* 17:291–317.

1906. "Hobbes-Analekten II." *Archiv für Geschichte der Philosophie* 19:153–75.

Trevor-Roper, Hugh. 1963. *Archbishop Laud, 1573–1645*. 2nd ed. London: Macmillan.

1989. *Catholics, Anglicans and Puritans*. London: Fontana.

Trinterud, L. J. 1951. "The Origins of Puritanism." *Church History* 20:37–57.

Tuck, Richard. 1979. *Natural Rights Theories.* Cambridge: Cambridge University Press.

1982. " 'The Ancient Law of Freedom': John Selden and the Civil War." In Morrill, 1982, pp. 137–61.

1988a. "Hobbes and Descartes." In Rogers and Ryan, 1988, pp. 11–41.

1988b. "Optics and Sceptics: The Philosophical Foundations of Hobbes's Political Thought." In Leites, 1988, pp. 235–63.

1989. *Hobbes.* Oxford: Oxford University Press.

1990. "Hobbes and Locke on Toleration." In Dietz, 1990, pp. 153–71.

1991a. "The Christian Atheism of Thomas Hobbes." In Hunter and Wootton, 1991.

1991b. *Hobbes: Leviathan.* Cambridge: Cambridge University Press.

Tulloch, John. 1874. *Rational Theology and Christian Philosophy in England in the Seventeenth Century.* 2nd ed. 2 vols. Edinburgh: Blackwood.

Tyacke, Nicholas. 1978. "Science and Religion at Oxford before the Civil War." In Pennington and Thomas, 1978, pp. 73–93.

1987a. *Anti-Calvinists: The Rise of English Arminianism, c.1590–1640.* Oxford: Clarendon Press.

1987b. "The Rise of Arminianism Reconsidered." *Past and Present* 115:201–16.

Van der Bend, J. G. 1982. *Thomas Hobbes: His View of Man.* Amsterdam: Rodopi.

Verete, M. 1972. "The Restoration of the Jews in English Protestant Thought, 1790–1840." *Middle Eastern Studies* 8:3–50.

Von Rohr, John. 1986. *The Covenant of Grace in Puritan Thought.* Atlanta: Scholar Press.

Walker, D. P. 1964. *The Decline of Hell.* Chicago: University of Chicago Press.

Wallace, John M. 1964. "The Engagement Controversy, 1649–1652: An Annotated List of Pamphlets." *New York Library Bulletin* 68:384–405.

1968. *Destiny His Choice: The Loyalism of Andrew Marvell.* Cambridge: Cambridge University Press.

Walton, C., and P. J. Johnson, eds. 1987. *Hobbes's 'Science of Natural Justice'.* Dordrecht: Nijhoff.

Bibliography

Warner, D. H. J. 1968–9. "Hobbes's Interpretation of the Doctrine of Trinity." *Journal of Religious History* 5:299–313.

Warrender, Howard. 1957. *The Political Philosophy of Hobbes: His Theory of Obligation*. Oxford: Clarendon Press.

——. 1960. "The Place of God in Hobbes's Philosophy." *Political Studies* 8:48–57.

——. 1979. "Political Theory and Historiography: A Reply to Professor Skinner." *Historical Journal* 22:931–40.

——. 1987. "Hobbes and Macroethics: The Theory of Peace and Natural Justice." In Walton and Johnson, 1987, pp. 297–308.

Watkins, J. W. N. 1973. *Hobbes's System of Ideas: A Study in the Political Significance of Philosophical Ideas*. 2nd ed. London: Hutchinson University Library.

Wedgewood, C. V. 1964. *The Trial of Charles I*. London: Macmillan.

Weiner, Carol. 1971. "A Beleaguered Isle." *Past and Present* 51: 27–62.

Westfall, Richard. 1958. *Science and Religion in Seventeenth-Century England*. New Haven: Yale University Press.

Weston, Corine Comstock. 1960. "The Theory of Mixed Monarchy under Charles I and After." *English Historical Review* 75: 426–43.

White, Peter. 1983. "The Rise of Arminianism Reconsidered." *Past and Present* 101:34–54.

——. 1987. "A Rejoinder." *Past and Present* 115:217–29.

Williams, George. 1962. *The Radical Reformation*. Philadelphia: Westminster.

Williamson, Arthur. 1979. *Scottish National Consciousness in the Age of James VI: The Apocalypse, the Union and the Shaping of Scotland's Public Culture*. Edinburgh: Donald.

Wolf, Lucien. 1901. *Manasseh Ben Israel's Mission to Oliver Cromwell*. London: Jewish Historical Society of England.

Wolin, Sheldon. 1970. *Hobbes and the Epic Tradition*. Los Angeles: Clark Memorial Library.

Wootton, David. 1983a. "The Fear of God in Early Modern Political Theory." *Historical Papers*, Canadian Historical Association, pp. 56–80.

——. 1983b. *Paolo Sarpi: Between Renaissance and Enlightenment*. Cambridge: Cambridge University Press.

——. 1988. "Lucien Febvre and the Problem of Unbelief in the Early Modern Period." *Journal of Modern History* 60:695–730.

1989. "John Locke: Socinian or Natural Law Theorist." In Crimmins, 1989, pp. 39–67.

1990. "Hume's 'Of Miracles': Probability and Irreligion." In *Studies in the Philosophy of the Scottish Enlightenment*, pp. 191–229. Oxford: Clarendon Press.

Wootton, David, ed. 1986. *Divine Right and Democracy*. Harmondsworth: Penguin Books.

Worden, Blair. "Radicalism between the Lines." *Times Literary Supplement*, August 5, 1983, p. 837.

Wormald, B. H. G. 1951. *Clarendon: Politics, History and Religion, 1640–1660*. Cambridge: Cambridge University Press.

Zagorin, Perez. 1954. *A History of Political Thought*. London: Routledge & Kegan Paul.

1982. *Rebels and Rulers, 1500–1660*. 2 vols. Cambridge University Press.

1985. "Clarendon and Hobbes." *Journal of Modern History* 57:593–616.

1990a. "Hobbes on Our Mind." *Journal of the History of Ideas* 51:317–35.

1990b. *Ways of Lying*. Cambridge, Mass.: Harvard University Press.

Zagorin, Perez, ed. 1980. *Culture and Politics from Puritanism to the Enlightenment*. Berkeley and Los Angeles: University of California Press.

Index

Index

Index

Index

Printed in the United Kingdom
by Lightning Source UK Ltd.
104933UKS00001B/145